THE WELL-TEMPERED SELF

PARALLAX ♊ Re-visions of Culture and Society

Stephen G. Nichols,
Gerald Prince,
and Wendy Steiner
SERIES EDITORS

Toby
Miller

THE WELL-TEMPERED SELF:

Citizenship, Culture,
and the
Postmodern
Subject

THE JOHNS HOPKINS UNIVERSITY PRESS ◆ BALTIMORE AND LONDON

The Johns Hopkins University Press
2715 North Charles Street
Baltimore, Maryland 21218-4319
The Johns Hopkins Press Ltd., London

Library of Congress Cataloging-in-Publication Data

Miller, Toby,
    The well-tempered self : citizenship, culture, and the postmodern
subject / Toby Miller.
        p.   cm. —(Parallax)
    Includes bibliographical references and index.
    ISBN 0-8018-4603-X (alk. paper).   ISBN 0-8018-4604-8 (pbk. : alk. paper)
    1. Politics and culture.   2. Political ethics.   3. Political socialization.
4. Criticism, Textual.   5. Foucault, Michel—Contributions in political
science.   6. Habermas, Jürgen—Contributions in political science.   I. Title.
II. Series : Parallax (Baltimore, Md.)
    JA75.7.M55   1993
306.2—dc20   93-13102

A catalog record for this book is available from the British Library.

Contents

Acknowledgments

The principal readers of my work during the production of this book have been Rita Felski, Lawrence Grossberg, Elizabeth Jacka, Meaghan Morris, Tom O'Regan, Horst Ruthrof, and an anonymous reader for the Johns Hopkins University Press. Their assistance has been invaluable.

I have also benefited from the help of Robert C. Allen, Tony Bennett, Ron Blaber, Merrylyn Braden, Michael Burton, Stuart Cunningham, Robyn Ferrell, Jock Given, Michael Gordon-Smith, John Hartley, Noel King, Alec McHoul, Tony May, Eric Michaels, Bruce Miller, Dan and Joanna Rose, Rita Shanahan, Stephanie Tchan, and Graeme Turner. In their very different ways, Michael B. and Noel were immensely important. My thanks also to Peter Dreyer for his excellent copyediting, to the staff of the Johns Hopkins University Press for their labor, and especially to Eric Halpern for being such a helpful business correspondent from afar.

Without Alec McHoul, none of this manuscript would have computed. Without Rita Felski, it would not have been produced.

Introduction

This book is principally about well-tempered, manageable cultural subjects formed and governed through institutions and discourses. These institutions and discourses work by inscribing ethical incompleteness onto subjects in a process of two-way shifts between the subject as singular, private person and the subject as collective, public citizen. These shifts, which can be discerned in the political technology of the subject known as policy, operate to produce loyal citizens who learn to govern themselves in the interests of the cultural-capitalist polity. This outcome is not, however, inevitable or unidirectional, and for this reason I also consider unruly subjects seeking to reform themselves.

The title to the book tropes Johann Sebastian Bach's *Das wohltemperierte Klavier* (The Well-Tempered Keyboard) of 1722–44, which uses all the major and minor keys of the clavichord across two dozen preludes and fugues and is regarded as an exemplary exercise in freedom and stricture—all produced from technique. Bach explained that one of his intentions was to train people in "good inventions and a cantabile manner of playing." The music is essentially an exercise in mutability, always within the domain of a polite, coordinated tone that does not jar and is consistent; it is a pedagogic work. The title itself functioned as an argument against the previously dominant method of tempering (i.e., tuning). This method, known as the mean-tone system, always left some keys out of tune, while others were well in tune. Bach favored small adjustments to the system that would find each key equally pleasant to the ear, even if none would have the mathematically perfect tuning available to certain digits under the existing method. In order to play *Das wohltemperierte Klavier*, one would have to follow Bach's new system, called equal temperament. The work's mercurial changes of direction across the keyboard were specifically designed to pick up the limitations inherent in the orthodox system, which most other writers studiously avoided exposing. For Arnold Schoenberg two centuries later, the outcome was a series of provisionally "horrible, incomprehensible dissonances" rendered beautiful. As a title and an intervention into musical technology, the piece represents a move toward *politesse* and consistency over unruliness and difference, a move that was to typify the incorporation of music into popular education in the nineteenth century as part of a training in equable citizenship.

Unlike the ideal subject produced by the careful pedagogic norms of Bach's tutelary text, some subjects are outside sweet reason. Their situation is akin to Lawrence Grossberg's 1980s distinction between the fan and the ideologue, and how it was that litterateur colleagues derogated his desire to teach popular music because of his absorption in the phenomenon. The power of Grossberg's "affective investment" seemed to differ from their own engagement with literary forms. They privileged the horizon of the disinterested expert that adjudicates via discrete sets of values removed from the everyday and applied across sites and categories of person. This was preferred to his principles of "relevance and effectivity."[1]

One might say that these colleagues favored a studied order over potential rancor and raucousness, a form of academic panic analogous to the "modernistic infamy" Theodor Adorno believed was attached to the saxophone's supposed capacity to "perversely subject the over-stimulated Western nerves to the vitality of blacks."[2] This is not, of course, to suggest that popular music or its incorporation into academic discourse represents systemic revolt. Popular music is clearly deeply involved with the structures of production and exchange that characterize the economic system in which it operates. (As Mark Crispin Miller puts it, "rock is a cry of revolt underwritten by major corporations.")[3] And it can easily be enlisted by cultural policy's developing propensity to engage with youth as a category of consumer and citizen. One might consider here the British government's 1965 White Paper on the arts, which welcomed a new generation's desire for "gaiety and colour . . . informality and experimentation" as opposed to the "drabness, uniformity and joylessness" of convention. Such approaches are routinely derogated for their clearly cooptive intent and execution.[4]

The hold that popular music can have on a politics of identity—or, rather, the shifting hold of various fractions of popular music on various fractions of the community at given moments—is, however, both different from and potentially unsettling for the project of government through culture exemplified by the pedagogic routine of *Das wohltem-*

perierte Klavier. The vitality of music not "made to order from the beginning" may paradoxically emerge from Adorno's "domesticated body in bondage."[5] Roland Barthes, for example, looks to music (be it live, recorded, or broadcast; classical or popular) for "an access to *jouissance,* to loss." Distinguishing, after Julia Kristeva, between *"pheno-song"* and *"geno-song,"* he abjures the first for its attention to an even-tempered structure and style in the service of "the tissue of cultural values," preferring the directness of the latter, which he says has a rawness derived from material bonds with language that transcends representational protocols, because it operates from a more elemental seduction and excess. This is "the culture of the 'grain' of the voice . . . the body in the voice as it sings." It is the special gift of this voice to eroticize the listener's world and loosen the ties of subjectivity through climax.[6] As Jacques Derrida reminds us, moving out of tune is frequently rendered as a tonic delirium, "a social disorder and a derangement, an out-of-tune-ness of strings and voices in the head . . . parasitising the voice of reason that speaks equally in each."[7] Such a condition becomes difficult to control, to order in accordance with the norms of adherence to the good citizen. In glossing his fantasies for *Hiroshima Mon Amour* (1959), Alain Resnais has emphasised the complex imbrication of private with public, deictic with distant that just such a counterpoint can produce. The vision Resnais enunciated to the film's scripwriter, Marguerite Duras, juxtaposed the intimacy of anonymous 1950s love with 1940s wartime horror, a personal and international tour of a museum of individual and collective memorial terror, exemplified by a Japanese man who missed the bombing and a French woman punished after the event for collaborator's sex. He wanted the film to be "a love story—in my head it was something like 'Moderato Cantabile' [a novel by Duras that was subsequently also made into a film, directed by Peter Brook]—but one in which the atomic agony would not be absent."[8]

Conversely, the unproblematic sweet reasonableness of *Das wohltemperierte Klavier* is clearly akin to the ordered obedience of the desired subjects of civic culture that I am seeking to address in this book. I examine four types of cultural subject produced by public policy under the sign of civility:

> the ethically incomplete subject in need of training into humanness;
> the national public in need of a dramatological mirror in which to recognize itself;
> the politically incomplete public subject in need of democratic training in citizenship; and

the rational consuming subject in need of alignment with this public citizen.

These four types have been chosen because they exemplify central issues for the cultural-capitalist state. That state needs to produce a sense of oneness among increasingly heterogeneous populations at a time when political systems are under question by new social movements and the internationalization of cultures and economies. It works to forge a loyalty to market economics and parliamentary democracy, as well as a sustainable society through the formation of cultural citizens, docile but efficient participants in that economy-society mix.

Following a theoretical account in chapter 1, the next three chapters of the book address cultural subjects produced by cultural policies designed to achieve this unity. Chapter 5 considers the unruly subject that seeks and makes a special truth for itself, in this case in sex. I shall elaborate on how the various chapters deal with this process later in the Introduction. First, however, I wish to define some critical terms and provide a schematic history of the person, which is the subject of this inscription.

This book is about a determinate indeterminacy. This indeterminacy is an ethical incompleteness, which cultural subjects are encouraged to find in themselves and then remedy. I am defining ethics here to mean the personal capacity to draw upon moral codes as a means of managing one's conduct. This becomes an exercise without end, a seminar of the conscience between desires, practices, collective and individual needs, and so on. Hence the concern, especially following Kant, to unravel the competing imperatives faced by Abraham over the call from God to kill his son Isaac, to decide between what is right and what is ordered from on high. This marks a change from pre-Enlightenment proclivities toward absolutes. After Hegel and Kierkegaard, the concern becomes something more, something that must contribute to a universe of the social as part of an active process moving, albeit asymptotically, toward completion. It is a world without end because it always needs reinventing with each dilemma.

If ethics seems to address the idea of "relations between an autonomous, self-determining subjectivity and a set of potentially, but never actually universalizable values," as Vincent Pecora argues,[9] then the inculcation and application of these values will be a determining influence on the subject itself as much as the other way round. The subject is not stable here, for it is itself reconditioned by the effort of interiorizing and exteriorizing such precepts. There is effectively no way out of the struggle between conditional and absolute answers to ethical dilemmas, a struggle that never decides finally whether there are always already contingencies of value, or whether we can somehow enter a domain of signs that needs no history in order to arrange ethical interaction. The canon of philosophical ethics is not characterized by the drawing of absolute distinctions between universally turpitudinous and worthy actions inside a static semantic field. Rather, the study of ethics has traditionally been concerned to interrogate what underpins contemporary conceptions of correct or incorrect action in search of general concordances that lie beneath such binarisms. This search for an overarching system of distinction that will adequately classify the good and the bad as systems of presumption, if not moral guides, has seen interminable difference of opinion. To participate in that debate is to sign on for a guaranteed indeterminacy of stay and activity. And even if we were in possession of all the categories and calibrations necessary for such a Manichean approach, the task of identifying the other subjects susceptible to our actions is never-ending.

To be aware of ethical dilemmas and their unresolvable nature is to be aware of one's own incompleteness and simultaneously be encouraged to unify these tensions into a single ethical substance. This encouragement takes the form of a series of exercises of the mind, dedicated to understanding both the maintenance of boundaries and the means to cross them via a debate about thought and feeling, desire and action, structure and agency, and the publicly concerned versus the privately concerned self. For the purposes of this study, these exercises of the mind are seen to be the substance of the connection between government and culture. For it is principally the training in subjectivity provided by this relationship that enables Michel Foucault's "mode of subjection *(mode d'assujettissement),* that is, the way in which people are invited or incited to recognize their moral obligations." This invitation/incitement is accompanied by a portfolio covering: the areas of judgment that will necessitate the use of this ethical substance; knowing how to develop it; and finding a goal of becoming. Together, these constitute the internalization and externalization, the individuation and the collectivization, of a subject's sense of its ethical identity.[10]

The process of formulating this ethical incompleteness works through the operation of technologies of governance, which are a means of managing the public by having it manage itself. This is achieved through the material inscription of discourse into policies and programs of the cultural-capitalist state. A technology is defined here, after Foucault, as "a matrix of popular reason." It may be divided into four categories. "Technologies of production" make for the physical transformation of material objects. "Technologies of sign systems" are about the use of systems of meaning. The two categories of chief concern to this book are "technologies of power," which form subjects as a means of dominating individuals and bringing them to define themselves in particular ways; and "technologies of the self," which are applied by individuals as a means of transforming their conditions into those of a more autonomous sense of happiness.[11]

Discourse here is understood not as a universe of meaning but as a complex that combines "the action of imposed scarcity, with a fundamental power of affirmation."[12] A discourse is a set of statements that determine actions and thoughts. So a given discourse is a particular vocabulary and grammar that permits the making of choices only within its own rules. It decides what can and cannot be said, done, or represented. At various times, different discourses may or may not intersect, producing meaning at their conjuncture and between their own constitutive vocabularies. Intertextuality, for example, may occur both via the meeting of discourses and the appropriation of one by another. Discourse is an area in which knowledge is produced and operates, both openly and in a less than overt way. It fixes norms, elaborates criteria, and hence makes it possible to speak of and treat a given problem at a particular time. So for Foucault, "the unity of discourses on madness would not be based upon the existence of the object 'madness,' or the constitution of a single horizon of objectivity; it would be the interplay of the rules that make possible the appearance of objects during a given period of time."[13]

These rules include: what it is to be human; what it is to be social; and the procedures and institutions that circulate such information. In the arena of the cultural subject, considered doubt is achieved through the attribution of ethical incompleteness to human subjects. They are thereby encouraged to recognize themselves as existing within an imperfect world of indeterminacy, which, like them, must be worked on. This is a strategy for training and reforming the subject. It is with this subject that I begin.

The subject has a distinguished history in social and cultural theory. For Georg Simmel as for many others, there is a grand and unassailable paradox: "Man as an object of knowledge is a product of nature and history. But man as a knowing subject produces both nature and history."[14] Modernity wrought havoc on the solid-state subject, which it inherited and proceeded to dissect. Marx finds history to be made outside deliberate human agency, by social forces. Freud finds identity to be a riddle made up of apparent clarity that is really self-deceit. Ferdinand de Saussure finds that language exists prior to its speaker and has the capacity to organize that speaker at the instant of its appearance.

Whether one takes its nominated referent of the person as a basis, a coefficient, or a product, however, the concept of the human formed through and forming knowledge has developed as a significant trope. The signs are there in the anthropomorphism of attributing human cognition, recognition, and misrecognition to entities such as nations, states, public and private bureaucracies, businesses, syndicates, and interest groups. They are there in doctrines of self and society, the double movement between categories so beloved of social theory from Aristotle through Hobbes, and on to sociology. They are present in the discourses of neoclassical or marginalist economics, with all its remarkable extrapolations from Benthamite psychologisms about consumers on to collective consumption and a vast array of nonhuman entities. They are present in the ambiguous relationship of consumers with their stalking partners—liberal citizens, permitted untrammeled access to themselves and their natural attributes in the name of personal development and contribution to social renewal through the alleged dynamism of what Isaiah Berlin calls a "free trade in ideas."[15] They are present in the exemplary pedagogue: an exemplary reader (exemplary because of a capacity to see the self in the text, translate the text to the self in the classroom, and identify and then treat the imperfections in each) who directs literary studies. This is the pedagogue who meets F. R. Leavis's "demand that the user shall be able, in the fullest sense, to read."[16] These signs are also present in accounts of true and appropriate personal practices, such as sexual technologies, which are held up for their ability to demonstrate, form, and discipline the true (if hence potentially alarming) characters of persons.

In his attempt to explain the collocation of Louis Althusser, Claude Lévi-Strauss, Jacques Lacan, and himself under the sign of structuralism, Foucault finds the subject to be their "essential point of convergence." Althusser queries the redisposal of alienation from the economic and political registers into the philosophical as a basis for Marxism, favoring instead a reading of Marx that does not rely on the perceptually dissociated human. Lévi-Strauss utilizes linguistics to perform structural exercises on myths in search of complementarities beyond the knowledge or agency of the human subject. Lacan problematizes the solid-state subject of experiential psychology because of its denial of the unconscious. Foucault seeks to explore the ways in which subjects and objects of knowledge are constituted via a "mutual genesis."[17]

Despite these projects, the dominant forms of the human sciences continue to display the power of the doctrines of evolution that appeared in the nineteenth century. The subject is said to have evolved through a complex process of differentiation. There has been a horizontal movement, extrapolating from the singular to the collective. But at the same time, a vertical movement founded on organized hierarchy has spread the sense of self down from the collective to the singular. For David Saunders and Ian Hunter, this is a trajectory in which "the public attributes of the person are internalized and identified with an inner entity."[18] The regularity, constancy, and velocity of this series of movements from self to public and public to self has worked to preclude the meeting of incommensurate doctrines whose junction might make for conflict. Such a junction would involve the dialectical interplay between, for example, the rationally selfish consumer and the rationally selfless citizen or between the ideal fealty of the "native" subject and the split loyalty of the migrant. Equally, it would establish a contradiction within the call to culture that asks texts to form persons at the same time as it claims simply to reflect them, and to do so through technologies of populism such as television that are said to narcotize and repress but are, relentlessly, expected again and again to enliven and develop.

Philosophical aesthetics tends to commence its deliberations with an ideal-typical subject. This subject is capable of artistic discrimination. But it is the product of the gaze and the rhetoric of this subject—the text it consumes and reproduces—that quickly draws the attention of aesthetic inquiry. The text heaves onto itself as an ineffable property the value it has received through the endorsement of the maker of taste. This fetishizes a process of reception by accumulating onto the text the force of a supposedly human process of approval. The ideal-typical subject that ushered in this reification is clearly critical as the source of objectification and, later on, the imagined person to be educated back into that original taste.

Foucault discerns three methods of manufacturing such subjects. First, the human sciences produce subjects by pronouncing the conditions and operation of speech, of material productiveness and of physical morphology. Second, various practices divide the subject within itself and divide it from others in terms of healthiness and appropriateness of conduct. Finally, the subject identifies as a subject. It works on itself in order to perform these classificatory operations and then to recognize itself within one or several of them. This process manufactures "two meanings of the word 'subject': subject to someone else by control and dependence; and tied to his own identity by a conscience or self-knowledge." The subject is thus both subject to institutions of power, such as governments, and subject to discourses, such as theories of the person. In fact, it is known through these very modes, as the subject of governance by itself via knowledge and administration; via policy.[19]

To accept this position on the subject and the state is radically to rewrite the classic account of government. It is to argue against the understanding of a "necessarily antagonistic" relationship between "subjects, or some classes of subjects, and the government" that juxtaposes "liberty and authority," "society . . . [and] the individual," in John Stuart Mill's *On Liberty*.[20] It suggests that there is no preexisting category of the person that is knowable outside the knowledges and categories enumerated through the governance of that subject. Put another way, there is no primal scene to be found, no meeting of person and government as chronologically distinct entities. Lacan refers to

> the drama in which the original myths of the City State are produced before its assembled citizens . . . [as a moment that] stands in relation to a history that may well be made up of materials, but in which a nation today learns to read the symbols of a destiny on the march. . . . [He argues, after Heidegger, that this manufactures the] subject as *gewesend*—that is to say, as being the one who thus has been.[21]

This raises a number of questions about what Althusser calls the "problem of origins." Which came first: the state legitimized by this drama of the public will, or the characters that formed that public? How could there be a public without a state? When did the citizen become a citizen? Or, as Robert Michels asked, what is "the nature of the act by which a people is a people"? And does that act make it possible for "the people [to] sin against themselves"?[22]

Derrida knows the difficulties in being clear about this. Imagining himself in the seat of Thomas Jefferson in Virginia, he asks who authored/authorized the U.S. Declaration of Independence. Jefferson drafted the document for fifty-six signatories, who were held to represent the rest of an emergent America. The document was actually signed on behalf of an entity called "the American people," operating "in the name of God." Which came first? The document that "the people" made sovereign? Or "the people" made sovereign by the document? Derrida knows one or two other things after having pondered this for a time, things about "the people":

> the American people did not exist as the American people before having signed the Declaration of Independence. And it is in signing

that they conferred upon themselves the right to call themselves the American people and the right to sign. It did not exist before the signature. Thus, the scriptor does not exist before the signature. The signature itself, which imposes the law, is in itself a performative act which in a certain way produces its own subject.[23]

This drama is a mythic installation and iteration of tradition, a tradition that argues for a compact with a polity and a belonging and fealty to a nation. The compact extends to a faith in particular procedural norms of debate and a particular definition of the tasks of the state in setting up and managing a framework of property relations and the definition of identity. Rather than being a point in past time that can be isolated, the "primordial 'moment' " that " 'has made a people a people' . . . is the always contemporary primordial 'moment,' " contemporary for Althusser because it is always being reinvented in accordance with the enunciation of an object the state calls the "general interest." This enunciative form relies on a mythic "general will" for its legitimacy and pretends that the latter preceded it.[24] This is the source of the paradox identified by Rousseau, the paradox "of making men free by making them subject." It is necessary to do this if one is to resolve the problem of needing a rational public allocation of resources while simultaneously guaranteeing individual rights to property; or to put it another way, to resolve the problem of believing in absolute individual liberty as a source of good government while also requiring absolute authority for that government over the individual.[25] Hence the installation of the mythic compact and the endless dialogue it encourages between those living under it and their imagined "ancestral citizens," to use Herbert Spencer's phrase.[26]

The original contractors lacked faith in each other beyond their preparedness to hold to the agreement to cede their governance to rules and representatives that created a timeless, depersonalized public aura. Jürgen Habermas provides a useful gloss to this: "According to the official version, political power springs from public will-formation and flows, as it were, through the state apparatus via legislation and administration, returning to a Janus-faced public that takes the form of a public of citizens at the entrance to the state and a public of clients at its exit."[27]

Habermas both historicizes and philosophizes in his prescriptive account of a public sphere that can make this relationship intellectually and politically valid. The public sphere is a space for the enactment of politics through talk, the site where subjects meet as citizens to discuss topics common to them that require collective deliberation. These may include criticism of the state; the economy; or the political or economic systems themselves. What was common practice for bourgeois men in Enlightenment Europe becomes a model for debate in a form that lays claim to the possibility of a homogeneous language as a guarantee of consensus. In the United States, for instance, such a model appears as overtly elaborated doctrine in juridical discussion of the First Amendment to the Constitution. And in Prague in 1989, the Civic Forum's "Rules of Dialogue" institutionalized conduct within such a space via the following precepts: "When searching for the truth together, your opponent must not be an enemy"; "Try to understand the other person"; "A statement without proof is not an argument"; "Do not try to have the last word in the discussion at all costs"; "Do not threaten the dignity of your opponent"; "Do not forget that a dialogue requires discipline"; and "Do not mistake dialogue for monologue."[28]

There is much history supporting the propositional value of this essentially procedural, enunciative mode. From the time of the Enlightenment, the emerging sovereign state took upon itself the task of producing modern individuals who would function effectively and progress singly and together toward the perfect meld of private and public advantage. From the position of elite theory, Michels refers to this, somewhat dismissively, as the "*amour propre* of every citizen."[29]

The French Enlightenment was said to have enthroned the human subject as a secular monarch, fit to rule without divine or metaphysical sanction or the fetters of a proactive past reaching out to dominate the future by forming the will of fate. Hence the model of the social contract, which presumes that history starts here and that rights derive from the human subject's own initiation of institutions of invigilation via systems of formal government. The accusation in response to this might be that such a project was fatally dependent on the very taste for metaphysics that it claimed to abjure. The new trinity was law, reason, and the human subject, a veritable substitution for divinity incarnate. For Engels, the apparently transcendental nature of rule through reason that was heralded by this Enlightenment simply indicated the realities of a specific point in history that saw the bourgeoisie breaking up an old regime and institutionalizing its power in new laws of property. The timelessness of particular philosophical claims merely reflected the power of their subordination to the economic conditions of the time. Marx put such claims into the category of a "legendary primordial condition . . . [that] asserts as a historical fact what it should explain."[30]

In fact, each of these positions turns on the rule of reason and the subject that Kant announced in 1784 in his reply to the query of a puzzled priest: "Enlightenment is man's emergence from his self-incurred immaturity."[31] For both the sense of persons learning to be themselves in a new way, which abjured dependence on others, and the drive of the state to define the available ways of so doing represent the impact of the emergence of the human sciences. This is a fundamental tension of the age, as great as those of public against private or of individual against collective. Foucault worries about the connection between rationality as a project of the West and the techniques of power that express and implement that project, such that the nexus between rationality and domination is problematic: Is this nexus necessary or inessential, inevitable or casual? Are industrial societies always tools of power and hence repression? He is concerned "that the promise of *Aufklärung* (Enlightenment), of attaining freedom through the exercise of reason, has been, on the contrary, overturned within the domain of Reason itself . . . taking more and more space away from freedom."[32] And yet the Enlightenment is routinely associated with the emergence of a knowledgeable and legitimate public that provides the basis for democratic freedoms.

How can we know that public? For Foucault, "rational discourse is based less on the geometry of light than on the insistent, impenetrable density of the object." This suggests that the establishment of knowledge of and as a public is no guarantee of freedom.[33] If "the public" is best understood as "the inescapable collectivity of any society," as Stewart Ranson and John Stewart would have it, the question remains of how this collection is made inescapable.[34] The *Federalist Papers* show evidence of the need to manufacture a single political public in their desire to do something about the ineffable fallibility of humanity, the way in which reason is said to be subordinated to passion. For just as the market is enshrined as a deity expressed through the drive to consume, so politics must be elevated beyond such immediate motives inside citizenship's "threnody on the corruption of political virtue by market greed," as Michael Ignatieff puts it.[35]

There are, in any case, practical difficulties with the ideal speech-act model of making decisions. If all the relevant information needed to decide a matter of public significance were to circulate, the chances of a workable outcome would be minimized by the time and space taken up by the process. And there are problems with the opposite system, one that imposes total control on people by the state, because it wastes productive resources in the task of policing. In recent formulations of this problem, it is often argued that government from on high is being displaced by governance of the self. This does the work of fulfilling the desires of the state by manufacturing a public comprised of subjectivities that can work toward that goal. Foucault suggests that: "To govern, in this sense, is to structure the possible field of action of others."[36] This is done in order to make people more productive and have them do this under their own cognizance. Self-governance as a set of technologies comes to displace the management of populations by material intervention. Just as the subject attains self-recognition via one set of discourses as a lone individual, even at this moment of loneliness, subjects are also expected to recognize themselves as part of a public. They know themselves as citizens.

The processes this book is concerned to look at are the following: how such a public is formed and governed via a technology of the cultural subject known as the cultural citizen, the virtuous political participant who is taught how to scrutinize and improve her or his conduct through the work of cultural policy; and what the limits are of that technology. The domain of the book may be defined, then, as the rules of knowledge and practice that describe a range of activities to do with the formation and governance of subjects. I argue that the human subject is a critical component in the formation of a discourse of "the public" and of distinct "publics." This discourse is not to be found in the domain of an ideal sphere of rationality, or in pure representativeness, or in the marks of class power. It is to be found and explicated in particular technologies of cultural governance. The subject may be split; but it is split in discourse, split in the sense that its characteristics are always described with an eye to their deployment as rationales for very diffuse types of conduct. So this is a policy book: it is concerned with policies for producing subjects that are about the formation of repeatable methods of conducting oneself, at the level either of the individual or the public.

The book draws extensively on work appearing under the name of Michel Foucault. It presumes as a starting point Foucault's accounts of the ways in which formations of persons as individual subjects and collective publics may be seen to operate with relative autonomy from each other. This is taken to be so in the sense that the rise and fall in popularity of these accounts, their constitution as objects of apprehension and their knowledge-effects, may not necessarily see them in dynamic relation to conventional categories derived from the sociology of knowledge, such as intersection with changing external reality or the work of research exposing flaws in argumentation; what Fredric Jameson calls "classical and paradigmatic scientific discoveries achieved by triumphant accident."[37] Foucault distinguishes between *savoir*, which refers to the overall domain of knowledge, and *connaissance,* or a specific knowledge. *Savoir* describes "the process through which the subject finds himself modified by what he knows, or rather by the labor performed in order to know. It is what permits the modification of the subject and the construction of the object." *Savoir* is the scene-setter, the determinant of broad movements of knowledge. *Connaissance* describes "the process which permits the multiplication of knowable objects, the development of their intelligibility, the understanding of their rationality, while the subject always remains the same." The movement between these categories is characteristic of Western subjects within modernity, "knowing a determinate, objective set of things while at the same time constituting themselves as subjects under fixed and determinate conditions," under the overarching, transformative sign of *savoir* and with limit-experiences designated by *connaissance.* Truth and the limit-experience thus become inexorably intertwined if one writes the history of the modern as the imbrication of a collective past with knowledge.[38]

Foucault's insistence on the corporeal, somatic, and historical efficacy of the knowledges emanating from the human sciences—his anti-idealist sense that only in such moments could these developments be regarded as significant occurrences—argues for an anchored account of modernity and postmodernity and the definite effects that these knowledges have on the exchange of terms of existence undergone by the body and its knowing subject. The operation of knowledge, then, becomes a tracing of power, power exercised by institutions formed by and themselves in turn forming knowledges about available subjectivities. At the level of political philosophy and political economy, this has very significant implications for ideas about individual rational actors; adherence to the state and capital; relationship to the self; and possibilities for making epistemological breaks that will allow new forms of subjectivity. I shall deal with some criticisms of Foucault in chapter 5. Here, I wish to signal that it is my desire to break down by attrition the allegation that his work is simultaneously impeccably radical and impenetrably apolitical. It is said that Foucault combines anti-humanism with a neglect of the specificity of political systems in such a way as to allow no analytic or practical logic for the organization of cultural activism within cultural-capitalist states.

Foucault's non–a priori account of the person does not deny the significance of the category, or its utility. Rather, he calls for an interrogation of the discourse of the human and the conditions of its emergence. Foucault thus hauls us away from both the conventional split between base and superstructure in Marxist accounts of the person "under" a given mode of production and the Romantic or liberal-humanist aesthetic of the individual, propelling us instead toward what Patricia O'Brien calls a "thesis of massive normalization."[39] Doctrines of free expression, of the individual realization of the self and autonomous self-governance, circulate plentifully. But these doctrines must limit even as they define; for to set out criteria for freedom and humanness is simultaneously to police conduct politely, to endorse the animated working hypothesis of democracy, in which to individuate is to normalize.

Paradoxically, this process of normalization may operate via differentiation. I argue that cultural policy is a normalizing power in cultural-capitalist democracies that inscribes a radical indeterminacy of the subject. Although the rationale for much cultural policy may be claimed to be the discovery and protection of real selves—even of inalienable ones—the following move is necessarily made: cultural policy exists to ramify what is apparently already there.

Foucault drew attention to this type of contradiction when he identified two critical philosophical postulates underpinning the development of the discipline of psychology: "que la vérité de l'homme est épuisée dans son être naturel; et que le chemin de route connaissance scientifique doit passer par la détermination de rapports quantitatifs, la construction d'hypothèses et la vérification experimentale [that the truth of man is exhausted in his natural state; and that the road to proper scientific knowledge must follow quantitative methods, the construction of hypotheses and their verification through experimentation]."[40]

Falsifiability is not natural. Experimentation is not natural. So "man" is not natural, since "he" does these things and is the professional embodiment of science. "His" scientific truth is assuredly not to be found in a "natural man," then. The preexistent self ends up, not uncovering itself to itself, but making a new self under the sign of the rules of scientific (or bureaucratic) method. But of course it is always also doing so in the name of an empiricism that claims not to disturb what its rules of discourse are, even then, beginning to form and cradle. So the discipline of psychology exists at the interstices and contradictory junctions of a consistent set of oppositions: totality and singularity; gene and environ; performance and potential; institutional law and individual conduct. This is akin to the contradictory maneuvers that cultural policy is called upon to make, maneuvers that oscillate between self and society, nature and reform, and selflessness and selfishness.

Although cultural policy seeks to make and govern manageable subjects, it does so within the epistemological framework of dispersal and chaos investigated in chapter 1, "Civic Culture and the Postmodern Subject," which describes the morphology of the citizen, both past and present, as a preliminary to establishing the connections between culture and policy as technologies that form citizens. It then situates this discussion inside a broader context of social theory by reworking some Althusserian positions into what is termed the social surface, concluding with a discussion of ontic, epistemic, and postmodern forms of knowledge and their relationship to these questions.

A backdrop of indeterminacy has, paradoxically, been made to function as the lodestone of cultural policy. It offers culture the task of aiding the subject in finding out the truth of itself, a truth necessarily of enigma. This radical indeterminacy is most prolifically constituted within textual analysis, the human science protocols of reading decipherment that institutionalize the impossibility, but necessity, of knowing the self. It is argued in chapter 2, "Textual Theory," that this is a critical component of literary and screen studies, as evidenced in a wide range of hermeneutic practices and proclivities. These disciplinary fields may be seen to take the discovery of the incomplete subject and its partial, essayistically achieved reformation into a satisfactory whole, as their reason to be. In the case of literary studies, this has made for its installation into the secondary curriculum in many countries as the mandatory point of entry into humanness, and within the humanities academy as the site of still further achievement of this set of reformations. It is argued that this is an exemplary instance of civics, of the building of the person that is central to governance and entry into full participation in the ethic of citizenship and the notion of a public. The theory underpinning ethical incompleteness as the touchstone of cultural criticism is expounded and justified in this chapter by tracing the contemporary *dispositif* of aesthetics. It is argued that the textual critic / pedagogue must be an ideal reader, ideality here residing in the propensity to find and transfer textual incompleteness from diegetic characters onto the said textual critic / pedagogue and the readers under his or her tutelage. This ethical manufacture of a preferred self and a preferred public through pedagogic guidance will be a recurring theme in my argument, which seeks to give an account of the cultural critic as tour guide to the self, a measure of the aestheticization of postmodernity. For inasmuch as cultural criticism is at the core of postmodernity, the overlapping of the aesthetic with the political is the conceptual core of this book.

Following these scene-setting chapters, the book branches out into establishing the different forms of subjectivity sanctioned/created by different discourses, arguing for a series of generally parallel drifts between differing accounts of subject and public that are occasioned and nourished by various discourses of the person. In a double move of governance, these discourses are frequently embodied in parts of the state as well as aspects of the person. I ask what happens in the movement between the constitution of the individual and the collective subject that informs our apprehension of both a person and a public, arguing that these technologies have been most obviously used in the analysis of texts. This is critically important for the formation of an interpretative, reading and receiving public that has learned to rummage for indeterminacy and incompleteness in cultural products and to map these back onto itself.

The next two chapters examine this contention about the separation of spheres of subjectivity and what may happen when they meet. In each case, the cultural-capitalist state is a motor of governance. Chapter 3, "Nation, Drama, Diplomacy," looks at the enduring qualities of a particular ethic of self-formation within aesthetics that is mapped onto public policy. Through an investigation of reactions to attempts by the United States to open up a free trade in television programs via the General Agreement on Tariffs and Trade, it is argued that a range of governments have responded in ways that indicate an abiding faith in reflectionist accounts of screen texts and their capacity to inhere in national cultural formations. This faith expresses itself in the name of forming an adequate (national and individual) self. Postmodernity finds the proliferation of televisual messages and a developing decentered internationalism mutually reinforcing; hence their centrality here and the choice of this site.

Chapter 4 is entitled "Making Citizens and Consumers." Via twin case studies, it further addresses the discursive construction of citizenship and how citizens are called up and taught. The first case study looks at the televising of parliamentary democracy and how this allegedly aims to teach the viewer to respect, value, comprehend, and participate in the institution of Parliament. My contention here is that this is as much about refashioning the politician as it is about detailing and remedying the inadequacies of the elector. In each case, a culturally trained citizen is being produced. The second study examines what happens when such disinterested notions of citizenship meet with an account of the utilitarian, maximizing consumer of neoclassical economic theory. It does this in the context of questions of authorship and the deployment of successful businesspersons to voice particular doctrines of human capital on behalf of fractions of the state against doctrines of critical educationalism, a move that sets up and then destroys an opposition between training and educating the person. Again, there is both a formation of the subject speaking—the apparent author of a given speech—as well as of the addressee. This works over the contradictory imposts of the two critical public forms of political postmodern subjectivity, the citizen and the consumer, and the important textual question of authorship.

The subject constructed here is, following Foucault, always already divided, ready, and readied to be redisposed: "According to a certain grid of explicit or implicit interrogations, he is the questioning subject; according to a certain programme of information, he is the listening subject; according to a table of characteristic features, he is the seeing subject, and, according to a descriptive type, the observing subject."[41] A similar set of moves is countenanced/required by connections to a series of theoretical domains in the bureaucratic, economic, and political registers. These are brought out in chapters 3 and 4.

Chapter 5, "New Technologies to Form New Selves," commences with a consideration of the criticisms of Foucault's politics and its utility as an analytic and pragmatic tool of social change. Following this dialogue, the chapter evaluates the possibilities of subjects reforming themselves in one of Foucault's principal fields of engagement, the domain known as sex. It is based on an ethnography of a disturbance by a male homosexual order of nuns at a university speech given by Pope John Paul II. The argument moves outside the conditions of the day, and how they were set up by various speeches given then, to consider the ethics of self-formation promulgated by the order. It asks why the nuns' preferred selves were deemed unacceptable at that time and place, although tolerated at others, as a consequence of a further problem that occurs when accounts of the subject that are habitually kept quite separate are permitted uncomfortable junction. This junction is notable for its emergence as an overtly dialogic and unruly moment, its significance deriving from the fact that the critical enunciators of self-formation in this case were quite outside the *politesse* of the civic public sphere. This marks them off from the official selves considered in previous chapters. It also offers a dialogue between what Habermas calls "expressive self-realization and moral-practical self-determination," the shift from alienation to utopia that he finds "rooted in cultural modernity."[42] Against an account of the ideal public sphere, the chapter also considers how dependent the notion is on incivility, on an account of unacceptable conduct and how such conduct may in fact be necessary in order to form an alternative sphere. This draws us back to the polite sociability ethos of recent theories of citizenship and suggests that they are logocentrically dependent on an excluded grotesque that is a different form of cultural technology, one that seeks to make the move from a technology of power to a technology of the self. To return for a moment to the well-tempered reference of my title, this chapter may be seen to problematize the reasoned sweetness of Bach and his attendant cultural subject. For Foucault, "listening to music is becoming more and more difficult, to the point that its notation is stripped of any recognizable shape or sign." The "conventional transparency" of classical music is gone, along with its "iterability."[43] This leaves some room open for the invention of a technology of the self, room for unruliness and difference.

It should be stressed that the book makes no claim to do more than aim at the surface. There is no desire or design to know what lies below or to place a value on the subjectivities or selves described in terms of their appropriateness as descriptions of or prescriptions for the actual conduct of living persons. Rather, this book essays an evaluation of subjectivity as a public cultural technology. No "real" person is found, no essence against which one might measure the subjects of policy.

The book does, however, claim to contribute across a range of disciplinary settings and methodologies. It presumes a competence to write authoritatively inside, between, and against such fields as literary and screen theory; international political economy; political philosophy; discourse analysis; public policy; neoclassical economics; ethnography; and gender studies. Further, it presumes to do so with a specific perceptual grid overdetermining the application of these knowledges and redisposing the fields of their intersection from the norm and onto the category of the formation and governance of persons as both subjects of knowledge and subjects to authority (authority from both within and without the subject itself). This reading against the grain presumes to uncover what Foucault called "rules of formation . . . never formulated in their own right, but . . . to be found only in widely differing theories, concepts, and objects of study."[44] Such rules are about the barely perceptible shift in gear made between constituting subjects as publics and publics as subjects, each category serving radically different purposes at different times, but with an apparently static conception of the "good" person and the "good" society underlying them. I argue in this book that these are actually radically unstable, mutually contradictory formations. They are conventionally kept apart but nevertheless share a propensity for this set of discrete double moves between "self" and "social" that mark all such forms out in terms of ethical incompleteness. It is the connections across sciences, the points of commonality, that produce this line of reasoning and, I trust, its warrant.

The human sciences emerged as objects "in which man had invested his very subjectivity even while transforming it," fated for eternity to fail to be co-present with "his own 'nature.'" The promises of a center and a totality, uncoverable via the stripping-away of layers to reveal a core, would remain necessarily unfulfilled, but promises that nonetheless guaranteed the subject's oblations at the feet of these sciences in the hope of becoming reconciled with its own essential self and hence, ultimately, of ceasing to inquire after that self or be in need of the human sciences. Instead, those sciences became "a general cultural experience," part of the great movements constituting and reconstituting subjectivities in search of a true self / in response to impossible promises across time. They managed to "authorize a knowledge of the individual" that made the definition of that individual "an endless labour."[45]

Ultimately, to be ethically incomplete, and engaged in an endless process of self-remedy, is to be the subject of this book.

THE WELL-TEMPERED SELF

Chapter One

◆

CIVIC CULTURE AND
THE POSTMODERN SUBJECT

TWO HUNDRED YEARS after the French Revolution, citizenship is a renewed and significant trope in everyday political discourse. Within a few months of the start of that bicentenary, free elections were instituted in Brazil, Uruguay, Argentina, Paraguay, Chile, and Nicaragua. Systemic changes of polity and economy were under way in Poland, the German Democratic Republic, Czechoslovakia, and Hungary. Further energy was being devoted to the infrastructural corollary of *glasnost* in the Soviet Union. And new debates were emerging in Western countries over how to define citizenship and whether it was necessarily related to particular forms of economic management. Alain Touraine's gloss of this period goes so far as to describe it as supplanting an age of revolution (1917–89) with an age of democracy, in a reaction against authoritarianism that shifted the rhetoric of the people and their interests away from vanguards and toward "the free choice of governors by the governed."[1] But as Claus Offe has shown, this was the first occasion of "a revolution without a historical model and a revolution without a revolutionary theory."[2] What can this occasion call upon in order to pass from the status of an event to that of a structure?

The Morphology of the Citizen

Classical political theory supports the notion of a "government which derives all its powers . . . from the great body of the people."[3] It therefore places much store on political virtue amongst the citizenry. In Aristotelian Athens, the search for the active expression of virtue and a rational world was the reason for political activity. In ancient Rome, the goal became the protection of the commonwealth. The Latin for citizen, *civis,* comes from the verb to hail or summon, *cieo.* The citizen can be called upon to perform certain duties as a quid pro quo for access to the processes of politics. For Rousseau, the "body politic . . . may be taken as an organized, living body, resembling that of man." Law and custom are the brain, business the mouth and stomach, and "citizens . . . the body which make the machine live, move and work" via a "general will." This will is the source of the law. It constitutes the conditions of intersubjectivity among "members of the State" and with the state itself.[4]

These positions are ready to prize "public over private good in action and deliberation." They recommend three ways of constructing the virtuous subject of such a polity. The options, as outlined by Shelley Burtt, are "the education of desire," "the accommodation of interests," and "the compulsion of duty." The doctrine of the education of desire wants to acknowledge human drives. It seeks to mold them, to transform them into public goods rather than private ones. Citizens are to be educated to define fulfillment in terms of public service. Pleasures will not be sacrificed. Rather, they will be redefined in the interests of putting personal satisfaction in alignment with the public good. Conversely, the position that accommodates interests identifies people as genuinely rational actors who calculate the costs and benefits for themselves of various possibilities. This essential nature can be made consonant with virtue where it is "structured by the norms and institutions of the commonwealth." Finally, compulsion of duty says that citizens serve because they understand rationally that it is their duty to do so. Denial of desire is important and self-aggrandizement is eschewable under the sign of service. Each option assumes, with Rousseau, the need to "create citizens," to teach them virtue as part of a process of "learning to deserve to live."[5]

The conventional pluralist political science position is much simpler. According to Harold Lasswell and Abraham Kaplan, citizens are "those in a body politic who share in the allocation of power."[6] But what form does this sharing take? It simply means that citizens are eligible to stand for public office; to vote for candidates for such offices; and to engage in a very vaguely intimated, more general participation in social life. Even with the revisions to pluralism that have come in the wake of decades of withering critique, this sense of the citizen remains relatively untouched.

Consider Charles Lindblom's influential book *The Policy-Making Process*, which was a volte-face from the sanguine nature of pluralism up to that point. Lindblom's previous work had argued that governments make decisions between competing groups that even out over time, but here he broke decisively with that view, noting that the bulk of the critical decisions taken by the administration in the United States favor] business interests over others. Nonetheless, although Part 3 of *The Policy-Making Process* is entitled "The Citizen in the Play of Power," the citizen in question implicitly overlaps with the "voter," and is nowhere defined. It is left to the reader to inscribe the citizen in the cartographic interstices of elections, parties, policies, and imagined satisfaction.[7] Citizens vote at elections. Their next act awaits the next election. They are, in Marxist terminology, abstract citizen-voters, subjects engaged in a repeated process of disaggregation and reaggregation.

Alternatively, citizenship is equated with patriotism: for three generations U.S. civics textbooks have had red, white, and blue spines, and their contents have betrayed no hint of social changes over many decades of momentous upheaval. Contemporary citizenship education continues to presume "commonality, sameness, universality in need, want and desire . . . in living as an American citizen."[8]

Some feminist accounts of what constitutes a desirable polity have entailed a return to the classical association of politics and virtue. Active citizenship is to be entered into as a Platonic search for the good life, independently of particular or personal necessities. Citizens must be treated equally, whatever the inequalities between them in other spheres of life, so as to form just and good persons. (The "natural" inequalities pronounced by Plato and Aristotle are, of course, rejected.) Other feminist critiques regard women's general economic dependence on men as so endemic and powerful as virtually to invalidate any apparent utility in citizenship. They point to the way in which defining citizenship as a public technology instantaneously creates a private sphere that is outside it, a sphere in which men have traditionally oppressed women. The timelessness of idealist theories of citizenship is said to sit poorly along-side a past that has either routinely denied women suffrage or set them up as problems complicating the disinterested exercise of male virtue. One might also point to the extensive connections between citizenship rights and the forging of brotherly bonds through war. Much of the idealization of the figure of the republican has been achieved via a series of oppositions or exclusions. Republican virtue is not-woman. The republican is austere and measured, but must be ready to be "virile" at times of crisis, as a former editor of the *Times* of London once put it.[9]

It is the loss of the certainty once offered by the patriarchal rule of tyrants, the certainty of straightforward firmness and obvious oppression, that troubles some feminist critics. Juliet Flower MacCannell characterizes the modern promise of liberty, equality, and fraternity as "the Regime of the Brother, of modernity." In true totemic fashion, the incest taboo imposed as guilt after the democrats' murder of the tyrannical father has led to a narcissistic assumption of an identical fit between their own selves and others. Modern democracy is consequently centered around ",the narcissistic ego" and not "the other." It is founded on faulty extrapolations by men from their own misrecognition of themselves, their needs, and their history, in a way that denies that anyone is outside the discourse of citizenship. This acts to prevent any arousal of the preconditions necessary for encouraging active participation in the affairs of state. Civil society is an imaginary projection that further denies the real democracy of "diverse, recognized relationships."[10] Such critiques are powerful today, when questions are already being asked about the status of women in the newly forming democracies of central and eastern Europe, which show signs of renewed influence on the part of the nationalism and religion that once consigned women to domestic roles. Anne Phillips gives this example of the limitations to the technology of citizenship that allow for such developments:

> We would be acting as citizens if we publicly campaigned for men to take a full share in the household tasks; we would not, however, be acting as citizens when we sort out the division of labour inside our own home. In the older language of democratising everyday life, each of these was equally 'political'. In the new language of citizenship, only the one that takes place in a public arena can seriously contend for the name.[11]

Against this, a return to Aristotle finds a useful problematization of the split between the private and public spheres. "Politics as the master science of the good" includes "household management" as one of its "most honored capacities." It is a space of equality.[12] Plato even gestures at a theory of difference when he suggests that women may need their own program for citizenship. And it is possible to point to critical moments in politics—such as seventeenth-century parliamentary petitions in Britain, the *salons* of eighteenth-century Paris, and mid-nineteenth-century U.S. presidential campaigning—when women have played powerful roles in expanding the morphology and significance of the public sphere.

The argument continues to be made with some force, however, that the idealized notion of the public sphere of citizenship has been created by the exclusion of women. A revived citizenship, in this reading, would have to be accompanied by a radical rewriting of the current relationship between public and private. This would reject the idea that difference and the particular, the peculiar, the microeconomic, or the domestic necessarily belong in the private domain.

Marxism is also cosmically ambivalent about citizenship. The early Marx presumes that there can be a community of citizens incarnated in acts of reason, but he comes to reject a Hegelian faith in the capacity of the state to act as an ethical agent against the naked self-interest of civil society. Marx took the concept of civil society, after Hegel, as "the material conditions of life," the domain of political economy that held the key to understanding a given polity and its legal relations. It was the "mode of production of [this] material life" that determined the shape of the state and its members' relationship with it. Any attempt to think through profound social change inside or outside this relationship could only occur once the beginnings of new social relations had put in an appearance. For without the signs of transition to a new mode of production there could be no methods for conceiving of real innovation: "mankind always sets itself only such problems as it can solve."[13] In 1848, what could citizenship offer to those who knew that "the executive of the modern state is but a committee for managing the common affairs of the whole bourgeoisie"?[14] Parliamentary democracy seemed to represent the petite bourgeoisie, a transitional class standing temporarily between the two great warring factions and blunting their violent meeting, a meeting that was a necessity if history were to move forward. Engels was clear about the fundamental problem with the idea of a republic and its potential for representativeness: "The state was the official representative of the whole of society, its concentration in a visible body, but it was so only in so far as it was the state of that class which in its time represented the whole of society." He argued that the state would lose its reason to exist if it were indiscriminately representative, because its foundation must lie in servicing one class over another.[15]

As the possibilities of action by the left within parliamentary democracy emerged with time, however, this position periodically seemed to soften. Consider Gramsci. At one point, he states that "within the general configuration of an industrial society, each man can actively participate in affairs and modify his surroundings only to the extent that he operates as an individual and citizen, as a member of the democratic-parliamentary State. The liberal experience is not worthless and can only be transcended after it has been experienced." But at another point, this is a distortion. Democracy is a technology of life "for large-scale production, for busy exchange, for the concentration of the population in modern, capitalist cities."[16] It must clearly be destroyed as a precursor to socialism.

The two classic left perspectives on citizenship as it would function under a socialist mode of production are as follows. Firstly, it is a prize granted as the pleasure of collaboration in pursuit of the good life. The citizen is a political agent of morality, actively engaged in the determination of the workings of society. Secondly, the citizen is a cooperative economic worker. As everyone is multiskilled in an interchangeable way and happily engaged in the physical manufacture of the good life, there is no need for a politics. There is nothing in citizenship as such. Civics is work. The problem with the legacy of this approach for state socialist societies was the absence of a lexicon for detailing social, economic, and political problems under socialism.

At a sociopolitical level, the sovereign state and the citizen of suffrage are perhaps the defining signs of modernity. In existence from the sixteenth century, this state and its members were theorized, endorsed, and sought after in the nineteenth century, and became a commonplace after 1945. But by the same token, modernity is also characterized by what Norbert Elias calls "self-detachment." The subject sees itself unfolding as an object of inquiry after the model of a scientific view of nature. Cognition conquers affect as a means of comprehending both natural and human phenomena.[17] All these morphologies seem to share the notion that citizens have a common or at least transportable code of conduct; a civics, or sociability. When the United States sought to replicate itself in a decolonizing Africa, it did so not only via the dogmas of industrial modernization, but also by ideas of civility. The infrastructure of modernity involved a landscape of subjects, modeled on a special notion of civic/civil conduct. David Apter refers here to "the double market place, i.e. the economic market place and the political. The

The Well-Tempered Self

inequities arising out of the operations of the first in social life can be rectified in the second to produce a moving equilibrium. The political problem is to find those specific instruments of economic and political organization which will enable those two marketplaces to work in tandem in an environment of increasing growth."[18] Today it is increasingly being argued, from a multitude of political positions, that in civility "lies the difference between a well-ordered and a disordered liberal democracy."[19] For Edward Shils "the institutions in which beliefs and desires or interests are proposed and confronted in argument and the institutions in which beliefs and interests are taken into account and digested discriminately into law cannot work acceptably without some constituent civility and consensus of the contending parties."[20]

The ideal type of reason triumphant and humanity freed that is prescribed for export around the world is, however, at risk of deracination at home. This loss of civic structure and virtue is of acute concern to the likes of Christopher Lasch ("in the hour of [democracy's] seeming triumph, its fragility is exposed more clearly than ever before, nowhere more than in the US").[21] In Lasch's eyes, public corruption, wastefulness, urban dross, and gruesome disparities in income call the moral standing of the United States into question even at the moment of its greatest self-congratulation with the departure of state socialism from Europe. Citizenship as a legal form must be supplemented and ramified by civic education, forging a nexus between rights and responsibilities. This is the means of manufacturing "a whole world of heroes." For Lasch, democracy is problematic when it fails to deliver "a workable social order" for want of "civic virtue" and the legacy of obedience and thrift granted by premodern religious and moral orders; in short, for want of civility.[22]

This concept of civility emerged in mid-sixteenth-century Europe with the publication of Erasmus's *De civilitate morum puerilium* (On civility in children) in 1530. Translations into English, German, Czech, and French soon appeared and the book was quickly adopted as a school primer. It was reprinted over thirty times in the next few years, and by the end of the eighteenth century, a hundred and thirty editions had appeared. The notion of civility entered everyday educational parlance across cultures as a key to the formation of young people and an index of the emergence of a problem of the social. The subject matter of *De civilitate* is very much that of proper conduct: how to look at others; how to present and maintain clean nostrils; how to dispose of spittle; and how to eat. So this is clearly a case of the public presentation of a decent self as both the sign and the mechanism of social cohesion. *Civil-*

ité signifies a gradual turn in the formation of the state, its shift from a series of decentralized and internally divided entities to centralized, externally divided relationships. Internal pacification—of both person and polity—is matched by external anarchy. Civilization comes to connote a broad variety of tendencies and practices, which occur diffusely in technology, manners, science, custom, and religion. From the first primers on the human condition as knowable through its surface look—Erasmus's contribution to behavior modification / depth psychology—there comes to be an equation of spirit with cloth, of dress sense with inner self, of seeing with knowing. Sight becomes the principal measure of character, now that speech is itself so measured that it betrays the signs of restraint. The same period ushers in a procedure of auto-invigilation, a requirement to evaluate one's own actions and appearance.[23]

Here we need return to the notion of civil society. Anglo-American meanings dominate its contemporary resonance in the refashioning of the geopolitical gazeteer in the postcommunist era. In the English tradition, *civil society* implies personal circles active in public life, but the various understandings of its German equivalent, *bürgerliche Gesellschaft,* show considerable change over time: in medieval German cities, for example, the adjective *bürgerliche* appeared in local identification documents, signifying the allocation of a place in the social order, whereas for Hegel, it denoted the equilibrium of relativities of liberty, safety, and subsistence between the subject and the social.

The different national careers of the term eventually begin to merge. By the nineteenth century, civility was institutionally located inside the modern sense of civil society, what Foucault called "the great fantasy . . . of a social body constituted by the universality of wills";[24] a fantasy that, it is argued, produced a sea change in the constitution of politics across central and eastern Europe in 1989 and continues a slightly different career on the left in the United States. For the new democracies, civil society has stood as an antinomy to state socialism and party dictatorship, defined by the absence of their salient features rather than any positive constitution of its own. For American radicals, however, the term equates with social movements of community that are opposed to formal machines of democracy or the market.

In political theory, civil society lies beyond the family, clan, or locale, but falls something short of the state. It possesses autonomous institutions in the areas of the economy, religion, intellectual life, and the political party (but not the legislature or executive government). The connectedness lies in a shared understanding of "civil manners." Civil subjects exist within this space and are known as such when their conduct is ordered by something other than basic collective identification or the force majeure of the state. Outside the formal laws of that state, everyday conduct is extremely autonomous, although routinely contained, constrained, and defined by respect for all sectors of the populace, because the Other is also part of the Self.

For Rousseau, however, civil society is a process of unending envy, initiated by the propositional form of reasoning about a state of being other than one's own. Whereas natural "man" simply dealt in the business of subsistence, civil society produces an incompleteness as part of its panoply of alternatives, plans, contingencies, collectivities, and individualities. The innate propensity to care for the self is supplanted by an amour propre that defines the meeting of needs in competitive relation to others, a relation engendered by reason and confirmed by reflection. Civil society is, in short, a mechanism of distinction.[25] One can see connections in this process to the elitism that marked its first emergence within pluralist American political science, which frequently argued that some citizens are cleverer, more decent, and more polite than others and can therefore best be entrusted with the management of those others.

There is another lineage to this pastoral tending, one that operates via an isomorphic relationship between the ideal elite officeholder and the ideal social order. It is most significant that this line is currently being publicly enunciated very audibly by Edward Shils, the high priest of such logics in the 1950s and 1960s, but long in relative eclipse. There is a clear return in recent deliberations within political science to the logics of that era, particularly as they were put to work within the Committee on Comparative Politics of the U.S. Social Science Research Council. It was the particular labor of that committee to explain the shared features of political systems and the process of "political modernization and development." Development was said to rely on an admixture of "equality, capacity, and differentiation."[26] The United States was itself a (mostly) implied gauge of other nations' achievements, especially those of the emerging sovereign states that seemed likely to adopt socialist principles. Making the modern state also necessitated making the modern person, with a civility to match the economic and constitutional movement beyond tribalism / village life.

Nevertheless, the referent for this civility seems to have changed since the 1960s. Andreas Huyssen argues that one of the key distinctions between modernity and postmodernity is the new relationship between the West and the Third World, which has come to be designated as one of respect in place of control, of difference in place of hierarchy.[27] The development studies that emerged alongside decolonization placed their faith in forms of knowledge that are now in question. Centralization, modernization, industrialization, modeling—in fact, development itself—are supplanted by dispersal, fragmentation, and the aesthetic. There is no center providing the criteria by which others are judged up-to-date. Under postmodernity, declares F. R. Ankersmit, "the history of this appendage to the Eurasian continent [i.e., Europe] is no longer world history." Its accounts of an industrial proletariat, of the emergence of reason, of the centrality of the West, are only of "local importance."[28] Weber's argument that the West developed in terms of a rational potential that is of the essence of human existence is now made to refer to specific, bounded rationalities inscribed in culturally particular technologies of the subject. While certain revived liberal tropes concentrate on an individualistic basis of citizenship, communitarian political philosophy emphasizes collective participation; but as Chantal Mouffe insists, this collective must equally be recognized for the proliferation of publics that constitute it and were denied by the Enlightenment's effortless ethnocentric and androcentric extrapolations from an "undifferentiated concept of 'man.' "[29] To confirm the idea that the Third World has been a key node of instability under postmodernity, one could turn back three decades to doctrines of *négritude* and find almost these very words appearing. Léopold Senghor, for example, differentiates between "European civilization and Negro-African civilization" as the difference between the Cartesian *cogito* and "I feel, I dance the Other; I am." This is still the outcome of reason. But it is "the reason of the touch" rather than the "reasoning-eye." Its talent is to set *logos* over *ratio* in blending logic and the material world.[30] The idea of an absolute, Western doctrine of progress has been leavened, if not discredited, inasmuch as the deployment of instrumental reason and the goal of growth has led to a multiplicity of problematic outcomes over the past century; "reason as despotic enlightenment," Foucault calls it.[31]

The question that still needs to be asked following the installation of the subject by Descartes and Kant is whether human subjection is ended by the advent of the citizen, whether the rupturous events of 1789 represent a break from domination, a departure from the era of absolutism that brings with it the desire and capacity to understand and influence events of government. The West's "local" history clearly continues to be made the center of many political and cultural typologies. This much is evident from the resilience of doctrines of civil society. More than a century ago, Lord Acton defined its task as "the establishment of liberty for the realization of moral duties."[32] Compare this with Michael

The Well-Tempered Self

Walzer's argument that "the words 'civil society' mean the space of uncoerced human association and also the set of relational networks—formed for the sake of family, faith, interest, and ideology—that fill this space."[33] We can discern a renewed interest in identifying the networks that make for the civility that animates this society. The motivation for such a search comes from two sources. First, it is a response by Western intellectuals and policymakers to the breakdown of codes of conduct in Western cities. Second, it is a response by intellectuals and policymakers to the new democracies and economies of central and eastern Europe; *civil society* is here a term to describe the wonder of the West and its non-Leninist rule, noted for its freedoms and the space it provides to influence public policy from outside the apparatus of government. Both responses still tend to focus on an idealized Western past or present, the second being exemplified by this quotation from Gabriel Almond:

> My most striking and moving experience during my 1989 teaching stint in the Soviet Union was my encounters with the members of Chairs in Scientific Communism at the universities in Moscow, Leningrad, and Kiev. With almost no exception, they were quite disenchanted with Marxism-Leninism and were turning to empirical Western-style political science, which they called politology. I carried back with me about a dozen *curricula vitae* of Soviet colleagues who would like to be retooled in the U.S.[34]

Uncertainty produces an invocation of a lost mythic certitude, here from within the former realm of state socialism. But one can see a similar sense of loss and appeal in Western social movements among those who might, on the above account, be responsible for "retooling." Their invocation is of sociability as a *telos,* a process guaranteed by the provision of equal conditions for communicability. Ernesto Laclau trusts that these conditions will "bring . . . to the fore a multiplicity of *limited, fragmented* and *partial* social agents, who together enter into the constitution of a 'collective will.' "[35] This model is much more oriented toward social equality than the one espoused by the pluralists, although such an outcome is to be achieved, not by the methods of command economics, but rather through the will of a community. This will must emerge from the conduct of the citizen, a new citizen who will appear and displace older models of political or economic "man." For these models have failed to deliver acceptable ethics in the eyes of many subjects to guide in the use of power (especially under Marxist-Leninist regimes), the management of the environment, and the status of women and people of color more generally. Environmentalism and feminism have been quite foundational in their combinations and per-mutations of broad-based social critique interspersed with a politics of the everyday that has broken up the anti-individualist certainties of the left. This new citizenship must in some sense be cultural if it is to be manageable by its bearers and enable them to take their places in what Barry Hindess terms "the political life of a self-governing community."[36] Opportunities appear to exist for a society organized by mutu-ally agreed rules of civil conduct, one in which meanings, not force of arms, bind subjects together in their identification with the polity.

As has been indicated, the desire for such a subject is ecumenical. While Shils is hailing the citizen, the *New Statesman and Society* is select-ing citizenship as its "radical theme of the year."[37] The citizen is a polysemic category, open to contestation; an avatar for all parts of the spectrum. Citizenship is an open technology, a means of transforma-tion ready for definition and disposal in dispersed ways at dispersed sites. My concern here is with how elements of the state work to make it a cohesive technology, one that binds its subjects in fealty, and how it may be problematized by other groups. I am doubtful about its ulti-mate utility as a technology of self-formation without subjection, but conscious of its significance inside the cultural-capitalist state.

Althusser argues that the "category of the citizen realizes the *synthesis of the State* in man himself: the citizen is the State in the private man." This technology ensures that subjects see themselves—and willingly—as such. It is a technology that produces a "disposition" on their part not to accept the imposition of a particular form of government passively, but to embrace it actively as a collective expression of themselves (even though this expression itself derives from preconditions for knowledge set by the state). Virtue comes to be defined as "the passion for the general" under democracy, in a way that derives from self-regard. Self and society are one.[38] Citizenship involves membership in a commu-nity and therefore political participation in the running of that commu-nity. This implies a doctrine of rights that are granted on a broadly based, social level, but, paradoxically, function on an individual level in such areas as freedom of association, speech, information, and personal liaison. Rights derive from a state that also polices their exercise through the doctrine of *e pluribus unum*. This doctrine requires the citizen to forge a direct link between "the defence of his ideas and interests and the laws or political decisions providing the basic framework for public life."[39]

For Foucault, the special feature of the development of the state in the West has been its deployment of "pastoral power" on the model of

The Well-Tempered Self

institutions of the Christian church. This power has four special facets. First, it promises heavenly salvation. Second, it lays itself down for others. Third, it promises care of both the community and the solitary self. And, finally, it needs to know those for whom it cares. It must know them so that it can direct them. This knowledge must be complete, its computation a critical production of the truth of the person, a truth that is hence only knowable within this mode of subjection. No longer ecclesiastical, this power has multiplied as it has dispersed over the centuries into a "modern matrix of individualization," normally called "the state."[40] The notion of a legitimacy attached to both private and public opinion founded on individual rationality best expresses and codifies ideas of natural rights that become the mechanism binding person and polity.

In the "modern matrix," salvation is to be had in the *hic et nunc*. It is a salvation that is somatic, to be understood in terms of being healthy, wealthy, and secure. The immediacy of this salvation necessitates many and varied forms of pastoral care, such as the hospital, the police, and a reformed family. And knowledge is now deployed toward two interconnected ends. First, the broad social body of the population becomes an object of care via quantification and extrapolation. Second, the individual body becomes an object of care via various forms of analysis that explain how and to what ends it is singular. So it is, for example, that attempts to understand the public mind will find "the level of wife, self and dream . . . most significant" as sources of truth and will seek them out with all the earnestness they can muster.[41] We must all confess and confide, if we are to uncover the truth of ourselves, a truth that is trained into us as we become cultural subjects through the operation of policy. This is part of the mission of the state to "gain access to the bodies of individuals," a necessary precondition to what Foucault calls "obtaining productive service from individuals" in a way that is "more efficient and less expensive" than by means of force.[42] This might be seen as a restatement of Rousseau's dictum that persons must quickly become "accustomed to regard their individuality only in its relation to the body of the State" as the most appropriate means of ensuring that they "identify themselves in some degree with this greater whole."[43]

Seeking to instill a new mode and degree of identification between people, state, and the integrity of individual life, an identification forged in a rejection of spectacles of punitive horror and their association with the work of authority, early nineteenth-century law reformers in Britain substituted the isomorphism of offenses and their punishment for the naked display of state power. The reformers spoke with great eloquence of the need for the "public mind" to engage sympathy and antipathy for criminals and crime in a processual relationship, and the British state embarked on a project of unprecedented significance, the calibration of popular conduct. In 1823, a need was identified to rewrite the penal code so as to make it "representative of the public conscience," able to unite the public by functioning jointly as "the fruit of moral sentiment" and "a school of public discipline."[44] This marked the invention of public sympathy and the formulation of a disposition to civic unity, operating under an index of respect leafed through and curated by state, citizenry, and society, and guaranteeing a relatively peaceable relationship between these levels. Coupling culture with policy was to be a cost-effective way of developing such a disposition.

Culture and Policy

Culture and *policy* might seem odd words to bring together and then match up with *subject*. The two most common definitions of culture do not suggest that it is the object of policy. On the one hand, it is often held to refer to the artistic output of a particular person or group, defined and valued according to aesthetic criteria and in some way emerging organically from a community of creative people. The other definition, less specific, takes culture to be an all-encompassing concept that incorporates how we live our lives, the sense of place and person that make us human. Conversely, policy is usually taken to refer to a regularized, systematized position statement or guide for action that has been adopted by an organization as an instrument for achieving a goal. In short, it is bureaucratic, not creative or organic.

This distance between the terms is nonetheless problematic. We should rather begin by collapsing the distinction between the two understandings of culture. Quite clearly, culture as a practice of representation participates in the construction of culture as a system of values and beliefs. In turn, that domain affects culture as a representational practice.

We could be endlessly inclusive here and follow Margaret Archer's trawl for culture to include "all intelligibilia, that is any item which has the dispositional capacity of being understood by someone." This leaves the term rather inchoate. Its importance can be agreed upon, but the direction and consequence of this significance remain obstinately difficult to specify. Archer's explanatory history of the term finds that "the status of culture oscillates between that of a supremely independent variable, the superordinate power in society and, with a large sweep of

The Well-Tempered Self

the pendulum, a position of supine dependence on other institutions."
It moves between a standing as the principal determinant of social structure and as a mere epiphenomenon accorded representational labour,
either "society's bandmaster" or merely its "looking-glass."[45]

We can specify the term more precisely than this might imply via four
critical frames that encompass the processes of culture: the market, via
the meanings attaching to commodities and their movement; the state,
as a force manufacturing identity as a subject of a nation and identity as
a citizen of a polity, while also organizing persons in terms of their
certification and aestheticization; the quotidian, the diurnal practices
of making a life; and social movements of identity politics. These in
turn may be seen as connected through the division of departments of
life engendered by the procedures of governance. Tony Bennett argues,
for example, that nineteenth-century Europe saw

> the emergence of new fields of social management in which culture
> is figured forth as both the *object* and the *instrument* of government:
> its object or target insofar as the term refers to the morals, manners,
> and ways of life of subordinate social strata; its instrument insofar as
> it is culture in its more restricted sense—the domain of artistic and
> intellectual activities—that is to supply the means of a governmental
> intervention in and regulation of culture as the domain of morals,
> manners, codes of conduct, etc.

Bennett concludes that we should redesign the technology of the word.
Culture is best reconsidered "as a historically specific set of institutionally embedded relations of government in which the forms of thought
and conduct of extended populations are targeted for transformation—
in part via the extension through the social body of norms, techniques,
and regimens of aesthetic and intellectual culture."[46]

Both the anthropological and the artistic senses of culture are by now
clearly linked to a notion of care, a duty encouraged and modeled by
government, which requires us to tend and improve ourselves and others through exposure to the best creative work produced by the best
persons at their personal best.

Looking more closely at these meanings of the terms *culture* and
policy, we can see that each is in fact quite related to the other. Through
the activation of policies, organizations educate, circulate, sponsor, cir-
cumscribe, and exclude actors and activities defined by the titles *artist*
or *artwork*. Governments, unions, training institutions, community
groups, and profit-making bodies all support, fund, regulate, advertise, train, and evaluate creative persons; in fact, they often articulate

the very criteria deployed to make possible the use of the word *creative*. This may be done through law courts that permit erotica on the grounds that they are works of art; secondary curriculum bodies that set texts on the grounds that they are improving; public film authorities that sponsor scripts on the grounds that they reflect national concerns; or private impresarios who print ballet programs justifying an unusual season on grounds of innovation. In turn, these criteria may themselves derive respectively from legal precedent; governmental education; citizenship or tourism aims; or the profit plans of large corporations.

The second, seemingly all-inclusive, understanding of culture amounts either to an ethnographic exploration of ways of living or to a glossy magazine account of the prevailing zeitgeist. It is quite significant that this sense of the term *culture* is best expressed in locations that once more involve the use of particular conventions and regimens of training to construct their categories. For instance, references to indigenous culture made by anthropologists before land rights tribunals are in part determined by the rules of conduct decided by the state in the light of a particular perception of political power and ethical rule. Similarly, references to merchant bank weekend culture made by "quality newspaper" feature writers are in part determined by the rules of conduct decided by their editors/proprietors and professional associations in the light of a particular perception of market segmentation and professional practice. We hear about these lifestyle/ritual practices because of—and through the utilization of—policy. And the arrangements that permit particular forms of knowledge to circulate as legitimate and distinguishable from others (the foreign and the juvenile) are, in turn, the stuff of culture. Jacques Donzelot brings the terms together implicitly in his concept of policing, by which is meant "methods for developing the quality of the population and the strength of the nation."[47] Cultural policy, then, becomes a site at which the subject is produced. This is to follow Saunders and Hunter in arguing that "the subject-form is not something promised by history or required by language; it is something brought into being and maintained as a definite mode of conduct by certain ethical institutions."[48]

It is only relatively recently that culture and policy have been bracketed and colonized by university study and become subject to regular high-level consultation via colloquia, mirroring the recency of the formalization of international cultural diplomacy as standard ministerial fare. The newness of the field makes the task of slicing it up into typologies difficult. Any survey of cultural policy would need to consider both the programmatic and the determinate, the discretionary and deliberate as opposed to the nondiscretionary and latent. Some account must be given of the difference between those policies definitely selected as positive interventions and those imposed by the requirements of a particular conjuncture of the social, the economic, and the discursive. To help in this, it is best to consider some history.

The model of the patron of the arts derives from the cultural subvention provided to ruling-class iconography by the absolutist monarchs of Europe prior to the advent of bourgeois democracy. The principal concern of the old absolutism was the maintenance of high aesthetic standards of culture within a very narrow social context, in part via the reproduction of the ruling classes through the training of their progeny. The topography of western Europe underwent a transformation through the tenth century via a process of *incastellamento,* which involved the erection of castles as sites of economic and juridical power wielded over peasants by seigneurs. The process both represented and facilitated the exercise of life administration. A hundred years later, the means of describing this authority, or putting it into discourse, appeared; it came to be known as "custom." Custom served to cover these practices of domination, to change them from relatively recent arrivals, with a repressive history, into the norm. Their translation into the everyday, through this process of naturalization, denuded them of the contingency and the violence that had made them historical agents. Granting castles a tradition worked to deny their past.

By the mid fifteenth century, Italian nobles were establishing instant libraries through the employment of copying scribes rather than the normal processes of collection. This marked the advent of an industrial process for producing symbols of power. Popular, general education was not part of this process. Pedagogic demotics had not yet had their moment. It is important to note, though, that we can already discern the two great wings of cultural policy—subvention and training—flapping energetically.

As Rousseau insists: "It is not enough to say to the citizens, *be good;* they must be taught to be so."[49] This model of movement between the collective, public tutorial and the individual, private one is clearly exemplified in the general education in civics envisaged, and partially implemented, in Revolutionary France. The Declaration of the Rights of Man was distributed to all schools in 1793. It was used to distinguish between public and private virtues and their gendered operation, but also to conceptualize a model of female citizenship and the rights of the child. The anxieties for the Revolution's future that were close upon reformers by that year encouraged them to release a multitude of publications for young people designed to create a new kind of public person. Instruction in citizenship appeared in manuals, secular catechisms, and alphabets. These publications established a close nexus between political and ethical principles. The citizens of tomorrow would be expected to know their Rights of Man in the same sense—and with the same purpose—as they could recite and live out codes of manners and lists of facts or recognize a variety of typefaces. But unlike other forms of conduct manual, such as the earlier Erasmus model and the variety that was to flourish in the nineteenth century, the revolutionary primer addressed a reader who was constitutive of a new social order, rather than standing ready to be integrated into an existing one.

This was, however, a temporary latitude. The more conventional state was meanwhile engaged in a process of incorporation in order to remake unruly practices and meanings as legitimate ones. The many carnivals and holidays of western Europe were gradually contained and incorporated between the early 1600s and the late 1800s. In the England of the 1640s to 1660s, for instance, the state made concerted efforts to coopt games and sports. The appearance of laissez-faire capitalism marked the desire to supplant automatic transfer of privilege by its earned equivalent. Capital was to take priority over the former system of inherited control of land and state. The development of modern industries brought with it cultural policy and, perforce, the emergence of the modern city. Although there have been cities for six thousand years, capitalism accelerated their growth dramatically. David Gross identifies four discourses determining the meaning of the city: as religious site; as public gathering place; as architectural structure; and as semiotic possibility. We might connect these shifts in discursive register with, respectively, the very ancient world of Mesopotamia, with significance on through the Middle Ages; pre-Christian Athens and Rome, with relevance also to late medieval and Renaissance cities; the Industrial Revolution, with precursors in the Renaissance; and postmodernity. The latter two periods are of principal concern here.[50]

With the modern city of the Industrial Revolution came the notion of public opinion and a public culture. Weber argues that its emergence was the precondition for an art history.[51] Production and its infrastructure certainly formed the stimulus to networks such as libraries and theaters, and there then developed the need to train a proletariat to manufacture and to consume; and hence to appreciate. Equally, there was the need to form a sense of belonging in the wider populace. This wider populace included new types of person inhabiting what Habermas terms "new *spheres of life*. . . . The diffusion of culture to the middle class and the formation of a broader educated public interested in the arts."[52] Sometimes in imitation of aristocracy and sometimes as an act of its own invention, the bourgeoisie becomes an innovator in the sense that it strives for T. H. Marshall's "consciously constructed culture" as a means of building a new social order.[53] For the first time, art and intellection were conceived, not just as mechanisms of distinction, but equally and also as techniques for molding a citizenry.

Citadin, citoyen, civic, civil, citizen; all were henceforth related to notions of a refined public civilization intimately connected to this city. The state's crucial defining factor became its capacity to divide itself up as an organizer of morality—its definition, encouragement, and execution, and the prohibition of immorality—and simultaneously to enunciate the values of obedience and patriotism. In the absence of what Elizabeth Wilson calls the "controlling paternosters of kin, clan or indenture," the modern city provided the first comparatively open site for people to meet promiscuously, if sometimes with additional policing of the movement of bourgeois women.[54] The abandonment of the country in favor of the city also marks a shift in generational terms. No longer did young people move through the same transitions as their forebears. From being a straightforward stage in a stable culture that processed aging in a stable way, youth now became an indeterminate social phenomenon. These developments coupled mobility with interiority, as the physical search for work was matched by a psychic search for self, typified in the bildungsroman. Youth was being refashioned in the eighteenth century to stand in for modernity, a specific manifestation of a broader restlessness. There was a grand ambivalence in all this change. Meaningfulness was always elsewhere, ahead, in the future; it was deferred. Georg Simmel's account of the "touch-and-go elements of metropolitan life" underscores the polysemic "reserve with its overtone of hidden aversion" that, paradoxically, offered an anonymous history and new "individual independence and differentiation" along with the "right to distrust."[55]

More prosaically, the appearance of factory life transformed people trained as peasants or self-employed artisans into workers in a system. This required a utilitarianization effect, whereby people learned to calculate potential benefits to themselves and act accordingly, to work for accumulation in place of subsistence. Marxist accounts stress the forcible disciplining that planned and implemented this trajectory of self-rule. But because the new forces organizing life simply ruled out the ways and manners of a passing era, these self-same situating modes of being had to undergo reform. This necessitated philanthropic and educational change as much as it did industrial and technical innovation. Alongside new modes of production such as the assembly line, there had to be an accompanying rhetoric accounting for life on this line and outside it and before and after it. This took the form of policing wasteful leisure activities; discouraging inefficient investments in recreation, such as drunkenness; and generally promoting a high degree of fit between workplace and home. A new definition of the virtuous person had to be assembled, one with appropriate quotas of selfhood and collectivity, of individuality and efficiency, of a sense of utility and a sense of obedience.

The evolution of the dynamic urban individual from his or her agrarian community forebear was one of the engines of industrial development. The European city manifested an end to this type of community and the birth of individuality as a political and economic locus of meaning, a paradox in the mass agglomeration that was the city of citizenship and self-aggrandizement. And as the great migrations toward, and hence formation of, cities took place in the nineteenth and early twentieth centuries in the emerging cultural-capitalist democracies, time and space were reordered outside the sense of them that had obtained in the sealed-off worlds of rural life. For the city requires of its inhabitants that they have a "cognitive map" as well as a strictly spatial one, a map that can encompass all the "vaster and properly unrepresentable totality" that Jameson attributes to the social.[56]

Cultural policy is the instrument used to provide this map. A classic, mundane instance may be found in the constitution of rules of the road, and hence of the footpath, with the arrival of the automobile in the early twentieth century. This exemplified a confusion about the relationship of the policing state to active self-governance by the citizenry. T. A. Wallace noted:

> In Sydney people promenading the public streets must always keep to the left of the footpath. For a long time the reverse was the rule. At the time of writing—1922—much confusion is still being experienced. . . . The new rule of the road, "Keep to the Left," is introduced because of the street traffic. . . . By keeping to the left, pedestrians face the vehicular traffic that is coming towards them.[57]

At a more overtly political level, by the nineteenth century the city had become a place of discussion and assembly, and hence a place requiring new forms of democratic control: the control of citizenship. This was to be the genius of the cultural-capitalist state: to ensure "that nobody may deem himself so humble as not to constitute a part of the body politic," as Woodrow Wilson put it.[58] Across Europe, the late 1780s and early 1800s witnessed a debate about the return of public trust that governments could make from an investment in press freedoms; quite a clear calculation on cost-benefit terms. Trust in the system cheapened the cost of its maintenance and renewal. And this trust could be engendered by a program of public education that took the onward march of the people toward freedom as its organizing principle while seeking to produce what Jean-François Lyotard terms *le projet humboldtien:* the simultaneous acquisition of knowledge by individuals, and their insertion into a subjectivity that legitimized the emerging social form of the nation.[59] Jefferson's method of dealing with the need for a new state born of revolution to combine an admiration of rebellion with a respect for law turned him toward cultural policy, via public schools, libraries, and galleries as systems of belonging-through-appreciation. The idea was to identify the state of Virginia in the public mind with precepts of tradition and beauty: history, philosophy, and fine art were to be the tools of public association. The project sought to render the people the custodians of their own liberty through a learned capacity to nominate the aesthetic. The appearance in the nineteenth century of the public art museum as a common cultural technology was directly related to a new duty for the visual arts as agents of civilizing discipline. Museum visitors were pressed into service as legatees of a national past and instruments of a collaborative national present.

This was frequently set up as a struggle between reason and unreason for "the public mind." The irrational aspects of subjects were to be made known to them as a preliminary to their mastery of life and its drives. Sir Norman Angell's speech in acceptance of the Nobel Peace Prize for 1933 might be said to stand as representative of the policies informed by such anxieties. In it, Angell called for public education to found itself on, effectively, demonstrating their own ethical incompleteness to subjects in order that this shortfall could be worked on in the interests of social harmony: "First, the ordinary citizen and voter must acquire a greater awareness of his own nature, his liability to certain follies, ever recurrent and ever disastrous."[60] In the fifty years that bracket the nineteenth and twentieth centuries, England urbanized so quickly that its chaotic lack of city planning and services unhinged policymakers and encouraged them to instill the virtues of thrift and self-help into the dross of the city via education of the poor for civility. Angell was articulating just such anxieties on the global scale.

The laissez-faire economy animating many of these developments only existed in a few places at the global core of world capitalism in the eighteenth and nineteenth centuries. Other countries, outside Europe and North America, came to be colonial and semi-colonial plots with huge debts to and limitations imposed by imperializing states and internationalizing corporations. With decolonization, the need of countries on the periphery of the system to progress beyond agrarian economies domestically while competing internationally produced a more planned approach to all kinds of development, including cultural development. Educational policies designed to produce a citizenry capable of speaking to other peoples and trading with them—in short, capable of competing with others—were formed. This presupposed a competence to recognize differences and the means of bridging them. The state and its citizenry / the citizenry and its state came to be connected by a complex of coercion, representation, provision, and mobilization that worked to define these differences. As a result, the peoples of the Third World have the longest-standing expertise in dealing with the Other. It has been well said that " 'modernity' was not born in Paris but rather in Rio."[61] And this was achieved through the exportation and customization of doctrines of cultural policy. Spencer influenced the efforts of Meiji Japan to forge a national identity in the nineteenth century. Emile Durkheim's precepts of civil religion largely organized the new Turkish republic after World War I. And *Gemeinschaft* and *Gesellschaft* were animatory doctrines in the East Asian region between the wars. The centralized systems of values and singular core identity favored by classical sociology as prescriptions for modern society were deployed in the Third World by later generations of social scientists playing at building new societies. For both such groups, the modern—which was isomorphic with the desirable—connoted specialized, differentiated markets for labor, administration, and politics operating within a constitutive framework of legal equality, universalist doctrine, integration, innovation, and bureaucratic authority.

These developments bespeak other shifts in intellection. Where eighteenth-century Europe has been characterized as the era that saw the emergence of the human being as the center of the new sciences, a center moving toward a new freedom in self-knowledge, the nineteenth century is thought to have required a specialized division of person and labor. By the middle of the twentieth century, there is seen to be a kind of crisis between the logics of civility and management: "In the sphere of politics there has been an overcoding of economic rationalism whose apogee is technocratic centralism," as Kristeva summarizes it.[62] American sociologists of the late 1950s and 1960s refer to a lack of fit between the logic of developing technology and the values it is supposed to serve. This is said to be an unconscionably quirky time, an unsettled moment of becoming that C. Wright Mills introduced to readers of the *Listener* as the "post-modern period" of 1959. Postmodern because the edifice of freedom and reason that was the heritage of the Enlightenment to liberalism and socialism had "virtually collapsed" in the face of the overwhelming priority given to efficient centralization in the name of rationality.[63] A decade after Mills, even the customary rules of rigor of instrumental reason had been problematized by this meta-term of the postmodern. Social scientist had been alienated from their profession when Daniel Bell declared in 1971 that "the post-modern, period or society, is not a definition, but only a question."[64] There is an important economic corollary of / influence upon these developments in the expansion of products whose properties of signification are of the essence: pedagogy, the audiovisual, publishing, tourism, and advertising. Information has displaced production of the physical necessities for survival as the trope of the postmodern economy by the 1980s, as the actual locus of production of such necessities has been removed to newly industrializing countries.

An enormously far-reaching process of urbanization is connected to these developments, making ever more relevant the issues of public management and identity that the modern city first threw up two hundred years ago. In 1950, the member states of the Organization for Economic Cooperation and Development encompassed thirty-eight cities with a population of more than a million persons. Projections for the turn of the century estimate three times that number. The rest of the world in 1950 had thirty-three such cities; a projection for the year 2000 multiplies this tenfold.

There are important cultural corollaries of this shift to the cities. Janet Staiger points to the significance of multinational corporations identifying themselves by means of global signifiers such as logos that reference the anonymous, mobile monumentalism of their headquarters, a significance located in imposingly immovable buildings whose inhabitants are nevertheless ready to influence life anywhere at any time. The contrast between this modernist architecture and the postmodernist chaos underneath and around it is drawn out for Staiger in such texts as *Blade Runner* (Ridley Scott, 1982), *Brazil* (Terry Gilliam, 1985), and *Max Headroom* through their sites of random protest by subcultures inside the dark decay of space—protests that serve to call up further surveillance and training by cultural capitalism in view of these insistent critiques of the identities formally available to people.[65]

The continued capacity to mount such critiques and elicit such responses is indicative of decentered fields of power. For all the desire to manage that world below, the very reach of the multinational is indicative of the dispersed operation of power, the fact that it can no longer be said to organize fixed, immobile spaces as part of a single movement toward centralized authority and a unitary subject. An example of this duality may be found in World Standard Time, which was introduced progressively from 1884 as a means of dealing with infrastructural/economic developments across and between different places. This made for a significant contrast with what had gone before: there were two hundred different zones of time between Washington and San Francisco in 1870. It might be thought that this innovation was a precondition for optimizing standardization and substitutability; but it both accompanied and stimulated a spatial mutability that has perhaps encouraged problems of human management rather than eradicating them, a theme taken up in much modernist writing, with its concern for the subject dissociated from any roots by such anomic life conditions. The cultural policy implications of contemporary urban life are manifold. Many cities, seeking renewal through commercial and cultural redevelopment, are now in active competition for the attention of large, mobile corporations, which they woo through economic subsidy, and as a corollary the urban quotidian has become a vital component in contemporary international business.

Bell's postmodern "question" of twenty years ago has become one of the public presentation of identity. It is far from a purely economic issue. The state's legitimacy is often drawn from its capacity to speak for its citizens, to be their vocalizing agent. This is achieved, depending on the type of society, at least in part through the doctrine of nations, the concept of particular space defined by the state itself but informed affectively by a sense of cultural belonging.

Faced with the loss of the sense of belonging flowing from "overcoding," Kristeva suggests that there are two options: "Either the state recognizes its moral prerogatives and integrates them into its economic rationalism—which would result in a fascist or Stalinist totalitarianism—or the state abandons this role and plays its part indirectly through technocratic liberalism—a course that entails a proliferation of aesthetic practices on the level that concerns us."[66] For Charles Taylor, this overcoding raises the specter of the loss of democracy to extremism because of the alienation of modern life from active political participation. He refers to the risks of instrumentalism producing "a desert of public space." Conversely, for Ernest Gellner, engendering a "self . . . underwritten by the social and general environment" is precisely a matter of

The Well-Tempered Self

instrumentalism, and worthily so.[67] On each side, the ideal space outside the scope of monetary and methodological individualism and technocratic reasoning-for-growth seems to be that occupied by citizenship. We can now hone our investigations of citizenship, paring them down to pinpoint the subject of this book by redividing citizenship into four moods.

In the first mood, classical political theory decreed that citizens had the political right to parliamentary representation in search of what, after Aristotle, might be called the arithmetic equality of political association. In the second, liberal political theory confirmed this right and added to it the doctrine of the civil right to relative freedom of personal conduct (short of contravening the same right on the part of others); the resulting identity was a community identity. The third, distinctively modern, component of the discourse of citizenship was the social right to a minimum standard of living guaranteed by a welfare state. Finally, the fourth mood, the most recent decisive innovation, is the postmodern guarantee of access to the technologies of communication as crucial integers in the set of polity and identity. Where the modern depended on subjects that would recognize their debt to the great institutions of the state, the postmodern derives its power from a sense that such institutions need to relearn what sovereignty is about in polymorphous sovereign states and transnational business and social milieux that are diminishingly homogeneous in demographic terms and increasingly heteroglossic in their cultural competence.

It would be misleading to presume that there is a direct empirical fit between material changes to populace, polity, and economy on the one hand and the discourse of citizenship on the other. For no idea of popular sovereignty can serve as a total account of political institutions. But we can discern significant historical changes within certain areas that combine accounts of citizenship with an institutional effect, such as the law. Common law formalism based itself on an account of the community as a collection of individuals in pursuit of liberty. The appearance of legal process shifted the focus of legitimacy onto the community as represented by the state acting as a neutral entity. Both these trends were called into question in the 1970s by a new understanding of public law resting on the notion of the community as a combination of interacting groups, whose relative autonomy from each other should be guaranteed by a guiding principle of formal and social equality. Elements of this new law, such as alternative dispute resolution, have grounded themselves in a critique of liberal legalism, arguing for a doctrine of the self tied to community norms and their relations, such that adjudication is neither the province of a remote civic authority and jurisprudence nor based on the rights of the individual. This position poses some problems for a totalizing account of what it is to be a citizen and the space of nature in which that citizen is located. We can see no unified subject of state law in such doctrines.

The discourse of citizenship now assumes that the technologies for calling citizens up and training them produce differing kinds of ideal subject as their preferred product, even if they continue to do so in the name of a preexistent, essential person. This book presumes that this tactic in part embodies Nietzsche's despised "snare of language . . . presenting all activity as conditioned by an agent—the 'subject,'" when in reality "there is no 'being' behind the doing, acting, becoming."[68]

It is cultural policy's object to find, serve, and nurture a sense of belonging through educational and other cultural regimens that are the means of governance, of the orderly formation of public collective subjectivity in what Mill termed "the departments of human interests amenable to governmental control."[69] Some of this is done in the name of the maintenance of culture, in the name of preserving senses of person and how to divide them up. This can be managed in terms of ethnicity, age, gender, faith, or class, though the last two are rarely cited as justifications for state intervention. Or it can be managed in other terms, which generate new modes of expression. The latter tend to embrace developments in the social technology of culture in ways that talk about the need for a citizenry to have available the latest and the best from wherever. Protagonists of the former want a type of cultural audit performed that takes account of the need for indigenous cultural production. They put a premium on locally made meanings and their systems. In this rendering, local culture exists to produce. In the other rendering, it exists to relay.

Celebrants of postmodernity frequently accord culture a privileged place outside utility. Ankersmit maintains that efforts to evaluate or "use" culture represent a category mistake, because culture is the arena of consciousness, a domain separate from advantage or disadvantage. It is the space within which such judgments may be made, but is itself outside their capacity to calculate.[70]

Matthew Arnold, by contrast, knew that there were definite, productive goals for culture, to be enunciated as part of policy. Culture was, in this view, neither autotelic nor accidental: "Culture is . . . *a study of perfection*. It moves by the force, not merely or primarily of the scientific passion for pure knowledge, but also of the moral and social

The Well-Tempered Self

passion for doing good." In this reading, culture is both the object of commentary and the site of metacommentary, simultaneously the means of recognizing and attaining perfection and the standard by which these means may be identified. Both the object to be evaluated and the criteria for evaluation are on offer. The "great aim" of culture is "setting ourselves to ascertain what perfection is and to make it prevail . . . through *all* the voices of human experience which have been heard upon it."[71] Arnold's *Culture and Anarchy* demonstrates how the "cultural values of the modern state" function via a dialectic of the Hellenistic and the Hebraic. Its crux is that culture is central to authority in its endless deferral of anarchy's play. Arnold is seeking to design the modern person, a person whose subjectivity is essentially that of the individual. He wants an architecture for this person that can enthusiastically contain and develop individuality by encouraging its belief in itself and its identity of interest with an authoritarian antisepsis to any possible democratic excess. An internalized aesthetic of truth and beauty becomes an ironically connecting chord of national harmony that binds individual goals to an implied national unity. For Arnold, "culture, self, and state" form the trinity of modernity, in the service of enlightened authority. Elsewhere, he writes that "culture is *reading*." This elevates interpretation to the level of a cultural right, a civic essential that is the secured debenture of the private self learned via public training.[72] Now as then, all such trainings require technologies to animate them. Let us move forward a century, to the site of one such technology: the business magazine.

The *Australian Director* advised its member-of-the-board readership in 1988 to invest in art, a recommendation made in the first place on grounds of the potential return: works of art might be expected to increase, or at least hold, their value. However, there is also the issue of taste, an unspecifiable human pleasure that exists in the domain in whose name capital is accumulated, but whose values are separate from it: "Art is certainly an investment for the future and not only in crass commercial terms. One can hardly imagine sitting back in the lounge room and staring at a pile of dollar bills on the table. However, art affords not only a handsome dividend, but unlimited visual and sensual pleasure in the meanwhile." The magazine goes on, less disingenuously, to note that the first modern private art patronage derived from American railway systems paying artists to depict scenes advertising areas through which the company's tracks would pass in future. This provides a bridge to a further statement that needs to be kept somehow separate from the first: "The prime motivation to initiate corporate collecting is probably most often generated through public relations consultants, the aim being to establish an image for a company entering the market or to adjust the image of an already existing company."[73]

This is clearly to do with the formation of a subject, or at least its refurbishment. In this instance, the subject is a business entity. Conversely, when the British Parliament first purchased paintings on behalf of the nation, in 1753, it did so as a means of forming a public by that very phrase: to buy "on behalf of" a public was also to form that public in discourse. Policies are neither static nor disinterested, and the public formed often changes as a result. Its changeability is part of the warrant for such subvention. Two hundred and forty years later, the British Arts Council enunciated three *raisons d'être/d'acheter:* the generation of employment; urban renewal; and the capacity for assisting and producing a spirit of enterprise among the British people. These clearly reference the political problems and codes of the time. They are objects of instrumental rationality that seek to be calculable means of reforming the citizenry. For my purposes, their legitimacy as aims or methods and their standing as pointers to history are less important than their mode of address. It is their work to constitute a public that is to be worked on. The contemporary British heritage industry fuses economic infrastructural development with what it is pleased to term new kinds of "visitor experience" and identification with a simulated collective past that is to be sensed as a collective present.

The Australian government's very ability to fund culture rests on an implied constitutional power to develop national sovereignty. In keeping with this license, consider the following rationales expressed in 1969 by Richard Eggleston, a board member of the Australian Elizabethan Theatre Trust, for state support of culture: elevation of taste; preservation of culture; education; indication of quality of life; awakening a dormant but natural facility in the public; preservation of heritage; and community inspiration through the presentation of excellence. H. C. Coombs, whose career included periods as governor of the Australian Reserve Bank and chair of the Australian Council for the Arts, accorded culture an a priori status outside economic and political cost-benefit calculation because of the lack of fit between high quality and high profits. Culture went beyond this, falling into the same realm as sport. National pride could be encouraged through the identification of art with Australia.[74] Twenty years later, his successors continued to stress the unspecifiability of the human value involved. As Donald Horne, then chairing the Australia Council, put it, "when we talk about arts support policies we are talking about the meanings given to existence within a society."[75] But if those meanings are widely understood and valued, why does the market not sustain their manufacture and circulation? And if they are meanings that fall outside the laws of supply and demand, what should the mechanism be for gauging public endorsement of different cultural activities?

The question of cultural policy clearly raises difficulties for ideologues on behalf of a state that is supposedly not paternalistic, but rather simply seeks to allow its citizens the opportunity to determine their own cultural wants and needs. If cultural-capitalist societies identify themselves as loci of free expression, as evidenced by the absence of state control of art, what is their appropriate cultural stance? Should they adopt one at all? Cultural-capitalist countries are wont to take one of two rhetorical positions here. The first offers the market as a system for identifying and allocating public preferences in matters of culture, denying the state a role other than that of a police officer patrolling the precincts of property and deciding who owns what. The second identifies certain artifacts as inalienably, transcendentally, laden with value but vulnerable to the public's inability to remain transcendental in its tastes. Heritage cannot be sustained through popular memory and preference. This latter position encourages a *dirigiste* role for the state, which may seem to coerce the public into aestheticization; it is routinely derogated by some critics for a certain cultural magistracy.

Ronald Dworkin divides these discussions of the public subvention of culture into "the economic and the lofty." The economic approach suggests that the need for and degree of community support for culture is evidenced through the mechanics of price. The lofty approach suggests that community support for culture is necessary because market processes emphasize desire rather than improvement, pleasure over sophistication. Dworkin specifies here the presumption that "it is more worthwhile to look at a Titian on a wall than watch a football game on television." As most people prefer to do the latter—a preference that may be quantified in terms of their preparedness to pay for the privilege—it is utterly paternalistic to force them to subsidize the former as part of their generic tax burden on the grounds that timeless art can in fact only survive if the vulgar are required to admire it.

Dworkin also identifies a third justification of support for culture. Although conventional capitalist logic is opposed to the deployment of public funds in the service of an ethically derived set of preferences, art may be seen as making a collective contribution to the aesthetico-intellectual functioning of the community via the mutual impact of popular and high culture. There is need for "a rich cultural structure" undergirding both the present social world and its imagined descendants, a structure identifiable as valuable not because of the contemporary pleasure it provides but through complexity, through difference; for in difference can be found the flexibility to produce pleasure at other times and places. Dworkin denies that this is an instance of uplift. The charge of paternalism is deflected in advance by an appeal to the notion of trusteeship, which is simply a force conserving the historically contingent (in terms of taste) in order that options not currently fashionable may nonetheless be available to future generations. Diversity is in this case to be supported over any notion of excellence, taste, or value.[76]

This approach seeks to submerge the loftiness of training in a heritage-inflected economism. Yet its simple paradigmatic swopping of excellence and difference presumes a capacity to differentiate between structure and content, singularity and normalcy, repetition and innovation, which must in itself involve a training in distinction, in cataloging people and their preferences in a way that encourages polyvalence. As categories and valencies are themselves historically and politically derived, this can never be a matter of innocent technical calculation. Rather, it must involve a contingent set of understandings of what constitutes the human and its cultural endeavor. In other words, it still presumes on a knowledge of the difference between what does and does not matter to an era. Just as the apparently timeless horizon of truth claimed for free market economics is bounded by a definite history (for which see chapter 4), so this attempt to broker a rapprochement between noninterference and preservation of cultural structure cloaks an inevitably tight connection between artistic work and social scaffolding, returning us to the overlapping definitions of culture advanced earlier.

The reconciliation of these twin definitions is part of the fabric of policy, and it is generally achieved as part of the need to elaborate the nation to itself. The Australian Labor Party's 1986 policy platform, for instance, maintained that the "basis of Australian society lies to a significant extent in the strength of its own artistic and creative expression. Government has a responsibility to encourage the development of an Australian culture."[77] Similarly, the law that brought into being the National Endowment for the Arts (NEA) and National Endowment for the Humanities (NEH) in the United States asserts: "It is necessary and appropriate for the federal government to help and create and sustain not only a climate encouraging freedom of thought, imagination, and inquiry but also the material conditions facilitating the release of this creative talent."

Looking back a quarter of a century later, one of the original congressional sponsors of this legislation, John Brademas, maintained that "the arts are essential" because "art and artists make an immense difference by enriching our lives as individuals and building a culture that illumines and enobles us." He argued that art would "nurture the creativity of our nation." The evidence given in support of this took the form of a quotation from a worker in the field, the late Robert Motherwell, that gives renewed focus to discovering real selves: "actually, what an artist is, is a person skilled in expressing human feelings."[78] In discussions of crises of reason and information, such elevation is now a nostrum for the likes of Saul Bellow and Octavio Paz.[79] This need not be in opposition to the more overtly programmatic economic or political goals revealed by Catharine Stimpson's tracery of successive NEH annual reports. This was the "official" mission of American culture in 1985: "The humanities are vitally important to the educational and cultural life of our nation, constituting as they do the soul of civilization, which has been formed over the course of the centuries. Preserving and transmitting this tradition serves to nurture and sustain our national character, helping to make the United States worthy of its leadership in the world."[80]

This mission reveals a significant degree of fit between the humanist faith in renewal of the social order through expression of the artistic persona and the more vigorously confident notion of an aesthetic underwriting of global leadership. Such a leadership needs more than financial, legal, or military coherence. As Marx said, "it is impossible to create a moral power by paragraphs of law." For him, cultural policy was "the *organic* laws supplementing the Constitution."[81]

The idea of beaming images of the people back to them in order to develop their sense of oneness also indicates some significant continuities in cultural policy. We shall encounter contemporary manifestations of the idea of drama reflecting the nation to itself in detail in chapter 3. But similar concerns animated, for example, cultural policy in the Third Republic in France and attempts to instantiate a republican sentiment via the theater. Where early Revolutionary theater made the occasion of performance into the originating text—with the canon residing in the decision of the populace to engage with drama, rather than in an inviolable textual classicism—this was quickly displaced by a core of tracts that would uplift the citizenry by the sheer virtue of their moral dance. Jules Michelet was very strong on the importance of using drama as an article of education able to connect people otherwise dissociated from one another; the theater was "*le meilleur espoir de la rénovation nationale* [the best hope for national renewal]." This itself displayed an unresolved tension between the desire for spontaneous publicness and the need for a careful general education. By the 1880s, the minister for the beaux arts was articulating the necessity to manufacture the people as a national entity, utilizing their comparatively recent literacy and enfranchisement in a double move of allegiance and participation that would bind them to the Third Republic even as it spoke to their drives for pleasure and accessibility. The same period in Britain saw an intimate connection between the call for a national theater and the notion of public contemplation and self-improvement.[82]

The exercise of authority has equally come to rely on the ability of historians to enunciate a partial past, an account of the history that gives birth to the present in an appropriately linear way and can be made to identify the concerns of the public with their collective heritage. (Tony Bennett describes the professing of history as "the locus through which the representations of the past circulated by the institutions comprising the public historical sphere are brought into contact with the historical record in order to be either corrected by it or allowed to change with it.") The historian produces a zone of endorsed public memory and learning, a zone organized by rules and colored by debates in historiography. Historians regulate the past, which is always understood in the context of the concerns of the present.

This is history both as a human science and as a technique of cultural policy, a technique that sees historians acting as referees in, for example, discussions over memorials in museums, heritage sites, and historical mini-series. The technique has been in increasing use since its emergence in the nineteenth century. Cultural policy hinges very much on the subjective rather than the objective side of this relationship, however: it is perpetually moving beyond questions of cultural maintenance and into the realm of contemporary taste, although always with a goodly component of appreciation of high culture thrown in.[83]

Having established some of the history and philosophy of cultural policy, there remains the need to assess the connection of culture with economy and polity. This necessarily raises broader questions of recent social theory and its accounts of the cultural subject.

The Concept of a Social Surface

The preexisting foundational subject of conventional social theory was done away with, or at least modified, by Althusser. What was once an ontology of the subject becomes something to be explained and situated, not uncovered as a transcendental truth. It is now a contingent truth that depends on the conditions of the social surface on which it is found. For Foucault: "One has to dispense with the constituent subject . . . to attain an analysis which can account for the constitution of the subject within the historical texture . . . that is, a form of history which accounts for the constitution of knowledges [*savoirs*], discourses, domains of objects."[84]

Althusser provides the following formulation of Marxism as social theory. The economic base is comprised of the productive forces and the relations of production. Its superstructure is comprised of the law and the state plus ideology, which in turn is subdivided into religion, ethics, and politics. One can understand the social order, then, as a place or building. Althusser develops the metaphor of base (or infrastructure, or substructure) and superstructure in the following mode, which has become extremely influential in a way removed from its historical genesis, because of the productivity of its meaningfulness and certain slippages between Althusser and Foucault; specifically, Althusser's contention that "a topography represents in a definite space the respective *sites* occupied by several realities."[85] Foucault uses the metaphor of the site in his material history of discourses; and this sense of the site, of a social surface, is integral to the formation of subjectivities investigated here.

There are difficulties with mapping all of Althusser's social theory onto that of Foucault. (As Althusser puts it, " 'something' from my writings has passed into his, including certain of my formulations . . . [yet] even the meanings he gives to formulations he has borrowed from me are transformed.")[86] I want, however, to consider Althusser's position more fully, prior to looking at a revised terrain. Much of his writing remains important, for all the denigration of it as obscurantist, arcane, incorrect, and alienating. Moreover, a clear understanding of Foucault's accounts of culture and society depends on a sense of their separateness from doctrines of the sovereign subject and an appreciation of how dialectical reasoning can be redisposed away from the grand stage of history and toward an analysis of conjunctures, and both these precepts appear to have come from Althusser. One recalls here Foucault's suggestion that we "open Althusser's books."[87]

The utility of a material trope of edifice resides in the foundational notion of the economy, above which lie the visible, daily workings of the social order. The foundational is a bedrock that must exist for the rest of the edifice to stand "to represent above all the 'determination in the last instance' by the economic base." But away from this "last instance," the superstructure has a "relative autonomy" and can even have a reciprocal effect on the economy.[88]

The state is a critical component of this social surface. It has two chief characteristics. The first involves the use of force and the threat of it as a means of eliciting obedience to authority. This characteristic is composed of the army, the police, the courts, the bureaucracy, and the prisons. Its work is done by sanction and interdiction. This is "the (repressive) State apparatus" ((R)SA). The second characteristic is the existence of numerous "Ideological State Apparatuses" (ISAs). These include religious and educational institutions, the family, the polity, the trade union, and the communications and cultural ISAs. So where there is a singular and unitary (R)SA, there is a "plurality" of ISAs. In addition, many of these belong partially to what is conventionally styled the "*private* domain," unlike the (R)SA. But, after Gramsci (or, for that matter, Durkheim), Althusser regards such a distinction between public and private as "internal to bourgeois law," a system of law that the (R)SA is not subject to because of its putatively legitimate monopoly on the exercise of force. And whereas this violence is the touchstone for (R)SA work, the ISAs *"function by ideology."* Ideology also exists in each part of the (R)SA, but it is secondary in importance to force. The ISAs may contain elements of force, but they are secondary to ideology as determinations on how ISAs function.[89]

Much of this analysis is convivial to the account of social surfaces used in this book, but as a methodological, heuristic base rather than a description of an organic society. Anthony Giddens argues that the central defining characteristic of (for him, a continuing) modernity has been how the social system organizes "time and space" in a cultural sense.[90] Hence my use of the term *surface* even as the metaphor of base and superstructure is mobilized. This then provides the means for conceptualizing the circulation of discourses and the formation of subjectivities within the sphere of governance in a way that can position such practices sometimes alongside capital and its critical economic role and sometimes quite separate to it.

The problem with the public-private division discussed above remains a critical one, as it determines a role for the state in policing the ownership of property. This is especially important given the methodological and political individualism of the rational consumer side to both the new citizenship and neoclassical economics. But even these discourses operate as technologies forming a public in ways that are primarily connected with their own internal logics of subjectivity. The best means of understanding such technologies is not simply to read them off against the absolute logic of capital accumulation but rather to treat them as formations of rules mobilized to manage populations. This is a micropolitical play of power in the governance of subjects.

Foucault argues that there is a risk of reductionism in concentrating on Marxist understandings of the subject. It may well be that subjection derives from forces connected to production, class conflict, or ideology. But he is skeptical about the assumption that these are the "more fundamental mechanisms," suggesting that there is a circularity in their relationship to modes of subjection. He points to the enormous impact of the sheer growth in size of the sphere of influence of the political domain of governance over the past five hundred years, arguing that the efficacy of the state's attempts to manage populations derives from two sources. The loci and logic of its power are not merely to be found among the interests or persuasions of the class that controls it, because it operates at a micro level as well as at the totalizing level of general economic forces. This micro level relies on the formation of various kinds of public subject, and the determining logics of those subjects may not necessarily provide intelligible accounts of action if they are always led back to the economic. In fact, the path of research that works with ideology may be said to presuppose the idealist subject of philosophy imbued with a consciousness ready to be worked on.[91] This line of reasoning illustrates a clear tension between: (a) the relative autonomy / relative reciprocity in Althusser's model of culture, state, and economy; and (b) his more mechanistic, totalizing account of ideology. Ideology poses a series of conceptual difficulties because it presumes that the real can be known outside its representations and called up as evidence as if it were external to any signification.

While acknowledging that they overlap, Foucault signals the need to distinguish between relations of power, relations of communication, and "objective capacities." Power works to transform the real world. Communication works to give that world meaning by establishing the conditions of semiotic exchange. And the "capacities" work to make for inequality and domination. Each is mutually imbricated with the others, but not in a coordinated or consistent way that would make for an equilibrium. Different sites will see different points of connection between them, with each sphere frequently operating by its own internal rules and regularities.[92]

When the issue of people as a collective public is addressed, developments since Althusser have in any case problematized his findings about who controls the apparatuses of the state and whose interests they may be said to serve. In fact, his crucial category of class may be unusable. Leaving to one side the accounts of class derived from self-apportionment of attributes through questionnaire sociology, or the Weberian stress on position within the labor market and the additional grids of status and authority, the Marxist tradition itself offers discontinuities in this area.

There are four distinctly different Marxist understandings of how class divisions may be discerned. First, there is a division between those with property and those without; second, between those with power or authority and those without; third, between those with control of the forces of production (machinery) and those without; and fourth, between persons in differing relationships to a shifting set of processes of the production, appropriation, and distribution of surplus value. It is difficult to find agreement within or between these positions. And it is also increasingly awkward to use class as a category of identifiable agency. When and how does a class "act"? It doesn't. For class is quite different from categories with signifiers that may be read against signifieds in the material world. It may lack any connection to real-world positions that become typified in signification. A counterexample is that of women inside a discourse of gender. Unlike their subject position, class is a theoretical object inimical to referentiality in any sense of social identity. It is not already constituted as a group of real persons. Jumping off from this issue, understanding that there are degrees of definiteness attached to *woman* that are different from those attached to *ruling class,* we might redispose the difficulty with class onto the broader terrain of signification, to break open these categories and indicate how they might be used methodologically rather than organically. The heuristic device of Althusser's social theory is reformed as a topographic map as it passes through a postmodern transmogrification. Ironically, perhaps, this takes us onto a path not dissimilar to that prescribed by T. H. Marshall, the recently reinstated high priest of the virtues of citizenship. This is a path that seeks "stepping-stones in the middle distance" as a guide to social analysis.[93]

It is instructive here to consider the "postmodern presidency," the concept marking the arrival of institutionalist American political science at the gates of cultural theory. The presidency was essentially founded as an agency of high foreign policy, removed from the everyday sphere, the argument runs. Congress was the site of domestic public policy initiatives. Theodore Roosevelt and Woodrow Wilson represented the coming of the modern presidency, which manifested itself in their customary practice of directly addressing the public and in their party organizations, as well as in their adoption and elaboration of doctrines of efficiency, reformism, and local intervention. The modern period reached its apex in the "personal, plebiscitary presidency" of Franklin Delano Roosevelt. It was his skill to govern discursively via a politics of identification, of culture. His radio broadcasts called up a citizenry and then called upon it to identify the best of each person and the best of society with the presidency. This identificatory process has heightened with the advent of the postmodern presidency, even as the significance of the incumbent is problematized via the developing reach of the un-elected into the management of the population. As the president re-turns, perhaps, to the domain of first lord of wars, he becomes ever more insistent on his rhetorical placement within the discourse of the domestic everyday.[94] The rhetoric of certainty expands in accordance with an actual uncertainty about its apparent essential basis in fixity. The uptake of postmodernity within public administration sees the discipline becoming similarly anxious about its own project of reform-ism and the public's faith in the validity of notions of preconditions for ideal argument and policy. What had been a thoroughgoing critique of Reaganism in the mid 1980s, based on modern premises of accountabil-ity and equity that promised a better order of principled debate and management, is transformed. It becomes "Public Administration in a Time without a Name."[95] It becomes indeterminate.

Consider this specific site of emerging indeterminacy, and the meta-indeterminacy placed onto the manufactured and managed subject that I have already outlined, alongside Althusser's account of ideology as "a 'Representation' of the Imaginary Relationship of Individuals to their Real Conditions of Existence." He argues that to criticize an ideology, for example, faith in God, is to presume that this ideology is illusionary, but that it at least alludes to reality and hence has grounds that are both true and germane to itself on which it can be criticized: "(ideology = illusion/allusion)." The next presumption is that the act of interpreta-tion can unfold this and give the lie to falsehood / underscore truth. It will be seen presently that this is quite critical as a hermeneutic well-spring for a stream of methods for reforming subjects and publics. Alt-husser maintains that such practices give rise to a query as to the sources and reasons for this "imaginary transposition of the real conditions of existence." For such an ethic of interpretation assumes that "what is reflected in the imaginary representation of the world found in an ideology is the conditions of existence of men, i.e. their real world . . . [when] it is not their real conditions of existence, their real world that 'men' 'represent to themselves' in ideology, but above all it is their relation to those conditions of existence represented to them there."

Let us now consider a little more closely what this signifies about the category of the knowing and doing individual subject. It suggests that ideas are material practices, rituals such as the act of prayer (material faith in religion) or the payment of a social debt (material faith in justice), that are simultaneously performed by the subject and define that subject. For the subject is hailing and being hailed through this set of practices.[96] (Although not all the practices will be compatible, this need not be a problem until and unless they come into conflict.)

The separation of potentially conflictual spheres, each of which may be necessary for the constitution of the ethical subject of cultural-capitalist citizenship and the maximizing subject of the free market, involves a further move, the emergence of a smaller unit of analysis than the ISA, and yet one that is constitutive of it. This is what Foucault terms "those systems of micro-power that . . . we call the disciplines." Liberties and disciplines are the dual inheritance of the Enlightenment, whereby the subjection of "forces and bodies" must accompany guarantees of sovereignty. "Mechanisms of power" travel alongside and stand as the guarantors of freedoms.[97] Power may sometimes silence, but it also hails, articulates, and requires speech. It works to produce truths. It is through the training or schooling of the subject achieved under the agency of disciplines, for example, that the subject may be known. And it is via similar methods that a "will to knowledge" appears. The emergence of categories of person produced by forms of knowledge ("the child, the patient, the madman, the prisoner") cuts persons up, making them the object of understandings that divide them into insides, outsides, conduits, and passages into and out of cohorts. This achievement is to be seen under the sign of a "technology of power," a productive manufacturer of truth: "The individual and the knowledge that may be gained of him belong to this production."[98] So the state, while "it" exists in a definite structural relationship to persons, executive governments, the market, and the delineation of these groupings, operates with and may be understood by the work of differing knowledges. This is Jacques Donzelot's "provisional bracketing" of "state" with "power." Neither exists other than relationally, as productive forces

The Well-Tempered Self

doing the work of "activating and managing a population."[99] Foucault is at pains to point out that he has no desire to replace the economy as an explanatory tool by a heuristic designated as power. But the latter is necessary to explain the normalization inscribed in mechanisms of the classification of madness and sexuality, mechanisms left unexplored by existing forms of knowledge, which should clearly be understood as exercises of power.

Such an understanding is in stark contrast to the two standard logics of the state. The social compact and functionalist views argue for a unified subject placing sovereignty in it because of a perceived community of interest. This derives from a foundational humanism that is clearly foreign to my argument. Neo-Marxist accounts, in some sense after Althusser, see the state as a set of fractions ultimately dedicated to protecting capital accumulation. Both discourses are totalizing and essentialist, one in its mythic first instance (the signing over of sovereignty) and the other in its mythic last instance (the servicing of capital). Each hour, be it first or last, is too lonely for this project to occupy. Neither discourse pays sufficient attention to the formation of subjects or the politics of culture, despite the fact that Althusser pointed in that direction. Instead, the tendency is to account for the state as a vehicle eliciting obedience and social actors as having definite, prediscursive, immutable interests (albeit interests that are frequently not self-evident). Once again we see Mill's self/society/state struggle, discussed in the Introduction. But what of the question of technology—that is, the question of power?

For some democratic theorists, the essence of the state is power. This power involves the production of intended effects, although it will also involve elements of give-and-take. Power can also be put in antinomic relation to knowledge, distorting the flow of information. For Steven Lukes, notions of power and the subject are all about interests. He proposes a final and conclusive level of its operation when "A exercises power over B in a manner contrary to B's interests."[100] Power thus offers a unifier for discourses about the state and the subject, promising both their union and their distinctness a mutual solidity. Power is produced here as a property.

It is possible, however, to reformulate the state and power as productive processes, fundamentally unfixed and relational in their circulation. The question "Cui bono?" is now displaced by "Qui parle?" Aspects of that question are reconceived by Foucault as "superstructural in relation to a whole series of power networks that invest the body, sexuality, the family, knowledge, technology, and so forth."[101] On this reading, there is no central field of force functioning as a logical, coherent whole to repress or order the social, and there are not so much determining interests as determining formations of interests and subjects to have them. Interests are epiphenomenal, in a sense, to the lines of power that form them. In seeking the shifting loci of power at different sites, Foucault chooses not to look for "the headquarters that presides over its rationality; neither the caste which governs, nor those who make the most important economic decisions which direct the entire network of power that functions in a society (and makes *it* function); the rationality of power is characterized by tactics that are often quite explicit at the restricted level where they are inscribed."[102]

Significantly for the domain of this book, the discursive tactics of cultural policy are frequently founded on accounts of subjectivity, of how to produce civil subjects. And the realm for so doing is that of conduct, which must mean culture if it means more than force. The logics and loci of power are here plural and often discrete, their rationality self-referential and restricted to particular inscriptive systems as means of keeping incommensurate accounts of the subject apart. Power is, then, the consolidation and dislocation of specific forms of speech at specific times. Power is the production of meanings in a decentered way. It does the work of demolition at certain points and construction at others because its principal task is the engineering of relations between subjects. The primary site of this engineering is at the level of governance through culture. This next section explains the terrain of available meanings that this governance must traverse and how that terrain has altered.

The Ontic, the Epistemic, and the Postmodern

The terrain of meaning has undergone significant epistemological and institutional changes over time, such that the relationship of signifier to signified has become increasingly complex. Foucault has systematized the question of the connection between discourse and object in the following terms: "There is a problem: how can it happen that real things, things that are perceived, can come to be articulated by words within a discourse. Is it that words impose on us the outline of things, or is it that things, through some operation of the subject, come to be transcribed on the surface of words [?]"[103]

Foucault points here to the central, critical foundation of the arguments enunciated in this book: namely, that three prejudices—the ontic,

The Well-Tempered Self

the epistemic, and the postmodern—have informed Western understandings of the formation of subjects. These three prejudices may be said to correspond to Umberto Eco's model of "conjectural space," which divides into three types of "labyrinth." The first labyrinth is *ontic*. It offers points of entry, center, and departure, clearly defined but complicated by the presence of the minotaur in the middle. Provided that the clear spacing of the labyrinth is kept in mind—or kept as a thread—it can be understood and traversed. Unraveling the thread manufactures a clear and comprehensive representation of the labyrinthine space's coordinates. The second labyrinth is *epistemic*. It can only be unraveled at the representational level. The thread can be unwound, but the labyrinth itself is full of oubliettes and culs-de-sac, a root-structure obedient to its own rules and with numerous "dead ends." The third labyrinth is *postmodern*. It is a rhizomatic network. Everything is interconnected. Center and periphery are no longer usable terms.[104]

The ontic register presumes that the world is stable, that a metaphysical realism is possible that renders entities perfectly recognizable on their own empirical footing. Signifieds beget signifiers. For Aristotle, a perfect match can be achieved between language and object: "An object of scientific knowledge exists of necessity, and is, consequently, eternal. For everything that exists of necessity in an unqualified sense is eternal, and what is eternal is ungenerated and imperishable."[105]

Since Aristotle, the ontic has undergone regular renewal and confirmation through its elaboration by English empiricism and sociological positivism. Its status is that of a certain kind of commonsense logic. On this account, we can know subjects in a positivistic way that is congenially realist. The value of meanings is determined functionally. Just as I am describing the postmodern as one of a series of prejudices, so Auguste Comte thought that his "positive philosophy" had emerged from a process of development through successive stages of "leading conceptions." The previous two were "the Theological, or fictitious . . . [and] the Metaphysical, or abstract." They were supplanted by "the Scientific," which was a "fixed and definite state" of reason and observation that connected "single phenomena and some general facts." With the "progress of science," the number of these general facts would diminish in the face of a program based on the certainty of "all good intellects . . . that there can be no real knowledge but that which is based on observed facts."[106] At an institutional level, attempts to utilize this way of thinking as a guide to the structure of society conceived of the ontic as a final stage of evolution toward order. Spencer presented the paradox of a nexus between heterogeneity and cohesion. The "structural and functional unlikeness" of the "civilized nation" correlated differentiation with integration. Where nomadism was chaotic, and charismatic authority only slightly less so, the fully achieved nation had organizational systems melding custom with law; the generic with the specific; and clarity with "multiformity."[107] Just as the world could be known on its own terms, so this empiricist freedom from cant could also deliver rational forms of life.

The epistemic register contradicts the ontic, asserting in its stead that objects are formed through knowledge. The signifier begets the signified. The subject is known according to a particular means of apprehension. In Durkheim's memorable phrase, "Thought . . . must become the creator of its own object."[108] For the "middle period" Jean Baudrillard, for example, "there is no reality or principle of reality other than that directly produced by the system as its ideal reference." The arbitrariness of significance resides both in the unmotivated connection of signifier to signified and in the restrictiveness that correlates particular signifiers with particular signifieds and those signifieds alone (a "one-to-one assignation").[109] Value is determined structurally. In *The Archaeology of Knowledge,* Foucault argues that a statement is tied to a " 'referential' that is made up not of 'things,' 'facts,' 'realities,' or 'beings,' but of laws of possibility, rules of existence for the objects that are named."[110] Similarly, Weber refers to "the discursive nature of our knowledge," a nature produced by the *Gedankenbild,* a system of analysis that brought disparate and dispersed phenomena together and made them relate anew on its own terms of trade, the terms of a "unified analytical construct." Meanings are henceforward never " 'true' in some metaphysical sense." Rather, they are necessarily the outcome either of the understanding of actual persons in terms of their own codes or of imaginary collectivities conceived and deployed in the practice of theorizing.[111] For Simmel, the task of epistemology is the identification of "the basic theoretical elements, the relationship between the theory and its immanent aims, and the status of the theory in relation to other theories." The epistemic, then, connotes a self-regulatory ability within the mature forms of knowledge that sociological modernity provided. Simmel is critical of "epistemological realism," which assumes that there can be a direct, mirroring correspondence between signifieds and pre-significatory objects. It has become a naturalistic fallacy to advertise knowledge as a replication of its material concerns. Every kind of knowledge is in fact better understood as a translation of data into "a new language, with its own intrinsic forms, categories and requirements." The defining characteristic of science is observable rules, not faithfulness

The Well-Tempered Self

to a disputed real; our "epistemic forms" determine our "objects of knowledge." Truth is a functional requirement of systems of meaning.[112]

The epistemic derives much of its force from modern linguistics and the elaboration of semiotics into a semiology across sites. Meaning is generated through the operation of binary opposites inside relatively discrete systems of signs that are carefully differentiated from one another and that assign value inside each system's *Eigengesetzlichkeit,* or sphere of self-legislation. The value of a cultural object is determined by the rules of the system within which it is discussed. These rules are relatively autonomous from the social world, in keeping with the miniaturization and differentiation of modernity.

The corollary for the subject is to be found in the task Weber set for sociology: that it ask about the conduct required of just such "differentiated" categories of person in order for "cultural uniqueness" to continue. This has great significance institutionally. In place of Comte's teleology of philosophy, Weber suggests "pure types of legitimate authority," founded on tradition, charisma, and the rational. Specifically, the validity of the most modern and complex of these systems, the rational, resides not in custom or personality but in "patterns of normative rules."[113] This may be seen to give a warrant to Foucault's removal of power from groups of persons and its placement inside institutional machinery and discourse. (To return to the allusion to Bach's *Das wohltemperierte Klavier* in the title to this book, it is significant that this was one of the first of what are called works of organic structure, which is to say that it appears to build via a logic of its own. The musical events that comprise it take on the task of building blocks that make each next step natural within the work's particular terms of reference or sphere of legislation. It is an epistemic piece of music in this sense.)

The postmodern is another set of problematizations again, following the dominance of the epistemic. It queries the very notion of there being an object and a history to its understanding. Here, signifiers beget signifiers in an endless, importunate array of meanings that denies a connectedness of signifier to signified. They are loose from one another; Baudrillard's assignation of signifier with signified can no longer be fulfilled. One might be in an epistemic or ontic register but the layers of signification, the sheer plenitude of signification, always already render these as category mistakes. Now there is what Gilles Deleuze and Félix Guattari call a rhizome, a chaotic root-system, in place of the logical trees of meaning that formed the knowledges of the past. The rhizome is founded simultaneously on "the principles of connection and heterogeneity: any point on a rhizome can be connected to any other point, and must be." Instead of a structural relationship between internal positions or points, the rhizome is made up of proliferating lines that lack any underlying force generating them.[114]

Each sign is predicated on an absence, on the non-presence of something that must be known or made present, but that is always elusively allusive and illusory. The interpretation of the sign cannot be confined to the presence of its signatory or to the material conditions or personal intentions of that subject. The sign has what Derrida calls an "essential iterability," which carries it along and ensures that it will always have meaning (if not the same one). Every sign can become a quotation, retroped for another purpose and cast adrift from its referent. This citational complex is in fact the source of the work of signification, rather than some isolable etymological diachrony or sociology of knowledge.[115] The postmodern derives from the promiscuous actual connection of all signifiers pointed out by critics of the binarism of the epistemic. Binarism is displaced by the logocentric interdependence of all aspects of a virtually indivisible set of signs. This is a prejudice driven by the proliferation of different language games, comprised of heterogeneous elements and rules and dedicated to a relentless antagonism between participants.

By analogy, then, it may be said that discourse is now seen both to form its object of study and to hide that productivity. Value is defined not by the use- or exchange-value of a sign but by an omnidirectional radiating force that refers to objects or processes via a momentary contiguity rather than a recognized system of referentiality. The idea of value as functionally, or even structurally, determined is lost. There is no referentiality in either reality or representation. All terms are commutable now and indeterminacy reigns. Baudrillard discerns this as the outcome of a passage through the three prejudices, at the end of which a "possible definition for the real is: *that for which it is possible to provide an equivalent representation.* . . . At the conclusion of this process of reproduction, the real becomes not only that which can be reproduced, but that which is always already reproduced: the hyperreal." The process sees a "mutual fulfillment" of "reality and art" via the exchange of "foundational privileges and prejudices." All life is now aesthetic. It is experienced as interpretation; and all interpretation is made as experience. Reality and fiction can no longer be poles.[116] Scott Lash calls this "de-differentiation" for its undoing of the processes of autonomous spheres of being and control that characterized modernity.[117] For this is not merely a shift in university knowledge, but in how to live, in how to talk and listen and make do with life.

The Well-Tempered Self

This aestheticization has considerable significance for any under-standing of subjectivity. Where the Romanticism of the eighteenth cen-tury had installed the artist as the model of the subject operating out-side commonplace rules of conduct, postmodernity aestheticizes the rules of both conduct and misconduct. What began principally as a debate within architecture, literature, and criticism, primarily in the United States, has shifted to the very condition of politics and culture in the Western world. The postmodern subject is known as many, never one; it is not it, but split. But this split cannot simply be laid at the door of the psychically divided subject of the psy-complexes. This is a subject that is split inside discourse. The amount of information available to the subject and required of it exceeds its capacities and turns it away from a transcendental view of itself. The television set and the screen-based knowledge of experience have institutionalized at public and private sites the "metropolitan blasé attitude" that Simmel found characteristic of the modern city's chaotically "swift and uninterrupted change of outer and inner stimuli."[118] Postmodernity is held by some to offer the chance of a reappropriation of the means of production of subjectivity. Alternatively, it is said to engender regression via a return to the ontic in an attempt to refashion restrictive concepts of *Bildung*. The corollary of this is that institutions are now critical, if contradictory, sites for the promulgation of subjectivity and struggles to define the self. This latter issue is addressed more fully in chapter 4.

Tracing the emergence and efflorescence of the human sciences in *The Order of Things,* Foucault travels two-thirds of this route across the prejudices, discerning a shift in the dominant Western mode of concep-tualization toward the conclusion of the eighteenth century: "Nega-tively, the domain of the pure forms of knowledge becomes isolated, attaining both autonomy and sovereignty in relation to all empirical knowledge . . . positively, the empirical domains become linked with reflections on subjectivity, the human being." When every conceivable mode of breaking up the person into a set of components named and known through the human sciences has been achieved, a total under-standing of a unitary subject is, ironically, forever dispensed with as achievable and forever inscribed as desirable: "Modernity begins when the human being begins to exist within his organism, inside the shell of his head, inside the armature of his limbs, and in the whole structure of his physiology; when he begins to exist at the centre of a labour by whose principles he is governed and whose product eludes him."[119]

This route has seen the person go through several transformations via the three prejudices discussed above. Once it simply was, it obtained, and was amenable to an act of description that could in turn be made accountable for its referentiality back to a presignificatory real (the ontic). Then it was formed through knowledge held by and about the person that doubled back on the person and made it the subject of that knowledge (the epistemic). Then it became a series of subject positions enunciated through intertextual games of language, no longer knowable within certain, hermetically sealed, discrete rules of those games. Slippage and indeterminacy predominated (the postmodern). The conditions of the production and interpretation of texts became the cradle of self-significance. Kristeva's essay "Postmodernism?" thus begins: "This question could be reformulated to read: first, in what way can anything be written in the twentieth century, and second, in what way can we talk about this writing?"[120]

We might set this challenge against Habermas's argument that the Enlightenment's "normative content" is to be found in "self-consciousness, self-determination, and self-realization." This self was publicly asserted in its individualistic organization and disposal of objects. Two hundred years later, says Habermas, "the paradigm shift that has occurred in the realm of theory speaks for itself: An anonymous society without a subject is taking the place of an association of free and equal individuals who regulate their communal life themselves through democratic will-formation."[121]

Habermas here seems a world away from the quotation from Kristeva immediately preceding. Her statement speaks its postmodernity in its epigrammatic indeterminacy. Habermas, by contrast, exemplifies explicitness and specifies, almost, the conditions under which he may be contradicted. And where one addresses inscription and analysis, the other turns more toward political philosophy. Nonetheless, they have a nexus in the mystery of subjectivity, the mystery of where it is, how it is formed and what this means. The link between them may be found in the concept of the *différend*, Jean-François Lyotard's formulation of "the unstable state and instant of language wherein something which must be able to be put in phrases cannot yet be."[122]

It is the hallmark of the era to seek to find words to speak *différends;* a hallmark of indeterminacy that must extend to person and polity from philosophy. When Lyotard amends his previous term *grand narratives,* describing the liberal, Marxist, capitalist, Christian, and speculative world-accounts that have collapsed with postmodernity, it is significant that he chooses *subject-systems* as his neologism.[123] For these have been models seeking to explain and modify subjectivity. They are, in short, models of human governance. It is now the surfaces that are to be molded

The Well-Tempered Self

in a contingent way, contingent not on finding the inner truth of subjects, but on the available means for manufacturing their outer truths. Foucault discerns a shift away from querying "What are we in our actuality?" and toward "What are we today?"[124] Critiques of metaphysics go in tandem with problems of intellectual and governmental legitimacy as, inter alia, the diffusion of technologies of communication breaks up established sources of the control of information and the definition and administration of persons. Rather than drawing on interiority, the subject is constantly reinvented "in order to satisfy certain requirements of personal advancement and of safety." For Saul Bellow, this reaches its apogee in the United States in the institutionalization of processes whereby "Americans have received advice on what to be like and how to behave."[125]

Of course, one could also break up these categories in economic terms. Clearly, the ontic preceded the modern economy, but also obtained within it. Fredric Jameson uses Ernest Mandel's work to periodize what he sees as the "three fundamental moments of capitalism," which we might redispose to describe the shifts in the organization of production, distribution, and politics that have been part of these changes over the past four hundred years. These moments are market capitalism, monopoly or imperial capitalism, and postindustrial or multinational capitalism. Each stage involves the progress of capital into previously uncommodified regions, whether they be new geographical markets and sources of production or new types of product and new technologies for their creation and transfer. Other terms for the period might emphasize the force of multinational capital, the predominance of image and spectacle and the formative power of the media. These issues are explored further in chapter 3, but for now we should note the suggestion that the relative autonomy of culture from the economy seems to have been succeeded by a movement of culture into all other realms. Far from having disappeared, its aestheticizing tentacles have merged with the direction of Western economies toward service industries and emotional labor and away from the production of goods. This is both informed by and informing the prejudice of knowledge called the postmodern.

There is a great deal of debate about the value of the postmodern era. For some, the formerly political doctrine of liberty has been displaced by the notion of consumption. The subject's freedom is marked by the capacity to acquire. This means that symbolic exchange, and hence the circulation of meaning and taste, is now the factor defining the person. Consumption provides the cognitive and moral center to life. It integrates and manages society; for the consumer has displaced the producer as the center of social engagement. Popular culture and democracy meet now; the engagement of quality and reason that typified the hierarchized link between an aesthetic sense and the enlightened citizenry at work in the public sphere is no more. For C. Wright Mills in the 1950s, "society in brief has become a great sales-room."[126]

This makes for an aestheticized politics of civic identity. Hence my argument that the objects of cultural policy are concerned with producing civil subjects. Whether or not Habermas's association of the free ever existed materially, its existence as a knowledge functions in a formative way, troped again and again in the discourses of liberalism and citizenship. This troping is more than political philosophy. It provides the foundation for the form of pedagogic Enlightenment that bureaucracies engage in, for the production of policies and programs that talk about self-discovery, autonomy, and identification; in short, for instruments that take the absence of an originating subject as an unspoken given and shore up the state by forming a governable subject. This is done in the name of an apparently transcendental subject, whose free will is magically always there but magically has to be formed and re-formed time after time, a move that is close to Kierkegaard's frustrations about the discursive power of doctrines of

> "the public," consisting of real individuals who never are and never
> can be united in an actual situation or organization—and yet are
> held together as a whole. The public is a host, more numerous than
> all the peoples together, but it is a body which can never be reviewed;
> it cannot even be represented.[127]

The postmodern condition of the displaced subject is resisted through an appeal to the ontic, as a warrant for intervention by the state. Cultural policy exists to confirm what is apparently already there. Social engineering becomes social conservation. But there is a contradiction. While postmodernity may be defined by absences, it calls up a sense of loss of something never had. This leads to a plenitude of representations —and hence formations—of publics and their appropriate conduct, as the remainder of this book will show. The postmodern acts in the name of the ontic despite the fact that it has substituted for the latter. For the postmodern is nostalgic for a historically ramified and derived meaning. Ironically, this means that, at the level of policy, the state is enabled to instantiate the new as the already extant, precisely by virtue of what Jameson calls "an age that has forgotten how to think historically."[128]

The Well-Tempered Self

Chapter Two

◆

TEXTUAL THEORY

THE DISCOURSE OF reflectionism in literary and screen criticism proposes that fictional texts portray/betray the sociocultural concerns of their
age. Whereas most contemporary cultural critics / textual analysts would
reject any absolute relationship or correspondence—not least because of
the productive nature of signification itself—it remains the case that textual commentary draws its legitimacy from the existence of a certain connection. Reflectionism provides the space for understanding the social
via the text. It is a sophisticated enabling strategy that can be used in a
variety of ways. For the purposes of my argument, the political valency of
such reflectionism is related to the extent to which it leads to the creation
of subjects both of knowledge and the cultural-capitalist state, as opposed
to offering the means of forming new selves. For cultural criticism is
more than a series of trends in sometimes quite marginal academic enterprises. It is a mode of self-formation inscribing incompleteness—but potential for something more—in an inexorable relationship that is the touchstone of the claim made by the humanities to manufacture civic subjects.

It was the special capacity of the humanities to instill doubt and *politesse* into citizens that so disturbed Rousseau. On one level he condemned "that numerous herd of obscure writers and idle *littérateurs*, who devour without any return the substance of the State," but he was equally horrified at the way in which the qualities necessary for warfare and the running of the economy, qualities encouraged by patriotism and religion, had been called into question by the processes of "rendering mankind more sociable" via "the urbanity of manners." The rise of philosophizing and the absence of what came to be known as a Romantic male self were the reasons he gave for the demise of a succession of empires from ancient Athens to his own time.[1] Although Rousseau clearly abjured self-formation through scholarly inculcation of doubt and *politesse,* he nevertheless certainly did not doubt its capacity to produce subjects of its own knowledge.

Rousseau would presumably have preferred a notion of personal transcendence that led to a strengthening of the passion of the public through Romantic renewal. But his position might also be amalgamated with an ethic of self-formation via textual analysis. Consider his arguments alongside the kinds of logic mobilized in the Declaration adopted by Mondiacult 1982, a world conference on cultural policy organized by the United Nations Educational, Scientific and Cultural Organization (UNESCO). Its litany of the critical components of what makes for "culture" and the reasons for its maintenance includes the following:

> It is culture that gives man the ability to reflect upon himself. It is through culture that man expresses himself, becomes aware of himself, recognises his incompleteness, questions his own achievements, seeks untiringly for new meanings and creates works through which he transcends his limitations.[2]

The Canadian Commission for UNESCO—operating in a First World context but with an ultimate purchase on the tribulations of unequal cultural transfer—called for a "proper cultural education" as a guarantee of the appropriate amalgam of auto-critique and auto-appreciation that would make for the well-rounded individual, an outcome that could be worked for by a combination of maintenance and renewal through critical reflection.[3]

Similar ways of thinking animate much contemporary literary theory. For Eco, fiction is indissolubly linked to ethics ("in stories about others we find models of behavior for ourselves"). These models, he maintains, need not be derived from a clear opposition of good and evil. Ethics means placing oneself in the role of characters—he instances

Emma in Flaubert's *Madame Bovary* (1857) and Ringo in John Ford's *Stagecoach* (1939)—who are always and necessarily themselves located in "a story of human conduct." In evaluating the worth of a novel, one is effectively making a judgment about its characterizations, which is itself always "an ethical argument." This is so because the primary burden of fiction is the narration of action, which involves a posing of and an accounting for choice. Each fiction offers alternatives at crucial stages, and it is these points of decision that form the very stuff of narrative. The reader then is able to identify with the selection made by the character, or dissociate from it: "The ethical response to a text is rooted in this identification."[4] But the process thus recounted is insufficiently self-analytical; for it is a process born of pedagogic exchange, of the professing of literature to the tutelary subject, of the learned transposition of ethical dilemmas and incompetence back and forth between diegetic persons and reading persons. The account of textual analysis presented in this chapter presumes that this reading subject and his or her proper education will be geared to positioning the self inside the text in order to know it better. This positioning will always have social ramifications, given the abiding proclivity of narrative analysis to the view that stories pivot on some breach in legitimacy; hence the abiding element of reductionism in even the most open of critical readings.

Approaches to Text and Society

As part of his attempt to work with a variety of approaches to Romanticism, Geoffrey Thurley opts for a symbiotic etiological and conceptual relationship between Romantic forms and their historical context. For the purposes of my argument, his position will stand for the conventional litterateur's sociology of culture.

"As symptomatic structures, works of art preserve certain homologies with the social and economic structures of their time," Thurley contends; "every work of art is, *inter alia,* an important social document." Nevertheless, his image of the male-bound social theorist requires granting art, not only a history of its own form that is a determination of each artifact, but a privileged autonomy both of quality and of type: "Whether he accepts art as being explained by the historical facts, or as, on the contrary, itself throwing light on history, the sociologist of literature is guilty of reductivism unless he accepts that the work of art is a source of experience otherwise unattainable and that this experience is its real value . . . the source of the identifying experience it offers."

The best of Romantic and lyric poetry and the realist novel can here be made to interact and forge a contest between the competing drives toward expression and mimesis, between a will to extension of the creating self's subjectivity and the capacity to represent the real social order. In its turn, modernism restores the reader to a position of prominence by drawing attention to the manufacture of the text. The figure of the author unites these strands of cultural formation. Authors are valorized as guarantors of an ultimately unitary culture by their status as speakers of what is known, hence of what is experienced, and hence, perforce, of what can or must be shared with their audiences: "the common ground occupied by author and reader: the ground of a common humanity . . . human experience . . . [offers an access to] inherited and public themes and contents [by] subjectifying the objective."[5]

It is this very sense of the best understanding the best that underpins the screen critic John Hinde's important distinction between "Cinema" and "Film industry." His contribution is significant for its rare facility with auto-interrogation and the unearthing of dearly held and barely debated foundational principles. "Cinema" here occurs at the junction of a fruitfully "disturbed local culture" and filmmaking. "Film industry" is a profit-making, export-oriented practice that does not aim at achieving any special fusion with the local community. "Cinema" provides a new mode of telling stories that is inexorably intertwined with an "entirely new concept of self—of self as individual, defying the gods." For a "national cinema" to assert itself, there must be a special, productive kind of audience seeking "a cinema of its own, not to be a mirror (although it is so tempting to say so) but to be a monitor and a comforter in the way a map can be when you're not sure where you're going."[6] This combination of Baedeker and polymath presumably finds its mystic expression in some kind of marketlike relay between the "right" audience and the auteur filmmaker.

Hinde has performed a great service here by acknowledging the role of the viewer as someone who is part of and subject to a public critical and pedagogic apparatus, thus pointing to the constitutive work of critic and viewer in setting up the text. Thurley's statement stops short of this. It remains a beguiling amalgam of the contradictory dictates of a faith in creative genius and idealism on the one hand and broader social, but never materially determining, forces on the other.

I want to turn now to the classic leftist position on the intersection of cultural products and their consumption. Terry Lovell argues that "any sociology of art must confront first and foremost the question of the relationships which exist between art and social reality, relationships both at the level of meaning and of cause/effect."[7] This is the world where authentic art displaces the rule of a misrecognizing imaginary domain and yokes the symbolic onto our apprehension of an art that goes beyond ideology and is adjacent to science. Raymond Williams humanizes such lines with his (always partial) insistence on the value of the avant-garde work's taste for the "fragmented ego in a fragmented world," defying as it does capitalist neatness and notions of a monopoly on quality in a unilogical realism. This is not, however, to disregard the importance of doctrines of representation or realist/reflectionist aesthetics. For Williams, "representation is not a subject separate from history, but . . . part of the history, contributing to the history."[8]

The division set up between truth and ideology that underpins this type of textual theory is prone to the constitutive double bind characteristic of models of false consciousness and their attendant, ethical insufficiency. The presumption that there is a domain that is ideological involves an identification of the knowing, speaking subject who dares to apply such a title to a body of work, simultaneously ripping the stuffing out of the concept. For once ideology is named, its work is over, because another kind of misrepresentative spy network of distortions must replace the revealed system. This reliance on failure, on never quite completing tasks, is a central problem in most theories of revolutionary cultural change. There can be no adequate predictive or programmatic metalanguage of revolt, because the subject required to articulate such a language would always be in a pre-, post- or current revolutionary environment and therefore a product of that environment and tied to available subjectivities. The corollary for criticism is a combination of certainty of the value of critique with anxiety over the act of criticism.

The British Film Institute's publication *National Fictions: World War Two in British Films and Television* (1984) is an attempt to explain the media experience of the 1982 conflict with Argentina in the South Atlantic. It mobilizes much of what has been discussed above in ways that exemplify the cultural- and screen-studies adoption of such left critical protocols. I read it here as a means of understanding mid-1980s militarism that assumes the presence of both realism and reflectionism in screen drama accounts of earlier conflicts, either in contemporaneous or archival mode, and claims that these are productive of a broader politics on the part of the consumer.

Geoff Hurd's introductory essay as editor of *National Fictions* sets the tone for an account that is almost constant throughout the volume in its reflectionist and pedagogic certainties:

> Wartime cinema played an active role in mobilising support for the
> war effort by successfully constructing an image of popular unity,
> one which placed ordinary men and women at its centre . . . cinema
> had to construct an image which attempted to resolve in its nar-
> ratives the social contradictions which challenged any simple no-
> tions of unity (class, gender, region, etc.) . . . the need to represent
> "the people" could not in itself determine the limits on what those
> representations might be.[9]

For Hurd, this set of requirements that the state has imposed on film
involves contradictions. It necessitates a direct address to the real, everyday concerns of people in their social location in order to interpellate
them effectively, but in such a way that inequality and difference can
ultimately be overridden by the pull toward national unity. He endeav-
ors to tie these elements together under the rubric of hegemony. It is a
theoretical move that continues to resonate in later work in the field.

This is done in isolation from evidence of readings at the time of the
first circulation of these texts and in isolation from specific textual analysis of the emergence and trajectory of contradictions and their suture.
Cinema is anthropomorphized and rendered nonspecific. It is a mere
extra product of history, which is rarely even described as specifically
visual and auditory. There is no explanation of the mechanism whereby
representations eluded the control of the state; whether the state found
this to be the case; or how it reacted to the fact. No concession is made
to the need for evidence of the mode, place, time, or even existence of a
site or sites of negotiation between and within state, filmmaker, distributor, exhibitor, and audience.

When the collection actually does the work of writing history, rather
than reading pictures unself-reflexively, it provides valuable information about how such texts have circulated—for instance, occasions when
Campaign for Nuclear Disarmament rallies were disrupted by groups
playing tapes of the theme music to *The Dam Busters* (Michael Anderson, 1954), a film about a World War II bombing raid on the Ruhr.[10]

The dominant tenor of *National Fictions* is set with typical force by
Colin McArthur's essay of the same title. He maintains that British
films of the 1950s and 1960s that looked back to World War II "repressed
the 'people's war,' presenting it as a series of heroic actions (mainly) by
middle-class white men supported by compliant other ranks with women
as waiting sweethearts or mothers. In retrospect, this can be seen as
contributing to the 'commonsense' construction of the war which was
animated, to such devastating effect during the South Atlantic War.

The Well-Tempered Self

There is a lesson to be learned here which will hopefully shape future film and television research and practice."[11] There appears to be no requirement for McArthur to trace the lineage of either this original putative " 'commonsense' " or its redisposal four decades later.

Leaving left screen history for the moment, distinct but related methods can be seen to animate various feminist critiques of representation, via powerful accounts of images of women in feature film, with the important work of Laura Mulvey encouraging a stream of research and teaching practices. As an instance of a politics that is concerned with reflectionism and the ethical incompleteness of its subjects, Mulvey's work will be taken as exemplary, both as a theoretical advance in screen and other textual studies and as the stimulus to a consideration of gender politics outside the fictive.

Mulvey's 1975 article "Visual Pleasure and Narrative Cinema" intervenes in the Althusserian and psychoanalytic accounts of classical Hollywood that were emerging in the 1970s in the journal *Screen* and elsewhere. These writings addressed the ideological inscription of positions for spectators to adopt, drawing on Freudian accounts of the formation of personality, particularly the process of first seeing oneself as oneself, as someone other than one's mother, that young children go through when they encounter mirrors. Mulvey sought to apply this approach to fictional treatments of gender, deploying it to look at the particular impact on forming gendered subjects of the gazing pleasure offered to men by classical Hollywood films. Here, films became mirrors. Subsequently, the approach has also been to describe sporting events; television situation comedy and other dramas; advertisements; avant-garde cinema; lecture halls; and a variety of public sites of spectacle.

Mulvey wants to apply psychoanalytic theory enmeshed with film history as a "political weapon" that will allow readers to see how "the unconscious of patriarchal society has structured film form." So already we have some significant assumptions. It is presumed that the formal components of film are determined by a very broad object called "society." It is further presumed that this object "society" can be specified as dominated by men and as having an unconscious. "It" is to be understood anthropomorphically. Mulvey argues that this society is paradoxically dependent on women to define itself, which it does by pointing to what it has and women do not. In other words, it defines by exclusion, pitting women as castrated subjects against itself as properly phallically formed. Unless it can show that their inadequacy and lack of fulfillment follow willy-nilly on the lack of the phallus, the phallus ceases to be important and worthy of its standing. In "the last resort," lack is all that women represent in the cinema. Men project onto these silenced creatures of their gaze their own other side, a side that might wish to give birth to children, but instead runs society. Women look on their child-bearing capacities as—simultaneously—the cause of and some compensation for their castration. Similarly, audiences use the gaze to project their own suppressed exhibitionism onto diegetic characters. This process becomes political once women realize that they can use the very tools of patriarchy—such as psychoanalysis—to discover how it works. The analysis of existing grammars of pleasure will ultimately help to subvert that pleasure.[12]

Despite its sophisticated discussion of the unconscious, this writing strategy depends on the inscription of incompleteness. "Society" is incomplete because for all its dominance it still requires the dominated both to serve it and help in its task of self-definition. Women are incomplete because they lack power and the phallus. Men are incomplete because they need to objectify women on screen in order to pleasure themselves and because they have to deal with their own inability to bear children. The audience is incomplete because it needs to project its inadequacies onto screen characters, who do the work of acting out audience desires for attention. The audience is like a child, always seeking mastery of its surroundings via relations extrapolated from the mirror; but such projections are always misrecognitions. And the analysis that allows the cultural critic and its pupils to reveal this truth is also incomplete because—like those in the pedagogic relationship that the article forms—it labors under terms of understanding that are patriarchal.

In her contribution to the *National Fictions* dossier, Tessa Perkins helps break up such certitudes. She asks whether women could argue that the BBC teleplay *The Imitation Game,* the political correctness of which was debated at the summer school that gave rise to *National Fictions,* "wasn't pro-feminist if it engendered guilt in men about patriarchy? Should we take women's anger as a mark of the play's failure (surely a pro-feminist play shouldn't make women angry at it?) or men's positive reactions to it as a mark of its success?"[13] There is, here, the litterateur's uncertainty about the residue of meaning. Does the ultimate referent reside in the text? Is that where battles over meaning can be fought, via reference back to it? Or is it in audience responses? And, if so, should these be ordered by political effectivity, emotional response, or category of person? In the last instance, a symptomatic reading is reinstalled that diagnoses via exegesis. But the issue of the audience has been addressed in a way that permits cracks around the analysis that are not observable in the unity of most criticism.

The Well-Tempered Self

Token references to spectatorship were common to textual analysis as far back as Aristotle. But the value of ethnography as a means of determining political utility is always and necessarily secondary to a process of close reading that seeks symptoms hidden within the text. This symptomatology is a yoking together of anthropological and literary studies' accounts of culture. Homi Bhabha refers to two key "traditions in the discourse of identity: the philosophical tradition of identity as the process of self-reflection in the mirror of (human) nature: and the anthropological view of the difference of human identity as located in the division of Nature/Culture."[14] The mechanism for their merger is an undercarriage of humanism. From a geographer's perspective, Yi-Fu Tuan has argued that "culture is near the core of one's humanity. . . . Without grounding in a specific culture, the world loses shape and focus. Culture may be conceived as a pair of spectacles that we need to wear so that the world can seem vividly particularized and real."[15] It is this way of seeing what touches the person that animates the manifestations of reflectionism gathered together above. For all the critiques of doxification by poststructuralism and postmodernism, mimesis remains one of the principal ways of assigning literary value. If anything, much current textual analysis is resurrecting mimetic evaluation.

On the screen front, the special triumph and quality of drama is said to be its inevitable commitment to detail, to hyper-relevant and recognizable trivialities. This drives the special anxiety attached to recorded images, in a way that Raymond Williams has effectively captured in his discussion of the shock that the mechanically reproduced picture can render, "that extraordinarily significant cultural moment which began with photography . . . [where] pleasure is found in the reproduction of wholly familiar people and places."[16] From its earliest days, photography established a realist aesthetic. Its special referentiality in the real was a source of one of the first arguments mounted over the authorship and ownership of images. The personal stamp given a painting by the artist did not immediately carry over into film, where it was questioned by the technicality and objectivity of the new apparatus. This had the side effect (or was itself a side effect) of the generation of a depersonalized hold on realism that immediately attached to the form. Reflectionism became an everyday hermeneutic code, routinely deployed by readers as a consequence of the realism of their personal collections of photographs as much as anything else. Of course, early film theorists were in little doubt about the mechanical reproductivity of the medium as a guarantor of its realism. They differed more over the political legitimacy and artistic value of, for example, the mortgage on authenticity proffered by the long take. But for Jean-Luc Godard in *La Chinoise* (1967), "art is not the reflection of a reality; it is the reality of that reflection."[17] Recent attempts to work through the implications of transporting something called "film theory" to the site of television have come back, when they address texts stylistically, to just this point, that truth is made in the work of photography and editing. As Foucault says, "by representation one must not understand screen or illusion, but real mode of action."[18]

The moving image relies on readers with similar skills in the registers of the iconic and the indexical, as well as the directive but also polysemic confluence of picture and sound that encourages a permissive intermingling of sign systems. Real world referents are interpreted phenomenologically because of the realist system of television. Written another way, one might point to how the coming of photography gradually elevated its authors to a status previously attained by poets, one that afforded them a privileged position from which to enunciate a staging of the self on account of the medium's effect of truth. This effect is sustained because of the photographic image's hold, as a classic material cross-referent between the natural and the manufactured, on the mirroring of the split between the two that is the foundational substance of both cultural/critical and anthropological accounts of self-formation.

Television Drama

Horace Newcomb has called for a conceptual placement of the television drama series alongside the novel and away from radio and film. This is because it is a form that can offer a "sense of density," exploring complex themes in very lengthy treatments with slow buildup and multisequenced sites of character problematic.[19] It has been convincingly argued that the continuous serial, like the novel, permits an asymptotic development. Beyond that, it offers travel through time that mirrors the time the viewer has passed since the previous episode in a way that makes for an intertextual merging of characterological acquaintance. This encourages a view of the television drama text as neither mirror nor window, but rather as part-generator of the manufacture of experience by the viewer.

Newcomb was making his claim in the context of an appeal to the central question addressed by the academic study of television in the mid 1970s—that is, whether it was worthy of formalist (or any) textual analysis, as opposed to behavioral investigation or generic condemnation. A decade later, a revised critical theory emerged. It could still condemn, but only in the context of detailed knowledge. Television is seen to be a medium and form that can reveal the traces of domination and the cultural politics of the prevailing mode of production. For Douglas Kellner, myths "provide stories which dramatize society's values, ideals and ways of life; they are enacted in story-telling media." Television is "the electronic ideology machine." Formulaic drama series offer "hegemonic ideology for advanced capitalism."[20] And their internal form would, of course, encourage such a functionalist reading. They are generally realist texts, meaning that they have neat etiological chains, an everyday mise-en-scène and continuity editing; their routine location is within everyday cultural competence.

There is still no accepted methodology for reading screen evidence as extra-diegetic historical narrative, however. So, attempts to account for the efflorescence of the detail-rich, sociology poor, anally retentive historical period piece television drama of the 1970s—what Rupert Murdoch has termed "drama run by the costume department"—have gone beyond the possibilities offered by the arrival of color television in Britain. Such explanations now tie this genesis to a realization on the screen of past days of class equanimity in order to remove or redispose attention from the real of the present.[21] Or, alternatively, these accounts argue that it was precisely the calling up of contemporary issues to do with class, gender, and nation that drew such sizable ratings.

John Tulloch's survey of television drama is an attempt to recuperate reflectionism to respectability by renaming it, allowing him to accept and recycle interpretations such as the one above. He works within a protocol that he calls "a counter-discourse of the real." This describes a domain in which extra-discursive, extra-subjective realms of the real exist and can be explicated via the application of social theory. Here, meaning occurs, not purely in the empty interstices between signifiers, but at the junction of signifiers, objects, events, and people. This is a move that reinstates symptomatology, a diagnosis of the times that continues to claim for artworks the status of encapsulations of prevailing political, metaphysical, and economic *tempora et mores*. Texts are accounted for as products and producers of the forms of consciousness available at a given period to particular categories of person, defined in relation to mode and means of production and/or reproduction. The putative warrant for these certainties is twofold. It resides equally in the form and content of the text screened and in the sense made of it by audiences. Hence the installation of ethnography as a new critical trope.

Or so it seems. But Tulloch continues to read meanings off from texts, except when he explicitly performs or reports the results of ethnographic research. An effortless—and unexplicated—move is made from the exegetic to the field and back again, with each approach seemingly providing the same type of result. It remains the case, for instance, that the police drama series "does its work as an agent of ideological control" by denying the class power aspect of the repressive state apparatus. But just to be safe from anti-reflectionist critiques, "*Miami Vice* and *The Sweeney* refracted, rather than reflected, their time." Where does one begin and the other end?

Australian historical mini-series produced by the Kennedy-Miller organization are valorized for giving multi-perspectival accounts of the recent past (the Vietnam War and the vice-regal removal of an elected government). This move argues that the offering up of different explanations and stories about apparently identical events is an approach that problematizes any notion of a single truth. Such an approach is said to be particularly effective when it involves the interspersal of documentary footage; reenacted historical figures; and other, more everyday units acting as emblems of the time (e.g., a family bildungsroman that develops via encounters with drugs, the contraceptive pill, feminism, conscription, etc.).[22]

The argument here is borrowed from Stuart Cunningham's work on the historical mini-series. Cunningham argues that the nature of the mini-series form, a sprawling yet condensed narrative sequencing that displaces a fixation with events by attention to etiology and outcome, makes for "an unparalleled upgrading of the terms within which historical information and argument is mediated through mainstream television." The multi-perspectival element is provided by the bildungsromanlike "multiplication of authorising perspectives," for example, within the family, which are set against maturational questions and historical debates and overlap the self and the social at a multitude of points of disagreement and negotiation.[23] Albert Moran valorizes this as "a grass-roots history that puts the common people on the historical stage. . . . The central strategy of the Australian historical mini-series is to portray the development of national consciousness inside emergence of an individual consciousness." He regards these tendencies as attributable, not only to the internal generic dynamics of television production, but equally to "the play of ideas within the larger society."[24]

These positions, like that of Tulloch, work hard to acknowledge problems with a mirror-image understanding of the relationship between cultural production and the wider world. In the case of Moran's work, they fall back on such protocols. Cunningham's material—hence, perhaps, its uptake by Tulloch—assumes the productive, if not necessarily realistic, power of the extended documentary-drama, arguing that its referentiality back to the historical record encourages its audience to discuss that history in other contexts. We are reminded here of Aristotle's distinction between history and drama, which finds the latter superior because of its capacity for the general and the complex, the explanatorily powerful and conflictual, over and above the empiricist: "The standard of correctness is not the same in poetry and politics."[25] Similarly, it is a referentiality in systems of knowledge, not an unalloyed conduit to actuality, that makes for television realism.

In keeping with the latter-day valorization of split narratives of history, though, such mini-series are ultimately deemed to be politically worthy because of the unresolved contradictions they present. Yet this is dependent on a particular array of pedagogic as much as textual norms. It assumes that audiences read methodologically, that the viewer is interested and able to analyze the text in historiographic terms. This historiography allows for contending purchases on truth and ultimately exposes truth as an effect of political contestation. Significantly, to repeat, it is that very narrative of self-discovery, the bildungsroman, that is the story's motor in all this, when allied to specifically nonrealist protocols of decipherment. One is drawn here to Walter Benjamin's position that all epic forms are closely related to historiography.

This line is identical to Althusser's when he valorizes Leonardo Cremonini's painting of the relations between objects and "their" people, although Althusser adopts a more anti-humanist position than would allow for so straightforward a support of the bildungsroman as Cunningham suggests. Both arguments rely for their championing of the products they discuss on the impossibility of absolute self-recognition and encourage a concentration on the multitude of relations that form an apprehension of history in the spectator.[26] There are resonances here, also, of the argument that ancient Greek tragedy's apogee lay in its movement beyond character and toward an account of actions; and a connection to Godard's line from *Pierrot le Fou* (1965) that finds Ferdinand yearning "no longer to write about people's lives . . . but. . . . what goes on between people, in space."[27]

Cunningham calls for an appreciation of the mini-series form as a moment in which the viewer is hailed "as knowledgeable citizen, rather than distracted consumer."[28] Similarly, the makers of the 1970s mini-series *Days of Hope,* a historical account of British working-class radicalism, have argued that it was read by the public as a commentary on latter-day events—that is, miners' actions against the previous Tory government.[29] (A modernism that would have satisfied Baudelaire.) Again, when asked his opinion of René Allio's 1976 film *I, Pierre Rivière,* Foucault stressed the worth of contemporary peasants acting the part of peasants from another historical time, not because of any purchase on authenticity that this might offer, or as a process of learning about one's class past, but rather as a junction of representing themselves to themselves and their history to themselves.[30] At the formal educational level, it is significant that the French Ministry of Education officially recommended that students watch the *Holocauste* mini-series in 1979; an act without precedent, illustrating the position that the form was attaining.

One can perhaps best summarize this revisionist reflectionism in the words of James Donald. Writing in a newly vocational *Screen,* he is concerned to detach himself from theoreticism of the sidelines that fails to engage with the practice of schooling and the context of the labor market. Donald argues for a non-utopic, grounded means of distributing screen studies knowledge. He continues to do so, however, from a position that empowers the set as a crucial device for hailing subjects. Again, we can see the social force—almost "merely" immanent, now, in the light of doctrines of active readers and multiple determinations on meaning—of television. It "constructs a calendar of public events and a schedule of private routines, as well as the pedagogic rhetoric of its address simultaneously to the listener/viewer as individual and to the people-nation as One."[31] Such continued faith in the cultural critic as the subject able to break the circuit between ideology and public is what places the textual analysis of television alongside older formats.

Reading Reflections

It is to this partially extra-exegetical mode of literary and other cultural studies that I now turn, taking as a beginning Terry Eagleton's characteristically pithy certainty about indeterminacy: "The hallmark of the 'linguistic revolution' of the twentieth century, from Saussure and Wittgenstein to contemporary literary theory, is the recognition that meaning is not simply something 'expressed' or 'reflected' in language: it is actually *produced* by it."[32] Meanings derive from language, then, in its actual use. "The" meaning of a text is indeterminate and beyond, to the point where the text's very existence is indeterminate. It has been supplanted by readers. The primary referent may be any or all of the following: the real; the reader's self; the intratext; or the intertext. Struggles enacted between total determination and total indeterminacy across the body of literary theory encapsulate the critical question here: whether symptomatic textual criticism subjectifies people undertaking it in terms of their relationship to various forms of knowledge; or whether it is amenable to a politics of identity, a politics of self-formation that abjures the subjection of others. We may proceed some way toward answering this question by examining the architecture that houses the relationship of textual criticism and the signs to be criticized.

It has been suggested that the extant terms of debate in the field are such that the internal structure of the text is either everything or nothing, and that referentiality to the world outside is either impossible or massive. The characteristically leavening but inconclusive evidence from empirical studies of readers suggests that literary texts have a regulatory structure that determines much of the reading process, but little of the content of readers' responses. (The reader will already have noted the cavalier way in which I am using the terms *audience, reader, viewer,* and *text,* such that the precision of form is lost. This is because, at a theoretical level, the cross-pollination between literary and screen theory has come to be very significant. It becomes commonplace for the metaphor of book usage to be applied to television and film in such a way that many of the best writings across forms, while paying due attention to the specificity of textual content and presentation, mobilize very similar hermeneutic and research protocols. Hence the terms of debate about reflectionism on screen are, to a certain extent, set by arguments over art, poetry, and the novel; and claims to the rare status of television drama by the traditional valorization of the immediacy and quality of live theater. All this in spite of the touchingly impressionistic prognostications of litterateurs and historians like Edward Said, Dominick LaCapra, Wayne C. Booth, and Leonie Kramer, who might argue for the specifically nonredemptive nonsensibility of television watching.)[33]

Where, though, is the text that people read? Consider the sense we might make of the following remarks by John Frow: " 'The text' is not given but is constituted and reconstituted in relation to synchronically and diachronically variant systems. Or rather: the text is given not ontologically but socially; and its 'meaning' is a function not of its origin but of the multiple historicities which constitute it."[34]

To what might this be made to refer? Does it mean that textual analysis itself becomes the point of reflection of its times? Catherine Belsey has maintained, in arguing along similar coordinates, that critical writings about *Othello* reveal traces of the racisms current at the time they were written. This is just as productive—and reflectionist—as readings of the play that hold the reflective meaning at a four hundred-year-past node of closure. Belsey distinguishes between the racism relevant at Shakespeare's time, which is tied to the conditions of an emergent system of sovereign states; the racism of the confident apogee of imperialism displayed in A. C. Bradley's account of the play; and finally, the racism of colonial *méconnaissance* exemplified by F. R. Leavis.[35] One might also look here at the prehistory to the installation of *Don Quixote* as the foundational modern novel. Its precepts include the notion that all people are the children of their actions. This position underpins Don Quixote's examination of subjectivity. It is directly opposed to the notion of inherited hierarchical systems and the discourse of the aristocracy. Now *El Quijote apócrifo,* the competing text to *Don Quixote* by Cervantes's mysterious contemporary Avellaneda, describes the path to virtue in quite contrasting terms. For that figure, honor and repute come from a combination of race, war, or art. The actual elevation of Cervantes to canonical status occurred in the eighteenth century, once the bourgeoisie was established in England as a dominant class, in keeping with the developing utilitarian ethos of individual responsibility and autotelic technologies of destiny that the Don's subjectivity endured and procured. England was the first country to adopt the novel, in keeping with its simultaneous formation of mercantile capitalism and a rhetoric of self-reliance. But of course we hear little of the choices on offer for the title of first modern novel, even when those choices share a title and topic, if one option degrades the autonomous, calculating subject. We learn little of the circumstances under which certain preferred accounts of public and private interiority circulate.

The division between reader, critic, and text is frequently unclear. Roger Chartier's project of "a history of practices of reading" has found that many systems of interpretation conclude with "interpretation of the self." He refers particularly to the contemporary hermeneutics of Paul Ricoeur here, but can also illustrate the point from the past. For instance, he mentions Fernando de Rojas's *Celestina* (1507), which contains the following prefatory instructions on how proper readers will make sense of what is to follow. Such readers "will understand its essential matter and profit from it, they will be amused at its wit, and they will store away in their memories the maxims and sayings of the philosophers, in order, when the proper time comes, to use them to advantage." This protocol is designed to encourage what Chartier calls "a plural reading that distinguishes the comic from the serious, and that extracts the moral that best illuminates each person's life, whose 'first person' is applicable to everyone."[36]

Like the metacriticism of Belsey, this acts to reinscribe the legitimacy of reflectionism in a way very similar to that parlayed by Tulloch, Moran, and Cunningham. It is a system of reading reading that suggests, in keeping with the empirical findings mentioned earlier, that meaning is fixed at the level of the structures of the text, but compromised by shifting relations between particular discourses of the human sciences and the representational text—for instance, the state of popular medical knowledge and its intersection with an account of science fiction medicine in a short story. It is a serious lacuna that even later accounts of the active television reader rarely appear to consider the role of the human sciences in prefiguring interpretation. This while litterateurs, in danger of becoming yesterday's pedagogues, are alive to the need for a teaching of reading that works across every kind of communicative study; that metaphor is, in some sense, always metaphor and hence amenable to a particular form of decoding. I shall return to this point shortly.

It is in tracing the deployment of these protocols of mapping, the actual cartography of superimposing nonfictive knowledge onto fictive, that we may find the meaning, the referentiality, and the political effect/affect of texts. No aesthetic form can be said to have a necessary meaning and therefore a necessary political effect. Rather, the latter is held outside, where people receive and make their intertexts. It has been argued that there is value for a feminist politics in an unambiguous, explicit, fictive borrowing from social experience in narratives of self-disclosure. This value can then be determined against a Habermas-derived, gyno-reformed group of what Rita Felski terms the "objectives of a feminist public sphere," in place of a text-bound aesthetic.[37] One could work other categories of person into such terms in addition to the category "woman," other elements of the human sciences than "experience" as motors of change in both the production and reception of texts. Where reflectionism was once a property, it is now an act. Cultural criticism becomes an active site of cultural politics, as in the uptake of Mulvey's work. This is a cultural politics that uses the connections drawn between text, reader, and world to rework existing relations of power in each of those domains. It becomes the site for generating a new realism for the reader, a realism formed by thinking oneself into and out of texts. I shall examine an instance of this type of politics in chapter 5.

Here, however, we might consider some of the work done in the journal *m/f*, a manifestation of the realization at the junction of British Marxism and feminism that discourse creates its own object. In seeking a political practice of feminism that acknowledged this, *m/f* described itself in opposition to unitary referential logics: "It is the shifting ground between the construction of the category woman that we have at present and that category that feminists struggle to construct, that gives rise to the temptation to fall back on the notion of a pre-given unity of women and a simple notion of women's oppression," an *m/f* editorial declared in 1978 (one could, for the purposes of my argument here, write any of the words *nation, person,* or *culture* over the word *woman,* and *formation* over *oppression*). Elizabeth Cowie's influential questioning of the practice of scrutinizing film texts for their appropriateness of representation is important here. She encounters two problems in evaluating women in film. First, there is the matter of the production of the category "woman"; second, the matter of the production of film as a signifying system. The latter is frequently undervalued in political analyses of film texts, which take an assured and unquestioned referent in the real as a means of weighing up the rectitude of gender representations on screen. Such symptomatic, nonformal criticism presumes to know that film merely reproduces, well or ill, already fully achieved accounts of what women are. Cowie problematizes this type of criticism: "What is important is not that film falsely signifies women, or appropriates the signifier (image) woman to another signification, but the particular mode of constituting woman as sign within film. What is of concern is the specific consequences [*sic*] of that mode of constitution both within film and in relationship to other signifying systems and discourses." Films, then, may be deemed to be part of the fixing of patriarchal values. They are more than reflections of a system that is already in place.[38]

In discussing the progressiveness or otherwise of the depiction of the female protagonist in Michael Crichton's *Coma* (1978), Cowie is thus dismissive of a reductionism that concentrates solely on the issue of women, because this "demands a fragmentation of the film into its elements and . . . denies the productivity of the film, both across the film as such, and in its insertion into structures and discourses of distribution and exhibition, and also film reviewing and even theoretical writing."[39]

Such fragmentation makes for a content analysis in which the critic adds up the number of progressive representations, subtracts the nonprogressive ones, and comes up with a final audit. Cowie finds this faulty because it assumes that what is shown has definite, fixed meanings in relation to a separate, accurate, and appropriate category of "woman-outside-representation." In place of such an approach, an audit of value can only usefully be made by asking about the text's deployment in the kinds of institutions and discourses listed above.

In his discussion of the attempt to downgrade the status of a particular poet for a supposed failure to achieve the supposedly possible—an adequate articulation of the social world of his country at a particular node of history—Ian Hunter makes the following assault on reflectionism that calls for a still further limitation: "What is it that gives all the things that might be located in the geographical and temporal boundaries of Australia in the fifties—everything from sexual manners and legal statutes through forms of economic and political organization to hair-styles and welfare policies—a single general articulation or movement, that a poet might align himself with or not?"[40]

These criticisms of blanket assertions about the inevitability of texts displaying the social world in which they were formed are powerful, whether they are made about the comparatively apolitical turn of a discourse of "art and society"; the Lukácsian-Hegelian call for the transcendent, and yet illuminative, *ur*-object of its generation; or a liberal reformist carping at representation of categories of person. Texts are most clearly the outcome of negotiations between conventions of genre, fashion, personal concern, industrial circulation, and the deployment of interpellative mechanisms by writers, teachers, and readers, with slippage between categories. How might such interpellations occur?

The subject is said to be a routine process of invention under modernity and its successor. Television is a prime site of this creation, especially under the prevailing sign of notions of freedom of choice rationally exercised. Hence the paradoxical argument of a columnist on television for Sydney's former *Daily Mirror* newspaper, writing in the 1960s. Her argument empowers the viewer while denying the effectivity of viewing: "A weekly injection of *Peyton Place* is not going to turn a Richmond River dairy farmer into an Idaho potato grower. . . . For television to determine our character or attitudes we would have to take it seriously."[41] This deploys the nativist view of David Hume in its elaborate dependence on the primacy of feelings or senses over representation: "All the colours of poetry, however splendid, can never paint natural objects in such a manner as to make the description be taken for a real landscape."[42]

The capacity to distinguish "authentic experience" from "televisual experience" may not be so straightforward, however, let alone determining which comes first. It has been television's distinctive contribution since its introduction to be at one and the same time possessed of the double status of community and industry, a people's medium precisely because of the absence of a critical apparatus—until the advent of media studies—informing people about what each text properly means.

There is, of course, intense argument about how different forms of texts can be read. In particular, the ruling Brechtian aesthetic of distantiation in 1970s *Screen* theory was arch in its derisiveness toward what became known as the "realist text." The notion of textually inscribed rules of reading—solid interpellations of viewers—as a function of naturalism/realism problematized the value of, for example, social realism. This orthodoxy viewed linear and resolved narratives that compelled closure as reactionary in their inevitable construction of the possibility of perfect knowledge (fore-echoes here of Cunningham and Tulloch's valorization of the multi-perspectival mini-series). Instead, audiences should be confronted with the constructedness of their positioning and the seams of weaving in each text made explicit via self-referentiality. It was more radical to address the camera directly and quiz the viewer than to demonstrate the condition of the oppressed. For the text was the real site of material relations, and that limit was also its potential benefit as a radicalizing force that could outlaw passivity. Great claims continue to be made for certain kinds of television narrative on the grounds that they refuse the "linearity and resolution" of other forms of communication.

This resonates with the preference expressed by Barthes for the "writerly" text that sees readers productively engaged via the problematization of a literalist signification that draws attention to itself in place of feigning a transparent realism. This is said to contrast with the "readerly" text, which denies its condition as a sign. The irony—the further leavening produced by the type of empirical work in this area to which I have already referred—is that the formally experimental metanarrative has been shown to generate an inevitable hermeneutic (of relativistic positions on truth). It is the realist text that routinely encourages divided protocols of decipherment. This suggests that there is a need to consider how and to what end people are schooled to read texts: to unpack the relationship of critic, pupil, and text.

Criticism, the Self, and Aesthetics

Literary studies functioned as a critical site in the late-eighteenth-century emergence of the human sciences, a site of Foucault's "double representations—representations whose role . . . [was] to designate representations."[43] Consider Benjamin's romanticization of the age of the storyteller and its spirit of communal experience—savagely displaced by modern, commodified life, which dislocated the self from its heritage—a process further developed in the displacement of the bildungsroman by the *monologue intérieure*. We might read this as an account of an emerging anomie that only literary history could redeem. Literary studies' longevity and influence under such signs of meta-incompleteness are striking. Let us examine some of the changes and continuities in the discourses of exegesis.

Up to the late eighteenth century, character in drama was often evaluated by critics through a set of rules organized around the quality of representation in the light of other, organizational elements within a play, be they prosaic or otherwise. The advent of the idea of a national theater in nineteenth-century Europe was coterminous with the advent of cultural policies that assumed that drama could represent the nation to itself. This necessarily embodies a dubiety, a sense of doubt that renders the witnessing of one's supposed collective unity on stage into an object for speculation rather than a matter of course. The signified is not also the onlooker; rather, it is a desired state of mind in that onlooker, whose actual disunity has created the preconditions for a distorting signifier founded on the need to manufacture a solid imaginary order of signification. The debates of the period, over theater *for* versus theater *of* the people, were conducted across a series of oppositions themselves determined by an agonistics: crowd or nation? participant or spectator? object or subject? target or source?

In the nineteenth century, existing rhetorical forms were supplanted as modes of decipherment by the quest for an ethical interiority that is in a dynamic relationship of homology with the reader's own inner self. Such readings borrow from the emergent human sciences, notably social psychology. In themselves, these shifts also amount to a change in the locus of moral supervision from the ecclesiastical to the literary-pedagogic, including the auto-literary (the confessional diary, biography, and autobiography). There comes to be a new kind of nexus between rhetoric and morality, which establishes for Kristeva the prospect of valorizing literature as the privileged site of movement "from the 'ego' to history."[44]

We have already encountered this shift in chapter 1 with Foucault's notion of the transfer to secular from pastoral salvation. For Raymond Williams, it amounts to a renunciation of metaphysical or religious concerns in favor of the "exclusively human terms" of realist drama. And for György Lukács, there can be "no such thing as unevaluated literature" because all literature is "inseparably bound up with the most personal, inner content of our lives."[45]

One might cite here a Third World postmodern cultural critic in evidence of the remarkable perennialism of this reasoning about the interior self and its relations with the world outside, a reasoning that abjures—or perhaps partially informs—the buffets given First World, or ruling class, or male cultural practices by alterities. For Ihab Hassan: "Literature . . . is literature of the self, a self in the world, self and world made into worlds."[46] The pedagogic-critical expression of this mode of symptomatic reasoning is further evident in a recent survey of the condition of television criticism: "It is the television critic's job—perhaps in concert with the audience researcher and surely in concert with the audience—to identify the unspoken or unenacted in a text."[47]

This installation of the social self into the decoding of texts is now complete. Pedagogy has long been the primary mode of cultural criticism/aesthetics. For the abiding norm of aesthetics is self-formation, the recognition and transformation of the person that are the touchstones of criticism as an ethic. I am presuming here that criticism makes its own object; that a latent but orthodox tendency to inscribe indeterminacy as a means of requiring work on the self is an integral component—and definite possibility—of textual analysis. In short, I am arguing that modes of criticism are not determined by representational connections to common objects. Once more, this is to work with the assumption that the political outcome for marginal categories of person of such analysis may vary between subjection to the norms of others and the prospect of manufacturing a new sense of self. This depends on the interests served by the particular protocols of the human sciences that are called into play.

This returns us to Foucault's position in *The Order of Things,* discussed earlier. To insist on the prevalence of ethical self-formation within criticism is not to deny the point made by Jonathan Dollimore and Alan Sinfield that "most struggles involve a struggle in and for representation," that "culture is the place where norms are specified and contested, knowledges affirmed and challenged, and subjectivity produced and disrupted."[48] Rather, it is to specify the realm of production and performance of the self as central to culture, to concur with their assertion of the signal triumph of literary studies in establishing itself as the key point of inculcation into civic conduct. Having done so, then one might begin to wonder about technologies of the self operating outside the technologies of power that subjectify through indoctrination.

A concentration in curriculum on the formal properties of texts makes for a mutuality of possession. There is a seeming equality of access to the apparent object of understanding; the document is, after all, in everyone's hands. In fact, this leads to an extrapolation from the hermeneutic of the pedagogue and other particular human science doctrines. These will determine the array of knowledges that can play with the text, with particular consequences for the treatment of alterity. "Resistive" pedagogy/scholasticism still depends on what Hassan has termed the protocols of "how the best readers read"—that is, with an ultimate determination of a sense of self.[49] Such a process is entirely in keeping with a routine drill installed along with the development of popular education in nineteenth-century Britain that sought a license for cultural criticism as the maker of effective and affective personality. From that time to now, as Hunter has shown, "knowledge of texts catalogued as Literature would be inseparable from the production of an endlessly repeatable knowledge of the self."[50]

Critically, though, expanding on the available voices of interpretation needs to be seen as a process, not so much of correcting representation as some absolute object all its own, but of encouraging new areas of training and civic presence. In the work that Dollimore and Sinfield want to have done, alternative sexual practices to those of the heterosexual male seem to be important. In a self-forming ethic of reading, this would not be about adequate representation in terms of the numbers of alternatives presented or the quality of their display. Rather, the concern would be to guide oneself and others to form a relation to, and thereby make real, this alternative or alternatives. "To be 'gay,' I think, is not to identify with the psychological traits and the visible masks of the homosexual, but to try to define and develop a way of life," says Foucault.[51]

This is itself insufficient for some; a still more radical incompleteness is expected in what E. M. Forster called "the proviso 'English Literature.'" In his lament over the failure of literary study to have a single ethical base or a technocratic appeal, Graham Hough emphasized over a quarter of a century ago that "a literary education is concerned with personal values; it does not really stand for anything, has no aim or purpose, without some ideal of personality behind it."[52]

In a manifesto that seems surprisingly blind to the emergent efflorescence of subjectivity as a critical component of radical politics, Fredric Jameson ended the 1970s with a frustrated call to close off the referent of the self to which Hough was referring. In listing what he regarded as anti-progressive trends in the study of literature, Jameson attached particular obloquy to "the rhetoric of the self and of identity, in which literary works dramatize the integration of the hero's psyche or personality, and in which thereby some psychologizing and subjectivizing stance is encouraged or fortified in the American student."[53]

His position here may be seen to stand for a general trend within literary theory in reaction against ethical criticism on the grounds that it fails to theorize representation. Yet ethical criticism has been consistently influential since the advent of German Romanticism toward the conclusion of the eighteenth century. Hunter argues that its longevity may result, not so much from its silencing of subjects or their perversion, neither from denial or cathexis as such, nor from "the power of prejudicial representations," but rather from "the stability of a specific ethical practice," which can be understood as "a set of specifications, imperatives and techniques for working on the self through literature."[54] At the center of this practice is to be found, not a preexistent subject to be fought over in a struggle for intelligibility, but an object to be worked upon. Such criticism operates without mediation by the subject, but rather by educational institutions and their drills.

We can see a connection in contemporary claims made for the humanities to Friedrich Schleiermacher's hermeneutics, born out of a sense of a radical separation of the people from their traditions, a process that had rendered them anomic. From Schiller's time on, citizens were to have their tastes and natures formed under the sign of the *Bildung*. The split between thought and feeling occasioned by the emerging industrial division of labor was to be mitigated by a process of cultivation. The homologous divide between content and form, evident in new types of textuality, could be deployed dialectically as models for the unification of the reader, who would interpret the private-public split of personal life in the light of this critical practice. The text here must be dragged down, its form unpacked and ethical moves displayed and performed. This is a turning point in literary analysis. The problem set up from now on is how to uncover signposts of well-being for the reader. In encountering the work, one is to be made aware of being incomplete. As a consequence, an endless dialectical process of self-transformation is entered into.

This process of dealing with the dissociation of the self matches a separation of reading and writing made possible by the technology of printing, which opens up the contemplative—but also potentially nontutelary—practice of what Hans-Georg Gadamer calls "silent reading."[55] The translation of this practice into the public domain of popular education in the nineteenth century was not merely a change in the techniques of criticism itself. More, it came to pass through new student-teacher technologies that Hunter calls "moral supervision." In modern education, then, "the self-problematising relation to the text that guarantees the reader's ethical 'incompleteness' also opens him to

The Well-Tempered Self

the aesthetico-ethical supervision of an exemplar who is above all else an exemplary reader." (Lyotard, recalling his time as a secondary school teacher, explains that the exegetical component of philosophy classes involved the inscription of three practices into the life of the classroom: "listening, anamnesis and elaboration" of a class identity that had to be founded on the presumption that "we, the students and I, were 'at sea.'")[56] This procedure imbues textual studies with a literally unbounded optimism. George Steiner has shown that in the nineteenth century "the study of literature was assumed to carry an almost necessary implication of moral force. It was thought self-evident that the teaching and reading of the great poets and prose writers would enrich not only taste or style but moral feeling; that it would cultivate human judgement and act against barbarism."[57]

Renaissance and eighteenth-century views of Latin and Greek as humanizing agents fed a nineteenth-century redeployment of this function onto literature that was necessitated by an association of the need to form the self with the need to place this self within a concept of nation. From Herder on, to know one's local literary history was to affirm one's national identity. And after Taine, this was also the conduit to a sense of the public.

Technologies for tracing the structures or experiences that are held to underwrite texts come to be heralded for their ability to express or expose forms of consciousness. But their productive capacity, their making of that consciousness, is rarely considered. This functions as a significant political force within institutions of education. It serves to establish cultural criticism as a transcendent pathway to humanness that is beyond technique in its access to the real nature of persons. It centers readership, however, quite decisively, by virtue of pedagogy's guiding hand on each reader-critic's shoulder. And recent trends in North American literary education, for example, may be seen to underscore a self-conscious turn toward an ethic of training students to put themselves into the text in order to remake themselves in the life outside. This extends to arguments for students of business administration to move into the literature seminar as the exemplary site for ethical training via the case study, a highly instrumental coefficient of what Daniel R. Schwarz is pleased to call "an intimate sharing of consciousness." His professional task is founded on the understanding that "in making people better readers, we do make them better people." Most of the time, the task of interpretation is concerned with deciding how to live life under the benign stimulus of the imaginative and engaging literary author, with the vital mediation of the imaginative and engaging literary pedagogue. This is ensured by our major task of interpretation, the one that finds us seeking to analyze "in terms of our most fundamental text: the story of our own lives."[58]

The appearance of this seminar of the subject through the nineteenth and twentieth centuries displaces the ancient support for etiology and plain plotting so that drama, for instance, pleases its audience by analogy to the unity of the human person or to specifics of category of person. Benjamin, the lyric belletrist in advance of cultural studies, comes to argue that the most memorable narratives do not offer closed, fully and self-evidently psychologized accounts of character. Rather, it is their special capacity to require readers to carve out plot and story etiology and relate them to the interiority of characters. For him, "the essential substance of a literary work [is] what it contains in addition to information . . . the unfathomable, the mysterious." So, too, for Gadamer; it is insufficient that the "work of art that says something confronts us with ourselves." More than that, it must do so in such a way as to replicate—or perhaps enforce—"the disclosure of something covert."[59] The human sciences have intervened decisively.

Geoffrey Hartman has made this more specific. He has indicated that we are dealing here with a technology of the subject: "Representation, in short, is Coming Out. The self makes its debut." Hartman concludes his essay "The Interpreter" with a dialogue between "Interpreter" and "Book":

> INTERPRETER: Who's there?
> BOOK: Nay, answer me; stand, and unfold yourself.[60]

Even the scientism of structuralist accounts of character finally presents readers with discontinuous signifiers and cumulative signifieds in the relationship between specific textual figures and a more global store of knowledge about individuals. And Patricia Spacks's adherence to the inevitability of ethical reading encourages her to find that the overt anti-humanism of much contemporary literary theory cannot help but return to the "fact" that "novels occur at the intersection of the individual with the social" such that an "ethical dimension inheres in the nature of narrative." Novels have a special capacity to train us in the linkage of cause to effect, requiring us to "function as ethical agents." But this is not just the province of the novel: Spacks's interpretative system is used to read New York answering machine messages as well as Samuel Richardson's *Clarissa Harlowe* (1747–48), because they share an unshakable nexus that creates an ethical arena, via the dual qualities of "ambiguity" and "inevitability."[61]

This ethical preoccupation is part of a move in Western thought, identified by Foucault, toward both the invention of the unknown self and a search for its insistent other in order to understand this self:

> In Hegelian phenomenology, it was the *An sich* as opposed to the *Für sich;* for Schopenhauer it was the *Unbewusste;* for Marx it was alienated man; in Husserl's analyses it was the implicit, the inactual, the sedimented, the non-effected—in every case, the inexhaustible double that presents itself to reflection as the blurred projection of what man is in his truth, but that also plays the role of a preliminary ground upon which man must collect himself and recall himself in order to attain his truth. For though this double may be close, it is alien, and the role, the true undertaking, of thought will be to bring it as close to itself as possible; the whole of modern thought is imbued with the necessity of thinking the unthought . . . of ending man's alienation by reconciling him with his own essence . . . modern thought is advancing towards that region where man's Other must become the Same as himself.[62]

Notions of misunderstanding and even the impossibility of ever understanding are crucial preliminaries to the emergence in the nineteenth century of the human sciences and their central postulate: the subject and its capacity for misrecognition as a systematic modus operandi and raison d'être for the task of interpretation. Textual criticism that uses semiotics, sociology, the psy-complexes, history, or politics must needs have misrecognition/misinterpretation as prerequisites, not occasional aberrations. All such modes depend on the notion that the unconscious or a dissociated sensibility is always already present and in need of attention. This is significantly redolent of the very ancient notion of the self as capable of representation, even to the self, only through a series of masks.

Lacanian criticism makes a similar move in its desire to work with the impossible necessity for literature of attempting to master unconscious desire; what Catherine Greenfield has productively termed "the textual production of individuals, that is, as missing or failing to see the element of human subjectivity."[63] Marx and Lacan are crucial innovators in the career of the symptom, because of their identification of identity with alienation. For one, alienated identity was sought and found in the fetishized commodity; for the other, in the fetishized person. But this preoccupation need not reside solely in such radical places. Even the most conventionally positive account of the poetic function, for example, may now sorrowfully note, with Joseph Brodsky, that "the atomization and fragmentation of modern consciousness" are "a market requirement," so institutionalized are they as tropes of the industries of interpretation.[64]

Recent surveys of the field of aesthetic theory have stressed the need for a consideration of how notions of truth have functioned within the field—a fairly clear nodding toward Foucault. This is done in a way that resonates with the postmodern politics of identity identified in the previous chapter. It is done very much in the name of the formation of an authentic subjectivity. Charles Altieri, for instance, stresses the requirement for theorists of aesthetics "to supplement our concerns for proper sense by processes of self-reflection, on who we become as interpreters and how that activity may be directed to improve the quality of individual lives or modify our approaches to social issues." As grand narratives fail, they are replaced by hope for "successful communication among agents who may not need thereby to surrender their most treasured differences." Altieri maintains that cultural critics are always working with three basic tasks in mind. The first of these is to search for cognitive measures that can be used as a basis for debating the value of an artwork. The second is the utilization of "first-person response" in the interests of being "self-reflexive." The third is the establishment of "enduring relationships with certain works based either on the intimacy of dialogue they offer or on the mode of authority they can take on for our imaginative lives." This is to enter ethics into the register of cultural analysis as a meta-standard, above the notion of validity of judgment that has been so dominant within aesthetics. The resonance of the "I" in interpretation is now held to derive from its access to a personal meaning that is beyond doctrines of accuracy of observation.[65]

The newer areas of aesthetic criticism display similar features to literature and art. Benjamin paid particular heed to the synchronous evolution of cinema and Freudianism, prefiguring the doxic status of psychoanalysis in screen critique. He argued that just as Freud perceived slips of the tongue to be worthy of greater characterological/psychological attention than conventional perception would admit, films permit a special view of the world. Both Freudian slips and movies are, then, privileged sites for the examination of conduct. As Lyotard notes, photography and the cinema confirmed the processes of "ordering the visible"—in the case of the still-photograph, in continuity with painting—and "the containment of diachronies within organic totalities"; in the case of the moving image, in continuity with the "exemplary educative novels" of the previous hundred years. The new media made their referents appear more stable than their predecessors had ever been able to manage; but that equally allowed for a still easier insertion of the self into practices of criticism.[66]

There are other effects of the coeval advent of the human sciences and photography. Romanticism and photography may seem an odd couple, but theirs is a powerful nexus. It is achieved as a drive toward the consideration of the self in the light of the relativity of experience and emerging questions of historiography. The photographic image is the symbol of the development of mechanical reproduction at the point of maximal alienation between public and work, such that anxiety emerges as to whether people will be capable of seeing themselves anywhere in it. Henceforth this is to be the critical test of form. *L'art pour l'art* may be situated in reaction to the threat posed by the casual availability of the image; even as anomie might prevent self-recognition, it might manufacture misrecognition by virtue of its very immediacy and propensity to demystify the ritualistic nature of production.

Calls for cultural studies to keep "the possibility of social change alive" have inscribed utopianism (the ultimate in incompleteness) as a sine qua non for qualification as feminist literature. Hence, Marge Piercy writes feminist fiction, but Iris Murdoch writes something else. Moments of dreaming the unachieved are prerequisites for readers making dreams come true.[67] The more conventional criticism of Irving Howe stresses the utility of a concentration on the subject in literature as a means of problematizing "modes of existence taken to be morally crippling," but only by projecting back onto the reader a method of exploration through "anxiety, a condition that grows in acuteness as awareness of self increases." For that self is the principal site of utopias, and hence can only ever represent "a provisional unity."[68]

Foucault notes that the classical *epistēmē* found utopias in "a fantasy of origins." The "freshness of the world" would gradually become clear to all. By contrast, the modern *epistēmē* places the utopia "with the final decline of time rather than its morning." It looks forward wistfully to "the shadow of the *dénouement* . . . the slow erosion or violent eruption of History [which] will cause man's anthropological truth to spring forth."[69] Ethical incompleteness based on textual indeterminacy is the contemporary manifestation of this principle of the deferred utopic vision. This incompleteness must be recognized before change is possible. And it should extend further, to a conceptual angst or sense of modesty on the part of the reader. It is a certain critic's failure to register these uncertainties that draws opprobrium from Elaine Showalter: "What

I chiefly miss in *The Rape of Clarissa* is any sign from Eagleton that there is something equivocal and personal in his own polemic, some anxiety of authorship that is related to his own cultural position."[70]

As part of the positive impropriety of claiming a textual knowledge of ultimate signifieds, Cheryl Walker has recently queried various developments in the discussion of authorship within contemporary criticism. She juxtaposes the authoritarianism of the conventional placement of meaning in the author's psyche with the need to reinstate the identity of the person writing as part of rescuing women thinkers hidden from the reading list. Walker calls for a selective iteration of questions of authorship, because of the necessity for "reading not for ultimate meaning but for positional readings." These readings will be nonauthoritarian and all-inclusive because of their combination of Marxism and feminism; but the all-inclusiveness will be guaranteed to avoid claims to exclusivity by its grip on positionality (and hence, implicitly, incompleteness). There will now be "persona criticism." This will look to a relationship between author and reader, because the status of the woman writer with respect to her work must not be erased in the name of deconstructive indeterminacy; to do so is to oppress. There must be some consideration of the mark of identification that the text constituted at the time of its manufacture and constitutes at the points of its redisposal.[71] This move away from singularity of meaning and experience but toward a personalized account of the trajectory of the work, its "feelings" status along the track of alignment between author and critical reader, is a further installation of this pedagogic move, a move that is equally perennial in the decoding of media texts.

As I stated above, the emergence of media studies in the humanities is clearly partly about the redeployment of litterateurs. Taking a new, apparently distinct object of study and locating it within familiar theoretical and institutional paradigms and practices is likely to result in a reading of the "new" form of text in accordance with established literary protocols: to alter the text while retaining the apparatus. One can perhaps see this process at work in screen studies in the English-language use of auteurism and formalism after Leavis and Vladimir Propp respectively.

Empirical research into screen critics and their trainings has been sparse. What there is suggests that from the earliest days of television drama criticism in Britain, Germany, and the United States, there was acknowledged to be a routine mapping onto the task of coordinates derived from literary commentary. Survey work suggests that American reviewers regard a college training in English literature as a favored starting-point for their job. It has been plausibly suggested that people watch television drama on the basis of the evaluative criteria imbibed through literary studies. Just as the visual media seem to be displacing the written, these ancient protocols of meaning raise themselves up to take charge of the task of understanding.

We can see abundant evidence of an institutionalized faith in the efficacy and prevalence of what has here been termed ethical incompleteness. For example, in trying to account for the simultaneous popularity in Britain of American ruling-class fantasy family drama and its local working-class realist equivalent, Michael Bywater has argued for a hermeneutic organized around the valorization of interiority, where the locus of significance resides in the degree of personal completeness in the narrative in a way unrelated to affluence or indigence: "The belief that it's what you are which counts, not what you've got."[72] This may take the form of a concentration on absences, as in elaborations of melodrama that take the gap and its fill as points of departure; or, it may identify homologies between the social experience of underprivileged (i.e., incomplete) categories of person and the appeal of certain types of text. So attempts to explain away the international success of *Dallas* have almost all presumed that it achieved an important degree of fit between incompleteness of narrative and incompleteness of domestic work experienced by women in the twin role of viewer and housewife. And for Stuart Hall, *Coronation Street* matters because viewers use it as a set of "fictional rehearsals" of "questions" about "how they really live their lives."[73] Studies of television comedy continue to work with an insistent dynamic of always-coming-never-arrived subjectivity within the audience, "its" fragile ego emerging and retreating in engaged laughter. Accounts of the way humor works dutifully concentrate on the primacy of the unsaid and the engagement this offers. In a move that is both more prosaic and more overt, some academic television criticism has recently moved into the area of Isocratean rhetoric. It was Isocrates' practice to give students an ethics grounded in how people live their lives. What citizens actually did each day became the object of their knowledge and training. Television's special place within everyday life becomes the raison d'être for screen studies, which is now able to work with the special meanings that the uniting of text and reader can have for a comprehension of how to live in "human association."[74]

Manuals of instruction on producing television drama institutionalize the mid-shot, the close-up of speech, and the reaction to it as dominant norms. This clearly makes for a concentration on evaluation of character. Leavisites are pleased to decry such easy identification as productive of an improper "relationship between viewer and performance" formed out of superficial access to surface signs of personality, to the point where this is held to be promoting an unwelcome "moral and aesthetic counter-education."[75] From a more radical position, we can discern an assault on easy viewer identification with texts, an assault that is in fact calling for easy viewer nonidentification, an oddly unself-reflexive double move. So the left polemic of 1960s British television, exemplified in Ken Loach's *Cathy Come Home* (1966), can safely be catalogued as "worse than bourgeois individualism." For all the pains it suffers and inflicts in order to bring us face to face with the rigors of welfare, it is naturalistic and deploys routine systems of encouraging empathy. This empathy is regressive because of the paradigmatic relationship that is held to inhere in the choices of personal catharsis and public action. Either one acts politically to reorganize the structures that have produced the inequities exposed in the text, or one cries away the anger in identification and ends up with emotional release in place of material intervention. The argument runs that spectators of naturalism are driven to believe that an emotional response to suffering is adequate.[76] The viewer here is ethically incomplete; vulnerable to offerings with an insufficiency of distantiation; and inexpertly tutored in the skills to compensate for this lack. The identification of an unfinished account in both originating text and viewing subject continues unabated.

Lauren Rabinovitz does something similar in setting up the portrayal of single mothers in situation comedy as a locus for discovering identity and its inevitable contradictions. She points to the taste that television critics display for finding lack of completeness in character (what Forster, in his account of the "right" sort of characterization in the novel, called "starting life with an experience they forget and ending it with one which they anticipate but cannot understand").[77] And Jerry Palmer's survey of screen humor organizes it as the place in which moral, rhetorical, and political dilemmas are enacted through the exemplification of conduct unpopular and popular and comedy's propensity for rejuvenation of "life." The doctrine of bifurcating characters as plausible or implausible is held up as a watershed between realism and fantasy, discerned through measurement by the audience of the narrative against its knowledge of itself. Complexity of character is the motor of a hierarchization of comic forms, with *Hancock's Half Hour* granted exemplary status because of "psychological depth."[78] In his notes accompanying the release of a 1991 film version of *Hamlet*, Frank Kermode was able to advise readers both that the "modern . . . popular, youthful audience" was significant and that it could be trained as Shakespearian, because of its familiarity with generic screen fictions, such as the police drama, which "at their best can, like 'Hamlet,' be about deep and anxious human relationships."[79] In her search to explain the genius of American television, Michèle Mattelart is performing a similar operation when she finds TV able to argue to all and sundry, "I am your Imaginary." In querying whether there can really be a "*discours de l'autre* or only an interrupted monologue," psychoanalysis is inscribing this indeterminacy as an argument for the need for vigilance.[80] The force of the human sciences as intertextual riffs of interpretation is thus given full vent.

What would happen if we ceased to care to interpret? This would mean nothing less than a conclusion to the practice of cultural criticism as legitimized under the rubric of entry into a true self. Feminisms seeking to work inside literary studies have clearly recognized that the discipline has made itself the privileged domain for retrieving the genuine self and reforming it. While Ariel Dorfman's claims for his denaturalizing of our reading of popular fiction reside in his certitude that "by asking readers to take another long . . . look at these cultural products, I am in fact challenging them to look at their own selves."[81]

This set of reasonings is solid with the account of the humanities provided by Hunter, who characterizes their sense of mission as twofold: first, to elaborate the person; second, to elaborate the truth. These are held to be mutually reinforcing goals; to be, in effect, double movements. Humanizing knowledge is dispensed, a knowledge that itself depends on humanization.[82] The aim of this schooling becomes utterly endogamous: to fulfill the requirements set by the humanizing enterprise (whether these are the appropriate display of drills held to be externalizations of a properly reforming subjectivity, or adequate treatments of great texts). Commentary works by continually reinvesting primary texts with new meaning, if in a way that—paradoxically—claims to be discovering what was already there. Even when the commentary is new, it religiously returns to the primary text in search of both its referent and its warrant. The commentary is consigned, in Foucault's words, "to repeat what had . . . never been said." The dismal task of criticism is to fill out "the critical space" with "a certain manner of coding and transcribing a book." It is on the basis of the rules by which it remakes such books that this criticism is best judged. It cannot be seen to have a referent in the text itself.[83] The very concept of a canonical store of literature involves a regular reinstallation of meaning via interpretation; the great works simply cannot be left alone or idle.

The mechanical limits of pedagogic exegetical drills, the endogamy of their process and destination, is not matched by a humility of intent. For Leavis, "to insist that literary criticism is, or should be a specific discipline of intelligence is not to suggest that a serious interest in literature can confine itself to the kind of intensive local analysis associated with 'practical criticism' . . . a real literary interest is an interest in man, society and civilization, and its boundaries cannot be drawn."[84]

Consider the recent complaint that people have lost both the taste and the capacity for ruminative reading and the contemplative reconsideration of the text that it is said to offer. Why should this matter? The answer comes back from James Sloan Allen, in the best global but nonspecifiable certainty of the ethos of the litterateur: "Reading is different. Because reading deals with words, not numbers, its contents are not disembodied quantitative relations but human experience." Reading at its best can force us to reach out and ask who we are by relating our sense of self to the great characters of literature: "It entails saying to a book: 'I will read you not to fathom your author's intention, or to add to what scholars know of you, but to learn what you can teach me about my life.' "[85]

In most cases, public policy or liberal humanist politics—depending on the sources of both funding and intellection—is able to carve from this self-view a rent-seeking and rent-finding role for the humanities in their productivity. Radical educationalism, for instance, now identifies itself as such by its claim to work on the self via the popular. This is decidedly not a productivity amenable to calculation via figured norms. Rather, it may be calculated, if at all, by proverbial ones, by the identification of the processes of the humanities academy with the processes of criticism, a criticism that is always named after renewal. This renewal is from the point of a knowledge that is disinterested on an individuated basis, from case to case as it were, but that amounts in sum to a caring, sharing social unit. To cease to care to interpret, then, would be to select another discipline as the formative mode of entry into personhood and active, academy-endorsed citizenship.

It is significant that the early calls for a semiotics of television were founded on the claim that "like going to school, watching television has become a fundamental component of social being, by now an obligatory requirement for full membership of the modern capitalist state. . . . The subject of television is a citizen in a world of communication." Equally important, this context sees the following claim made for textual analysis as a critical intervention into this field:

The Well-Tempered Self

Such a procedure is absolutely necessary in that it is only in the detailed consideration of particular instances that the effective reality of television production can be grasped (it should be noted, too, that there is an immediate intervention made, and a potentially decisive gain to be won, with those working in television, by the very fact of "stopping" programmes, "exposing" them in all the detail of their functioning).[86]

Although there may be an instantaneous reward for such a practice in alerting workers to what critics know they are really doing, the longer-term goal is clearly a general reeducation of the viewing and reading citizen via the elaboration of critics' truths and textual/personal absences or distortions. The indispensable element of symptomatic readings has always been to contrast bearers of dominance, be they called "Hollywood" or "the BBC," with adequately self-reflexive texts that exhibit an awareness of their plasticity and the contingent nature of their accounts of themselves and others. Even critiques of such accounts may be seen to rest their own signifying ground in notions of inadequate spectatorial knowledge. We must all learn to ruminate on that which we do not know: criticism's beguiling paradox.

Literary, Television, and Film Studies: Three Recent Metanarratives

This interdependence under the sign—sometimes a secret one—of self-formation is a continuing theme of cultural critique. To demonstrate this, I shall make some extensive use of three significant recent meta-texts in the field of cultural theory: Gregory Ulmer's claim to rework the pedagogical and research trajectory of communication studies in *Teletheory: Grammatology in the Age of Video;* David Bordwell's excoriating critique of symptomatic film criticism in *Making Meaning: Inference and Rhetoric in the Interpretation of Cinema;* and Terry Eagleton's magisterial *Ideology of the Aesthetic.*[87] I want to use *Teletheory* and *Making Meaning* to reinforce claims already made about the automaticity of transference from literary theory to screen theory, as well as the seemingly deeply inscribed, if not in fact perennial, tracks of the self as characters found outside, inside, and around the text and its available human science readings. Prior to that, however, it is necessary to consider the claims I am making about the longitudinal continuity of self-formation within aesthetics by using (perhaps against its grain) Eagleton's book.

I read *Ideology of the Aesthetic* as a work of political philosophy addressing ways of knowing the self and the things around it, in the sense that its terrain is how subjectivity is formed, or thought to be formed. For the purposes of this chapter, there is an especially productive tension running through the text between the notion of self-formation as a worthy ideal and its actual exercise as an entry into an imaginary domain, where ideology reigns and subservience to a class-laden state is masked within various brands of individualism or misallegiance. Eagleton positions Burke and Hume as the starting-point for the treatment of the aesthetic in this way. From their time on, it became customary for Western social formations to discuss and protect themselves by referring to culture, here understood as "a plea for the values and affections richly implicit in national tradition."[88]

Common means of reasoning and feeling become the grout holding together eighteenth-century British social order. Taste is provided with an objective and necessary status as a semi-automatic psychological affect. The suffering engendered in the audience to a tragedy is held to mimic and explicate its interiority of sensibility, vital to the functioning of society. In gender terms, this is seen as a blending of a profoundly womanly aesthetic of emotional identification with a man's sense of moral duty. Both rely on a confidence in extrapolation, in the universality of governance guaranteed by the universality of the senses. Learning a balance between these poles, uncovering one's capacity for self-restraint via aesthetic awareness, is a prerequisite for stable social governance. Here a kind of community of spirit can be formed that will work to minimize the need for a coercive state, an apparatus of consanguinity through cultural consent being preferred to one of repression.[89] Inevitably, this is a developing trend. For Foucault, the history of political life in the West since the nineteenth century can be deemed to be "the manner in which power gives itself over to representation." The body of the society, not the monarch, becomes a binding that is to be attended to; less obviously literal in its manifestation than the body of one ruler, a mythic "universality of wills" is formed.[90]

Through the nineteenth century, with major economic change under way, this story becomes ramified and further elaborated, coterminously with the commodification of artifacts. The advent of factorylike production and the elevation of individual authorship to transcendental genius occur simultaneously. The recovery of the self alluded to earlier in Schiller's anomie cure sees art made into "a paradigm of more general social significance—an image of self-referentiality which in an audacious

The Well-Tempered Self

move seizes upon the very functionlessness of artistic practice and trans-
forms it to a vision of the highest good."[91] This is seen to be an autotelic value, deriving paradoxically from a mimetic connection to the
otherwise unspecifiable nature of existence itself, in a way that harks
back to Aristotle's suggestion that the propensity to imitation is the
essence of humanness.

Eagleton stresses that with Kant the aesthetic moves outside cognition. It has the force of law at the level of affect, producing a "reciprocity of feeling" that unifies subjectivity in a way that politics and morality are unable to achieve. This force becomes the Schillerian foundation
for the exercise of rationality in the public sphere. Without an adequacy
of aesthetic self-awareness and contrition, the citizen cannot function
effectively. Thus for Wittgenstein, "ethics and aesthetics are one."[92]

The Romantic version of personal identity sees the act of creation as
one of self-discovery via differentiation between Self and Other, subject
and object, just as the economy continues to develop to the point where
contradictions between two spheres become apparent: in civil society,
civility is prized; but economic society values competitiveness. More
will be said of this in chapter 4.

Hegel is a critical figure in any aesthetics because of his standing at
the crossing point between idealism and materialism, his defining status with regard to the former being matched by his methodological
generation of the preconditions for the latter. The lectures on aesthetics
position drama as the highest form of art because of its capacity to
resolve the distinction between objective and subjective sense. This is
said to be critical in the education of persons through and in the phenomenology of spirit because of the form's proclivity for presenting
ethical actions. Drama, Hegel argues, moves a step past the evocation of
feelings and adventures found in lyric and epic poetries respectively. It
brings together the inner world of the subject and the outer of the
subject matter. Yi-Fu Tuan's elevation of the West for its propensity
toward self-reflexivity takes *Antigone* and its treatments as exemplary of
this. Nature is mastered via the assemblage of the human sciences. Self,
society, and nature are controlled through cultural armatures.[93]

Rarely, however, is this sort of concern addressed to questions of
governance; rather, it has tended to operate within a field that opposes
self and society as objects with an existence independent of discourse. It
is Eagleton's particular achievement to deal with the aesthetic as an
ethic of citizenship, in the sense of the articulation between person and
polity and the invention of subjects out of a dialectic between the indi-

vidual and the "corporate." Radical literary criticism and its pedagogic lode/load are made to meet in *Ideology of the Aesthetic* under the sign of philosophy.

In contrast to the relatively congenial and familiar approach adopted by Eagleton, which pays due obeisance to cultural theory's apparatus of referencing, commitment, distance, and—principally—survey work that cares to consider all the arguments that matter, Ulmer's book works on very different terrain. Their differences seem to match the comparative academic status of literary and television studies.

Teletheory is a polemical call to destabilize the pedagogic and research protocols and relativities within college life. It calls out to be read under the sign of Derrida, which is to say—in this instance—a playfulness that is irreverent of teacherly subjects, while requiring that they be examined as much as they are examining. Ulmer matters as an articulator of Derrida, and he matters as the critical point of entry for a television studies that looks at itself as an institutional object. (All of this regardless of the possibility of reading the book as a paradoxically unselfreflexive confession owing more to a call to "own" one's feelings, and hence "grow as a person" within a particular therapeutic norm, than to deconstruction or anything related to screen products or critique.)

Ulmer seeks a new admixture of three levels of intellectual work, what he terms the "private, public, [and] disciplinary" prongs. He regards these as structuring forces determining academic output, which are customarily left merely implicit both in their impact and in their actual existence as formative elements in intellectual work. It is the putative denial of the putatively determining efficacy of the personal that the book aims to uncover and reverse. The import of this resides in the fact that *Teletheory* is perhaps the first major work of communication theory that cannot be cataloged as either a survey text, an empiricist exemplar, or the outcome of critical politics. *Teletheory* announces itself as a new genre, or at least its first marker. This genre, founded on the Benjamin/Derrida trope in its subtitle of *Grammatology in the Age of Video,* takes as its generative basis the presumption that it is both a true and an interesting statement to say that identity is partly the outcome of "a life story that people believe in and tell about and to themselves." Ulmer produces just this account of himself at the end of the book in a way that seeks to blend the three levels of academic determination. It is anticipated that there will emerge from out these revelations a new version of college writing about the screen, a collage genre that seeks a *telos* only of doubt/skepticism. This is based in part on psychoanalysis and the unity of subject and object that it achieved via the union of Freud's emotional history and his cultural accounting. Critically for my purposes here, Ulmer maintains that even if the articulations that the psy-complexes claim to make between screen criticism and other domains are inaccurate, if they in fact fail to deliver a finally compelling account of the social, they can still be rendered serviceable. Their value lies in the fact that they offer a "calculus of composition, as an invention."[94] They offer, another might rather say, a new servicing of a much older imperative: to uncover personal incompleteness—each reader's unfinished self—and encourage an unendable odyssey, if one that is challenging rather than eldritch.

The book ties this in to the specifics of the domestic screen via another kind of subjectivist warrant. Ulmer argues that we are presently the prisoners of a culture that ascribes television-watching to the right brain and artificial intelligence to the other. This results in an inimical splitting of intelligence that disables the folk. It is left to criticism to offer interlocution and the possibility of integration. Feminist quests for a new aesthetics are valorized because they are said to be voyages in search of a nonreificatory practice of knowledge that will displace the habit of presenting objects for the inspection of the dominant. In this sense, they are the hook back to a new communications pedagogy, one in which "the student and teacher are the object of the exploration, engaging their own stories in the information set forth as scholarship." The semiotic outcome of this will be undying semiosis, a processual move of "Post-meaning" that will refuse ultimate certainties. The new form is to be "mystory," a riposte to logical positivism that denies any chance of the researcher being positioned as satisfactorily knowledgeable. Our very ignorance will make for an openness to finding the truth of us, a conduit to adequate apprehension of individual interiority.[95] There is a gaze, but it is known and valued as a gaze at the self.

It will be gathered that there is an arresting quality of self-disclosure to all this, and it comes complete with photography of the author's father; cartography of his sense of Custer's Last Stand; and lengthy explanations of John Cage's collection of books on mushrooms and why this opens us up to indeterminacy, all done with liberal use of the pun and the academic reference. The book *is* what it wants its readers to institute and thereby become: a *bricolage* that wants to be ready to change. In one sense, this is massively to anticipate, if it anticipates anything at all, possible moves within the television-studies academy that appear quite aberrant and idiosyncratic. In another, it is an unusually open move by a senior scholar to claim a new trajectory for research and teaching that does nothing of the sort at other than a rhetorical level. So the success or failure of *Teletheory* is not to be. It can only be effectively known as an emblem of the stickability of the inscription of exegetical indeterminacy, and its homology within the textual analyst, that is criticism's reason to be. This is so even when we appear to be at the outer limits of academe.

If the political within the personal and the personal within the pedagogic are the concerns of Eagleton and Ulmer respectively, then Bordwell's labor is to uncover the very morphology of exegesis itself. *Making Meaning* is a similarly bold claim to rewrite how people should read. Its central topic is "the conventionality of criticism . . . a significant American industry." The book uncovers sets of conventions subtending even those critical moves that seek to differentiate themselves from each other quite radically. These unifying tendencies derive from the systems through which "an institution constructs and constrains what is thought and said by its members, and how the members solve routine problems by producing acceptable discourse."[96]

It will be gathered that the sense of place is very American; *Making Meaning* seeks to look at college critique, but it does so via a narrative and analysis that range across *Cahiers du cinéma, Movie, Screen, Positif,* the British Film Institute, and other institutions. And while the rhetorical analysis of the moves made to situate political and exegetical positions within critical fields is compelling, the institutional correlatives drawn out may be said to suffer a forced homomorphism of different orders of knowledge: none of the above may be seen in the same space of history, it seems to me, as the rise of screen studies in the United States.

The argument distinguishes between comprehension of a film, which is said to involve "apparent, manifest, or direct meanings," and interpretation, which seeks "hidden, nonobvious meanings." It sets up four typologies of the construction of meaning in the act of criticism: diegesis and *fabula* (the referential); explicating abstractions (the explicit); calling up wider meanings (the implicit); and extrapolating to make the hidden knowable (the symptomatic). These moves match those made by the philologist Gustave Lanson in the nineteenth century, whose ultimate point of explication de texte was to be found in the evocation of morals as part of the decoding of a "secret." Bordwell discerns links here with the infiltration of the symptomatology of the human sciences and the structured indeterminacy of psychoanalysis and Marxism as part of the desire of film and television academics to associate with established university reasonings (initially, New Criticism and moving on—with due timelags—down the line of fashions in literary studies until postmodernism). So even when screen studies' trajectory affronted institutions politically, or argued with itself, it was also enshrining itself in the academy. The shift from literary to film criticism by students and critics is managed routinely, easily, and competently because of the disciplines' mutual history. Bordwell points out that this consanguinity was first signed by André Bazin in the 1940s through the act of mobilizing writing metaphors to account for cinema.[97] They have been a continuing trope since then.

Although he is far from concerned with discussing cultural subjectivity, or publics, or citizenship—in fact, the issue of the value of watching films and being taught about them is utterly absent from the book—Bordwell gives magnificent detail on the ascription of indeterminacy to which this chapter has laid claim. He discerns trends in North American criticism of the 1960s and 1970s toward treating modern avant-garde works as analogues of consciousness in their epistemology via mirrors to the "movieness" of the text, thus encouraging the viewer to an awareness of the act of signification. Bordwell then extrapolates from these early days to the further development of symptomatic readings founded on the presumption that "the text *cannot* say what it means; it tries to disguise its actual meaning."[98]

In his account of the history of the psy-complexes, Foucault explains how such a symptomatology operates. There are clear ties to criticism and its attempt to mortgage truth as the secretion of the secreted:

> Dire qu'un symptome reproduit symboliquement un traumatisme archaïque implique que le passé n'envahisse pas totalement le présent, mais que le présent se défende contre sa réapparition. Le présent est toujours en dialectique avec son propre passé. [To say that symptoms reproduce symbolically the experience of ancient traumas implies that the past can never really be evacuated from the present, for all the efforts of the present to deny such reappearances. The present is always in a dialogue of struggle with its own past.][99]

The repressed will return everywhere and always, but often camouflaged. Only the cultural critic, it seems, can find the true self within this thicket of repressed meaning. Being unable to say what it means makes the text, like the person, subject to the ancient tag "*Quae negata, grata*—what is denied is desired."[100] For Baudrillard, this preoccupation with "latent discourse"—presuming as it must that the latent overdetermines and properly explains "manifest discourse"—denies the reciprocity of the relationship. For him, the surface may frequently determine what is beneath it. But to deny the primacy of the latent is to refuse the "moral law" that requires of the subject that "you know your will and your desire."[101] It is to accept, with Wittgenstein, the "completely veiled" nature of the subject.[102] (The next move in a cultural politics is to allow that veil its completeness and turn toward a politics of actions that refuses the search for a true self within dominant subjects of knowledge. Again, this will be addressed further in chapter 5.)

Bordwell refers to the doctrine of "repressed meaning" as a mnemonic for the denial/revelation couplet of textual criticism. Even in the period between the 1930s and the 1950s, he argues, psy-criticism manufactured Hollywood as at one and the same time both the symptom and the denial of questions of collective fear and anxiety. The advent of criticism influenced by texts signed by Lévi-Strauss, Foucault, Barthes, and others is itself symptomatic for Bordwell, as he stresses the fact that it is in their exegetical modes of writing that these authors have been taken up and redeployed by others. Similarly, the utilization of Lacanian visual metaphor work is correlated with the transfer by the literary critic into films, as part of the grand cultural shifting of sites for the public search for the self.[103]

There is one significant problem in *Making Meaning*. Bordwell's admirably tight rhetorical analysis has no account of these trends in other than careerist or institutional terms that find rational academic actors carving out lives for themselves within the limits of an industry. He never offers an explanation for why there should *be* any criticism; whether there is any ideal viewing or projected subjectivity and intersubjectivity; or why any forms of politics do in fact emerge from criticism. (There are symptomatologies and symptomatologies: one might valorize the experience/worth of certain categories of person over another because of correlation with material, noncinematic areas of practice.) There is no address of the purposes—the imposts within the selected ethical register—for which criticism has made itself a pedagogic necessity.

Making Meaning nonetheless remains a fine retracing of the critical trope of anthropomorphization, of seeking out opportunities to "find" personhood in cinema. For "to ascribe . . . voyeurism to movie cameras, and duplicity to narrators is to make meaning by 'making persons.'" It then becomes necessarily commonplace to articulate the spectatorial process as a series of movements (of course never straightforward) between identification and detachment, a fecund trope that Bordwell directly attributes to trainings in literary decipherment.[104] (One might render this observation more specific. Consider the propensity for left critique to suspend disbelief in its treatment of certain texts, a suspension discernible via the reinstatement of peculiarly liter-

The Well-Tempered Self

ary forms of analysis in the name of a solidarity in charity. So we see the return of the disabling oppositional couplet feeling/theory and the reassertion of the requirement that there be a strong degree of fit between criticism and its object in preference to a counterindicative reading. In addition, as one might anticipate, there is a reinsertion of authorial intent as the measure of rectitude.) Bordwell concludes that:

> Interpretation takes as its basic subject our perceptual, cognitive, and affective processes, but it does so in a roundabout way—by attributing their "output" to the text "out there."
>
> . . . Interpretation answers to a widely felt interest in motives, intentions, and ethical responsibility by showing that artworks which do not offer explicit guides for behavior can raise significant issues of thought, feeling, and action.[105]

Interpretation, in short, ensures that fictional texts become measures of life.

The issues raised in a traversal of these three metatexts are central across this book. They are issues to do with how the cultural subject and public are thought about and formed in terms of an appropriate politics and an understanding of what cultural criticism can realistically achieve. For to repeat, this volume addresses the formation of citizenship through ethical incompleteness and whether it is feasible to fill such an empty pedagogic *donné* with a politics that responds to democratic and demotic notions of what comprises a citizenry, its training, and its tastes. The practice of textual commentary is greatly implicated in that politics, perhaps irretrievably so. Foucault was deeply concerned that the practice of "commentary" necessitated "an excess of the signified over the signifier." There is, then, "a necessary remainder of thought that language has left in the shade." The task of this remainder is to open up the space for commentary. But "to comment also presupposes that this unspoken element slumbers within speech," thereby assigning to itself a place in life for the duration, a comfortable niche in the "supposed space" where signifiers and signifieds each speak for and about themselves. Exegesis is thence "ever secret, ever beyond itself," the unwrappable secret that has displaced religion as the site to look for revelation.[106] The educational corollary of this procedure is the loss of inquiry into how words work in favor of an inquiry into what authors mean.

In place of this dismal parthenogenesis, Foucault wonders whether it might instead be possible to evade the putative search for the signified while continuing to read the work of others. This would substitute a statement of the emergence of a discourse and its effect for a search for that discourse's remainder and its interpretation. The editors of Routledge's "Popular Fictions" series of books exemplify such a project when they explain the need for textual study across forms, reasoning that popular fictions "help to define our sense of ourselves, shaping our desires, fantasies, imagined pasts, and projected futures. An understanding of such fictions . . . is thus central to an understanding of ourselves; of how those selves have been shaped and of how they might be changed."[107]

This prospectus realizes these twin needs as dictates of "relevance" operating under dual, shifting heads of power: one, the increasing utilitarianism of educational policy and the need to protect a space for texts and margins; the other, the responsiveness to voices of dissonance from the conventional and how they might renew that sense of what a citizen might be. This turning away from grand anti-statism and toward a recognition of an always-already-achieved compromise with the institutions of learning, teaching, and making entities is a response to both the enunciation of "new" subjectivities and the falling by the side of the road of monist accounts of the social. We can see similar moves being made in Meaghan Morris's utilization of the poetry of John Forbes to consider some complex questions in the area of economics and cultural theory. Morris finds that Forbes's work gestures toward a "sociable disjunction" that allows the reader to "surpass or even confound . . . *aesthetic* performative closure." The value of this approach is that it models the way that "ethical and political dilemmas" traverse "everyday cultural practices (spreading tea [i.e., setting the table for dinner], watching television, talking economics)."[108] Instead of complaining about the remainder component of the truth that was left out of the sign, this uses cultural criticism straightforwardly to position the reader inside political debates rather than to set up a grand touring guide to subjectivity and its lack of fulfillment.

To repeat, the crucial question politically that has been forwarded under postmodernity and the collapse of grand narrative explanations of all and sundry has been the issue of subjectivity. Hence the irony of a return to these issues, their reconsideration by the most eminently qualified anti-humanism. In his essay "What Is Enlightenment?" Foucault answers that for Kant it is a moment of maturation, which is to say a following of others, a deferral of authority away from the self in certain areas in order to render the self autonomous in others. This knowing of oneself inevitably leads to auto-critique.[109] It becomes the basis for a redeployment of the subject by the state. But this is not a simple, straightforward exercise of domination. Rather, it is a relationship between the state, the self, and the ceded subject that is especially important in the field of culture, a site of noncoercive adherence.

Aesthetics is about the production of value, not mimesis. Art forms reality anew, but never as a utopia. Instead, it is made into an insistent, infinite process, a mode of becoming that is criticism's unacknowledged touchstone. This ethic, not crises of criticism over representation or quality, has been an abiding theme in aesthetics and cultural policy. The implication of a call for representation is that it is insufficient for a subject to be "present" in its own person or substance. It must have a form of advocacy lest it be inadequate to itself. This is an implicit recognition on the front of cultural protection that the citizen, the public, the consumer, or the nation is insufficiently self-evident. And for those consumed by the burden of the Enlightenment, this is a lacuna that must be filled in. Habermas refers to the (apparently absolute) value of "a communicative rationality in whose forms modern societies, that is, societies which are not fixed once and for all and which have no guiding images, must reach an understanding about themselves."[110] This is a revival in the secular of the Augustinian imperative, that requirement to uncover what Foucault describes as "a mind in profundity . . . a mind folded back in the intimacy of itself which is touched by a sort of unconsciousness, and which can develop its potentialities by the deepening of the self."[111] The systematic incorporation of writing as a practice of everyday cultural life went hand in hand with the elaboration of invigilating doctrines of the self and its institutionalized mysteries, over and above the apparently more outward world of orality. In terms of the allocation of resources, the question for those dealing with the formation of cultural subjects is finally: "How much does it cost the subject to be able to tell the truth about itself?"[112]

This truth will be known through a process of cultural subjectivity. For if modernity offered earthly salvation through a pedagogic, rather than an ecclesiastical, tending of the flock, as was argued in chapter 1, then postmodernity has struck back to require the replaying of errors of the self that can never be worked through. The sentence imposed by the promise of finding a true self in literature is that the process cannot be brought to a conclusion. And the particularity of postmodernity is that of an "age without instruments" to take the "temperature," but nevertheless an age that Jameson almost celebrates for the accompanying directive to take "uncertainty as its first clue."[113] Such is the burden of an aestheticization of politics, when identity is central and the available technology for forming it is in the thrall of cultural critique, unless that critique abandons uncertainty as a reason to search for coherence, and embraces the use of textuality as a possible means of remaking oneself outside the subjection of the human sciences.

The Well-Tempered Self

Chapter Three

◆

NATION, DRAMA, DIPLOMACY

THERE IS a continuity and coincidence between cultural policy and textual analysis in their utilization of hermeneutic protocols of ethical incompleteness, if not in any transfer of interest to political critique. There is evidence of this in the debates in progress between trade negotiators at the recent culture round of the General Agreement on Tariffs and Trade (the GATT) in this context, which juxtapose the position enunciated by the U.S. team (with its internationalist laissez-faire logic) against the "no-go-zone" discourses articulated by legatee cultures. Numerous governments and culture industry workers around the world have mobilized a reflectionist protocol to justify what amount to ripostes to American cultural dominance, the unequal exchange of cultural goods and services that marks so much of U.S. textual traffic with Second and Third World countries. From all brands of politics and polity, concerns are raised about the imaging that, it is held, flattens out and homogenizes with a view to a Pax Americana Pollyannaism that fails to address the special needs and discrete histories of people living in other cultural formations. This American product clears its costs by a combination of huge domestic sales and a broad international reach, which allows it to drop into foreign markets at costs that no local producer could possibly match. There is no basis for real "competition" between the parties in terms of the taste of the viewing public.

These policy anxieties are all about the need to form national subjects, about the need for cultural maturity to be expressed or invented in that moment of automimesis when an anthropomorphized nation stares back at itself via the privileged site of drama. Without this shock of recognition, it is held, we fail to know ourselves. In addition, we fail to open ourselves up to the excoriating, searing, uncomfortable but finally amelioratingly liberal gaze of the artist. For the artist is a creature that can know us by being of us, but who stands away from the everyday cycles of accumulation and dispersal in order to see what we fail to be but might have it in us to become. In turn, reading such output becomes a cultural right. Hence, the humanities academy's justifications for training readers in reading texts often amount to the dispersal of an assembly of technologies designated as "developing critical thought." But in fact these technologies operate at the level of a set of quasi-Polonial imposts organized around means of knowing oneself as part of a national culture. And this quite critical end of cultural production—the point where meaning is finally invested, the moment when protocols of reception really determine signifieds—is left unable to touch the discourse of sovereign cultural production that sets all store by the nationality of texts themselves. Points of origin and inaugurating registers of address overdetermine the relatively autonomous procedures for investing such texts with local significance. It is assumed that readers will interpret in terms of self and nation.

Such anxieties have gathered around them a contour of urgency in the context of recent developments in the freer trade negotiations conducted under the sign of the GATT, an agreement originally forged between states from the industrialized market economies (IMECs). The GATT is the principal forum for the IMECs to work through discrepancies among their policies on a whole realm of issues, negotiating the complex terrain that makes for sudden plenipotentiary disjunctures between the discourse of the imaginary market enshrined in the neoclassical school of economics and the political pressures already deriving from the real material conditions of constituencies at home. It is of course also subject to the everyday tactic of diplomacy that calls insistently on negotiating representatives to have lists of items that they will give up and lists that are sacrosanct. With the capitalist world order

The Well-Tempered Self

increasingly emphasizing services, in its First and Second World manifestations at any rate, attention has moved to free trade in this sector. The United States has a huge balance-of-payments surplus in the area of cultural property, for reasons already noted, and pushes very hard for the removal of all barriers to free trade in screen texts. And the implication of such yearnings extends beyond the negative aspect of state intervention—keeping things out—and into actually proscribing active modes of subvention, such as government-assisted film industries.

The General Agreement
on Tariffs and Trade

From the time of its emergence as one of the capitalist world's key trading and monetary protocols of the late 1940s until the shifts and shocks of the 1970s, the GATT enshrined the key principles of the world trading system: multilateralism; nondiscrimination; and codified methods of regulation in place of sovereign administrative discretion on the part of individual states. It became, rhetorically, the bureaucratic champion of free trade, dedicated to the removal of trading blocs and restrictive blocks to the "natural" operation of a perfect market organized around the preferred rhythms of supply and demand under the intersecting signs of pure comparative advantage and consumer sovereignty.

This was very much the U.S. agenda, and it worked well for the great and powerful until the appearance of the European Community (EC) and Japan as fields of real economic force. This effect was doubled by some internal loss of faith that a liberal trading regime necessarily coincided with the best interests of the United States. By the 1980s, the rules of discourse of international debates on trade set up binary opposites of liberalism and mercantilism, but with no major player staking lofty moral terrain other than on a contingent, site-specific basis; protectionism was accepted when it worked for the speaking subject, rejected when it worked for some other entity to that speaker's detriment. The IMECs have differing material interests in different spheres of their formations, such that today's laissez-faire representative on issue x is tomorrow's insistent voice declaring issue y to be outside the spirit of the agreement. In addition, the GATT's record has suffered through the very success of its legalism, which has encouraged resistance via the emergence of new forms of protectionism appearing under the signs of nontariff implements and, latterly, industry policy. This comes as no surprise to dissident economists, who have reacted against the neoclassical model over the past hundred and fifty years for its tendentious dependence on individual human preference, natural endowments, and technology. In particular, they have noted that the signified of "free trade" is the self-interest of the most powerful. U.S. demands for a deregulated domain of cultural openness have been criticized as a form of corporate libertarianism. By the end of 1990, the influence exerted on the U.S. executive to increase or at least sustain its own protectionism in the area of both agriculture and services was a most significant counterpressure on policy. This was possible because the U.S. president's right to strike agreements on these matters is limited by legislative sunset clauses providing for automatic termination at the end of a given period. It does not reside in freestanding constitutional authority and is therefore highly contingent. The United States may have been planning a less totalizing approach to service industries diplomacy, one that relied on bilateral discussions until and unless the GATT paid dividends.

The late 1980s saw a massive expansion in the quantitative importance of trade in services (TIS), with obvious significance for the realm called "culture." TIS now comprises about a quarter of world trade. Prior to this period, it was a convention in economics to downplay the significance of TIS, because of technological limitations and networks of domestic regulation. Traditional colocation of production and consumption militated against international development of the sector. This was always less true of noncontact services, particularly service products. And with changes to the American and British macroeconomies, in particular, knowledge has expanded to encompass tests of neoclassical theory in this domain. TIS expressly includes broadcasting, film, television, and television commercial (TVC) production and distribution within the terms of the GATT. Current negotiations on freeing the sector from market distortion could affect such areas as legislation by particular sovereign states for local content quotas in the media; foreign ownership of radio and television stations; public subvention of screen industries; and state assistance given to indigenous bourgeoisies to move into export markets. The problem with active assistance is that it contravenes one of the principal formative elaborations of GATT logic—namely, that state aid should be via tariffs instead of restrictions or nontariff measures, in order that such distortions to the market be visible, predictable, and thus capable of being planned around as well as verified. None of this, of course, denies the desired *telos* of GATT: the eventual elimination of all actions by states that hamper free trade.

The theoretical logic underpinning this critique of state protection of industries is that economies will eventually attain a mutual natural equilibrium if they are organized around already-extant (i.e., nonlegislated) factor endowments that provide them with a comparative advantage over others. Despite their awareness that this has favored the already-strong, over ninety sovereign states are signatories to the hundred-plus agreements that constitute the GATT. When the United States put TIS on the agenda, it threatened to exit the general agreement if others rejected the move—which coincided with a decline in the relative importance for the United States of its traditional secondary industry and a clear expansion of its advantage in the services sector. After failing to cover the culture industries under the Free Trade Agreement with Canada signed in 1988, representatives of the U.S. Trade Department were briskly lobbying the EC against the threatened imposition of quotas on television programs from outside the community.

The United States is especially scathing of the notion of a pan-European culture. After years of supporting European unification, there is now something of a reaction in the light of terrors about what *Forbes* magazine has called "a protectionist, corporatist, anti-American Frankenstein."[1] In reality, the proposed limit of 50 percent of broadcast time devoted to imports would make very little difference to existing practice, with the United States currently providing a (sizable) fraction of this amount. But the developing proliferation of stations in the wake of deregulation across western Europe means that new entrants, faced with high start-up costs, have already shown themselves willing to ignore or abuse any directives on localism in the interests of filling airtime with cheap U.S. product, and this will presumably develop as a problem in the near future. It has been claimed, for instance, that some years in the recent past have seen more than half the drama on British television imported from the United States, despite an 86 percent local content quota. In the first half of 1992, British stations screened 600 feature films, 370 of which were imported from the United States. And this predates deregulation. At the end of the 1980s, television in western Europe was using about a hundred and fifty thousand program hours a year, which was expected to rise to three hundred and fifty thousand hours by 1995 because of new technology and deregulation. If one may anthropomorphize, it could be said that the U.S. archives were waiting. And as they waited, lobbyists for the American screen industries and U.S. trade negotiators were mounting increasing critiques of the Community's "Television without Frontiers" directive on the 50 percent limit for being in direct conflict with GATT principles; ironically so, as it may be the services trade element that puts culture within the legal power of the EC to consider, as opposed to any general authority to make directives in the name of the conservation or production of identities. (One might, however, also note an oft-cited comment by Jean Monnet, a founding parent of what became the European Community: "Si c'était à refaire je recommencerais par la culture [if I had my time over, I'd begin the process with culture].")[2]

We can gain some sense of the relative dispositions within the GATT on this matter by reference to the August 1990 meeting to discuss the TIS subtopic document entitled "Draft Services Trade Framework for Audiovisual Services." Most states represented in Geneva referred in debate to "the cultural importance of the audiovisual sector." India and Canada argued for the addition of a clause that would exempt "assistance measures imposed for cultural reasons" from laissez-faire protocols. The European Community preferred a "sectoral annotation" that would allow for greater flexibility by permitting space for future assistance measures that might be required to develop various aspects of the audiovisual continuum. Japan and Australia spoke favorably of the need to maintain cultural sovereignty but were noncommittal on the specifics of the draft. The United States was unequivocally and implacably opposed to any form of exception or notation. Its negotiating team was quoted as saying that the GATT should "agree to disagree on motives—cultural sovereignty or business opportunity—and then start negotiating."[3]

There is more than a little irony in this, when one considers that U.S. government diplomacy, information-gathering, quotas, and tariffs were critical to the establishment of Hollywood's success in setting internationally attractive cost structures in place and expanding monopolistically through the 1920s; moreover, the deflection of significant Italian, German, and French film exports from the United States was occasioned by government action: the commitment of those countries to war economies in the previous decade. But then history is not the motor of neoclassical discourse. One might, however, have expected some reflection on two decades of generous tax credits for U.S. investors in American film and television, in addition to numerous tax shelter schemes and evidence that U.S. businesses operate a selling cartel each year at the Cannes Festival.

In another sense, though, this laissez-faire stance represented strong continuity in U.S. policy. During the first GATT negotiations in 1947,

The Well-Tempered Self

the United States pushed for free trade in film, which was inscribed in Article IV of the original agreement; and the early 1960s saw attempts to have trade restrictions on television removed. One might equally question the consistency of attempts by the United States to uncouple business from culture; it would be quite wrong to see U.S. trade policy in this area as politically agnostic. The Motion Picture Producers and Distributors of America brokered the industry's interests to Congress and the departments of State and Commerce in the 1920s by advancing both arguments of trade, which would supposedly follow film, and arguments of political culture, summed up in Will Hays's promise, "We are going to sell America to the world with American motion pictures."[4] The allegedly exemplary anticommunist message of the good life carried by mainstream Hollywood product gave the industry significant leverage in its dealings with government after World War II. The continuity of such concerns—and their careful elaboration to politicans and bureaucrats—may be seen in the fact that the U.S. House of Representatives delivered a vote of three hundred and forty-two to zero in condemnation of EC television quotas in 1989. Representatives of the industry had assured Congress that this protectionism would inhibit choice, minimize the dissemination of American ideals, and encourage governmental determinations of culture. In the 1990s, the Department of Commerce stresses the modeling effect provided by the audiovisual export of democratic ideals and values that will promote free speech and individualism.

On the other side of the ledger, there is almost no importation of television programming by commercial networks in the United States. In contrast, more than 10 percent of TV time in western Europe is taken up with U.S. programs. The figure is 30 percent in Canada and Latin America. Drama varies significantly in these statistics. Fiction comprises 37 percent of European television, but just a quarter of that is produced locally; imports from the United States account for 44 percent of the rest. Only the United Kingdom and the former Federal Republic of Germany made more television than they bought in the 1980s. Since 1972, the global number of television sets increased 160 percent, from 270 million to 700 million. In 1983 the United States had 75 percent of the value of all international television trade, mostly in drama. U.S. $5.5 billion was earned in 1988 from overseas sales of entertainment, the nation's second largest source of export revenue after the aerospace sector. That year saw export earnings from television go up by 30 percent over 1987. In the five years from 1983 on, sales of television to

Europe went from U.S. $212 million to $675 million. The Columbia Prix Entertainment company's overseas revenues from television doubled in 1988 to U.S. $200 million. Sales to EC countries account for two-thirds of U.S. television trade. The United States also dominates exports to East Asian television systems, with the exception of China. Intra-regional trade is much less developed. Predictions for 1991 suggested that world exports of U.S. film and television would generate U.S. $6.7 billion in foreign earnings, up 13 percent on 1990 and nearly double the 1985 figure, although some buyers in Asia are increasingly substituting domestic programs for imports, especially in economies big enough to support indigenous drama production, and the U.S. majors exported first-release films to the tune of U.S. $1,426 million in 1991.[5]

All of this should be seen in the context of an an overall U.S. trade deficit of $100 billion in 1989. The stakes in television were high for the United States, which had become the world's most indebted nation and was moving toward being a net importer. Positive contributions to the balance of payments were critical, and as the image market trade paper, *Variety,* put it, the prospects for the 1990s were that "as old borders come down and old ideologies give way, preach the true believers, the *lingua franca* of motion pictures will command a greater worldwide audience than ever before."[6] More prosaically, the majority of U.S. television drama was being financed on a deficit basis. Producers were selling programs to the U.S. networks at well below cost, having planned to recoup and profit through domestic syndication and sales overseas. What had once been the source of super-profit was now effectively a standard component in the servicing of debt. This matches the state of films since the end of World War II. At that time the industry empha-sized to government that, in Will Hays's words, the "approximate forty percent of motion picture revenues which is foreign, *is the margin by which supremacy of United States pictures is financed and maintained,*" indi-cating that product for the domestic market might decline in quality without this source of funds. And this remains a critical source of reve-nue. The ten top-grossing U.S. films of 1992 all had greater returns overseas than at home, sometimes by a multiple of two.[7]

Importantly for my purposes here, there are correlative cultural pol-icy views of this dependence. As Sandra Braman has argued: "The focus on information as a commodity by the US is part of an overall rejection of cultural, social or political valuation of international information flows that is embedded in background studies for policy-makers, con-gressional hearings and policy statements in a quite self-conscious way."[8] The intellectual training ground that might have provided a locus of calculation in this domain was simply absent at the policy and academic level outside critical communications scholarship. The area of left scholarship that has considered these questions has tended to do so from within a realist media effects paradigm. It uses a conventional content analysis of news flows from North to South to pronounce on media imperialism, without any consideration of readership protocols or, significantly for my argument, the specificity of screen drama. The realm of news and current affairs is privileged in a way typical of the political science discipline.

Policymakers in Europe from the 1950s on routinely conceived of television as a critical pedagogical instrument in the formation of citizens and the elevation of public taste, primarily via the disciplinary genre of current affairs. The officially endorsed genre never proved to be as popular as American entertainment programs, however, and even the capacity of the public broadcaster to guard and produce morality was called into question by developments in satellite and cable transmission and U.S. marketing. It may well be that the flow of television makes for a transfer of what has been called the "aura of truth" from news and current affairs to fiction.[9] Quite clearly, this presents a dilemma for cultural policy. It is a dilemma with historical contours wrapped around the development of a series of policy constructions of the United States by others as the mountebank of twentieth-century visual culture.

The International Cultural Order

Before shifting to world systems economics and the terrain of recent debates within the GATT, it is as well to consider in more global terms why it might be that so many countries have adopted strategies of special pleading with regard to cultural property and how and when they have gone about it.

In 1926, the League of Nations sponsored an International Film Congress to discuss the issue of American dominance of the market, but attempts to act in concert as particular trading blocs against Hollywood failed. The British Cabinet Office issued a paper to participants at the Imperial Economic Conference that year warning of the perils implicit in the fact that "so very large a proportion of the films shown throughout the Empire should present modes of life and forms of conduct which are not typically British."[10] By the following year, the *Daily Express* newspaper worried that the exposure of British youth to U.S. entertainment was making them "temporary American citizens."[11] This has been an enduring complaint. Nearly sixty years later, the Commission of the European Communities was prescribing "a common market for television production . . . if the dominance of the big American media corporations is to be counterbalanced."[12] As Ian Jarvie aptly phrases it: "Was Hollywood, by means of selling films, also selling something to the world that the world might have reason to resist buying?"[13]

The contemporary posing of this question might also be read as a reaction to the simple magnitude of the U.S. presence in the global economy. For all its huge debts, the United States continues to be the industrial focus of the world. In 1989, the five hundred biggest multinationals were located in just nineteen urban centers, ten of them in the United States. This kind of concentration makes for perceptions of imbalance, particularly when it is allied to an aggressively interventionist and moralistic foreign policy presence. U.S. companies and the U.S. government tend to be perceived as coterminous, and their ideological work is seen as being done through the culture industries.

A dynamic new force emerged in the 1960s that provides some conceptual link between these spheres. The cultural imperialism thesis, as developed in Latin America in particular, argued that the United States, as the world's leading producer and exporter of television, was transferring its dominant value system to others. There was said to be a corresponding diminution in the vitality and standing of local languages and traditions, and hence a threat to national identity. (Latin America was the cradle of this research tradition, because it combined features that standard development theory deemed incommensurate: long-term political independence and sovereignty and a perennially unequal economic exchange relationship with the industrialized powers.) In this view, cultural imperialism is isomorphic with other forms of imperialism. As Herbert Schiller expresses it, "The media-cultural component in a developed, corporate economy supports the economic objectives of the decisive industrial-financial sectors (i.e., the creation and extension of the consumer society)." The Third World was seen to be in a dynamic position, "not yet frozen in class relationships" and alive to the need for "a comprehensive restructuring of the world information system."[14] International organizations became the domain for the implementation of this approach by government agencies.

Since 1973, in particular, via UNESCO and the Non-Aligned Movement, Third World countries have been lobbying at a series of meetings and conferences for what has been variously termed a New International Information Order or New World Information and Cultural Order

(NWICO), mirroring calls for a New International Economic Order and a revised North-South dialogue. This is a dialogue that is reenvisaged as an ideal speech-act, one where it is possible and indeed necessary for the sovereign state to question relative differentials of economic power and call for an end to processes of unequal exchange whereby First World countries create and manage markets in other places. What began as a concentration on news flow and the television presentation of Third World countries has been broadened to include the place of the computer in economic and social development and the allocation of telecommunications frequencies. This has continued to occur under the imprimatur of what was announced at the 1973 meeting of Heads of State of Non-Aligned Countries as "the need to reaffirm national cultural identity."[15]

UNESCO was the agency with an infrastructure to implement policies flowing from such a rhetoric, but it has operated under a complex set of imperatives, combining the proclamation of a universal humanness and tolerance, which sees culture as singular and inalienable, with a more specifically politico-diplomatic drive toward the recognition and veneration of difference, obedient to the founding dictate of an organization based on sovereign states. UNESCO has now ceased to be the critical site for NWICO debate, in part perhaps because the Americans withdrew from it in 1985 as a consequence of the organization's supposedly illegitimate politicization. (It has also been suggested that Ronald Reagan's faction of the Republican Party envisaged withdrawal before NWICO had even been acronymized.) UNESCO administrators have increasingly modified the organization's program and rhetoric in the hope of encouraging the United States to return, but this has always been balanced against the need to satisfy the majority of member-states.

Australian diplomats have argued that the United States chose to debate TIS in the GATT because, as a forum, it "is not strongly influenced by ideological controversies."[16] Less-developed countries have fought hard to resist the U.S. push for the GATT to open up TIS, on grounds both of cultural sovereignty and of the desirability of establishing their own industrial infrastructure of culture for economic reasons.

It would be misleading, however, to isolate this—as opposed to the very broad debates on restructuring global inequality—as exclusively a Third World concern. At Mondiacult 1982, the Mexico City world conference on cultural production referred to in chapter 2, Jack Lang, the French minister for culture, caused a major split amongst First World nations with the following remark: "We hope that this conference will be an occasion for peoples, through their governments, to call for genuine cultural resistance, a real crusade against this domination, against—let us call a spade a spade—this financial and intellectual imperialism."[17] U.S. representatives reacted to this by accusing Lang of chauvinism.

One recalls Diogenes' mocking of Demosthenes for claiming to provide a lead to the people of Athens while himself being sexually "passive" in bedroom relations. The homology between sexual and civic standing arches across history to the homology between cultural and national independence. As Foucault puts it: "When one played the role of subordinate partner in the game of pleasure relations, one could not be truly dominant in the game of civic and political activity."[18] (We could also find points of comparison in the modernizing struggles waged by intellectuals and business in Greece from the 1820s on against imperial and religious influences, struggles waged in part over the question of language and the ability to capture national identification through aesthetic culture. These struggles frequently referenced the supposedly high age of Greek intellection as one of their sites of contestation.)

The fact is that the notion of cultural identity as a discrete and superlegitimate phenomenon becomes highly questionable when it serves primarily as a warrant for an asphyxiating parochialism created and policed by culture bureaucrats. Its principal effect under such conditions has often been to champion narrow, hierarchical accounts of culture. NWICO was characterized, for example, by an extraordinarily complete exclusion of women from the UNESCO agenda. And its moralism may also have cloaked the interests of emergent bourgeoisies keen to advance their own market power. *Dallas,* for instance, is routinely held up as an exemplar of 1980s cultural imperialism, notably by Lang himself. One response to its commercial success has been for local producers to model other programs on it within their own milieux, to render its textual referent local while recycling many of its generic components. This has driven some authorities to more and more prolix accounts—very limiting accounts—of what may be termed authentic and local. The net effect has been a quaint dynamic of interpenetration and symbiosis between discourses and movements of capital going under the apparently diffuse signs of globalization and regionalization, but both dependent on very homogeneous, integrated understandings of culture.

This is just one illustration of the tendency in European debate to conflate the sign "mass culture" with the sign "American," denying in the process the power of the extraordinary heterogeneity of the domestic U.S. audience and conflating source of supply with impact at point

The Well-Tempered Self

of consumption. At the Symposium international sur l'Identité cultur-elle européene in Paris in 1988, the leitmotiv was terror in the sight of "la déferlante américaine—the American wave."[19] One is reminded here of a gibe in Billy Wilder's *A Foreign Affair* (1948): "If you give them food, it's democracy. If you leave the labels on, it's imperialism," says a U.S. congressperson of postwar relief efforts in Europe. Nevertheless, it is worth noting that Brazilian audiences watching customized versions of *Dallas* had their viewing of a supposedly local text punctuated by adver-tisements for Levi's, General Motors, Volkswagen, and Coca-Cola. And when considering what can go into a public's constitution of itself and its surroundings, it is hard to decry the presentation of facts such as that 87 percent of English-language Caribbean television was imported in 1988, up 10 percent in ten years, with most of it in the field of drama.

Of course, having identified this as a problem, the next move for the subordinated is to form oneself as distinctly different and able to repre-sent that difference via the concept of the nation. There is little agree-ment over what nations are, what national identity is, or how to explain national movements. But culture is clearly important here at the level of the constitution of community, the performance of typical words and actions. Elements such as idiom and syntax are important means for the transmission of retraining at times of economic change as well, so that these matters quickly become of formal, instrumental concern in the governance of populations. A standard language—Parisian French—was, for example, an essential component in the emergence of a bour-geoisie after the French Revolution.

To repeat, however, the point has been well made that the valoriza-tion of traditional cultural formations is frequently profoundly repres-sive of particular categories of person. The enunciation, disposition, and protection of a culture may be done by and for local elites in the name of a romanticized harking after authentic community spirit. Such practices "emphasise distinctions between one nation and others at the same time as they work to *suppress* internal distinctions."[20] The devel-opment of publicly funded telecommunications systems in Nigeria, India, and the Philippines provides instances where the rhetoric of "technology transfer" and "community access" has essentially served the interests of multinational corporations and local elites. And the notion of the redemptive powers of drama may also serve the interests of particular categories of person. In noting the results of a recent poll, David Russell emphasizes that the survival of "quality drama" is of far greater concern to television executives than it is to the British viewing public.[21]

On the score of the European Community's television policies, there is great force behind former U.S. Trade Representative Carla Hills's uncomfortable question about whether "English culture is promoted more by a film produced in France by 'Europeans' than by a film of New Zealand origin."[22] After six years of trying, attempts to bring together the "quality" stations of Europe in order to create a deliberately European drama series continue to encounter difficulties with notions of discrete national dramaturgies and fears of creating the ultimate blandness of "un *euro-pudding.*"[23] And aside from the attempt to create the alchemical European, Jack Lang's plaintive appeal to national specificity in the language of freedom from media domination rings hollow given that his own ministry worked strenuously to wrest the balance of TV programming away from the United States and Britain via the formation of an audiovisual Latin bloc consisting of France, Iberia, and Latin America. It may be that the rhetoric of a single Europe is not much more than an attempt to cut the costs of advertising through standardization. In addition, early evidence suggests that although the new channels in Europe may have increased the presence of U.S. programs, they have also greatly boosted production by local entertainment corporations, while diminishing the prospect of increased production in the EC's smaller member-states.

Most conceptions of cultural conservation are put forward by particular groups that claim to possess a particular geopolitical space and to guarantee its cultural validity and authenticity. One might question whose interests were served by Israel's decision to hold up the introduction of television until 1968 because of the supposed dissonance between American entertainment messages and appropriate local values. Such a line of questioning is encouraged by the eventual enabling legislation establishing an Israeli television system, which called on the medium to be constituted around "the life, struggle, creative effort and achievement of the State."[24] And the dominant definition of today's "new European" is organized in terms of a Judeo-Christian set of religious beliefs; Hellenistic accounts of the polity, arts, and science; and Roman jurisprudence. EC directives of this kind are, however, increasingly under attack for the partiality of such an amalgam and its connection to imperialist tropes. Critics refer to the EC bureaucracy as "the official magisters of culture."[25] When she was prime minister of Britain, Margaret Thatcher always insisted that the EC eschew any fantasy of "some identikit European personality" on the one hand and a Leviathan-like "super-state" on the other. She was very dubious about an extra-economic component to the Community.[26] At the same time, a

The Well-Tempered Self

powerful position is being enunciated on the left about this, as the following quotation from Michèle Mattelart indicates:

> How will commercial logic be aligned with the social logic govern-
> ing the interests of groups, the widening base of audiovisual pro-
> duction, the participation by citizens in the choice of technologies,
> and the definition of their use? Is a "local product" one that would
> permit a particular collectivity to express and to reappropriate its
> sounds and images, compatible with the international market? Is
> there an "alternative" product that could be international yet not in
> the mold of a transnationalized mass culture?[27]

The old concept of the global unity of workers suggested that the international class struggle would be entered into not merely because of
specific, local conditions but as part of a wider emancipatory promise,
what Lyotard calls "an Idea to be realised." Emergence from the misery
of proletarian existence was the promise that could unite working people otherwise separated from one another in every conceivable way. But
the past hundred years of socialist activity has been resolutely nationalist, notwithstanding the fantasies that have circulated in Moscow and
Washington respectively. It has been capital that has managed to loosen
its moorings and locate where necessary in order to increase profit and
influence. The "Idea" of an international working class has been super-
seded, a fallen icon of modernity.[28]

Yet in governmental terms, Hans Kohn was right when he suggested
in 1945 that, paradoxically, the "age of nationalism represents the first
period of universal history."[29] What is apparently by definition an enclosure may in fact provide the first prerequisites for *inter*nationalism,
particularly in terms of the internationalization of commerce. That
process is dependent on formal entities organized along national lines
and speaking for different peoples, especially in the provision of legal
and organizational infrastructures for the accumulation and investment
of capital. Same and Other can only be understood individually in relation to their apparent opposites. The nation is fundamentally a constantly reformed remaking of tradition and coherence on ever-altered
terrain. The original account of the nation as "a body of people with a
common history and descent, a common language, common customs,
and a long-standing attachment to a particular piece of ground" is no
longer tenable, as J. D. B. Miller points out. The polyethnic nature of
most nations now sees them bonded together "by the fact of the state's
existence" and the detritus of the diplomatic cartography of decolonization.[30] Hence the state's need for vigilance in forming, surveying,

and reforming cultural subjects. More often than not, however, the rhetoric of cultural difference essentially promotes commodities.

Writing two decades before Lang's outburst, Harold Anderson, a vice president of NBC International, said of difficulties with lip-sync dubbing in the eport of television programs to Saudi Arabia: "This problem has been encountered before with such languages as Japanese, and will be overcome as American television know-how continues to expand throughout the world."[31] His position as an aid consultant provided a fine degree of fit between expanding markets for U.S. products overseas and promulgating doctrines of modernization and development. This may be seen to typify the dominant industrialization and democratization logic of the 1960s, the era when mainstream U.S. researchers and trainers valorized "the 'free flow of information' principle" as a powerful instrument "for achieving the announced goals of socioeconomic modernization, national integration, and cultural expression."[32]

There are strong institutional and theoretical links between this logic and Edward Shils's recently revived doctrine of civility, outlined in chapter 1. Auto-critiques and those from outside the paradigm flowed both from the failure of the model to deliver its planned Panglossian outcomes and as part of the questioning of U.S. overseas conduct connected to the war in Vietnam. Its proponents were accused of imposing Western goals on notions of progress/development by misrecognizing the political and problematic nature of the nexus between tradition and modernity; applying a transcendentalist social psychology; and neglecting issues of dependency/unequal exchange. Cultural imperialism was regarded as a means of eliciting consent to economic domination from outside, not least through the formation of endemic consumption via advertising.

In turn, however, the functionalist and statist underpinnings of dependency theory were called into question for their failure to account adequately for factors outside the sovereign state and inside national boundaries (viz., respectively, the operation of effectively undomiciled multinational corporate capital and the emergence of bourgeoisies within developing countries). World systems theorists would assert that class formation is not necessarily to be found at the site of production, but rather in relation to core-periphery connections, specifically the multifarious locations of different aspects of the delivery of services. This will be considered in more detail in the following section.

The point about Harold Anderson's remark is not that it is of itself wicked or even interesting as an expression of self-confidence, but that

The Well-Tempered Self

it could be made in the form that it was. It should be recognized as a method of forming foreign populations in one's own image, itself of course necessarily partial and an ideal type. This can only lead, assuming that I am correct in setting it up as emblematic of a wide range of similarly positioned utterances, to the kind of restless desire for counterpower evidenced in Lang's outburst and other critiques of textual imperialism. In 1960, for instance, the European and African Societies of Culture held their Rome Conference. It broke up after the Europeans had claimed to be the only group ever to have conceived of the universality of culture.

Anderson fits into the 1950s and 1960s logic of aid, which rested on the presumption that the media were a means of dispensing knowledge—the West's owned object—to those less fortunate. This applied equally at the levels of the development of the polity, the economy, and what was called the "modernized individual" (again, as per Shils's notion of how to form public subjectivity). Throughout those decades, the United States and UNESCO promulgated research paradigms that directed less-developed countries to reinvent themselves in the image of the First World. The Anderson mission and its confident report fit this period's command metaphors and material manifestations, the process of enabling "taste transfer."[33]

That process can be contrasted with statements made two decades later by Josh Elbaum, then a sales representative with the U.S. overseas distributor, Telepictures, about exports to the Soviet Union: "Knowing their political sensitivities and constraints, we gave them a catalogue that took these sensitivities into account." He went on to note: "The hardest thing to sell in the Caribbean are music specials, because music is a very strong component of their own culture. Even a Bette Midler special with computer enhancement—you couldn't give it away there."[34]

This demonstrates a fully achieved business sense of the need to blend international sales with import cultures' own patterns. A shift has occurred since Anderson, since a time when knowledge was brought to the willing simpleton. The center now understands, with Elbaum, that shifts in the global political economy require a dedomiciling of corporate thought and planning to embrace local cultural contours as one more configuration to be labeled a "market niche." This is one of the critical turns toward the postmodern outlined in chapter 1. Models that extrapolate from an ideal West are in question, but remain a dynamic force; the consumer is a critical trope; and a politics of identity is determinate.

Along with the boom in services that it was created to manage and alter, and despite the forces it confronts, the NWICO paradigm has had real effects. It has encouraged a discursive and marketing streamlining that acknowledges the senses of self expressed and determined in the world according to the Other. Sony's in-house term for this is the splendid oxymoron "global localization":

> The aim is to be present in many local (or national) markets simultaneously, in order to reap global economies of scale in distributing products across different markets and different media. The challenge facing global companies is to transcend vestigial national differences and to create standardised global markets, whilst remaining sensitive to the peculiarities of local markets and differentiated consumer segments.[35]

This is not uncontested terrain, however, and this counter-counter-power in turn elicits responses, such as parodic local production that offers a sardonic critique of its own status as an import culture. To position the South as hopelessly weak in the field of culture is also to ignore the tremendous contribution to balance-of-payments figures that, say, exports from the Indian screen make to India's economy. And it is worth noting that in 1990, the fifth biggest U.S. television chain was the Spanish International Network. Owned by a Mexican, it fed more than three hundred stations with Mexican, Brazilian, and Argentinian drama, reaching between six and ten million viewers. By the end of 1990, just three of Hollywood's seven biggest studios were owned by American capital. Many U.S. cultural industries have a high proportion of overseas ownership, including Japanese interests in films and television, German and Dutch in publishing and music distribution, and British in advertising. A critique of foreign control of American business has even emerged, on the grounds that "self-determination is the solid core of citizenship motivation."[36] Internationalism has become a keyword, a keyword both of opportunity and constraint. As Richard Collins points out, "Quite who is the Coca-Colonized and who the media imperialist is hard to identify exactly here."[37]

This is not to deny that the entertainment powerhouse remains the United States. In a recent feature on co-productions of television drama between different countries in the U.S. trade magazine *Broadcasting Abroad,* for example, the interviewer put it this way to a panel of television executives and producers from Britain, Australia, and the United States: "Let's look at the harsh reality of co-production. Rather than seeking a true creative co-venture, aren't American producers just looking for silent overseas partners, bankrolls, facilities houses?"[38] The primacy of the United States is undeniable, but shifting in its impact. To

The Well-Tempered Self

see how these shifts may have occurred and what their future form may take, we need to theorize the global economy and its effects on culture.

The Global Economy

Immanuel Wallerstein is installed as the key historical theorist of world economic systems. He has argued persuasively for the globally determined nature of business, in particular the understanding that, regardless of the economic and political formations internal to sovereign states, if they trade, they are part of a capitalist sphere. In his reading, capitalist production is seen to move through various processes. Initially, goods of a certain type are produced and consumed in the center, by an IMEC. The next phase sees these goods produced there and exported to peripheral economic points. The cycle concludes with production moving to that periphery once technology is sufficiently standardized and labor in the right mix of docility and skill. But products owned at the periphery rarely make their way to the center.

In response to accusations of economic determinism and the exclusion of categories of person and practice eluding this approach (categories such as women, ethnic minorities, and various forms of cultural distinctness), Wallerstein has latterly considered other areas to broaden the support for his basic position. He suggests that two critical and distinct definitions of culture have centered nineteenth- and twentieth-century Western debates. These are: (a) "the set of characteristics which distinguish one group from another"; and (b) "some set of phenomena which are different from (and 'higher' than) some other set of phenomena within any one group." The key element mobilized in the process of difference described in system (a) is a means of self-formation that permits a recognition of relative sameness in some but not others: "some kind of self-awareness (and therefore a sense of boundaries)." Both usages can be understood in the context of their position and deployment within the emergence of the capitalist world economy. System (a) sees culture signifying a field of constancy in a space that is actually undergoing, necessarily, constant reinvention because of the dynamic of growth and newness that emblematizes capitalism. System (b) is invoked to justify inequalities emerging from this process. The valorization of modernity in the West, Wallerstein maintains, has amounted to a convergence between the West's own view of itself and modernity; they have become indistinguishable. Those entities that fail to thrive are held to have made the mistake of following the hermetic conservation precepts of system (a) instead of the competitive ethos of system (b).[39] This binary opposition regards cultural maintenance under the sign of relativism or charity as a form of retardation. Attention to the "rights" of minorities or formations of persons that are not culturally strong in the face of globalization, nationalism, or masculinity is regarded as an act of economically irrational folly.

Wallerstein may be right about certain aspects of the impulse toward hierarchization in culture, but he seems to make the discourses of modernization and rationalization applied to economies and polities into the masters of modernity. In doing so, he overrides a significant autonomy and reciprocity across these domains. It is a commonplace of the Enlightenment and modernity to fetishize representation because of the complex interrelationship that it is held to have with reading protocols and the structure and operation of the public sphere, in such a way that a cultural openness and relativism are regarded as integral components of the resulting discourse of liberalism. This has become a heterogeneous and confused process, which is much less totalizing than Wallerstein's account allows. There has also been a significant impact on the politics of subjectivity deriving from the confluence of an expansion in trade and a relocation of production (to the point where distribution is now a critical site). This is a process in which capital formation, state-corporate relations and dispensations toward ethnicity are constitutive of TIS rather than supplementary to it. As a consequence of the world's greatest industrial force trimming itself toward services because of its comparative advantage in the area, there has developed what Jonathan Friedman has called the "intensive practice of identity . . . this desperate negotiation of selfhood."[40]

Such is the discursive quintessence of the postmodern part of the century. It is an immensely productive force, ushering in Pollyannaish McLuhanites to speak of the new cosmopolitan subject. That subject relates permissively to a plenitude of cultural forms and formations because of its desire to confront and integrate alterity through a new practice of expansive cultural competence. Its self becomes reformed in the interstices that describe the contiguity and disparity of different cultures; the self becomes an intertext in a new phenomenology. This auto-management achieves a collective, hybridized expression in transnational cultures—namely, business and state outpourings from North America and western Europe. Persons and meanings are thought to be globally networked to the point where "there is now one world culture."[41] Certainly, every society is now beholden to external dynamics, ecologically and economically, and to the work of both other sovereign

The Well-Tempered Self

states and public and private international organizations. Cultural-capitalist corporations seek to naturalize and localize themselves to fit the norms of their hosts, but in a way that still amounts, in Stuart Hall's eyes, to a world in which "the global is the self-presentation of the dominant particular," a particular that stifles difference.[42]

It is assuredly true that much of daily life is increasingly determined in distant places and time zones. We can all acknowledge the time-lessness, placelessness, and permissiveness of multinational corporations and their awkward meetings with local cultural norms that are precisely historical, geographical, and indigenous, at least rhetorically. This has, though, been seen by some as a fairly straightforward search for a lingua franca of the commodity, not for a new world citizen. Yet this account, too, has been found wanting by the celebrants of sub-cultural resistance. They might not wish to go the distance with the unitary world culture position, but they refute the view that cosmopol-itanism is always and everywhere imperializing. The new form of image-tourist may be anybody with access to a television service, the immediate audience to dynamic shifts in the world order. Contemporary global capitalism is organized in terms of worldwide supply and local demand, and hence a developing overlap of the economic with the cultural. Creating effective patterns of consumption on such a broad scale requires multinationals to customize merchandise to sophisticated markets. And this customizing does not end with the producer. Audiences for television drama make their own sense of what is put before them. For example, much Nigerian television programming consists of ancient U.S. serials—a clear case of cultural dumping. But they do not engage Nigerians to the same extent as locally produced situation comedies. Rather, such texts are air-fodder to satisfy programmers and schedules. Similarly, the showing of imported feature films, standard practice twenty years ago, is now secondary to the use of stage-space for traveling the-ater. Oddly, the pro-development pieties of a *mission civilisatrice* are iso-morphic with the anti-cultural imperialist miserabilism that presumes an incompetent and culturally indigent Other. Nor does it now seem so easy to identify the guilty party in any revised account of cultural impe-rialism. Even Herbert Schiller acknowledges that four decades of eco-nomic dominance by the United States are problematized by the global circulation of names such as Philips (the Netherlands), Samsung (Korea), Unilever (the Netherlands and Britain), Daimler-Benz (Germany), and Sony (Japan).[43]

Rupert Murdoch is not alone, though, in rendering the terms *nation* and *information* substantive, as in his celebrated suggestion that Adam

Smith writing two hundred years on would have retitled his *Ur*-text *The Wealth of Information*.[44] It is clear that the terms of the debate on traded moving images must now consider a cry to address (which is to form) particular subjectivities, whether as a response to pressures from the right or from the left. Utopias have shifted from the domain of free labor and free will to free communication. For cultural policymakers, this has often meant an equation of such freedoms with an idea of national sovereignty that is not always identical with immediate economic concerns.

Australian Screen Drama

This next section of the chapter is particularly concerned with Australian positions on television trade, which have to be apprehended in the context of the overall diplomatic and trading imperatives of a middle-range power. Australia has a particular need to go with the flow of the GATT's liberal logic because of the country's dependence on natural resources and vulnerability to barriers to agricultural exports. This is in the context of an increasingly unfavorable set of balance-of-payments figures from the 1970s on. Australia had to struggle—first tempestuously, then carefully and in coalition—to get the GATT to address agriculture, everyone's favorite protected zone. The government's formal technical advisor, the Bureau of Agricultural Economics, has repeatedly called on trade delegations to argue against protection across the board. (Although it would be as well to note the cynicism with which some commentators have disparaged Australia's faith in free trade. The removal of overseas rural subsidies may not in fact assist Australian agriculture because of the competitive advantage of U.S. and European technology.)

The economic policy discourse in Australia has been dominated since the early 1980s by a faith in the imaginary market unparalleled anywhere else in the world. So it was automatic for the Industries Assistance Commission (IAC), an advisory body to the Australian government, to be charged with the task of informing the Treasurer about "how Australia may liberalize its trade in services" after the GATT had adopted the area for scrutiny. There was no element of doubt about the efficacy of this logic. The IAC acted from the explicit presupposition that Australia would ultimately benefit even from unilateral action to remove barriers to TIS.[45]

The Well-Tempered Self

Formal (that is to say, spoken and signed) responsibility for the carriage of Australia's negotiations in such matters rests with the Department of Foreign Affairs and Trade (DFAT), which initially regarded the audiovisual sector as an area that could usefully be traded off in return for critical concessions by other countries in matters of greater significance for Australian balance-of-payments figures. It was commonly held that a liberalized TIS environment would in any case be of direct benefit to Australia, but in such domains as education, finance, and consulting. Of course, the argument was also made that removing restrictions on market forces would ultimately make for the right conditions for a private sector screen industry anyway. Some government economic advisers even maintained that the export success of Peter Weir's *Gallipoli* (1981), Peter Faiman's *"Crocodile" Dundee* (1986), and the television series *Neighbours* evidenced an Australian advantage in the entertainment field, justifying a reduction in protection for the services sector. And 1988 did see seventy Australian drama and documentary programs on British TV, with *Neighbours* screening twice a day, whilst U.S. pay television was showing two Australian dramas each week. Australian programming is very strong in New Zealand, and to some European critics, Australia is one of the principals in the television drama trade.[46] But such exports were born of the stimulatory side of regulation, something that appears to escape marginalist economists.

The U.S. Embassy in Canberra had already responded to pressure from the Motion Picture Association of America by protesting the 1989 announcement that Australian commercial networks would move up to a 50 percent local content policy as a result of government pressure. It had indicated that restrictions on overseas content and participation in Australian TVCs might offend GATT obligations. The Office of the United States Trade Representative placed Australia on the splendidly named "Priority Watch-List" in 1992 as punishment for its broadcasting policies (while Australian beef, dairy, and sugar exporters had access to between 0 and 4 percent of the U.S. market). As anti-protectionist pressures increased, the Australian Writers' Guild (AWG) and the Australian Film Commission (AFC), a statutory authority acting multifariously as a source of script development assistance, film investment, and policy advocacy, sent representatives to the GATT negotiations in Geneva, in part to lobby Australia's own diplomats. The Guild official said on return of the DFAT mission: "They now understood that serials like *Neighbours,* and TV commercials, were aspects of Australian culture."[47]

This sort of lobbying is typical of disputes over economic paradigms within a policymaking constellation. The formation of public policy globally over the 1980s tended to privilege a faith in the market over demand management, but both approaches lacked the capacity to theorize culture in ways acceptable to workers in the field who used it in the name of the uplift and governance of the populace. "The trade-restricting effects of some interventions may be insignificant when weighed against the broader social purpose for which the intervention was instituted. *It is beyond the scope of this inquiry to comment on the merit of these goals,*" Australia's IAC flatly explained with reference to the cultural aspects of services protection.[48] The AWG pushed hard for extension of the draft exception clause to the TIS agreement to include "a clear statement of principle that questions of cultural development are not made subservient to those of trade policy."[49]

One also, of course, encounters precisely this sort of opposition in analogous cultural formations in other second-tier powers. Consider the line enunciated by Canadian filmmakers in the Winnipeg Manifesto of 1974: "We wish to state unequivocally that film is an expression and affirmation of the cultural reality of this country first, and a business second." Success for this logic would have the effect of positioning culture alongside other "no-go zones" for the GATT, such as "public morals and order, safety, health, the environment and essential security interests."[50] Put another way, it would seek to assign cultural values to a sphere of calculation that rejects a locus of power organized around the formation of prices in favor of one concerned with the formation of subjects.

At the level of television drama, there is a process of deliberation that is now a routine policy *donné* across different polities, a nostrum with no need of justification. This process is about reconciling the commercial imperatives enunciated by television proprietors with the imperatives of cultural formation enunciated by policymakers. Within this debate, Australian screen cultural nationalism has been remarkably constant in its themes. Consider a letter sent by David Williamson to the national daily the *Australian* in his 1989 capacity as president of the AWG. Williamson argued thus:

> It is not to protect an industry, or even employment, that Australian content in commercial television is so crucial. It is for the sake of an Australian culture. We as children grew up seeing ourselves as exiles from real life which only happened in the rest of the world. That is not what we want now for ourselves or for our children.[51]

The Well-Tempered Self

In describing the impetus underlying the lobbying of the Australian government for screen subvention in the early 1970s, former Film Commission chair Phillip Adams has spoken of the desire "to dream our own dreams," making special reference to a famous cartoon from the Vietnam War period of an Australian family watching a television set that had emblazoned on it: "Have your emotions lived for you tonight by American experts."[52] And calls for the protection and promulgation of a "national literature" continue to be couched in terms of what John McLaren sees as the "need to strengthen local voices so that they are not lost in a global homogeneity . . . [and to protect Australians from] becoming passive consumers of the product of the metropolitan centres. . . . Cultural independence is the freedom to take part in the global conversation on our own terms." There are preconditions and externalities of this move, which overlap in such a way that their conceptual and chronological relations of primacy become unclear. But they all pick up the critical theme of knowing/forming the self: "The most important argument for supporting Australian writing—and Australian film and television—is . . . that we need to carry on a continuing dialogue amongst ourselves if we are to understand ourselves and our place in the world."[53]

This line has had far-reaching effects. In its search for numerical justifications in a public policy world dominated by rhetorical flourishes borrowed from marginalist economics, the Australia Council (the Australian government's policy advisor and distributor of public subventions in the non-screen arts) recently asked a selection of citizens a series of questions: Did they gain a sense of achievement from the success of Australian artists? Did the arts have an important role in making Australians look at their way of life? Did the arts help Australians to know their country better? These are questions of metonymic self-knowledge. They give culture the task of mirroring the nation, a mirroring that presumably leads eventually to better images, as those looking at themselves begin to practice self-help.

We might advert here to P. R. Stephenson's argument in the 1940s that the country would gain self-respect and the respect of others when it had a "distinctively Australian culture . . . [a] *genus loci*—the spirit indwelling in a Place."[54] This tradition of litterateur nationalism is a discourse of self-awareness and self-improvement that anthropomorphizes and unifies the nation, deploying the search of the subject to know its own body and mind in a teleological metaphor that glides toward the apotheosis of competent adulthood. Along the way, this knowledge is mobilized as one sometimes of appraisal and evaluation, sometimes of discovery, and sometimes of development.

In 1969, the Australian Council for the Arts' Film Committee reported to the government that the need for public subvention of the screen industries was "self-evident" because of the necessity for Australia "to interpret itself to the rest of the world."[55] Similarly, a Senate Select Committee of 1963 had called for the export of Australian screen texts to Southeast Asian television in the interest of showcasing the nation. But this restless search for knowledge that characterizes public policy on the screen was equally self-directed. In 1965, Sylvia Lawson argued that there had been a halcyon period of neorealism in Australian feature films of the 1920s, foreshadowing the work of Vittorio de Sica. In doing so, she referred to a "sense of identity which a community's own film-making confers upon it as nothing else can. Now, when most of our diversions are processed and packaged elsewhere, we probably need it more than ever."[56]

In his survey of the history of Australian television drama, Moran has noted the divergence—in fact the intense separateness—of the discourses of Australianness mobilized in broadcast regulation and producers' and writers' rhetoric on the one hand and in drama texts themselves on the other. In the case of the former, great play is made of the role of television drama in opening up a multifaceted awareness of the country and its people. But the actual product is monomaniacally concentrated on the heterosexual nuclear family; specificities of Australia in terms of geography, demography, history, and social relations are almost utterly marginalized.[57] Recent studies have shown the lack of correspondence between the demographic proportion of people from non-English speaking backgrounds and their appearance in TV drama.[58] Protectionism and state subvention have at times provided *cordons sanitaires* for a very conservative cultural politics. Significantly in terms of the concerns of the Romantic author, the publicly funded Australian Broadcasting Corporation (ABC) has traditionally been valorized by scriptwriters because, in the words of one such person, the genre dictates of commercial television "gave very little room for them to explore their own personalities."[59]

Local commercial determinations have been vital to the state's requirements of both regulatory bodies and state-owned broadcasters. At license hearings prior to the introduction of television to Australia in 1956, it was commonly held to be the case that there would be no more than eight or nine hours a week of overseas programming on the commercial stations. But by the end of the first year of operations, technological developments meant that American television series were available on film. Such series had already cleared their costs domes-

The Well-Tempered Self

tically and thus had very elastic pricing opportunities at the point of onsale. But growth in audience figures for television was slowing by the early 1960s as the networks flooded the market with U.S. materials. While the absolute number of viewers continued to increase with the population and the distribution of sets, time spent in front of the screen was decreasing. Advertisers reconsidered their departure from print and radio. When allied to the licensing of a third commercial network in 1963, this led to a shortage of American product. The commercials rethought the quick fix of imports. In a move that consolidated these influences, the ABC began to show more local drama, with a commensurate improvement in ratings. So the eventual imposition of a drama quota on the commercials in 1966, requiring thirty minutes a week of locally produced material, was effectively institutionalizing what market forces were already configuring.

Nevertheless, twenty years after the plaintive calls for a local film industry and a locally concerned television industry, it is still possible, in fact necessary, for a key academic text on Australian feature film to refer thus to Australians' multifaceted dependence on Hollywood: "They feel second best with their own markets and culture, forced to second guess what their authentic indigenous culture should be." For Lawson, the country remains "a colony of Hollywood."[60]

Yet this flies in the face of the actual operation of much of Australia's screen market. Throughout the 1980s, the key profit centers were local television, U.S. home video, and co-productions with British broadcasters. And as indicated earlier, the end of the decade saw international financial movements that resulted in Japanese and expatriate Australians in fact owning much of this supposed imperial center.

Nevertheless, 1992 saw Australia purchasing 80 percent of its program imports from the United States at an annual cost of more than A $500 million. And in spite of an increase in the cost of foreign programs of 40 percent between 1987 and 1989, an hour of Australian drama still cost several times its American equivalent. One has to question, of course, the relevance of these concerns outside cultural policymaking. The evidence is complex. It is not that Australian production is comparatively uneconomic; drama costs more to make everywhere than sport, light entertainment, and news programming. Thirty minutes of U.S. drama might be sold to Australia for A $12–14,000, despite an initial production cost of A $1 million. *LA Law* is sold to an Australian network for A $12,000 per episode, despite an hourly production cost of A $1.25 million. The same network could expect to meet a much higher proportion of equivalent production costs for Australian drama (between A $150,000 and A $200,000). As was pointed out earlier, Australian drama is exported to over seventy countries; but even in 1987–88, a fiscal year distorted by the huge success of the *"Crocodile" Dundee* pictures, Australian film and television trade amounted to a balance-of-payments deficit of A $224 million. (This is not, of course, aided by the fact that Australia and Canada routinely pay what are exceptionally high prices for U.S. programs; in Australia's case, twice the amount paid by Britain for TV movies.) It has been estimated that Australian television producers recoup no more than 10 percent of their production budgets from sales overseas.

A recent survey undertaken for the AFC found that Australian television advertisers show little if any concern about the country of origin of programs in which their products are showcased.[61] And some of the fairly sparse empirical work done on spectators and texts has suggested that Australian children accept the dissonance between their own cultural domain and that presented to them in U.S. drama as attributable to the operation of television's conventions of form and style, if in a way that denies the specificity of the experience portrayed. Extrapolations from American programs do produce opinions about Australian society, however, for example in the area of crime.[62]

It would be wrong, of course, to identify such anxieties as new, specifically Australian, or restricted to television. Before Canadian confederation, the 1850s saw pressure for the imposition of cultural protectionism in the shape of a tariff on books as a means of promoting national identity through indigenous literature. One might consider this in the same light as the proliferation of Canadian government investigations of cultural nationalism since World War II (three Royal Commissions and two major policy reviews, going into such matters as the need for locally owned and locally textual culture industries) and the eleven major surveys of public opinion on cultural identity over the same period.[63] Surveys such as these, like the Australia Council and AFC findings discussed above, represent an anxiety about cultural identity, in particular about the desirability of transmitting the cultural capital of putatively "discrete" national entities in the face of multinational/American homogenization.

Commercial pressures to make local drama that can be sold elsewhere may, in any case, lessen the claim to a specific cultural address. In Britain, the requirement to produce with an eye to the audio dub has led to the predominance of "inauthentic" "air-traffic-English" in television drama.[64] Such issues are gone over in Phillip Noyce's 1978 feature film *Newsfront,* which traces the history of competing newsreel companies and their coverage of current affairs in Australia. Toward the end of the

The Well-Tempered Self

film, expatriate Frank Maguire returns after time overseas, replete with American accent. He is back to complete a Cain-and-Abel relationship with his brother Len, to kill, not by force, but with the kindness of an export culture. Frank offers Len, who has stayed with the local company, a job as the Australian end of an American-funded TV series. It is to be shot in Australia, but with U.S. iconography. Len is tempted by the prospect of on-set control, but is dissuaded by the prerequisite that the series have American themes and unimpressed by Frank's insistence that it will be Australian simply as a result of being filmed there. Len's position, well enunciated academically by Elizabeth Jacka, is one that seeks textual signifiers "applying to particular and specific sets of circumstances and forces that operate at any given time and place, be they signs of place, accent, and idiom, or more diffuse but no less vivid ways of hooking into the social unconscious or social 'imaginary' of a particular subculture."[65]

The search for the resistive, progressive object is never-ending, it seems, and influencing policy is the latest route to encouraging its production and reception. An elitist critique of mass culture as a manufacturer of cultural and political incompetents has been supplanted by a valorization of popular culture at sites where it is held to reflect localisms. This presumes that in a mass-produced, -consumed and -analyzed culture, the local can become a powerful, shifting, slippery yet isolable icon of radical change. Ultimately, this further presumes that the cultural policymaker and the cultural critic can offer an unmediated account of the social world, to be enshrined in governmental regulations and textual analysis respectively.

In his discussion of the processes of simulation, Baudrillard calls this certitude into question. He talks about the impact of recognizing the arbitrariness of its preeminence, about what it means to discover that there is, for example, no ontology beneath iconography. He identifies four phases in the development of our understanding of the image:

1. It is the reflection of a basic reality.
2. It masks and perverts a basic reality.
3. It masks the *absence* of a basic reality.
4. It bears no relation to any reality whatever: it is its own pure simulacrum.

The reaction to a loss of referentiality in the real is to heighten efforts to manufacture it.[66] So while policymakers retain the tenets of reflectionism, they add to it a complex weave of innovation/administration in response to the internationalization of images. Ultimately, as will be shown below, this amounts to precisely the self-referentiality to which Baudrillard alludes, a kind of desperate desire to form a definite root system in the face of the rhizome. One does not have to fantasize as touchingly as does Laclau about the decline of the sovereign state to discern the urgency of such moves.[67]

Cultural critique became policy formation in the late 1980s when the regulatory Australian Broadcasting Tribunal (ABT) decided to reconsider television drama in this particular way, a way that became known as "the Australian look." Instead of using production indices—the locus of creative control—as a means of determining the Australianness of drama, it decided to move toward a policy of on-screen indicators of "theme, perspective, language and character."[68] A bureaucratized form of cultural nationalism had replaced the old arrangements, when regulators and programmers had basically been in step.

A representative of the AFC used the Jacka material to criticize this new logic, claiming that the disruptiveness, newness, and self-formative potential of TV drama would be lost under such a proposal. In its stead, a pan-Australianism constituted from essentialist protocols would preclude the hitherto inevitable emergence of local political concerns flowing from the participation of Australian production personnel.[69] But it is precisely a reflectionist protocol, I shall argue, that drives this argument for localism. It continues to mobilize accounts of an authentic Australia in just the same fashion as the Tribunal's "Australian look," but in a less overt manner that requires a more mystical—and unspecifiable—manifestation of Australianness to appear in order for an inexplicit cultural mission to be accomplished. What binds these putatively disparate positions inexorably together is their conceptual undergrowth, a thicket of unstated assumptions about the formation of the self that is an amalgam of reflectionism and pedagogy. This connectedness emerges on such occasions as the Australian minister for transport and communications announcing in 1990 that the government would restrict foreign (i.e., U.S.) ownership of local television networks to 20 percent because of the need to ensure "the exploration of cultural identity"; and when the AFC calls for a broad exception for audiovisual materials in TIS in the name of "cultural development."[70]

ABT policy in general has often been read by the AFC and academics as crassly essentialist, unworkable, and ignorant of critical literature in this and other, adjacent domains. But the Tribunal was deploying a set of logics here that was identical to the Australian Film Commission's in Geneva, for all the apparent differentiation by the latter between these positions. Such logics demonstrate an abiding concern with a particular

The Well-Tempered Self

aesthetic practice of self-formation that has remained relatively immune to the criticisms leveled at it by litterateurs, screen theorists, and sub-cultures. Paradoxically, it necessarily subtends both those critiques and what they ostensibly seek to bring into question. Toward the end of its deliberations on local content—considerations related to amount, genre, and testing methods—the ABT maintained that "drama . . . enables Australians to see themselves in their own environment and experience their own stories. . . . There appears to be a growing consensus that 60% [of prime-time television programming] represents the desirable level to preserve a national identity."[71] In 1989, the Tribunal announced that 35 percent of broadcast time between the hours of 6 P.M. and 12 A.M. would be Australian, rising to a top limit of 50 percent in 1994 (the consensus had lost 10 percent over twelve months). It also established a quota system for drama and confirmed the limit of 20 percent of foreign content in advertising.

The revised Television Program Standard (TPS) 14, covering local content, had the following objectives:

1. To encourage programs which
   are identifiably Australian;
   recognize the diversity of cultural backgrounds represented in the Australian community;
   are developed for an Australian audience; and
   are under Australian creative control.
2. . . . to encourage Australian drama in which:
   (a) the theme (if set in Australia) is recognisably Australian, that the subject matter portrays aspects of life in Australia or the life of an Australian or Australians; or
   (b) the perspective (if wholly or partly set outside Australia or if the subject matter is not Australian) is Australian, that is, the subject matter is presented from an Australian viewpoint;
   (c) the language is Australian, that is, the speech of Australian characters is the speech, including idiom or accents, found among people who meet the definition of an Australian; and
   (d) the character of the production is Australian, that is the visual depiction of the scenes set in Australia including locations, back-grounds, props and costumes is recognisable as Australian, the interpretation of the material is Australian and . . . casting accurately reflects the Australian characters portrayed.[72]

The Standard represents the contorted outcome of negotiations between competing determinations. These include actors' industrial requirements; producers' investment requirements; and the Tribunal's sense of its cultural task. TPS 14 is a prolix attempt to make Australianism non-American while not specifically saying so. At the same time, it must encompass and thereby forestall potential criticisms for excluding the polyglot demographic nature of the local populace. When the U.S. Embassy protested that this amounted to a quota on goods of trade, the reaction came back that "the rule is not a trade barrier, but an integral part of domestic broadcasting policy designed to encourage not only the local film industry, but also an Australian cultural identity."[73] But was that the actual point of reference? It is possible to trace a lineage from the classical *epistēmē* described by Foucault to the kinds of logic at play within TPS 14 and its cultural critics. Although Foucault discerns the disappearance of this *epistēmē* in the nineteenth century, just such logics were being institutionalized in cultural policy in the late 1980s to make for new selves. I shall summarize Foucault's gloss and bracket its application to Australian television content.

The classical *epistēmē* took resemblance or similitude to be the key to representation and exegesis. It operated through four assumptions. First, that the adjacency of objects could be a sign of the type of relationship that they enjoyed (audience with text, production personnel with hermeneutic referent). Second, that emulation was achieved via reflection, a form of imitation in which primacy accorded by origin was impossible (mimesis of story setting over generic origin). Third, that a process of analogy incorporated elements of these first two assumptions (the mix of on- and -off screen indicators). And fourth, that taxonomies of Same and Other were constructed and organized around sympathies and antipathies engaged in a dialectical relationship (the association of local cultural politics with local themes or creative agents).

TPS 14 is, like the discourse encircling it, a document with a lineage in much earlier doctrines of verisimilitude. It is quite immune to notions of the specificity of individual subjectivity or the formative influence of signification. In this sense, it has another home, in early writings on something called "the study of communication." There are clear links to the sender-message-receiver account in the presumption that laying down textual regulations of what is "Australian" can make for the maintenance of a national patrimony. This is not to embark, with the likes of Stephen Heath and Gillian Skirrow, on an argument to the effect that the concept of "communication" must be eschewed for its resolutely humanistic anti-materialism.[74] As will be indicated below, rules like those of the ABT are material determinants of the pro-filmic text and its reception, and are amenable to a sender-message-receiver account, pro-

The Well-Tempered Self

vided that this is not regarded as unequivocally and necessarily humanist, but rather as a stipulatory norm of textual regulation. Reconsidering TPS 14, one could essay a still newer mode of reflectionism. This is a policy reflectionism. Its desired referent is not "Australia," but TPS 14 itself, albeit with prescribed notions of "Australia" and proscribed versions of "not-Australia" as indexical adjuncts. Here, the reality that precedes the pro-filmic moment is given by the rules laid down by the ABT. They become both authorizing subject and zero signified, moving on through another transmogrification to provide a critical apparatus by offering an ultimate accounting of "Australianness." They thus are sender, message, and receiver rolled into one. Their claim, like that of cultural nationalist bureaucrats, is to manage what Foucault identified as the principal raison d'être of the human sciences: "to define the way in which individuals or groups represent words to themselves."[75] This process of management takes place at all stages of the production-distribution-interpretation continuum: it stipulates the nationality of certain creative principals in production (for example, scriptwriters or directors); it requires the manifestation of specific textual features that will appear local; and it polices the observance of these rules.

In the collection he edited on Australia's first *Ten Years of Television*, Mungo MacCallum argues that "drama is as much part of a community's culture as its sport. In its range, from banality to brilliance, it reflects us to ourselves, helps us to know ourselves and passes on the information to the rest of the world. A community without drama is undeveloped, or maimed beneath the skin."[76] Similarly, just after the advent of Australian television, the former radio and future screen drama producer Hector Crawford lobbied publicly for the protection of local TV drama as a means of constituting "a consciousness of national identity and pride in our nation, and a regard for our own cultural ideas and patterns."[77]

This is to go over the territory already established, but it is necessary in order to get a little closer to the theoretical mechanics that work through such arguments. It is important that lines being run thirty years ago are still current. Consider, for example, the oft-cited cultural nationalist journalism of Tom Weir, "No Daydreams of Our Own: The Film as National Self-Expression," in which he speaks of the screen as "the most important means for heightening a people's feeling of communal personality, bringing them the shock of recognition that Herman Melville was concerned to give when his own America was a dependent culture. . . . [Film] plants one's feet on the ground. The workaday world is integrated with the world of one's imagination. . . . It is typical of the undeveloped personality of our [Australian] people that we have practically no indigenous films."[78]

There is little doubt that this desire to form a national identity underlay much of the argument produced for state subvention of film and television. Similar rhetorical moves apply in, for example, Canada. Consider the following, from the president of Quebec's Régie du cinéma et de la vidéo in 1985: "A given population should from time to time be able to see itself on the screen. That just seems fundamental and not even for nationalistic reasons but because of questions of identity."[79] This could be related back to Aristotle's formulation concerning the pleasure of the audience in "learning or inferring, and saying perhaps, 'Ah, that is he.' "[80] It is well in keeping with much of the material covered in chapter 2.

Like those approaches, however, this search for cultural identity is characterized by necessarily conflictual narratives of incompleteness. Hall suggests that there are now two principal forms of conceiving of cultural identity. The first of these defines the term as a "collective 'one true self,' hiding inside the many other, more superficial or artificially imposed 'selves.' " Excavating for this indissoluble oneness of history and nature is deemed to be the mission of a national audiovisual culture. The second definition qualifies this view by insisting on the irreducible points of difference within culture that are as abiding and meaningful as those of sameness, that cultural identity must always be considered in the plural.[81] This still relies, if it is to be operationalized as a cultural policy, on a correspondence between the social and the aesthetic that is crucially constituted by an endlessly unknowable quintessence that must nevertheless be sought after. To form and manage the means of cultural subjectivity in this way is to create the preconditions for a national public to recognize and conduct itself as such under the sign of textual analysis; reading as cultural policymakers would wish. Such is the logic of plaintiffs before the GATT who approach the bar with culture as their trouble.

Chapter Four

◆

MAKING CITIZENS
AND CONSUMERS

I HAVE ALREADY ALLUDED to the complexity of the notion of the liberal subject. There is a clear potential for contradiction between the doctrines of subjects who seek a democratic society via free and equal participation in the interests of the public good and those of subjects who seek to maximize their own utility in the market, a mechanism that will supposedly counteract their selfishness with the competing self-ishness of others. There is a superficial fit between these models if one presumes that the sphere of government embraces those areas that the market could never cover (for example, laws of private property and standing defense forces), but the purely laissez-faire economy is a myth. Most capitalist democracies have mixed economies, which often see not so much intervention in industries by the state as action by the state to generate industries. Inasmuch as this is always done in the name of a preference for private sector initiative and management and with refer-ence to a ruthlessly competitive Social Darwinist world, it is necessary for the state to forge two kinds of subjectivity: the selfless, active citizen who cares for others and favors a political regime that compensates for losses in the financial domain; and the selfish, active consumer who favors a financial regime that compensates for losses in the political domain. This self-interested consumer is more than a rhetorical trope or a description of an already-extant subjectivity. Because of the extraordinary completeness of the permeation of liberal discourse by marginalist or neoclassical economics, the notion of such a consumer is also part of the principles of certain interventionist aspects of public policy, especially in the area of human capital called, variously, education or training. Moreover, it is the very plenitude of consuming possibilities that drives attempts to develop public policies on citizenship as correctives to such excess.

This chapter examines two sites at which these imperatives operate. It illustrates some of the contradictions inside and between them. The first part, "The 'Visible Scenario' of Politics," seeks to explain how moves to televise the Australian Parliament can be understood in terms of the formation and display of particular subjectivities. It argues for an assumed incompleteness on the part of the potential viewer that is to be rectified in the name of citizenship education via exposure to what is generally regarded as having been a source of this incompleteness—namely, television. The actual texts of the broadcasts are found to generate a very different form of television from the routine continuity system, one that may not in fact achieve the desired outcome of audience respect. The chapter maintains that the particular mode of televisuality required by the Parliament indicates a further anxiety about the appropriate display/formation of politicians as ethical subjects, as exemplars of assiduous work and icons of cultural-capitalist democracy.

The second part of the chapter, "Authorship and the Public Speech," has three tacks. At one level, it is a fairly straightforward analysis of speeches about industry training made by two businesspeople on behalf of the state. As such, it can be situated within a constellation of relations described by the following formations: relations between and within business and government; the role of nonstatutory public advisory bodies; and the nexus of economy and training. At a second level, it may be read as an attempt to address the techniques of speechwriting within the civil service and how these resonate with "famous names" to produce authored—and authorized—documents, in a way that borrows from many of the traditional concerns of textual theory. And at a third level, what I am seeking to argue is that neoclassical economics is a structuring discourse determining the terms of truth and subject positions within the speeches. The speeches personify both the rational, consuming, maximizing private subject on which a free market is based and the caring, sharing, disinterested public subject on which a democratic polity is based. The irony is that the speakers are articulating a market-oriented discourse produced by elements of the state favoring a neoclassical model of educational development in opposition to other elements favoring one based on civics.

The "Visible Scenario" of Politics

Citizenship

Following the establishment the previous year of the Australian Parliamentary Education Office (PEO) with the primary aim of redressing "the low priority given to 'active citizenship' education [in schools and to stress] . . . the important role of parliament and parliamentarians in educating young citizens for democracy," the Australian Education Council, the government's advisory body on curricula, adopted ten national goals in 1989. Among these was "developing skills in students to enable them to participate in a democratic society."[1] The PEO followed up with a conference designed to devise strategies for "incorporating parliamentary and citizenship education into courses for teachers in training." This in turn led to the formation, with the Senate's blessing, of an Australian Association of Parliamentary and Citizenship Educators and an affiliated journal. A citizenship visits program was also introduced, which subsidized trips to Parliament by school students who lived more than a thousand kilometers from Canberra.

When Australia's new Federal Parliament House was opened in 1988, it included A $50 million worth of television technology, initially deployed to send closed-circuit pictures from the House of Representatives and the Senate to the offices of members of Parliament (MPs) and an edited service to the press gallery. When debate then commenced about the value of broadcasting proceedings, the president of the Senate suggested that the expense already gone to was an argument for public televising, although there had been stirrings toward this for some time. At Parliament's suggestion, 1990 saw the Australian Broadcasting Corporation (ABC) commence live coverage of Question Time in the Senate, proceeding on to the House the following year. The commercial stations did not show the same interest, perhaps because of an initial prohibition of edited highlights.

These innovations were institutional responses to three related perceptions: a putative lack of public familiarity with Parliament and its distinctness from the executive; a putative lack of public knowledge of citizenship, sovereignty, democratic participation, and related concepts; and, overlapping with these, the additional problem of how to form channels of communication between the public and politicians that avoided the mediation/determinations of media owners and professionals. It was as though the instatement of a direct connection between sender (parliamentarian) and receiver (citizen) would magically make for knowledge, responsiveness, and respect. As citizens came to understand what parliamentarians did and said, they could learn to articulate their own needs and preferences in the correct pose and tongue. This understanding was to be manufactured by intervening in the secondary curriculum and via a reassertion of Parliament's right to be seen and heard on terms and terrain that it controlled.

Such concerns are not confined to Australia. Rather, they are part of a common reaction within cultural-capitalist democracies against the discipline imposed by political parties, a reaction led—and in most cases barely sustained—by parliamentary officials and junior MPs who will never make the ministry. In 1988, British backbenchers successfully pressed for a trial televising of proceedings as a method of reclaiming the public as an active constituency; in effect, a pressure group on all issues, formed through tele-sovereignty rather than any specific material interest or organizational form. So while the public is questioned and—supposedly—empowered, hailing it in this way also provides a power base for MPs.

This reaction represents the public as a subject that has hitherto been formed and ruled by a less desirable entity than its own sovereignty: by the mass media. Government at one time favored professional journalists as expert mediators between public and politics. In 1944, the British War Cabinet argued that "proceedings in Parliament were too technical to be understood by the ordinary listener who would be liable to get a quite false impression of the business transacted."[2] In the age of television, however, the public is seen as an audience that must be made into a body of citizens, and that can be once civics has been instated as a pedagogic norm. "To televise parliament would, at a stroke, restore any loss it has suffered to the new mass media as the political education of the nation," observes the British parliamentarian Norman St. John-Stevas.[3]

Quite apart from the question of who should be educating whom, there is a dependence on the media explicit in St. John-Stevas's position that is oxymoronic. As Lesley Johnson has pointed out, live broadcasts of Parliament bring politics to the public but—crucially—thereby spell and define politics with a capital *P*, perhaps impeding the development of a sense that equally important and equally political debates and struggles occur around and over the lathe, sink, or word processor as the mace.[4] In addition, the stuff of much parliamentary talk is impenetrably procedural. Whatever substantive debates emerge, it has been argued, are ultimately flattened out by television's norms, thereby robbing the event of any genuine capacity for public education. Politicians learn how to reform themselves as objects of the photo-gaze along the lines of the personable, evenhanded, bland talk-show host.

This returns us to the Derrida/Jefferson dilemma of chapter 1, the quandary that political theory has been faced with since the invention of the idea that when we are born, we enter an implied social contract with the state. This contract—to cede a certain autonomy of action in return for a certain amount of protection, service, and identity—is one that we are then said to be able to survey and utilize through the technologies of sovereignty: the parliamentary system and, latterly, pressure groups. The quest for origins is without end, so to speak, as fruitful as it is interminable in a realm where "what came first" is equally hard to establish in archival and conceptual senses. Did I exist before the country in which I was born honored me with certification of the fact? Was it then that I made the mature decision, after all due consideration, to agree to the Constitution? Or did that come later?

As was seen in chapter 3, many countries ask broadcasting to resolve this uncertainty. Publicly owned radio and television stations are routinely required by legislation to encourage unity in the sovereign states that fund them. They are there to perform a variety of functions simultaneously, some of which paradoxically involve both responsiveness to taste and its formation. Public service broadcasting is meant to shape as it tames as it delivers. It is expected to manufacture citizens (citizens who have contributed to their own creation) even as it attracts an audience. When allied to the fear that it is precisely the "mass" aspect of the mass media that has made for an ignorant public, this can lead to a logocentrism that places all its faith for renewal in a kind of sociological homeopathy: television is one of the villains, so television must be given a position of trust to take advantage of its abilities and make it responsible.

Benjamin argued more than fifty years ago that the new mechanical forms of the reproduction of information made for a reduction in the effectiveness of parliaments. He addressed squarely, if epigrammatically, the alienation of person from parliament that citizens felt in terms of their interaction with the state: "I think of the modern citizen who knows that he is at the mercy of a vast machinery of officialdom whose functioning is directed by authorities that remain nebulous to the executive organs, let alone to the people they deal with."[5]

The attempt to ameliorate this situation may be seen as the post-modern adjunct to citizenship. Classical political theory accorded the citizen representation through and by the state. The distinctively modern addendum to this was that the state guaranteed a minimum standard of living, provided that citizens recognized their debt to the great institutions of welfare. The decisive postmodern guarantee falls in the area of providing access to the technologies of communication as crucial integers in the set of the polity. This promise derives its force from a sense that such institutions need to relearn what sovereignty is about in polymorphous sovereign states that are diminishingly homogeneous in demographic terms and increasingly heteroglossic in their cultural competence. Contradictory accounts of this citizen emerge from the presumption that it is the work of a parliament to tell the people why they should be interested in and faithful to it, while at the same time claiming their considered acceptance and support as the grounds for its own existence.

The recent turn within social theory toward an interest in the idea of civil society can then be seen to run alongside the anxieties expressed from within the state apparatus. Opportunities for marginal groups to express themselves and fears on the part of the dominant about its own legitimacy become part of a double movement of renewal under the sign of the citizen. Hence Taylor's contention that civil society can be said to be an entity that "exists over against the state, in partial independence from it."[6]

How practical is this distinction?

In 1979, Britain's Conservative Party made the free market a cornerstone of its manifesto by claiming that it would not only make people wealthy, but also make them better able to deal with public services and the private sector workplace through a combination of opening up the former to competition and the latter to employee shareholding. It is possible to see the Conservatives' "Citizen's Charter" of 1991 as a delivery of part of this, not at all as a diversion away from the supposedly naked market of the preceding decade. *Citizen* means something very special here; not "the activist, the campaigner, the lobbyist—but . . . the consumer." The delivery of services is given priority over questions of representation and participation to the point where an editorial in the *Times* termed the process "mimicking the market" and the *Indepen-*

The Well-Tempered Self

dent announced the birth of "citizen-consumers."[7] These are not citizens who exist to act politically inside or outside the state; not citizens concerned with questions of policy or of political ideology. Rather, they are users of public services who are being offered a limited power of redress when those services are delivered unsatisfactorily.

Further to the left, debates over the Charter 88 movement in Britain—an attempt, inter alia, to construct a scripted basis for being British, but in a way that claims a genesis in the *New Statesman and Society*—have occluded the question of the notion of the individualism of the citizen. Is this the "nice" side of the person who is also the utterly selfish utilitarian? Was the Tory minister Douglas Hurd's advocacy of "active citizenship" a cipher for a government that needed to appear caring and sharing (or perhaps needed its policing done at below cost)? Is there some kind of contradiction within the human subject if it is made to combine the communitarian togetherness of citizenship with the dynamic competitiveness of the participant in the market? This tension has been called "the duality of publicness." It troubles theorists from all parts of the political spectrum. Lasch claims that the drive toward "private satisfaction" via the material consumption of objects associated with fantasy in fact weakens both the private domain in its hold on personal relationships and the public domain in its hold on attention to matters of civic concern.[8]

At the site of parliamentary television, we are more directly returned to the ideal speech-act of communicative perfection. For it is fairly clear that Parliament is being set up here as a model. It is not only important in itself as the site of fealty and access. More than that, it is being used to manufacture citizens as participants in a particular mode of discussion. Habermas argues that there are three critical elements to the formation of a public sphere under democracy. These elements provide a popular justification for political authority. First, each participant in a debate must have the charity to assume that the others involved are acting rationally. Second, this charity must be seen to apply to parliamentary rules and conduct. Such "practical discourses" may then claim to offer a conduit to "the universalizability of interests." There is a nexus between high-quality debate and the very ability to express particular interests. Third, the formation of the "public will" must involve compromise. This is a compromise whose conditions of appearance can be evaluated by all the parties. In doing so, they can ascertain whether the discursive conditions under which the compromise was struck were conducive to open discussion. These elements collectively comprise the domain of "public discussion guided by arguments." The gift of modernity is the displacement of the "substantive rationality" offered by religion and metaphysics in favor of this "procedural rationality."[9]

In the conventions of parliamentary politics and much left critique, there is an evil that stands between the people and their representatives, that precludes the exercise of this rationality. This evil has a name. It is called television. The claim is made that television forwards image and emotion as opposed to sound and rationality. But the next move is often for television to become the source of power and the warrant/technology for training publics into a citizenry loyal both to the state and to a particular model of dialogue. Consider Lyndon Johnson's rationale for supporting public television; it would, he said, "make our nation a replica of the old Greek marketplace, where public affairs took place in view of all the citizens." Yet in an equal, opposite, but intimately connected sense, Johnson feared that "in weak or even in irresponsible hands, it could generate controversy without understanding; it could mislead as well as teach; it could appeal to passions rather than reason."[10]

For his part, Winston Churchill knew that television was "a red conspiracy" because it had a robotic component that combined undifferentiated mass access with machinelike precision and reproduction. On the other hand, televising the Bundestag in postwar Germany was said to be critical for democratizing the public.[11] Such discourse is a critical concern of this chapter for its description of the culturally overdetermined public subject. It involves a conception of television that amounts to a will to infantilize. John Hartley has neologized this will in another context as a regime of "paedocracy." The institutions of television construct an account of their audience that calls it up as a subject for training and protection.[12] This is in keeping with the medium's duality, its capacity to produce a combination of fear and fascination on the part of its guardians. This will seems to be shared by MPs and parliamentary bureaucrats alike. The current issue in question is the potential for learning how to engage in rational debate that is offered by watching brief discussions of politics on television news and current affairs programs. Fifty years ago, it was the degree of rationality encouraged by brief articles in the popular press.

A routine struggle is going on here. It balances out the sacred and the profane, the potent and the barren of the media. Consider the decision taken in July 1990 by a New South Wales parliamentary committee not to proceed with a proposal to televise the proceedings of the Indepen-

The Well-Tempered Self

dent Commission against Corruption (ICAC) on the grounds that "visual images were 'tremendously powerful.'" Even proponents of telecasting ICAC acknowledged problems with "television's propensity to trivialize and merely entertain," as the *Sydney Morning Herald*'s editorial put it. At one and the same time, then, it was held that television would wreak havoc in the orderly conduct of ICAC and yet have no real effects. It narcotizes as it stimulates. Similarly, within a single report, the Brisbane *Courier-Mail* could advise that before the March 1990 federal election, the opposition had refused coverage of the Lower House because it believed that this would give the government an unfair advantage, and then go on to say that the government believed no one would watch such television.[13] Television is an omniscient beast welling up and controlling everything; but its end result is nothing.

Austin Mitchell, a British Labour MP, has labeled this "fear of television." Using the old hypodermic model of media effects, where television enters the *soma* sometimes to drive to madness and at other times to instill quietude, he refers to concerns that "TV politics may even inoculate against understanding and build up antibodies against politics itself."[14] Consider the recent special issue of the Australasian Study of Parliament Group's *Legislative Studies* journal on "The Media and Parliamentary Education" (note, not education *of* the Parliament, but *by* it, *in* it). The contribution from a Senate official included the following observation about the threat to "Australian democracy" posed by "an impotent television-bound nation, trusting in politicians and parties that are as reliable as any other television commodity that must be dressed up and pushed."[15] A patrician certainty of ignorance on the part of the Other is an article of faith in this discourse about the television audience. The ignoble savages who devour television do so in a way that is herein always already connected to their failure to know enough about parliamentary politics. Such baleful attitudes toward the popular have a distinguished lineage. Plutarch, for example, recounts the following story about Solon. Having enjoyed a performance of a tragedy, Solon spoke with Thespis, who was developing this dramatic form into the shape that is now so familiar:

> He went up to Thespis and asked him whether he was not ashamed to tell such lies in front of so many people. When Thespis replied that there was no harm in speaking or acting in this way in make-believe, Solon struck the ground angrily with his staff and exclaimed, "Yes, but if we allow ourselves to praise and honour make-believe

like this, the next thing will be to find it creeping into our serious business."[16]

The public space was an honored location, not to be cheapened. The hold of reason and truth on participation was tenuous, so the public was to be safeguarded from its own frailties. These weaknesses could easily be brought out by the dangerous imaginings of popular fictional culture and turned into a source of distraction from more important matters.

It was a cognate move two and a half millennia later that saw the first day of the trial telecast from the Australian Senate begin with ABC commentators explaining how Parliament "worked." Vox-pops were used to prove the ignorance of the public: no one interviewed on the street knew how many MPs there were. This is reminiscent of an American survey reporting that children aged between eight and twelve could identify more brands of beer than they could presidents of the United States.[17] But it would have met with the approval of Australian Democrat Senator Paul McLean, who was disturbed by the "great ignorance, indifference and apathy in the community about things parliamentary"; or, indeed, with the views of the leading commercial network in Australia, Channel Nine, which argued for ICACTV on the grounds of its "educative function."[18] The public is here an object to be worked on. Once it is shown the extent of its own ignorance, it will take up the need for reformation by in turn working on itself. This, of course, denies the "*Sesame Street* problem," where programs designed to uplift the informationally underprivileged are lapped up by those more privileged, leaving preexisting power relations of knowledge undisturbed. It also ignores the evidence from Britain, which suggests that those most likely to watch Question Time Television (QTTV) are the people who are already familiar with the parliamentary domain.

At a more theoretical level, there is no sense here of the paradox of dependence on the alleged source of the problem to remove that problem in a wave of homeopathic self-transformation. The flatness of television, the fact that its physical form is relatively stable, along with its physical positioning, is seen to override the actual content of ideas raised in debate because this content can be processed in such a routine manner by the mythic public. Television now is held, not so much to destroy participation in public life, but rather to be a revolutionary force unraveling established power within the private domain. Alternatively, one might redispose these positions and suggest that a culture of appreciation of televisual technology and communicative form, learned in

The Well-Tempered Self

the home, is critical for the development of direct citizen participation via the electronic town meeting or new ideas about the dialogic and the plebiscitary as sites of the technological experimentation and the formation of spaces in which the public can appear.

Local Consumption

It is important to consider what this public might be that was under construction, and what it had already shown of itself. For Australian surveys of television audiences indicate that their interest in "Politics" in news bulletins is greater than their interest in "Sport." This is especially true of professional people over the age of twenty-five. So perhaps this is not the same public that is being spoken of as in need of parliamentary education. But it may be a public that is tired. For it is perhaps not insignificant that although the 1987 Australian federal election saw a 137 percent increase in expenditure on television advertising over the 1984 figure, which indicates a developing reliance on the medium, half the viewers watching television in Sydney turned off their sets when all the commercial stations screened the same campaign speech simultaneously. One could argue that such partisan interruptions fail to constitute a litmus test. But three-year parliamentary terms and a proliferation of state and local government elections at different times mean that the parties are, in one sense, always already campaigning. The electoral questioning of citizens is excessive.

In any case, just as television is ambivalently perceived as a threatening solution (an oxymoron worthy of standing beside that of the selfish, but considerate, consumer-citizen), so the much longer history of interaction between radio and the Australian Parliament has been full of contradictory disjunctures. When the duchess and duke of York came to Australia in 1927 to open the temporary Parliament House, the promised broadcast of the duke's speech was advertised for four weeks prior to the event to encourage people to buy radio receivers as a contribution to uniting the nation. Nonetheless, a few years later, the ABC briefly banned the broadcast of all speeches by politicians for the three-month period prior to elections. A Labor Party government introduced legislation requiring the ABC to broadcast proceedings after World War II in part because of the perception that the party was being unfairly treated in the press, although the official reasons given had to do with raising the standards of debate, improving Parliament's image, and developing community awareness of it as an institution. We shall return to these themes, which are startlingly redolent of the reasons forwarded for televising the legislature forty years on.

Whereas radio coverage had begun on the mainstream ABC, it was relegated to a special parliamentary network in 1988. This was, in part, recognition of forty-two years of dwindling audiences and listeners increasingly dissatisfied by the interruption of other programs. A survey undertaken for the Dix Committee of Review into the ABC in 1981 had found that only 26 percent of respondents were content with the amount of time devoted to such broadcasts. Ratings have regularly been below 1 percent.

There is a striking similarity between the trajectories of parliamentary broadcast policy on both radio and television. Each starts off with an inimical view of the media: in one case, perhaps the outcome of a mistrust of privately owned newspapers; in the other, the product of a much more general misgiving about the mass media in general, a more profound mistrust that was social in the sense of being related to the audience, but unrelated to any account of the ownership of the means of production. Second, both had a brief to reform MPs themselves, of which more will be made below. Third, both sought to upgrade public knowledge and opinion of democratic institutions. Given all the evidence of the radio experience, one might ask what was likely to eventuate from televising the proceedings, but before addressing that question, we need to look further at relevant practice outside Australia.

Overseas Consumption

Belgium, Bulgaria, Canada, China, Costa Rica, Cuba, Denmark, Egypt, Germany, Greece, Hungary, Israel, Italy, Japan, Luxembourg, Malta, Mongolia, Norway, Poland, Portugal, Singapore, South Korea, Sweden, Switzerland, Thailand, the United States, and the erstwhile Soviet Union all televised their legislatures before Australia did, with varying allocations of control of the coverage between media entities and officialdom. There are now close to sixty nations doing so.

Proceedings in the Netherlands' Staten Generaal began to be televised in 1962, with three types of coverage: live for topical issues; summaries of less important debates; and "flashes" on magazine programs. The first years of the system saw considerable public disaffection because of members' on-camera proclivities for dormancy, absence, novel-reading, and jargon. Over time, members came to attend at the same time as producers, viewer familiarity with procedural norms grew, and ratings increased on occasions of moment.

"Whether one likes it or not, television is regarded as the Voice of France," President Georges Pompidou intoned resignedly in 1972, and two years later a clutch of broadcasting reforms required certain stations to cover the French National Assembly.[19] Here was a president installing television as sovereign, as Jefferson/Derrida did the act of writing. The people watched and believed and created the people.

It is no surprise, similarly, that during the extraordinary events in Czechoslovakia at the end of 1989, the opposition Civic Forum movement made the televising of the Federal Assembly one of its principal demands. Sometimes such moves have amounted to a defensive reaction, at others to a positive innovation. One thinks here of the video chariots that go into the Indian countryside with video recordings of political rallies and speeches to be shown on screens that can be viewed by five thousand at a sitting. Millions of voters in the rural hinterlands who are unable to receive state-run television thus gain electoral and ideological information. Uganda adopted color television to coincide with a meeting of the Organisation of African Unity. And the first live broadcast of the Soviet Union's new Congress of People's Deputies in 1989 attracted a record two hundred million viewers across a dozen time zones, a 25 percent increase over the previous figure. A side effect was the formation of a new image overseas. For American journalists, televising parliamentary sessions helped to bring the Soviet Union into the field of political normalcy.

Of course, we should also consider the cognate use made of new communications technologies, which are said to have broken down the extent of mediation between politicians and publics in North America. Direct contact between congresspeople and their constituents has positioned them at the leading edge of applications of cable, satellite, video cassette recording, and computer-aided interaction. Alaska, for example, has a Legislative Teleconferencing Network that permits committees to receive audio and computer messages from citizens. Ross Perot linked six American cities by satellite in 1992 to convene a "nationwide electronic rally," a metonym for the "electronic town hall" that was to administer the country had he become president; he would debate policies with Congress and have citizens respond through modem or telephone.[20] Political talk-back television in Italy has produced notable events, such as the call from a viewer that persuaded the defense minister to admit that a North Atlantic Treaty Organization missile had brought down a local DC-9 aircraft, with the loss of all on board.

Arguments are now made to the effect that such programs represent a major shift from the days when audiences were simply something to be counted or points of reception. Instead of being educated or entertained, "ordinary people" now have "access" via phone-in, feedback, discussion programs, and access television. The audience discussion sector (which includes *Donahue* and *Oprah*) is said to open up a new angle on America by drawing the active viewer or concerned citizen into debate.[21] Nevertheless, it has also been suggested that the proliferation in the 1980s of television programs claiming to give a voice to the people is symptomatic of a general crisis in news reporting and a response to perceptions of public powerlessness, rather than a genuine innovation in access broadcasting. The United States suffers the lowest rate of electoral participation in the industrialized world, part of a trend toward apathy that has been in evidence since 1960. And all this despite—or perhaps because—the 1988 election saw U.S. $200 million expended by presidential candidates. Perot's 1992 candidacy evoked contempt from Carl Bernstein because it was "created and sustained by television" in a way that mocked the complexities of working democracy.[22]

It is useful here to consider Robert Karl Manoff's discussion of the history of journalism. The standard account locates the nature of the media in its eighteenth- and nineteenth-century origins. The press is thought to express an emergent bourgeoisie's revolutionary attitudes to knowledge and preferences for empirical and material writings rather than speculative or spiritual ones. Newspapers become not only the sources of this mode of being, but creatures of it, business entities themselves, conceived and managed along the new lines of capital investment. An alternative history to this "sociological and political-economic" one might consider "journalism as discourse." Such a history would emphasize parallel movements in the nineteenth century toward independence from particular pecuniary or political interests but dependence on a particular political system or thesaurus. On this account, the United States, and the state of its journalism, developed together and in mutually determining ways. So the "hierarchy of the profession" puts Washington at its apex, a formalization of the processual relationship that sees affairs of state as the real business of the press. This serves to stress still further the identification of state and people.[23]

This second history may help to explain the tardiness of direct actuality reproduction between politicians and publics. Despite the introduction of a bill in 1922 providing for electronic media coverage of Congress, with a trial the following year, the United States had no regular radio broadcasts of proceedings until the signing of the Panama Canal Treaties of 1978. The opening of the Eightieth Congress in 1947 was

The Well-Tempered Self

carried on television, but this was generally proscribed until 1971. The major drive for change stemmed from the results of public opinion polls from the early 1970s that suggested that politicians were held in low esteem. Regular trials were instituted in 1977, but only on closed circuit. Publicly available coverage was routine in the Lower House from 1979, and the Senate agreed to the same in 1986. The service is available on cable, fifteen million subscribers having access to the Senate and thirty-nine million to the House. Again, twin goals are claimed for all this: "Most observers agree that television has improved the general quality of debate and has contributed to a more informed citizenry."[24]

Of course, debates between presidential candidates have been valorized for their instructional impact, and Watergate saw the Senate Select Committee on Presidential Campaign Activities gain high ratings through thirty-seven days of coverage. But ratings for U.S. party conventions, on all three networks, declined throughout the 1980s, with 1988 figures down 9 percent on the previous campaign. During the 1984 conventions, one network interrupted slow periods with a drama re-run of a live car chase until the Democrats agreed to move proceedings along at a faster rate. Television had made the primaries into a political Olympics. Winning primaries had not been a prerequisite for presidential nomination; but television made it seem as though it was, and reforms motivated in part by that very perception ultimately made it so. Once more, television is constructed as simultaneously formative and destructive of an active electorate. Great concern continues to animate moral panics over the supposed decline in civic education since the 1940s and alleged connections to television and progressive curricula, despite evidence that the U.S. public's level of political knowledge has remained remarkably stable over that time. One reason for the delay in televising Congress derives from the histrionics of early committee broadcasts, such as those of the House Un-American Activities Committee in 1948. In fact, committee coverage temporarily ceased in the 1960s, although these powerful investigative instruments have often been the most dramatic sites of television politics on offer.

The most spectacular recent examples have been the Senate Judiciary Committee's hearings in the confirmation of the Supreme Court appointment of Judge Clarence Thomas in 1991 and the appearance of Oliver North before a congressional committee in the 1987 hearings into funding the Contras in Nicaragua. The evidence about Thomas and Anita Hill was so "popular" that its competition, Minnesota versus Toronto, drew the lowest ratings ever for a baseball play-off. C-SPAN had over fifty million subscribers even before this issue arose. North's evidence had five times as many viewers as *General Hospital,* its closest daytime soap opera competitor. And most commentators on the event clearly read it intertextually by referring over and over again to acting, entertainment, and stars in their analysis. CBS actually juxtaposed images of North with clips of the Rambo and Dirty Harry characters, emphasizing the lone warrior against an establishment state that would not live up to its responsibilities. North assisted this process by alluding to Clint Eastwood in his promise "to tell the truth, the good, the bad, and the ugly."

Later critics have fetishized the North "character" by contrasting it—and in fact the entire hearings—with the heroic Jefferson Smith from Frank Capra's *Mr. Smith Goes to Washington* (1939): the anomic citizen puts his faith in constitutional ideals and homely virtue and is punished for doing so. Much media attention was given to President Ronald Reagan's words of admiration to North: "This is going to make a great movie one day." The reaction of the public was similarly remarkable. The polls, which had previously showed that years of government propaganda still left 70 percent of Americans opposed to funding the Contras, saw a 20 percent switch in opinion after the hearings. Once the policy issue became personalized in the form of North, and opposition to him could be construed as the work of a repressive state, congressional television viewing became popular and influential—but in a way that led Richard Bolton to attack the "highly manipulated forums for public speech now operating in the United States [which] encourage citizens to participate only through the consumption of images."[25] Congressional hearings were so intertextual that the notional distinction between legislative proceedings and current affairs—or for that matter fiction—had become spurious. Stark contrasts are evident between the revelatory wildness of the Watergate hearings and North's mannered, televisually literate presentation. But because the personal, sexual vilification was so intense and so hurried in the Thomas hearing, Senator Joseph Biden, the Judiciary Committee's chair, wondered aloud whether truth could out "under the hot lights of television." The irony lay, of course, in the fact that this plea/critique itself took place, was publicized, and led to debate under—if not thanks to—those very lights.

In Britain, debates over televising proceedings were common from 1965 on, with twelve separate parliamentary proposals to do so discussed between 1985 and 1988. Arguments for television rested on constitutional importance and on the medium's capacity both to involve the public in making politicians accountable and to involve politicians in making the public interested. Arguments against coverage centered on the intrusiveness of broadcasting equipment; the trivialization through editing of the circumstance and pomp integral to British politics; the undue attention to the major parties and to adversarial division that television would encourage; and the concern that established procedures and conduct would change to suit television.

Channel Four screened a program called *Their Lordships' House* from 1985. The Lower House rejected a proposal for coverage that year, but trial Commons telecasts commenced in late 1989—despite the then prime minister's opposition—and drew a domestic audience of ten million and thousands more via cable in the United States. Television coverage was regarded both as an advance and as an acknowledgment that parliamentary politics had been overrun by the media as the major formative political influence on the people. For until 1956, the BBC had not even been allowed to broadcast discussion of any topic due to be debated in Parliament over the coming fortnight. And the 1980s were a disjointed, disturbing period of frequent Conservative Party interventions into BBC programs on the Irish Republican Army, the South Atlantic War, American attacks on Libya, and *Spycatcher*. This led to hopes on the left for a less fettered form of MP-to-citizen communication of public issues than had been the case.

Against these instances of established democratic systems agonizing over their relationship with the perverse instrument of television, we might consider a political arrangement encountered in chapter 3 in the midst of inventing itself: Europe. The European Parliament has been directly elected since 1979 and has used television coverage for the past decade in search of attention and legitimacy. Recordings and live material are made available to broadcasters without any cost to encourage a more positive image of the new Europe. Second-order coverage of the Parliament had always been minimal owing to lack of media interest, but it increased markedly with live television material. And the new opening presented all the difficulties that this *bricolage*-polity routinely experiences: proceedings take place in three cities and nine languages. In keeping with such newness, the rules on coverage are more liberal than elsewhere, even encouraging reaction shots and film of the public gallery. (When Ian Paisley, a Northern Ireland member, pushed in front of Margaret Thatcher to display a poster in 1986, and interrupted the pope's speech in 1988, his demonstration was broadcast and made available on tape.) It is to the minutiae of such issues that I now turn.

We can gain a clearer idea of the subjectivities being produced within QTTV from a consideration of the protocols used to maintain control of parliamentary telegenics. I argue that this control is as crucially constitutive of the conditions of possibility for debate as are standing orders. Despite the intention behind them, these protocols are so at variance with the discourses of professionalism animating mainstream television that they make for a new kind of program and viewing subject.

Parliaments require control of how information about them is presented. The rules of Australian radio coverage, for example, preclude ABC announcers from mentioning the presence or absence of MPs. They are "confined to a straight description of procedure."[26] The putatively empty signifiers of "balance" and "value-free" talk mystify through their silences on crucial matters and valences on others; but they are at one with the process of constituting the electorate as needing a (carefully circumscribed) education-as-protection / protection-as-education.

Rules enunciated by the British Select Committee on Televising the Commons prohibited cutaway reaction shots, other than of those named in debate. Close-ups, shots of sleeping members, and wide-angle shots of empty seats were also proscribed. Disruption must automatically lead to a cutaway to the Speaker. These restrictions persuaded Channel Four to abandon plans for live telecasts, although the House decided to permit wide-angle shots in 1990 in order to increase the televisuality of the occasion. How should one read instructions that insist: "Coverage should give an unvarnished account of the proceedings of the House, free of subjective commentary and editing techniques designed to produce entertainment rather than information"?[27] This surely encourages a respectful, fearful distance on the part of the audience; a stately removal that is worlds distant from the participatory engagement of active citizenship. It stands in stark contrast to American ABC News President Roone Arledge's response to falling public interest in watching convention politics: "The two political parties should sit down on their own, or maybe with the networks, to come up with something more appealing to the American people."[28] The Iran-Contra hearings were said to be characterized by reaction shots that encouraged concern for Oliver North via cross-cutting between close-ups of him and medium shots of his questioners. The use of split screens set up congressional counsel in direct opposition to North, while a persistent high angle on him contrasted with low-angle shots of the committee. It was to get away from the very televisuality of this presentation that the Australian and British rules were brought into being.

What this once more illustrates is the tension between different forms of subject. On the one hand, we have the citizen in need of training, who must be shown the grandeur of constitutionally endorsed debate. The processes of filming, editing, and narration must not be anything "natural," in the sense of being ordered around action, display, or commentary, but must follow very strict procedures for the creation of the appearance of orderly work. On the other hand, we are seeing the subject as a consumer to be wooed, a subject who is a television watcher and sovereign for that reason. But emerging between and behind these, there is a further subject, who has perhaps all along been the key entity in need of reformation: the politician.

Consider guidelines on the use of file footage of proceedings issued by Australia's Joint Committee on the Broadcasting of Parliamentary Proceedings. These guidelines are similarly concerned about the unruly gazes of directors and publics. They insist on maintenance of continuity, avoidance of freeze frames, and a guarantee that material "not be used for the purposes of satire or ridicule."[29] And when the then Acting Speaker explained the presence of a film crew in the House in 1989, making a film to be shown to visiting schoolchildren, he was quick to emphasize that shooting had occurred during a division and that only a full House had therefore been revealed. This is part of a wider anxiety over the need to conceal any absence from duty that makes television a threat to MPs. The fear of a focus on reclining repose, or a neglect of the process and form of tradition or good governance in favor of visual style or investigative exposé, drives the debate over presentational protocols. This debate brings to the fore the figure of the professional politician as in need of cleansing and purging both of its own, presently flawed self and the distillation of that self by the media. A Senate bureaucrat's "Case for Television," made to a parliamentary seminar convened on the topic, included the promise that it would "eliminate possible selectivity in the media and similarly affect interpretive television journalists."[30]

One can see a striking and significant parallel in the *Rules for Film Documentation in Ethnology and Folklore* published by the West German Institute for the Scientific Film in 1959, which require that "filmmaking be done by persons with sound anthropological training or supervision, and that an exact log be kept; that the events recorded be authentic (technical processes can be staged for the camera, but not ceremonies), filmed without dramatic camera angles or movement, and edited for representativeness."[31]

The notion of "editing for representativeness" signals a fear of the camera as unrepresentative in its look. But more than that, there is a sense here that the gaze of the audience is powerful, minute, and expressly judgmental; that viewers are quite excoriating in their evaluative processes. They are able to pick up the merest blemish. It is, perhaps, the citizen who is also an MP who is the subject in need of redress. I shall consider this in the next section.

The actual output from the Australian Senate's QTTV has been quite different from the textbook ideal (not least in that it has attracted very low initial ratings). The story world of QTTV is conventional in narrative terms. An equilibrium is indicated, in which the president or acting president of the Senate announces Question Time. A disequilibrium occurs as speakers dispute and engage with each other, often in unruly ways. At the end of an hour, the presiding officer calls a close, and equilibrium is restored. We are returned to the state of the story that applied at the beginning of the program. As a credits marker of this, a parallelism is established between the introduction and the conclusion, with a fully groomed boy and girl opening and then closing doors to welcome and farewell us. In a lot of ways, then, this fits the description of *paléo-télévision,* a term coined to describe the era of institutionally defined television. It was a project founded on cultural and popular education, with the audience the subject of lessons delivered and controlled by television professionals. Francesco Casetti and Roger Odin identify three features characteristic of this form of pedagogic address. The first is that knowledge is transmitted from *savant* to *idiot.* The second is that this is achieved in a way that is based on the separation and hierarchization of roles. The third is that each program is a series of contracts offered to the spectator and a request to identify and be engaged in different ways according to the genre of the program and the age, interests, and taste of the viewer. The project seeks to structure people's days by calling up their interests and organizing them via flow (for example, Saturday is sport).[32]

At first glance, the purposes underlying televising parliament would seem to sit well within such a regime. But QTTV also breaks many rules of the continuity system. Apart from the usual oddities of outside broadcasts, the lack of fit between action and sound and disruption of shooting conventions make a case for QTTV to be acclaimed as an anti-realist text that questions the possibility of perfect knowledge on the part of the viewer. Cuts from speakers to interruptors frequently leave us with sound coming from off-screen while a truculent interjector is in-shot but silenced. When AIDS activists protested very vocally during QTTV in June 1991, they could not be filmed, even though MPs stopped talking to watch the disturbance. This was followed by a sermon from the Speaker of the House about due process and the need to balance democratic access with proper form. To the viewer, who had no idea of the nature of the disturbance to the program until it was reported in other media, this amounted to censorship. Only those outside the audience were denied access to the action engaging those within the text.

Most routinely dislocating of all is the refusal to abide by the hundred and eighty degree rule of camera placement. The Australian Film, Television and Radio School's recently released *Guide to Video Production* advises users to envisage an imaginary line between aspects of the mise-en-scène so that their camera positions will not cause objects to move to opposite sides of the frame in alternating shots. Crossing the line—deploying the circumference of a circle—will appear to make the action occur in reverse direction. The myth of seamless editing / realism is generally held to be threatened unless, in Graeme Turner's phrase, "the viewer is given a consistent representation of the spatial relations between the actors and their surroundings."[33]

QTTV radically subverts such conventions. Like a film by Yasujiro Ozu, it uses three hundred and sixty degrees, which makes it very hard to be clear about who is speaking; what his or her party position is; or, indeed, who is being addressed. The viewer is encouraged to work with the text. Dialectic shot / reverse shot relations *are* deployed to set up a duel between questioner and minister, but so are disruptive cutaways to MPs talking on the phone, laughing boy/girlishly, and reading. Wide-angle master shots dwarf the process. Shifting sound levels, graphics that identify speakers' affiliations by an isolated map of their state of origin, and a complete dissonance between the prearranged narcissism of government questions and the semi-spontaneous spleen of opposition ones, produce a quite hysterical program at a formal level, for all the apparent pomp. This is actually television of people at work, with all the non-Tayloristic chaos, as well as order, that implies. So its directors' attempts to get away from the tedium of talking heads disrupt the realist text (an apprehension doubly engaged by our knowledge that robots operate the cameras in what may be the biggest television production studio in the country). So much is available to produce so little that the outcome is excess. It is of little surprise, then, that QTTV has been attacked by the ABC's leading film reviewer for having "more production blunders than you'd really like to shake a stick at."[34] Such is its capacity to flaunt the conventions of the continuity system.

In short, this is more in the realm of *néo-télévision,* a form in which the pedagogic model is played with. Didacticism is displaced by interactive processes.[35] QTTV is a constant incitement for the spectator to interpret, because there is no commentary, no practice of coordinating the direction of sound and image, no context given to discordant discussion; and above all, there is no sense of anyone inside or outside the text being in a position of perfect knowledge. Perspective is an author, and perspective is clearly indicated as partial. This partiality goes beyond content. It goes to questions of form. The set of debating rules valorized by Habermas and exemplified in parliamentary law/lore is shown itself to have determining effects on what can be said, heard, and seen. The referent for debate is a complex combination of the history of the particular topic and the rules of the legislature. A topic can never be fully explicated on its own terms because of time constraints and the placement of questions without notice in the midst of specific controversies. Question Time functions as a technology that produces metacommentaries. These metacommentaries are set in the center of the controversies to which they allude, accusations and answers on the run to fetishized subsections of well-established areas of disagreement. The publics they address are confronted with disarray and the inevitability of a multiplicity of authorizing perspectives/constitutions of the problem under discussion. The combination of parliamentary and screen conventions is quite chaotic. As debate frequently organizes itself around the terms of debate themselves, and is always adjudicated by an officeholder, it is in authority, not process, that the form of communication finds its juridical ground. A recognition of this could see the spectator moving from being the subject of a technology and making a new self. Chapter 5 addresses such possibilities in another context.

Perhaps our referent here should be Lyotard's account of communication. Distanced from Habermas's valorization of process, it specifies distinctions between the referent, signification, addressee, and addresser of phrases. Each determines and is determined by its disposition alongside the others. No primacy is given to the purity of conditions for reasoning. Instead, like a political poster, the parliament becomes a model for a "desired treatment of social space"; but not a model for "perfect" communication.[36] Form is one more site of struggle rather than something that has an innate meaning and quality. The potential for a new treatment of space is also examined further in the final chapter.

The Well-Tempered Self

When QTTV began in Britain, there came with it an associated micro-politics of the body that provided a clue to the other subjectivity being produced here; for professional charm schools were hired to train MPs in deportment, debate, and habiliments. After the first day, a Conservative member stated that "some of the men—I happen to know—are carrying powder-puffs in their pockets to beautify their sallow complexions."[37] The rule restricting cameras to shots of the head and shoulders encouraged a past leader of the House to versify thus:

> The shampoo approach to public affairs
> Would not have us over the moon,
> With members less worried by currency scares
> Than comment from Vidal Sassoon.[38]

Who can forget U.S. House Speaker Tip O'Neill's sensational findings on television coverage of Democratic and Republican party conventions: "If a delegate was picking his nose, that's what you'd see. . . . No wonder so many of us were skittish"?[39] It is easy to write this off as characteristic masculine and institutional vanity, pomposity, and tightness. But the issue of manners and appearance is a critical one. Consider the following from an Australian senator, spoken when the decision to commence the trial was taken: "It is a very common practice for the Ministers and people on the other side to stand in the way that men do and put their feet up on the furniture. I find it appalling. The furniture belongs to the Australian people and the Australian people will see those feet on the furniture, if parliament is televised."[40] It is just this element of concern that motivates others as well. In opposing the televising of proceedings, the manager of government business in the Senate made telling parody of Parliament's attempt to constrain reuse of file tape: "The producers cannot use an excerpt to satirise and ridicule anyone. Half the clowns who jump up here ridicule and satirise themselves. Does that mean half the senators are never going to get any television exposure?"[41] Conversely, the opposition whip argued that "Senators normally hope to encounter television in the course of their work and they should be dressed for it."[42] This respectful attitude of obedience to the aesthetic of the medium—here, one senses that television *is* the electorate, that it is metonymic for the voter—is in a constant state of tension with the view that televising Parliament will trivialize it. But more than that, there is a multifaceted ambivalence at play: television is all-powerful as an instrument of apathy; television is all-powerful as an instrument of education; television is evil; television is our salvation; and television is the ultimate arbiter of the fitness and style of MPs.

Such concerns have a long lineage. Theodore Roosevelt advised his successor, William Howard Taft, to police mechanical reproductions of himself very carefully: "photographs on horseback, yes; tennis, no. And golf is fatal."[43] And even the developmental stages of television in the 1920s saw suggestions that presidential candidates would come to use television for their campaigns. From Dwight Eisenhower on, it became standard for U.S. presidents to employ professional consultants on televisual presentation and deportment. Robert Montgomery's duties for Eisenhower ranged from locations to cosmetics, from the inaugural televised cabinet meeting to the wardrobe departure of white suits and striped shirts. Reagan staff policed his archival image with great care, preventing the Dick Clark Company from airing outtakes of his acting errors. A bizarre movement, between the jazzy and the dour, the exotic and the conventional, is required of television politicians and those who mind them. We can see traces of this in the observation by the Speaker of the Canadian House that "televisual MPs are at the top of the whips' list" because "performers" are preferred to "the thoughtful."[44] In an Anglo-Saxon democracy, successful politicians need to be simultaneously glamorous and pure. "But he can't be president if he's had sex," Madonna objected on hearing a rumor that Donald Trump was campaigning for the presidency, but she later relented, conceding that the country might sometimes even be keen to elect "a guy with a dick."[45]

To return to my earlier point about the supposed lameness of party politics, this concern with telegenics is particularly interesting in the context of Parliament's will to find its own significance. The countercyclical attempt to rein in executive power that has been a recurring theme in the auto-panegyrics of parliamentary bureaucrats and romantic political scientists is as much about control of the image as anything else. But it is founded on contradictory understandings of the image. Consider a recent *Business Week* cover story on the problems associated with the U.S. Congress as a democratic forum, which lauds the passion and commitment that come from ideological positions policed by strong party machines, lamenting that "in the television age, political organizations are withering."[46] This calls into question the idea, popular in Britain and Australia, of a necessary nexus between centralized party power and an ignorant electorate vulnerable to television.

It is meet to think here about the *Code of Ethics* that has been promulgated for the producer of Australia's QTTV, the Sound and Vision Office. The *Code* advises that the Office operates in "the special and sensitive context of serving the Parliament" and that its staff must conduct themselves at all times in ways that "respect the institution of the Parliament."[47] Just as the people most affected by Watergate on television were said to be its principal actors and those who followed them, so the real subjects of television, the people genuinely "affected" by its gaze, are the politicians. They, after all, are the product.

In arguing that televising Parliament would increase the standard of debate, the leader of the opposition in the Australian Lower House maintained: "You would only oppose a decision like that if you had something to hide."[48] Similarly, it has been suggested that QTTV will have the long-term effect of rendering Question Time less vilificatory but also more cautious; a way of halting the decline in "classic parliamentary principles and behaviour."[49] Research into the impact that televising the House of Lords has had since 1985 suggests that the practice has altered the people on-screen much more than those watching it. In the Commons, speeches from the front bench have increased in length, backbenchers' time has been more carefully policed, and the minor parties have been marginalized at Question Time.

The critical point is this: since the Parliament and its apparatchiks—along with the rest of us—are so divided about what television *is,* they need to concentrate on treating what they presumably *can* know—that is, themselves. Max Harris saw in QTTV a "sea of nonentities" without any "sense of . . . self-absurdity."[50] And *Blitz* magazine's survey of the new Commons television coverage found a "hopeless dominance of custom over democratic function."[51] In a world where no one can decide whether television is God, Beelzebub, or A. N. Other, perhaps the real regime of education needs to be that between parliamentary institutions and themselves, their self-interrogatory auto-critique and reformation before the mythic public. This much may already be clear from the force of QTTV. For it stands as sturdy evidence for the need to reshape the viewed subject, not the viewing. It has already provided us with "a visible scenario, that one can see, like proof in a court of law," as Godard might say.[52] It is a scenario that offers hilarity through incomprehension and abnormality to the viewer; as Godard himself might once have wished, and as the unruly subjects of self-invention examined in my concluding chapter have sought to produce. But prior to moving on to the operation of a technology of the self, I want to look at the subject of cultural policy that has the most obvious already-extant claims to autonomy: the construction known as the desiring consumer, devouring and reconstituting the materials of supply and demand economics.

Authorship and the Public Speech

Macrosetting

In 1985, three public speeches were given by Brian Pickett and Trevor Prescott, members of the now-defunct National Training Council (NTC). The council existed to advise the Australian Federal Government on labor force training policies and programs via a tripartite structure incorporating representatives of capital, labor, and the state. Its charter required it to assist in the development, operation, promotion, and funding of training, its claim to legitimacy residing in this three-way "partnership." The list of full and deputy members of the NTC from 1982 to 1984 decomposes and informs this rhetoric: six representatives of small to medium-scale business enterprises, six business bureaucrats, four trade union bureaucrats, three state government bureaucrats, six federal bureaucrats, and two Technical and Further Education (TAFE) bureaucrats. In terms of "grass-roots" experience of delivering, receiving, and paying for training, such people are prima facie spectacularly unqualified. They perform, rather, representational functions, standing for aggregated groups and peak organizations. In any case, despite claims to being an "independent, tripartite, national body," the council effectively functioned to voice and sanction the free market philosophy of the then Department of Employment and Industrial Relations (DEIR), favoring "competency-based training as opposed to time-serving" that would signal the needs of consumers to providers.[53] (The NTC was succeeded by a more formalized and coordinated version of the same: the National Board of Employment, Education and Training was established on a statutory footing. The latter body's inclusion of education is an important development, of which more later.) It is best to begin with some biographical and conceptual context to the authors of the speeches under review, because of the critical effect of their names and status as both determining and determined structures of the conditions within which "their" words were produced, circulated, and consumed.

In addition to his role on the NTC, Brian Pickett was a member of the Kirby Committee of Inquiry into Labour Market Programs. The Kirby Committee recommended that the Australian government set up a new method of structured vocational preparation for jobs outside the trades, jobs not covered by the apprenticeship system or professional accreditation/credentialism. All of these duties were against Pickett's backdrop as a personnel manager with Email Australia, a "white goods" manufacturer. Trevor Prescott, deputy chair of the NTC and chair of the TAFE Research and Development Centre, ran a car-fleet maintenance service. Both men exemplified the multifaceted subject of latter-day capital, working as they did not only for their companies as executives (the particular self-good) but also for the reproduction of certain forms of social relations by expressing a "business perspective" as "industry persons" (the general civic good). This perspective was presented in both consultative roles (advising government through the council) and coopted neocorporatist ones (making public statements under the NTC's public banner of tripartism).

To give these speeches an economic location will help to indicate that they derive from somewhere quite other than the individual experience of "industry persons," while calling up and demonstrating that category of knowledgeable subject as their warrant. They should first be situated within an understanding of the lengthy historical interconnection of business and government in Australia, via the granting of land, the early allocation of convict labor, and the frequent stimulation of particular economic sectors. A series of international recessions and trade conflicts since 1974 has produced inflation and unemployment, rocky financial markets, unstable commodity prices and balance-of-payments deficits for the Australian economy, developments that have provided further stimulus towards cooperative links. Successive Australian governments have sought the input of labor and capital into the development of programs of intervention in the economy. The aim is to organize the simultaneous advent of certain tendencies that theoretically only occur sequentially in a pure market economy: a decline in unemployment and inflation; an orderly restructuring of industry under the sign of comparative advantage; and an increase in investment. Of course, these tendencies are far from unique to Australia. In Britain, for instance, to indicate how caring and sharing capital could be, Sir Alastair Pilkington and others formed a group called Business in the Community, which developed what it called "corporate community involvement policies" as part of "enlightened self-interest" at a time of economic and social crisis.[54] There was an equally clear trend in North America from the early 1970s on toward bringing business closer and closer to the heart of policymaking.

Australia moved quite distinctly to the global margin during the

1980s because of its reliance on export commodities with small value-added components. Repeated economic crises saw a concentrated and continuing critique of the local education system, which went hand in hand with an obsessive reliance on it. This was identical to public policy responses to the depressions of the 1890s and 1930s. Doctrines of human capital, of calculating economic subjects who would respond to being given informational skills by maximizing their own potential, became crucial investments in an economy of policy discourse that presumed to train as it responded, simultaneously adopting the postures of knowing what is best for others and of acting in the name of the rational consumer.

This is another expression of the eighteenth-century rehabilitative project (in that case managed through a combination of work and isolation) that sought to "rearrange not only the complex of interests proper to *homo oeconomicus,* but also the imperatives of the moral subject."[55] It also saw the formation of a singular subject that could express and in some sense unite the divided national self. One might point here to the way in which the independent entrepreneur was valorized in North America toward the close of the nineteenth century as a civil society exemplar of the success that every person could realistically aspire to emulate by virtue of being a citizen of the United States. Such rhetoric served to work through the tensions identified by Simmel in his analysis of the transformation of primitive societies into modern ones. For Simmel, the old, cohesive world of collective identification and sociability was displaced by the institutionalization of money. The new system of exchange encouraged a substitutability of person and labor that encouraged individuality even as it established itself as the most social of currencies.[56] Hence the need to institute a supposed unity of civic and economic subjectivities. That unity is now integral to the processes of policy.

Prescott and Pickett stood for the reunification of the economic and civic subjects, subjects split along psychological, policy, and disciplinary lines for all their mutual origin in Hobbes, Locke, and Mill. Some confusion results from the consequent need to yoke together rational citizens who think of the greater good of the greater number and rational consumers who valorize themselves. Both are called up by this set of policy desires inside the one subject. The subject must be taught to distinguish between public goods, where one person's consumption does not preclude another's, and private goods, where it does. This is to instate doctrines of civility as collective and doctrines of commodity as singular. It is a technology for dividing those areas that are to be the objects of policy discussion (public goods) from those that are basically the province of inviolable, undebatable protection via the law of property (private goods). One might rephrase the issue more prosaically by calling into question the ahistorical nature of free trade, free consumer, free business, free market logic for its fantasy of countries without societies or governments. (Hong Kong may be the only example of such an arrangement, the outcome of a unique colonial pattern.) From the beginnings of laissez-faire as an analytic doctrine, it has always suffered from what Comte regarded as the substitution of the "barren aphorism of absolute industrial liberty" for consideration of material practice and history.[57]

This sphere of methodological self-legislation is classically epistemic, so much so that Weber used it as an example of the problems connected with reasoning through ideal types, a process that selectively picks up on certain types of observed conduct and then repackages them as sealed systems of interlocking logic. Such systems are internally consistent, but they depend on bracketing like with like to the exclusion of other factors of conduct unsuitable to their purity of analytic synthesis, or *Gedankenbild*.[58] For example, neoclassicism depends on the certainty that consuming decisions are made entirely outside the influence of producers and via an unalloyed, absolute rationality. Two discourses of the subject, which are conventionally left separate, run across one another here. They have enormous internal contradictions and may often be mutually exclusive. But they are presented, as Marx said of marginalist economics, as ideas "independent of history . . . natural laws of society *in abstracto*."[59] Both discourses are imaginary states of grace, which must be exemplified in order to be replicated in lived history. The attempts to create popular interest in operating within markets and democracies that began in the Soviet Union in the late 1980s exemplify the need to manufacture the putatively natural in these domains. It was the work of the public speeches under review in this chapter to spread just such a process as widely as possible.

Speeches as Texts

Prescott's speech to the printing industry forum, like the others under discussion here, was produced in the period immediately following the release of the Kirby Committee's Report and—significantly—the government's announcement of its intention to construct an Australian Traineeship System (ATS). The talk begins by praising the printing industry as one that "has always adjusted effectively." This is immediately linked to a preparedness to invest in training.[60]

Although a different form of politics would not unify labor and capital as one subject with one interest under the rubric of "industry," because of their differing practices and relationships to the means of production, Prescott's formulation presumes an axiomatic and indisputable unity. Notwithstanding that the two positions would appear to be at odds, Prescott proceeds to argue paradoxically that training can only be undertaken because it pays, but that capital must have a sense of corporate responsibility that transcends the profit motive and acknowledges the needs of the individual undergoing training. He calls on employers to enunciate their requirements clearly to providers of training in order to ensure its relevance, particularly in the developing areas outside the trades.[61]

There is, in this sense, a recognition of the macroeconomic move away from a materially productive industrial structure and toward consumption capitalism, but of course this kind of language is not employed. In keeping with Prescott's function as enunciator/lobbyist of capital-inflected state policy, he provides the requisite advertisement for traineeships. They "are not just another labour market program. Rather, they herald an entirely new training system." Of course, the new system must be constituted within the logic of oneness, of industrial unity, that was mentioned above: "The responsibility for training and retraining must be shouldered jointly by all parties: governments, employers and employees should all play their part."[62]

A collaborative model of mutual interest and action (semi-planned and negotiated, semi-self-interested) is the implicit driving force of this logic. In particular, the claim that employees will benefit from the ATS, and should therefore contribute toward its cost, is an implicit rejection or ignorance of the possibilities of a labor theory of value: "The three parties are partners in training, locked in a cycle of mutual need." At the same time, Prescott acknowledges divisions within this industrial self. He sets up a fraction of the state—the TAFE system—as a vendor to capital: "It is offering a service. That service must be attuned to what the marketplace decrees."[63]

Pickett's speech, to a conference on the hardware industry, displays similar concerns. It describes the NTC as "bringing the partners in industry together." Tripartism "mirrors the responsibility for training that the social partners share." The emphasis is on the council as a body that formalizes what is already there. An implicit functionalist streak is already emerging from both these talks, premised on putatively mutual

The Well-Tempered Self

interests and desires. This mystifies the debates and material conflicts going on between and within the so-called "social partners." For despite their consanguinity, it remains the case that training must be developed and delivered in the direction dictated by capital. So training should be "more relevant for the enterprise and the individual"; the "private sector is the leading edge of technological innovation. It is best placed to address the training needs which it generates."[64]

The meaning of *industry*, a term used throughout these speeches, becomes clearer at this point: at the level of the power and legitimacy to make and enunciate decisions, *industry* means capital. But when it comes to funding the process, this responsibility lies with the now-familiar "partners." Like Prescott in his printing address, Pickett proselytizes on behalf of traineeships, because they promise reduced youth wages and an "adaptable workforce."[65]

Prescott's second speech was addressed to a conference on "the changing context of TAFE." Introducing himself as "an industry person," he provides further clarification of the term, via an implicit differentiation of industry from labor; the latter is required to mold itself to "the needs and realities of the marketplace." He proceeds to acknowledge that equitable public policy outcomes are a national priority: "But as an industry person, I have to place the greatest emphasis on efficiency." Here there is some recognition of the division within the disinterested citizen who is also a business executive. But the stress on the knowledge of the workplace guarantees other concerns as well. Prescott asserts that "TAFE needs to see industry as a consumer to be wooed and satisfied, not a captive user." He is critical of "education moguls," arguing that "overly academic approaches, with the attendant luxuries of time and minimal consequent responsibility, are inappropriate . . . we must beware any attempt to pad out skills training courses with pseudo-relevant educational components."[66]

The consumer must be all-powerful. This is the consumer of public education in the name of its own business efficiency as a corporate entity. Its operations are sharply distinguished from the notions of the "well-rounded person" imbued with "life-skills" (such as citizenship / civic conduct?) that the educating subject is held to desire to impart to others. The way to avoid this educationalism is through a system of "consumer sovereignty . . . a fee-for-service method which would encourage greater responsiveness, putting TAFE more clearly in the marketplace."[67] TAFE is to be reformed, from educationalism to vocationalism, by the imposition of a new system of allocating resources to it, a system that rewards popularity rather than civic delivery in the name of improving others. The new system redisposes TAFE from a disinterested subject that caters to broad social design into a semi-person, semi-business entity that is competitive. Such a system is opposed to automatic recurrent funding of TAFE by the state. Instead, it favors a structure driven by demand from the users of training. (DEIR was pushing this line at the time and giving grants to business with which to purchase TAFE courses of its choice; the significance of this conjuncture of Prescott and DEIR will be explicated below.) The clear implication is that civics, or person-building—the task of creating a socially responsible citizen—is either irrelevant to this domain or will occur naturally through learning to be a docile worker. Skills are abilities tailored to jobs, and skills must be the basis of learning. The rigor of market economics requires the "discharge of business according to *calculable rules*" and "without regard for persons . . . in the pursuit of naked economic interest," to use Weber's phrase.[68]

Authorship

Within the domain of literary studies, it is a commonplace to problematize authorship. Everybody knows that the author might now be a "what" rather than a "who," and that he, she, or it is far outnumbered and outsignified by readers; or if they do not hold to this, "everybody" inside literary studies knows that a case has to be made against it. But the burden of decades spent institutionalizing the category of the author as the creative, imagining—and responsible—heart of texts continues to be carried in much of the history of thought and, of course, in everyday logics of attribution. In opposition to this, factors such as genre, history, popular discourse, audiences, publishing/speaking conditions, institutions of interpretation, and components of the very forms of texts are increasingly being deployed in the task of critical writing by a scholarship that abjures strategies seeking the origins of texts in the individual biographies of their authors. Such approaches contend that to read texts using orthodox critical procedures is to under-read. Privileging the category of personal experience as the lodestone of writing involves buying into a particular moment in textual history, specifically the emergence of authorial discourse as part of the rise of Romantic aesthetics in the nineteenth century and its later modification and professionalization in the Leavisite search for the best novel by the best of souls at his or her personal best. In place of this, there is a certain tendency now toward an examination of how particular sites and practices in fact produce the author, via an apparatus of critique and ped-agogy. This examination frequently extends beyond a consideration of the formal characteristics of texts—the repeated, regular components that can be discerned across a range of compositions—and asks how texts circulate, the contexts in which they are known, and the rules that govern their interpretation. Such an approach contends that technolo-gies produce authorship, technologies of interview, criticism, publicity, and curriculum, and that even purportedly personal inspirations must intersect with a set of conventions for telling stories.

Yet it would be quite wrong to suggest that authorship as a category is ended or irretrievably problematized. The reinstatement of inten-tionality under the aegis of Donald Davidson and doctrines of "the greats" has even been matched by structuralist recantations derived from the category of experience. Saunders and Hunter argue that authorship continues to be a "magnetic topic for literary studies" because of its fecund play with the author as either an "exemplary consciousness" or a point of articulation for "unconscious determinations that bring this consciousness into being and speak through it." Each of these modes is central to a cultural approach to accounting for subjectivity.[69]

For the purposes of this chapter, there is great significance in the reasons for the intense anxiety induced by problematizing authorship. David Lodge, for example, has attacked Foucault for discrediting the author because he believes that this also serves to discredit humanism and the Enlightenment and thereby the freedoms associated with them: freedoms to speak, worship, and move about. Lodge instances the case of Milan Kundera, who lost his Czech citizenship because of his writ-ings and then came to act as a symbol of resistance in a way that would not have been available to anonymous discourse.[70] This case could, of course, be analyzed from a Foucauldian perspective. Such an analysis would concentrate exactly on how "Milan Kundera" is made to circu-late via certain institutions and forms of knowledge and recognize the political significance of that. But it is easy to see how the anti-subjec-tivity of the "new theory" is writ large in the responses of its oppo-nents, because of the uses to which the human subject's "instincts," "feelings," and "rights" have been put in cultural-capitalist and popu-list discourse as signs underpinning and exemplifying doctrines of free-dom. The continuing impact of overlapping notions of originality, pla-giarism, and individual worth expressed in doctrines of authorship is evident in recent controversies surrounding the written work and per-sonal character of Martin Luther King, Jr.

Locating responsibility for a text in the name appearing on its cover tends to downgrade other forces shaping it, because of the associated tendency to decipher the place of its "real" meaning as contained in the author's imagination and experience and their distillation. The author is held to form a text individually. In the case of Prescott and Pickett, their pronouncements use a number of disparate legitimating forces. Contradictorily, as "industry people," they claim personal experience and enlightened self-interest / possessive individualism as generators of authenticity, while their positions on the council establish them as concerned for the greater public good. As exemplars of successful selfishness, they can become exemplars of successful selflessness. This is a happy resolution of Rousseau's dilemma of how to make the consuming subject's "profit in the misfortunes of his neighbour" mesh with broader community needs.[71] And the technology for this resolution is one of authorship. Reconsidering Foucault on authorship illustrates that he had no problem with the argument that it "is legitimate to ask whether a person whose work manifests a certain set of modifications was a genius." But to research in such a way—and only in that way—is not sufficient as a procedure of analysis because it disenfranchises discourse in the act of centering the subject, at the price of understanding: the field of possibilities confronting that subject; its constitution; and its practice of writing.[72] Hence the need to locate authorship within concerns such as Rousseau's, when this practice of writing addresses civic issues.

In what sense did Pickett or Prescott "write" these texts? They were, of course, based on the product of the NTC's secretariat, an arm of DEIR. As such, they represent a negotiated situation, a set of meanings born of the meeting between different forms of knowledge. The hands on the keys were those of middle-ranking bureaucrats, in their part-time mode as professional public sector writers. They were producing words that the private sector could speak in order to endorse what these fractions of the public sector needed to have authorized as authentically private. Such bureaucrats were borrowing from a departmental rhetoric that both informed and was derived from the council's logic on training matters. Neoclassical economics here functions as a discursive tactic that is used variously, but never with the aim of a complete evocation of its logic in material policy. In the case of the speeches under review, the tactic is a balancing act between the very poles of public subjectivity that bring its purism into doubt. The backdrop in this case is of DEIR using its relationship with private sector employers to articulate a market-oriented opposition to the civics currriculum favored by the then Department of Education and academic educationalists.

The NTC secretariat effectively published an "industry" person's "thoughts," following a departmental approval process. Pickett and Prescott would certainly have read drafts prior to accepting their speeches for verbal delivery, and may indeed have proposed certain amendments. It would be misleading to imply that they were duped by officials, that they either did not understand or did not concur with the positions they enunciated. But it is similarly misleading for them to be positioned as "authors," as this denies the actual process of production. What little we know about how such speeches are written suggests a multiple authorship.

Since the revelation that Larry Speakes invented "quotations" from Ronald Reagan, there should be greater public awareness of the dangers inherent in denying this kind of multiply constructed practice of writing and attribution of knowledge. The *Washington Post* was moved by that incident to editorialize thus: "For years, speeches that were never given were made to seem in the Congressional So-Called Record as if they had been. Ghosts write reams of prose purported to have originated with someone else."[73] One is drawn here to Gerald Ford's splendid distinction between the acceptable and the unacceptable in this area. Speaking at a conference on press-presidential relations, he felt able to term it "totally wrong" for a press secretary to attribute a statement to the president he had never made. But "the press secretary oftentimes has better phraseology than the President. And if that, in the mutual discussion, ends up in what the President says, there's nothing wrong with that."[74]

This matters. It matters both because, in the case of the DEIR-endorsed speeches, it distorts the role of bureaucracy in enunciating and creating a free market doctrine; and because it buys into authorizing logics that may be quite inapplicable. Peggy Noonan, who wrote some of Ronald Reagan's most notable speeches, has argued that "speechwriting in the Reagan White House was where the philosophical, ideological and political tensions of the Administration got worked out. . . . Speechwriting was where the Administration got invented every day."[75] In reviewing her book on the subject, the *Economist* felt compelled to ask: "Should a speechwriter, however gifted, really make policy?"[76] The question received further attention following George Bush's 1991 speech denouncing Lyndon Johnson's "Great Society" programs. As controversy mounted, its "real author," a speechwriter, was interviewed to give Bush's remarks the correct interpretation: the administration's view of Medicare, Medicaid, food stamps, consumer protection and auto safety legislation, voting rights, and federal aid for schools was, he said, "more complex and nuanced than the speech suggested."[77] This need to call on the original begetter of such rhetoric should be of little surprise; a speechwriter for Bush is also said to have remarked that "the man doesn't know how to use verbs."[78] Perhaps not surprisingly, this is the president who mistakenly autographed an unemployment benefits book handed to him by a protester during the 1992 primaries.

The anti-educationalist, laissez-faire rhetoric appearing under the names of Pickett and Prescott needs to be seen both as the outcome of speechwriting and as part of a discursive system. This system is a network of power that has material effects on education policies, programs, and administrative arrangements, premised in part on incorporating a particular form of *doxa* in public statements as tools of circulation and naturalization. Suffice it to say that Prescott's speech was well-received at the printing industry symposium ("it's realistic" and "he knows about the real world of business" were representative comments). Conversely, a speech delivered at the same forum by a DEIR bureaucrat with a Ph.D. was derogated ("not in the real world in Canberra"; "he's too academic"). Both speeches were based on contributions by the same officer of DEIR/NTC, and written within a particular form of neoclassical discourse. The public response to their delivery is indicative of the propensity to accord statements the value of truth because of the category of person making them, a displacement of public function onto personal capacity that Richard Sennett notes as characteristic of the times.[79] It further indicates the importance of the authorizing function provided by Pickett and Prescott and the complex nature of the circulation of economically rational subjectivity.

Economic Subjectivity

Wages have traditionally been set within advanced industrial cultural-capitalist democracies through a rapprochement between the discourses of civics and consumption, which as I have indicated are typically in need of some separation, at least rhetorically. The sheer productive power and share of the market available to such countries once offered something of a license to set the price of labor in response to bargaining and questions of equity. This was part of a design to remove humanness from the factor costs of production, to render the exploitation of people external to the calculation of distribution and planning. But the swing toward neoclassicism that accompanied the downturn in the economic fortunes of these states internationalized their calculus of labor, making it clearly superordinate to citizenship. Henceforth, "productivity wages would align on what is now the world shadow price for labour, i.e. subsistence, given the enormous and growing global labour surplus."[80] The marginalists claim that this subsistence level of wages will be only temporary, but it was, of course, something predicted as an enduring future crisis by Ricardo. Before Marx, before Trotsky, before Mandel, Ricardo saw the long-term propensity for wages to fall.

The apparently straightforward nature of neoclassicism makes it attractive when compared with much other social theory. It is founded on the congenially familiar unit of the person, the Benthamite utilitarian who operates from self-interest (in Mill's felicitous phrase, "the self-regarding virtues.")[81] The actions of this rational maximizer spread from the individual to all economic organizations, making for a long-term equilibrium between supply and demand that forms a perfect market. But even some of the *Ur*-texts of nonintervention raise doubts about the desirability of an educational system driven by consumer sovereignty. For Mill

> utility does not consist in ministering to inclinations. . . . This is peculiarly true of those things which are chiefly useful as tending to raise the character of human beings . . . any well-intentioned and tolerably civilized government may think without presumption that it does or ought to possess a degree of cultivation above the average of the community which it rules, and that it should therefore be capable of offering better education and better instruction to the people, than the greater number of them would spontaneously demand.[82]

The dominant model of consumer choice, the market metaphor, has become so pervasive that it is a convenient carriage for a host of aims. As Sandford Borins has noted in the Canadian context, "the notion of self-interested, utility-maximising rational choice . . . has vigorously entered general discourse, even if it goes by other names."[83] Despite the relative recency of its appearance as technical orthodoxy and common sense, neoclassical dogma lays claim to a transcendental apprehension of the subject as a desiring and calculating machine. This assertion should be understood, not by its claim to an absolute truth, but in the light of the specific conditions that have led to its success as a mode of producing and circulating knowledge (paradigm shifts in economics faculties in conjunctural relationship to capitalist crises) and shifts in its internal rules of signification (specifically, what it does about the political subject).

What is needed here is an epistemic appreciation of "technologies and techniques of representation."[84] Such an appreciation encourages investigation of the particular truth-effect of particular axioms and practices; in other words, it drives us to see that the realism of a given form of knowledge will always be constituted within its own rules of evidence and method. Neoclassical economics now becomes a historicized system of narration, to be contemplated by reference to the conditions under which it arose and its own rules (the theoretical rigor of an imagined market) but also by other rules (rules that render the human subject a possible member of a class, a gender, or an ethnic group prior to being a consumer). Like utilitarianism itself, the model is rooted in the exercise of technologies of power that produce a particular type of subject. Its narrative is about a desiring subject that wants goods and services. Other desiring subjects seek to meet those desires and compete for the return promised.

As a first step in unpacking the history of the use of this narrative in the making of public policy, we need to consider the anthropomorphization of "the economy," whose popular public identification as a subject with needs and desires dates from the Great Depression. Attention was drawn away at that time from discussing relations between producers and consumers of goods (an industrial relations discourse on the part of the popular newspapers that was in fact at odds with conventional economics) to relations between different material products of labor, with a similar shift from use-value to exchange-value. The discursive commodities "the economy" and "the market," themselves now valorized signs, became transformed into agents with their own needs. With the crisis of the 1930s and the popularization of the ideas of John Maynard Keynes, "the economy" entered popular knowledge.

Keynesianism was discredited in the 1970s by stagflation: inflation combined with stagnant demand and high unemployment. It was supplanted as a dominant discourse first by monetarism and then by neoclassical economics. The latter "asserts that *market* forces typically unleash growth, innovation and efficiency, whereas *governmental* regulations and expenditures impede growth, stifle productivity and entrepreneurship and generate inefficiencies in both the private and public sectors."[85]

There are echoes here of the Pickett speech's insistence on the private sector as the epicenter of innovation, a product of competition. But Pickett and his "real writer" were following on from the conversion of a whole range of professional economists in colleges, governments, banks, and so on. (A study of the Australian government's senior management has found that 42 percent favor less state provision and "more individual initiative" and 52 percent support deregulation of the labor market.)[86]

Now it is clearly the case that entering the logic of the imaginary market manufactures its own particular rules of what can and cannot be said, as per Weber's notion of the ideal type mentioned above. It is interesting to note the comments of the 1987 Nobel laureate in Economics, Robert Solow, in response to criticism of his practice of parodying the neoclassical school instead of debating it on "technical" grounds: "Suppose someone sits down where you are sitting right now and announces that he is Napoleon Bonaparte. The last thing I want to do with him is to get involved in a discussion of cavalry tactics at the battle of Austerlitz. . . . Now . . . [the neoclassicists] like nothing better than to get drawn into technical discussions because you have tacitly gone along with their fundamental assumptions."[87]

In other words, a "respected" economist is simply not in the same world of language as these people; but their doctrine is nevertheless applied as a revealed truth, not a contested logic, both by most professional economists in Australia and in the discourse of the speeches under review. The dominance of market faith is such that speechwriters and journalists conventionally query trade union power, but not big business power; and that they propose reductions in government activity that neglect the positive role that might be played by increases in state services. Thea Lee offers an important account of the internal inconsistencies of neoclassical economics, in addition to its absence of referentiality in the realm of the real. The established rhetorical move is to provide assumptions about markets that have never existed, but that might in a good world. But if firms really do seek to maximize profits, as is conventionally asserted, then there would never be the equilibrium countenanced and desired by a disinterested, civic public policy, because such firms would never be satisfied by Paretian optimality (in which no other result than the one obtaining could occur without some participants in a transaction losing out).[88]

There is a stolid determination within the discourse of neoclassicism. The executive director of the New Zealand Business Roundtable knows, for example, that Keynesianism is not a theory because it is tied to "the circumstances of the 1930s" (for which read that it is anchored in material history). He also knows that unfettered markets lead to social equality and that "the first duty of the economist-adviser is to be a seeker of truth" dedicated to "increasing knowledge" and the correction of "wrong ideas . . . errors . . . [and] mistakes." Similarly, the official Australian statistician and ex-secretary of the Department of Finance, Ian Castles, fancies "scientific economics."[89] The warrant here is access to an absolute, transcendental, technical truth, with no history and no politics either to its object of study or to itself as a regime of knowledge, other than as a neo-Whiggish coming-into reality and the freedom to know.

The Australian Treasury has been a critical point of neoclassical advocacy, ensuring a gradual growth of interest in relative prices as determinants in the allocation of resources: the consumer as sovereign. Under the Labor government of the mid 1970s, economists spread through other government departments and instrumentalities, a trend that has developed since. A new subject of policy, one that is called upon as a justification grounded in its desiring rationality, has emerged to stalk the needy, political, and civic subject of other discourses. And this discourse has become pervasive through much of the Australian community. As an Australian Treasurer put it, "In every pet shop in Australia, the resident galah [a type of cockatoo] is talking about micro-economic reform." Meaghan Morris argues that the successful career of neoclassicism should be understood as "a politics of consent depending not on mass spectacles or massifying events, but on a continual assertion of the magic of expertise—on eroticized images of teaching, learning, (controlled) debate, (limited) consultation, and exquisite mastery of data."[90]

This politics continually stresses the power of the state to enunciate its own demise, at least rhetorically, in the name of modernization. Castles, for example, is very keen to indicate the disinterested practices of bureaucratic economists. He insists that the Treasury has never been run by people from ruling-class backgrounds. But the survey of senior managers cited above demonstrates a close correlation between privilege of background and opposition to state participation in the economy (and vice versa). Senior officers of the Treasury were four times more likely to have attended expensive fee-paying schools than representatives of other departments analyzed and were keenest on nonintervention. The spread of neoclassical economics is indicated by the fact that 54 percent of the group surveyed had degrees in economics, business, or accounting. There is precious little room for alternative paradigms here, or indeed for narratives invested in other than the factor endowments and preferences of unified individuals. It is significant that the weekly magazine *Australian Business* reported the survey's findings about support for the market while ignoring its data on class.[91]

Of course, significant differences exist within and between different departments. Coming from representatives of fractions of capital with different interests (for example, farmers and manufacturers on the question of tariffs), it could hardly be otherwise. But the key point here is the overall rhetorical impact of a broad market logic on instruments for popularizing the consuming subject, as in the talks under review.

This has been especially crucial in discursive distinctions between "education" and "training" and the struggles between their institutional bearers, who have set up a binary divide polarizing the civic and the employable subject via the concept of human capital. I have already shown how the NTC fought a battle for other public sector training bodies to offer courses in line with the requirements of business rather than any concentration on a core curriculum dedicated to such concepts as personal development, social responsibility, or generalized pedagogic notions of citizen-building. And the Kirby Committee on which Pickett served did "not consider it useful to make a distinction between education and training."[92] Such positions inform the entire shift in power relations between the federal bureaucracy and actual providers of tertiary education. The demise of the "arm's-length" source of advice on policy and funding, the Commonwealth Tertiary Education Commission (CTEC), was announced late in 1987. It resulted from the pressure exerted by DEIR and others via arguments founded on the same premise as the Kirby Committee's. Here, "really useful knowledge" finds the consuming subject to be specifiable and the civic subject less recognizable. Just as funds that DEIR gave to business to purchase courses from TAFE had increased from A $0.6 million in 1981 to A $12.1 million in 1984, so lines of force were being redrawn discursively and administratively. CTEC was effectively excluded from providing a broad social perspective to the development of traineeships. Person-building citizenship was to be a side product of the needs of employers, presumably. DEIR became known for its successful promulgation of neoclassicism because it "advocated a narrow job-specific approach and had a reputation for regarding students as 'units of labour.'"[93]

DEIR may well have used NTC vocalists in just the same way, as units of labor enunciating the tropes of the sovereign consumer and the concerned citizen / experienced businessperson within a universalist discourse of economic "science." The precise significance of such speeches is twofold. In the first place, they illustrate broader theoretical and public policy trends to do with disciplinary fashion. And secondly, they are a means of popularizing *doxa* without the attendant negativity of any association with the bureaucracy or academia. This does valuable service to populist notions of the market in general and the need for business-oriented training in particular. Clearly, the origins of these speeches lay in DEIR distillations of neoclassicism, not in the names that authorized them. But DEIR required private sector authorization by virtue of its own rules of truthfulness.

The subject produced by these two narratives is split. It is divided between its selfish self and its public-spirited self. The peculiar task required of the civic subject is to know when it should throw off the logics of the consuming subject and vice versa. Consider the tenor of a letter sent by the Australian minister for administrative services to the *New York Times* about the government's decision to prohibit political advertising. He was responding to an article critical of the policy: "The Australian Government does not regard advertising as 'free' speech, but very expensive purchased speech, available only to those who possess the financial means to buy it. . . . Participation in the democratic process should not rely on the size of one's bank account." In addition, he expressed a horror at any opportunity for "wealthy interests to buy influence." The Australian initiative—later disabled in the High Court— is now cited in the United States as a positive move.[94] We can see a clear distinction being drawn here. On the one hand, the government places great faith in the generic value of the capitalist system, a system that necessarily produces inequalities of income and that operates via the desiring machine of comparative advantage in association with the educational and policing functions of the state. But conversely, this same government is critical of the specific advantage that might "unfairly" accrue to fractions of capital within the political process. The citizen is expected to understand these distinctions. It is to be a rational maximizer of its own utility within the marketplace and a disinterested supporter of equality of speech within the polis. In general, the government finds advertising desirable because it offers choice. It is a successful mechanism for the manifestation and allocation of rational desire. Advertising about politics (the site of the delineation of the overall public good) is undesirable because only some can afford it.

Similarly, the consuming subject is a valuable model for training policy because it is a model of competition. The civic subject, by contrast, is a valuable model for politics because it is a model of cooperation. The spheres must be separated, the subject split by what George Armstrong Kelly calls the "basic cleavage."[95] Of course, there are times when collective conduct assists the individual more than apparent self-interest, as for example in the prisoner's dilemma. But in terms of the cultural subject formed in a discourse of policy, this is uncommon. Whereas some future world might be able to unite the consumer and the citizen by saying that utility can emerge from the shared values of a collectivity, the burden of existing economic discourse is a reliance on individual

The Well-Tempered Self

preferences and satisfactions. This is to step into Marx and Engels's "icy water of egotistical calculation."[96]

Unlike their hagiographers, the early economists understood the indissolubility of a vision of the good society and the operation of immanent competitive laws. As Adam Smith's later work shows, even the writing hand behind the invisible hand acknowledged the need for an ethical subject to underpin—perhaps by disciplining—the potentially disabling nature of such calculation. An ethical sense is finally critical because the nature of people is frail; and Adam Smith was finally unable to conceive of a society that could function without ethics. He was equally unclear on the source of those ethics or how, when, and where such a source might intersect with market forces if not via a civic conscience schooled in self-doubt. The French physiocrats of the late eighteenth century also emphasized the need for the economy and populace to be wound back from an ultimately counterfactual hedonism through the restraint of decorum.

The actual data in support of notions of rational calculating actors and entities are thin on the ground. Murray Milgate and John Eatwell maintain that economic theory is frequently constitutive of political and popular discourses rather than the obverse, for all its claim to be determined by its own object, the individual in nature operating with perfect knowledge.[97] Because neoclassical economics is essentially a normative, prescriptive doctrine, no amount of counterindicative "evidence" about economic psychology works to undermine it, even though it is hard to isolate the development of preferences and harder still to trace the actual process of deciding how to satisfy them.

The neoclassical subject and its parent discipline are struck from a high modern mold of a self-legislated domain of truth. It is a mold that will allow consumers an a priori and apolitical legitimacy that is denied to producers and to any act that can be termed "political." By contrast, citizenship has venerable antecedents in opposition to older notions of self-aggrandizement than the sovereign consumer. In Plato's *Laws*, Cleinias merges the two momentarily in the imperfect communicative form when he declares that "not only is everyone an enemy of everyone else in the public sphere, but each man fights a private war against himself."[98] The self must defeat itself in the name of the general good, just as the state must defeat itself when it is tempted to make decisions in favor of enslavement. The skill to be learned is how to articulate between these technologies: when to be consuming and when to be civic, how to move toward what Michels called the "ideal sun" that such a transcendence of the consuming subject presumes. This is Bryan Turner's paradox of individualism, that "while citizens are required to be individuals in order to exercise conscience and choice, the institutions which make citizenship possible promote equality and bureaucracy."[99]

As Offe has pointed out, market economies have always originated "under predemocratic conditions" as part of the requirements of "original accumulation," a history that dogs the new eastern European democracies in their attempt to introduce the two conditions at once.[100] The new discipline of socioeconomics is one attempt to address this problem by defining a domain in which decisions are made for reasons other than individual utility. Theorists on the right seeking ways of simultaneously producing market politics and market economics in the former Soviet Union responded to Mikhail Gorbachev's instability by shifting from a faith in "orderly reform" toward a "radical populism" that would operate via "one angry man's ability to raise the masses in a rage." For the *National Interest,* people on the frontiers of rational politics became the most effective forces working for democracy. They were given the oxymoronic title of "liberal demagogue" and praised for their ability to create the right environment for the new synergy by nominating the culpable, naming those to blame for the economic and political settings that had gone before.[101]

To throw off the dichotomous views of consumer and citizen, and thereby refuse their paradox, would be to seek a technology of the self in place of technologies of the subject presently on offer, to move beyond a situation where people can "recognise themselves and their aspirations in the range of representations on offer within the central communications sector."[102] Such is the burden of chapter 5.

Chapter Five

◆

NEW TECHNOLOGIES
TO FORM NEW SELVES

PREVIOUS CHAPTERS have established how a disparately ordered network of relations of power operates through cultural policy to form civic subjects. The book has focused on the formation and deployment of cultural subjects as a technology of governance. In doing so, it has not yet looked at the actions of living persons in opposition, in resistance, to such protocols. By contrast, this chapter addresses the potential for contradiction when quite different accounts, accounts of a cultural self, are produced. It does so through a study of incivility. This is an incivility distinguished by a public conduct that breaks rules in the name of a technology of the self. This technology of the self operates against the technologies of power that form the subjects examined in earlier sections of the book. But it continues to be concerned with a formation of the person. After Foucault, this formation abjures an identity known "through a system of signs denoting power over others," in favor of a "sovereignty that one exercises over oneself."[1]

Although it seems that this system cannot escape some reference in conventionally derived notions of the individual, if it operates in a way that evacuates the notion of disciplining others, it may be said to have avoided many of the pitfalls of cultural subjectivity outlined in the preceding chapters. Obviously, there can be no absolute independence from the categories of person enunciated by the powerful discourses already encountered. Attempts to resist dominance always implicate themselves with what they struggle against. But the notion of a technology of the self that questions a subjectivity of orderliness and of influence over others does instance the potential for a project of freedom that might seem implausible in the light of much of Foucault's work. It may also serve as a heuristic device limiting the value of a reformist politics that opts to work exclusively inside the exemplifications of a civic cultural subjectivity.

This is especially important in the light of two interrelated critiques of Foucault: that he fails to deal adequately with the human subject as an active, sentient being; and that he cannot distinguish between forms of domination and the extent of their effect, such that the Gulag and *glasnost* are elided. Anthony Giddens applauds Foucault's contribution to an understanding of "administrative power," but finds him essentially lacking as a theorist because of his view that "events that govern human social affairs are determined by forces of which those involved are wholly unaware." This, Giddens asserts, is a wrongheaded and unnecessary rejection of the notion of "knowledgeable human subjects." This notion has been unproductively linked by French structuralism to the more legitimate—but essentially unconnected—disavowal of a Hegelian "transcendental subject." For Giddens, there is no need to dispense with the idea of history as "the outcome of human projects" simply because one wishes to discard history "*as* a human project." People have agency, and a determining agency, in the circumstances of their lives, both as willing and resistive subjects. To place all notions of repression and freedom together as disciplines of power is, for example, to deny the significant differences between totalitarian and liberal regimes. It is also to deny that the successful struggles to win rights to free association and contractual law, and the significance accorded to such victories, have basically occurred through the acts of persons.[2] One might connect this objection to certain feminist criticisms of the imperialism of anti-essentialist accounts of the body. Monique Plaza points to the regressive implications for an analysis of rape that may derive from Foucault's denial of the existence of sexuality outside discourse and his consequent assault on punishing crimes of sexuality. To unite all bodily invasion as a set of lesions is to deny sexual difference and the

The Well-Tempered Self

specificity of rape as an act complicit with male power, on this account. Not all acts of oppression are commutable, transferable.[3]

For Walzer, Foucault's failure to be a political scientist or "scholarly" seems to be the means of defining his politics as "infantile leftism" that simply seeks to be more radical than the rest of the world. Foucault's account of dispersed relations and networks of power has "conservative implications" that tie it to the pluralism of American social scientists, without even their leavening commitment to an ultimate center of legitimate power in popular sovereignty. No center means no object of critique, such as a ruling class or the state, and no subject of history, such as the public. Nevertheless, Walzer manages to make Foucault a subscriber to "functionalist Marxism" in his account of power, and an ahistorical theorist for his reliance on site designs of discipline rather than "practices and experiences." This latter point is crucial. Foucault is brought to the bar for failing to distinguish between subjection to a form of discipline and actually "being in prison." This is said to be emblematic of what is wrong at "the heart of his politics": a prison is a prison is a prison, and "liberalism is nothing more than discipline concealed." This makes it impossible for Foucault to differentiate totalitarianism from democracy.[4] Here, Foucault's work is flawed both because it does not homogenize an absolute truth from manifold perspectives and because it fails to deal with the politics of the everyday.

Giddens, Plaza, and Walzer were writing before the publication of the second and third volumes of *The History of Sexuality*, Foucault's principal writings on ethics and his major attempt to address the issue of the rule of the self and of others in a way that is very aware of the specific operation of, for example, male power within a given political system and the privileges it carries over the lives of women.[5] But a stream of critics writing since that time have continued to level similar critiques. The lack of preparedness of these later critics to address the work on ethics, even as they accuse Foucault of failing to consider the subject as a space for action or resistance, leads Barry Smart to suggest that the new dictum on his work is "rubbish it, don't read it."[6] As John Frow points out, disciplinary power may be an endless category of effectivity in Foucault's work, but not always in a repressive way because of its contradictory and dispersed operation and effects. Social relations are never to be transcended, but that does not mean that there is no means of transforming them, if people know—which is also to set—their limitations. This is the achievement of the later writings.[7] In addition, Foucault is quite explicit that he understands a prevailing *epistēmē* to be "a space of *dispersion*" that is discontinuous and relatively open. It is not a "sovereign, unique and constraining form." The *epistēmē* is instead to be seen as a "complex relationship of successive displacements," not something moving toward a grand synthesis or "syncopated transcendental."[8] This is not functionalism, or anarchy, or a denial of the effectivity of subjects.

Nor is it an answer, however, to the second allegation, about forms of polity and power. When Larry Ray restates Habermas restating Nancy Fraser as an objection to Foucault, it is for failing to answer why domination should be resisted. Ray adds that the inevitability of power as part of resistance that Foucault insists upon only lends weight to the heraldic cry of "real" theory "to distinguish normatively between legitimate and non-legitimate power."[9] Such a phrasing amounts to the pure and impressive pleas that can best be sustained in textbooks of ahistorical political philosophy. It denies the fact that the primary sites of Foucault's extramural interventions and intramural research—carceral institutions and discourses of illness, insanity, villainy, and sex—all saw his work informed by involvements with the subjects formed at those sites. This answers, in the case of Foucault, the questions one might ask of Ray's nostrum: why distinguish normatively? on whose cognizance? to please whom? inside which totality? deriving from which historically determined contingency? and to what end? No warrant in material practice is offered to pose the critique in the way he has. Quite clearly, Foucault finds that the grand failing of alternative conceptions of politics has been their very location within a coming-into-consciousness of the subject in history, precisely because such tropes amount to a triumphalism that is forever mired in "uncertain ideality" in preference to tackling "the difficult problem of historical change."[10]

Nevertheless, this latter issue about the legitimacy and effect of different forms of power continues to be particularly galling for a number of American critics, notably Richard Rorty: "We liberals in the USA wish that Foucault could have managed, just once, what Walzer rightly says he always resisted: 'some positive evaluation of the liberal state.'" Rorty divides Foucault up between "the Romantic intellectual" and the "citizen of a democratic society." Foucault's "moral identity" existed inside "democratic institutions," but he believed that his "self-description" should be extended beyond that canopy, beyond the domain of intersubjectivity and into his "*rapport de soi,* his private search for autonomy." For Rorty, this search becomes a yearning for what I shall call *différends de soi.* Rorty's problem with Foucault is the conflation of the two domains, the moment when his private person's pursuit of an autonomous self is projected onto his intellectual's right to speak that is

The Well-Tempered Self

granted by the public space that democracy alone can offer. When Foucault spoke self-consciously as a citizen, discussing such matters as prison reform and the classification of madness, he worked with a humanitarian liberalism that was caring and sharing. When he spoke as a Romantic, he abjured any involvement with others as part of his desire to manufacture an identity unfettered by tradition or contemporaneity. This latter Foucault used a different vocabulary from that of the former, replacing morality with a negation of the value of all *donnés,* including the institutions of the cultural-capitalist state. This vocabulary lacked the moral imperative required by Rorty to demonstrate its dependence for its own existence on liberalism as a discourse of high moment. Rorty is effectively speaking about creating networks of cultural civility when he pleads with an absent Romantic Foucault to see that there is nothing wrong "with whatever networks of power are required to shape people into individuals with a sense of moral responsibility."[11]

Taylor's epic attempt in *Sources of the Self* to account for the modern sense of identity is most unsettled by the absence of any explanation of what it is to be good in the writings of Foucault. He finds a parallel failure in utilitarianism's refusal to value the "ordinary life" of "production and reproduction." This refusal is indictable for its correlative lack of a map of dignity and decency with which to assemble an effective case for arguing "just what makes human beings worthy of commanding our respect." Foucault is to be commended for his weightiness of argument and for revealing that ethical ideals are interwoven with practices of exclusion and domination. But he is at fault in assuming that all moral orders are "equally arbitrary"; overtaken by a "neo-Nietzschean position," Foucault denies the truism that he can only be correcting others from a stance of elevation that prefers itself to the alternatives on offer. The further problem is that Foucault has only accepted the segment of Nietzschean philosophy that abjures the Romantic self. He has neglected the epiphanic possibility of Dionysian transcendence that is equally critical to Nietzsche. Even the last studies of sexuality and ethics are derogated; for although they do essay an aesthetics of life, this is done without adequate reference to social responsibility. For Foucault to operate as a public intellectual in such a fashion is to hide a commitment to absolute liberty that must underwrite such conceptions. In short, Foucault is denying the underlying presence in his work of a sense of "the good."[12]

Attempts to recuperate Foucault from within this type of reasoning tend to veer between two directions. The first is an intellectual trajectory. It sees Foucault slowly realizing that his findings on the historical nature of truth and subjectivity are in fact reliant on an implicit account of the reading subject as capable of remaking itself by engaging with the revelations of a genealogical or archaeological method. He emerges at the end of his life as a child of the Enlightenment. The second trajectory is personal. Here, Foucault moves away from his early anti-humanism and toward a more open and evenhanded account of subjectivity in accordance with his own private career as a sexed person. Reading for the "hidden level of homosexual reference" in his writings permits us to see a shift away from the *"discretion sur lui-même"* of the repressed days in Europe writing works of theory and studies of oppression and toward a self-revelation via the "belonging and comfort" of summers in California writing works of ethical intersubjectivity and personal style.[13]

Rather than tracing the influences on Foucault in an attempt to find either a solid-state authorial voice or a developing pattern of thought, it seems more useful to me to take of the texts what they say about subject and institution and redeploy those insights where possible. That is the most practical approach if one is to use the works of Foucault as an author-function, rather than to add to the establishment of that function within the reams of exegetical commentary. We should seek to go beyond histories of ideas and toward histories of truths as technologies that locate those truths inside embodied, disciplinary regimes, to acknowledge that the universe of freedom associated with the Enlightenment was itself historically situated, whatever the claims made about its ontology. This is to deny neither subject nor polity, but rather to account for their conditions of operation and mount a study of the feasibility of autoinvention—of *différends de soi*—within those conditions. For the Rorty critique and others fail to heed a clear message in Foucault's account of ruling-class male ethics in pre-Christian Athens and Rome, to the effect that the relative autonomy within particular fractions of particular social formations to manufacture and manage oneself is dependent on the institutions of those formations. When Foucault spoke in his utopic mode, it was to find lessons from the past that might be applied in the present in order to give voice to those whose conduct currently evaded the good grace of conventional civil society, but not to deny the value of that society in making the conditions of possibility for his own enunciative mode.

His view of the task of the intellectual did not feature the formation of a public "political will." Instead, he favored presenting information that would allow the people to take "a new measure of rules and institutions" and form their own will. This process saw the participation of the intellectual, but in "a role as citizen" rather than as someone "tell-

The Well-Tempered Self

ing others what they must do." The idea was to establish the complexity of social problems in order "to shut the mouths of prophets and legislators: all those who speak *for* others and *above* others." As Teresa de Lauretis notes, it is precisely the contradiction of contributing to theory even as one is contributing to practice, where the former is a domain of piety and the latter of effectivity, that gives Foucault a productive inconsistency.[14]

In response to the criticism that he fails to distinguish between totalitarian and liberal regimes and their systems of discipline, Foucault emphasizes that the presence of a concentration camp in a cultural-capitalist democracy (such as England, which was an early exponent) does not make that society identical to a totalitarian one. In fact, its existence there gives the camp a different meaning, and offers different information about the overall constitution of that society, from the interpretation to be drawn from the existence of such camps in a National Socialist state. But this overall constitution—of, say, democracy—does not provide an alibi for the specific technology of concentration camps. Techniques of coercion may run alongside and assist conditions of social and economic freedom. Democracies utilize networks of power, and to say so is not to problematize democracy *tout court;* but nor should it legitimize those networks indiscriminately. Such networks may bear some comparison with, or even emulation by, totalitarian regimes. That should not cancel out the validity of categorizing these micropolitics of technique without constantly elaborating and excusing them through the drawing of connections to preferences for an overall narrative of social or political order.[15]

There is, despite the debt owed by the intellectual to liberal democracy, a clear limitation emerging here, and it is to do with the notion of cultural capitalism. For this notion not only requires constant active obeisance from its subjects, but also a form of obeisance that allows no space outside itself for such a subject to obtain or best be represented. And ultimately, that very notion of representation and its running-mate of the public interest become a homogenizing force that incorporates many differences into a single, enunciable need by conceiving of difference on the basis of equivalence.

This equivalence serves to deny the prospect of *différends de soi*. The search for new meanings that characterizes Foucault's later work is not, it seems to me, part of a thoroughgoing desire to unpack the social world and live out the anarchy that Walzer and perhaps Taylor attribute to him; nor is it an endorsement of the technology of subjection described in the mythic originary social contract. It is a limited, definite activity undertaken within democracies. It needs no account of other forms of political regime and their comparative worth. And it is clearly anchored in a series of human constituencies, as was indicated above. Hence the narrative drive of this chapter, which seeks to examine an instance of the problems that arise when *différends de soi* are so unruly as to be outside the norms of cultural civility—norms of equivalence—available within cultural-capitalist states. It is not a totalizing, systemic critique of the operation of those states; rather, it is an investigation of cultural resistance at a particular time and place that has implications for the politics of identity available inside such states. This is not to suggest that a politics of identity is unimportant. Let me use Lyotard here, who provides the source material for my neologism: "Le différend est l'état instable et l'instant du langage où quelque chose qui doit pouvoir être mise en phrases ne peut pas l'être encore [The *différend* is an unstable condition, a moment in language when something that must be put into words cannot yet be]."[16]

The case study selected here is particularly notable for the category of unruly person it describes: the white male. For the most innovative politics of identity in cultural-capitalist democracies has generally come from the work of feminists and people of color. The study is doubly significant because it presents persons operating on the edge of a very conventional notion of the cultural subject, a notion animated by "sexuality" as an all-encompassing way of typing personalities, what Guy Hocquenghem refers to as the "triple equivalence 'choice = exclusive choice = personality.'"[17] Here, these persons are making a limited truth of themselves via public presentations connected to sexual practice, but in a way that rejects any necessary correspondence between such areas of practice and a valid means of categorizing people as subjects of a wider discourse, even that of the citizen.

The Ethnography

On November 26, 1986, Karol Wojtyła, also known as Pope John Paul II, addressed an audience of invited guests in the main quadrangle of Sydney University. As he rose to speak, two men stood up from their seats holding pink triangle flags and chanted:

ANTI-WOMAN
ANTI-GAY

FASCIST POPE
GO AWAY.

They were immediately dragged by security men or police (versions vary) to the covered area of the quadrangle and beaten against a red brick wall. The men, identified as members of an order of gay male nuns known as the Sisters of Perpetual Indulgence, were later charged with offensive behavior. In May 1987 a Sydney magistrate found the charges proven, but dismissed them.

This was, clearly, a case of incivility.

After the removal of the two men from the quadrangle, about a hundred people in "Polish national costume," carrying pro-Solidarity banners, pushed past barricades toward Wojtyła and repeatedly interrupted him to cheer his speech and make statements of their own. None of these people were forcibly removed or charged. At one point, Wojtyła responded to their interruptions, saying, "I understand."

This was not a case of incivility.

There are two powerful critiques of ethnographic practice, with a third flowing from them. First, anthropological method has long been delineated in a highly culturally specific (but allegedly universal) way. It has been something "done by" white people "to" nonwhite people, suffused with ethnocentric assumptions and reificatory operations. Industrialized democracies have been presented as a teleological referent against which other cultures are to be measured. And claims on the part of practitioners to the dualistic legitimacy of experience and distance have objectified the lived mores of others. It has been argued, often simultaneously, that participant observation can admit of both immersion in a foreign way of life, thereby acting as a guarantor of authenticity, and also distance and objectivity, via the methodology of academic research. Statements are generally not forthcoming on how, when, why, and where distinctions are made between the experiential and the distanced, although the claims to truth of the two kinds of understanding rest on diametrically opposed grounds.

Second, assertions of truth made in ethnographic accounts are based on a neglect of the specificity of experience and the productivity of its inscription. To write about the mythico-symbolic valency of particular rituals is already to perform an important—and ethnocentric—operation upon them: namely, their removal from the realm of practice, from a lived context. To argue for a weltanschauung or unconscious based on myth or ritual, for instance, is a new function. It introduces rules of knowledge that lay claim to replicate practice, but in fact involve different, intellectualized, items of manufacture and places of consumption. Pierre Bourdieu's recantation of his own anthropologizing in Algeria, combined with his attack on Lévi-Strauss's interpretism, provide a telling series of statements against these approaches.[18]

The third, and related, critique is the lack of political rigor in such treatments, best evidenced by the absence of reflexivity. Homologies can be traced between the carving out of academic careers through the intellectual colonization of other cultures and the carving out of empires through its physical equivalent. The stimulus to starting university departments of anthropology in Britain during World War II was a response to the prospect of an uncontrolled decolonization once hostilities had ceased, and U.S. Central Intelligence Agency funding is said to have animated a set of research and espionage connections via participant observation in Latin America, India, and Thailand over the years. Many researchers were also involved in the forced resettlement programs of the Vietnam War. It has also been argued that the breast-beating self-revelations of the latest breed of male ethnographer are a very particular form of discovery and guilt, confessions tied to a post-colonial anxiety that does not apply to women. The new ethnography is said to have plagiarized technologies for becoming the Other from feminism without acknowledging that legacy.[19]

The application of field technologies on home ground may redefine the field, but suspicions remain about the alleged differentiation of student and studied. In addition, a reliance on the category of the personal—"I was there and I know"—can be seen as specific to an ontic form of knowledge. Derrida argues that the ethnocentrism of this method "is irreducible; it is not a historical contingency," because of the tradition of knowledge that constitutes it, a self-serving view that defines itself as a center not subject to the determinations used to structure the lives of those being examined.[20] Nevertheless, the lived experience of an event—not a claim to total comprehension of a culture—may offer important insights. This particular telling of such an event takes a set of moments and utterances from which to theorize some elements of the social. Rather than laying claim to authenticity, it offers a reading of this event that concentrates on the intersection of discursive knowledges about the extra-discursive and the types of subject called up.

There are further difficulties in setting the Sisters' actions into a frame of general cultural theory. Referring to some forms of critical ethnography, Morris has identified the following standard approach:

The Well-Tempered Self

first comes "a citing of popular voices"; next, "an act of translation and commentary"; and finally a "play of *identification* between the knowing subject of cultural studies, and a collective subject, 'the people.'" The warrant for this type of analysis lies in its isomorphic relationship to populism: resistance can be identified as a practice of self-as-text; the method for identifying this practice is also that of reading; and so cultural theory itself becomes resistive. The critic has delegated his or her own pastimes to the people and then reappropriated those pastimes once they have been made popular.[21] And I have clearly applied theoretical categories here to a set of practices that would be described differently by the participants. Nevertheless, my focus here on an event-based politics does reference a group that is overtly in protest against forms of public and private subjection.

The invitation to Wojtyła's address that day described its audience as "representatives of those associated with tertiary education in Australia." The document detailed a set of policing practices surrounding the event: entry would be by presentation of the card itself; only certain roads on the campus could be used; and particular guests should appear at particular times. It was essential that spectators be clearly positioned as such prior to Wojtyła's arrival. Arrangements for achieving this extended to a policy on what to do with chauffeurs. The card provided a number of clues about the day, to do with exclusivity, wealth, systems of control, and the wide range of functions surrounding the academy (the governmental and industrial as well as the intellectual).

The audience was divided into two distinct groups: eight hundred and fifty invited guests and two thousand people who had gained places via a ballot in the university newspaper. The list of academic invitees had been drawn up by a committee of the vice-chancellor and registrar of Sydney University and two priests. Situated in a quadrangle and flanked by a bell tower and assorted gothic structures, the audience was facing upward and toward a podium, with loudspeakers near jacaranda trees. Nature, technology, training, tradition, and police thus intersected in a context of obedient reverence. Syntagms were made of apparently incommensurate items, as when a listener to the public address had her eye caught by a poster advertising the *Papal Tour Guide* attached to a semi-Doric column. Commodification of the spiritual was integral. Wojtyła, himself formally trained as a philosopher, was to speak from a spot directly between contending Departments of Philosophy at the university, bifurcated during the 1970s in a split over the place of Marxism and feminism in the curriculum. Behind the podium, on a board watched over by gargoyles, was a sign reading: "Notices will be removed immediately if placed on this board without authority." So many of the formal and informal institutional conflicts and authorities of the university were apparent without people being needed to articulate them.

The crowd itself was highly differentiated, a former social democrat prime minister in one of the front seats as an invited guest and people in "Polish national costume" in the balloted seats in back. Banners read TOTUS TUUS and AUSTRALIA SEMPER FIDELIS. A page from an afternoon newspaper headlining fears for Wojtyła's security acted as a sunshield for one person, the headline "Pope Power" for another. A priest sat during the wait reading an article entitled "Aspects of Feminist Theology." Four television cameras looked down and across, offering a gaze to that night's television viewers. Fresh-faced guides in academic gowns moved people to their seats. The police looked casual, leaning against columns and smiling. Compared to their demeanor at other public spectacles— not only political demonstrations, but also sporting events—they seemed relaxed and friendly. Press photographers were required by Vatican order to stand in a single group. They were given very poor angles to work from. People up the back—the balloted rather than the invited—chanted "Papa, We Love You" and "John Paul Two, We Love You." Announcements were made about the form of the afternoon. The university choir's chant of "Gaudeamus igitur" provided a sign that the pope's arrival was imminent. The balloted crowd moved toward the wing of his entrance, offering hands when he appeared. Wojtyła waved. This contrast in response and positioning between the "cheap seats" and the front rows was dominant throughout. Those guests "associated with tertiary education" sat quietly and still. The people behind were loud and peripatetic. The difference between them offered a metaphor for the myths surrounding the academy's combination of privilege and quiet removal within industrial society. Academicians were placed close to the seat of attention, but were withdrawn from the activity of adulation, the positive rendering of adherence, the physical work of positioning Wojtyła as charismatic even before the first official words were uttered.

Textual Analysis

Keith Jennings, the university registrar, addressed the assembly before Wojtyła arrived, welcoming people "to this great occasion." The occasion was thereby rendered other to the crowd, separate from *hoi polloi*. Rather than being partially constitutive of the event, the "audience" was made the spectator to a spectacle. Speaking about the event con-

The Well-Tempered Self

stituted it. A registrar in charge of invitation and administration—and himself a speaker—took his own work as referent, and did so from the position of commentator. One is reminded here of Lyotard's discussion of the endogamous proclamations of academic openness by university officials.[22] At the same time, Jennings established a system of obedience and reverence to Wojtyła as "His Holiness," following this with a briefing on other speakers and a set of detailed instructions to the crowd. All were to stand when "he" appeared. The information was didactic, but delivered from a smiling face, in the same spirit as school prizes. Jennings explained that the vice-chancellor and chancellor would greet Wojtyła in front of the quadrangle's clock tower. The fatherly authority of time-policing would provide a meeting point for religious and university bureaucrats.

Jennings then introduced those further down in the podium's hierarchy: the deputy vice-chancellor; a student; and fifty or sixty members of the "pope's party," who would enter before him and sit between dais and audience. The term "party" unifies and jollifies the range of technical functions performed by representatives of the Curia, Wojtyła's bureaucracy. Research, surveillance, speechwriting, education, and security jobs were subsumed by a signifier of ease and disinterested amity. In describing the speeches to come, Chancellor Herman Black was slated to thank Wojtyła on behalf of Sydney University and the "Australian academic community" in general. No representative structure existed to give Black authority to speak for students, teachers, bureaucrats, manual laborers et al.; the "right" was simply arrogated. (Similarly, Black's later statement that Sydney University was "honoured" at being "chosen to host the pope's address" indicated that he had no appreciation of the important fractions working within the institution for gay and women's rights.) When Jennings finished, the Australian folk song "Waltzing Matilda" was played. Although not the national anthem, it holds a special place in a series of myths surrounding Australia's bush country, inscribing a set of outback practices connected with pioneering, isolation, all-male company, and work. The signified of a white male bush subject operates via second-order meaning when "Waltzing Matilda" is heard by Anglo-Celtic Australian audiences. It spreads meanings across the specifics of the song's words to stand for Australia as a whole, in spite of the highly urbanized, bureaucratized, and ethnically differentiated character of its people.

After the main group arrived, Chancellor Black spoke. He termed the "distinguished visitor" a "Man of faith, head of the Vatican state, poet and author, an indefatigable traveller." This presented a series of complex binary oppositions. Where "Man" signifies corporeality and masculinity, "faith" signifies ethereality; "traveller" and "head of . . . state" stand for movement and stasis respectively; "head" and "poet" juxtapose control and creativity. These opposites were kept apart, precluding any possible dialectical process by ensuring that they did not directly encounter one another. The ultimate configuration was one of compromise, producing Wojtyła as "a Renaissance man," of sensibility and gentility in one subject position, authority and firmness in another. Within each of his "professions," these characteristics were identified as absolutely appropriate, their combinations discrete and unproblematic. But there is an inversion between these binary opposites not dissimilar to the potential contradictions encountered in the selfish consumer / selfless citizen dualism commented on elsewhere in this book.

Black then claimed that Wojtyła was "speaking to the poor and lowly in developing countries and the more fortunate in the developed nations." This essentialized the internal and interrelated aspects of First and Third World economies, ignoring poverty in the first, highlighting poverty in the second, and denying any causal relationship between the relative prosperity of one sector compared to the other. They were the outcome of "fortune," perhaps related to a naturalized "fate." Within this reading, there can be no definite conditions of production, circulation, and exchange created from modes of production and the relations prevailing within them.

Having performed these operations on Wojtyła and the international political economy to create a just and peaceful man using power to do good for the "lowly," Black went on to associate this good with the institution of which he was titular head. Sydney was positioned as the "oldest" university in Australia. The simple fact of longevity bestowed legitimacy and hence exchange-value. The university sought to offer a "liberal education" to all classes, regardless of "sex, race, creed or politics." This apparently unprejudiced accommodation in fact allowed for a particular type of cultural subject. It became clear later on that various forms of conduct designed to break away from the manners of civility were untenable within such a system.

The one woman in the group, Thérèse Byzannes, a third-year Arts student and convenor of the Sydney University Society for Welcoming the Pope, who was introduced next, continued the valorization of "a courageous defender of peace, human rights and the dignity of man . . . profound philosopher . . . outstanding scholar . . . a professor and a promoter of academic freedom." Byzannes told the pope that her society had been conducting "talks on your teachings," which had received a "wonderful response," and then called on him to "guide us in our pursuit of truth and justice." This hagiographic treatment postulated a leader embodying the academic virtues associated with Sydney University by Black, but going beyond the academy to step into the realm of the real, to struggle for peace. These capacities were finally coupled in a request of the pope that he direct a hunt for preexistent "truth and justice," academic and "real world" objects respectively. The practice of writing "truth" does not herein produce a truth-function on its own terms (within its own rules of speech). The effect of an utterance is to reveal reality, not to constitute it. We are clearly within an ontic frame of knowledge. Subjects, for instance, are not formed in discourse. They are real human entities whose activities are more or less accurately described in language.

Wojtyła spoke last, by now effectively identified with Sydney University, equality, truth, tolerance, and peace; and thereby also bestowing these qualities on his adherents. There was thus a symbiotic connection between audience, visitor, and institution. The audience created legitimacy because sovereign consumers provided a verification of value. The visitor bestowed quality because to listen to the blessed was to show sense. The institution provided both physical setting and intellectual validation. And these three elements were then unified and personified in the trinitarian guest. The carriage of peace and truth was made Wojtyła's responsibility, rather than the result of specific political tactics (in the first instance) and discursive formations (in the second).

His response was to act as a counter-donor. He returned this gift: "Man . . . [is] the owner of truth." God is at the center of learning, and academic institutions exist in the pursuit of this truth "in order to embrace it and to live according to it in the context of Australia, and her needs and challenges." So the relationship of deity and people to truth was intense and immovable. But this essentialism was mediated by the cultural-economic specificity of the sovereign state. The needs of this entity were to be met—and defined by—the application of truths discovered by universities. The scientists and economists of the academy set tasks, which others should work to complete. Such reasoning presented a series of givens: "God," "man," "academic institutions," and "truth" were in a timeless relationship to worthiness.

Wojtyła proceeded to state his appreciation of "a society that protects human rights." This was, however, a profoundly contingent notion of human rights. Such things were in no sense absolute or inviolable; for the applause that met this statement was immediately succeeded by his eulogy for "a society that encourages the family." The category "human rights" was thus dependent on holding a position within a definite domestic structure. To be outside a system of monogamous procreation was to be outside "right humanity." There was a strong implication that to deny the act of procreation—in particular to reverse it once under way—was to deny the most fundamental "human right" arrogated by Roman Catholicism: the requirement that a woman carry a fetus and be responsible for it but have no rights over the courier, her own body.

Wojtyła concluded by claiming a special connection between church and academy because of their "relationship to truth." This relationship derived from a "supply" of "structures of dialogue." These structures were clearly the province of civilized, polite conduct. One took one's turn and agreed not to question the domain of the ontic, here seen as the irreducible capacity of the Church to pronounce on the sexed body; but the secular salvation of the Enlightenment was an additional offering. Where "Jesus told the gathered: 'You shall know the truth and the truth shall make you free,'" universities "must recognize the right to freedom of study, inquiry and research, so that truth may be attained." Finally, Wojtyła advised that the function of truth was "uplifting and transforming power." Following and finding knowledge displaced and transmogrified power. Then he departed, content in the certainty that he had been "at home, among friends, among my own": the truth-tellers.

The Tour

Having analyzed the events and speeches of November 26, I want now to look at the public circulation of knowledge about the tour and how it was interwoven with a narrative of the pope's life that mapped out a path of virtue for the public to admire and measure itself against. Marvel Comics' official biography of Wojtyła, reissued in conjunction with his Australian visit, positions his life's work as a narrative being told by a hard-bitten New York newspaper reporter looking to explain the man's street significance. The reporter appears in the strip with a hat on the back of his head, the top button of his shirt undone, and his hands in his pockets; a city credibility roughly hewn, echoing Philip Marlowe and Carl Bernstein. Fifty pages on, having traced the pope's life via flashback, the comic concludes with the testimony of "street kids" at Yankee Stadium who have come to one of his public addresses in order

The Well-Tempered Self

to jeer, but are made to listen, their dramatic transformation proof positive of "WHY THE POPE IS GREAT!"[23] The grail has been found. This textual system—constant cross-validation of pope and people by each other, via a mix, respectively, of blessing and consumption—is emblematic of the general newspaper treatment of Wojtyła's Australian trip. He addressed the crowd, which made it significant. The crowd turned up to watch, which made him significant.

During the Brisbane phase of the visit, he called on the press to be "the lens through which others focus on reality."[24] Systems of meaning were thereby produced as external to "reality," rather than constitutive of it. Such a position was entirely congruent with the field described by private newspaper owners' defense of the concept of the sovereign consumer, the ratiocinative *homo oeconomicus* who acts with "perfect knowledge" to choose preferred products. Even those newspapers that printed stories approving of the then Nicaraguan government or that took liberal attitudes to birth control could rejoice at the advent of Wojtyła and regard his arrival as a sign of togetherness, despite his attitudes on these very issues. All the ruptures and lesions for which he stood, and that he helped to recreate, were put aside. This was partly done for the sake of the myth of constructing a unifier for spectatorship, the symbol of enclosure that encircles an audience and makes it what it is.

This draws us back to the question of postmodern knowledge. As Raymond Lémieux puts it in his essay on media coverage of a Wojtyłan visit to Canada: "Sont-ils producteurs des charismes qu'ils mettent en scène, ou simple reflets de réalités qui leur sont étrangères? [Do the media manufacture personality or merely reflect something that exists independently of them?]."[25] The two are simply not separable in such a tidy, chronological fashion. In a sense, the forces of textual production situating the media as neutral "windows on the world" are identical to notions of consumer acceptance of Wojtyła as sage and holy. Each set of statements is founded on assumptions about the unity and rationality of the speaking subject, the legitimizing function of choice when executed en masse. Yet any charisma attached to Wojtyła cannot exist prior to signification, any more than a research methodology can precede or complete the circulation of meanings. These media reports clearly set Wojtyła up as an exemplary cultural subject. He is not just an important institutional figure. More than that, he is properly serious, properly selfless, properly civil. He is, in short, dignified in a way that interruptors are not.

The official Papal Visit souvenir record described the Sydney University event as "a meeting with representatives of the Australian academic world." Byzannes was said to have been "speaking on behalf of students." No consideration was given to how a series of monologues constitutes a meeting or how Byzannes was authorized to speak for hundreds of thousands of others. The *Australian,* the country's only nationally circulating daily newspaper, acknowledged that: "Not everyone loves John Paul II, though the protests by gay groups or those opposed to him on religious grounds had little more than gimmick value." While the official record contrasted Byzannes with the gay interlopers: "A welcome of a different and unfortunate kind took place as the Holy Father rose to speak, when two men confronted him. They were quickly removed from the quadrangle by police, while the pope commenced his address without comment on the episode."[26] Gays are rendered apolitical and asexual, their message unvoiced. Conversely, the *Sydney Morning Herald* was more specific: "So-called Sisters of Perpetual Indulgence [were] hauled off in short order by the blue-capped men of university security, handed over to the secular arm. . . . The Pontiff, perhaps in the interests of freedom of speech, did not appear to find their action offensive. He observed them with a half smile."[27] This investiture of bemused evenhandedness and tolerance from on high raises again the question of the origin of papal-popular relations. Does the blessing come first, or the consumption?

An advertisement appearing in Australian newspapers around this time consisted of a photograph of Wojtyła and an invitation to non-Catholics wanting to learn about the Church to send off a form for some informational booklets. Wojtyła signified both familiarity—a recognition factor in product differentiation—and allegiance. The advertisement emphasized that a response would not result in visits to private homes or any obligation. In fact, anyone deciding to write off for the booklets was gratuitously enrolled in a correspondence course of twenty lessons, sent out over time in batches and with periodic question sheets to be completed. This amounted to a form of enlistment, alongside a renewed investment in Catholicism; an invitation to become the credulous subject or to remain it.

Wojtyła's visit was an important reinforcement of Roman Catholicism in Australia. Quite clearly, the proselytizing work of the Church is concerned with the appropriation of a (metaphoric) surplus mendicant value. A quarter of Australia's sixteen million people described themselves as Catholic in the 1980s, compared to 17.5 percent fifty years earlier. Large proportions of Italian and Irish settlers make the country a significant outpost of the Church, with potential for growth in numbers and strength of adherence. As I indicated above, the papal visit did

The Well-Tempered Self

not merely lodge its appeal to the captive. In its conception, the trip was "a recognition by the Vatican that for a largely secular country, blatant evangelism will not work. Thus, a program in which the pope met representatives of virtually every sector and age."[28] It was also part of an attempt to reverse the worldwide trends of reduced donations to the Church and a wholesale loss of numbers in training for the clergy.

Officially, this was "yet another opportunity to preach his message of peace, justice and human dignity," to meet "politicians and parish priests, young unemployed and homeless men." In this way, Wojtyła's munificence would "help to make Australian Catholics better Catholics and better Australians";[29] a rendering to Caesar of what he is due, in a linguistic formulation akin asking, "Have you stopped beating your husband?" The bind is double and intradependent. Better Catholic practice and better Australian practice are syntagmatic. To be an anti-Catholic subject is to be anti-Australian, and vice versa. "Good" "Australianness" is always already theological.

Of course, the visit was also a commercial venture. Recent estimates put the Vatican U.S. $63 million in debt, a substantial incentive toward commodification, and the pope's six-and-a-half-day stay resulted in the licensing of a hundred and twenty Official Papal Visit products in Australia, with a brewer, a sugar-drink maker, a car firm, airlines, and tobacco, communications, paint, and oil companies among the major sponsors. The National Papal Visit Office formally acknowledged "the generous support of the corporate sector and the Australian community in planning the visit."[30] This may also have helped to pay for an entourage of thirty-one, which included a butler, a doctor, a valet, security guards, a journalist, and television camera operators, all costing A $40,000 an hour.

The Body of Papal Thought

This materiality should not be regarded as incommensurate with public accounts of Wojtyła's theological or philosophical positions. Much is made of the fact that he has completed two doctorates, one on Saint John of the Cross and the other on the thought of Max Scheler. The second doctorate is described as a phenomenological attempt to combine feeling with reason. We are told that he has published half a dozen books and over five hundred other works and formerly held a chair in ethics at the Catholic University of Lublin.[31]

Rather than provide an exegesis on his oeuvre, I want simply to consider here the popular accounts of his teachings. My referent is not "his philosophy," but its description and redisposal within another, journalistic, mode as a model form of cultural subjectivity. Within this mode, the solid-state subject is a given for Wojtyła. This stable human is the basis for thought, the fundamental way in to reality via experience. Theologically, this sits easily with a materialistic theory of transubstantiation, in which the physicality of the Sacrament guarantees truth. Christ's body is an essence, not an idea. "It" is to be somatically experienced. This experience itself is a total, all-enveloping one. Touching and sensing become referents for perception and representation, rather than their constituents. Again, truth is rendered external to discourse; it is an entity that transcends terminology. Hence the reported direction of Wojtyła's desire: "I want to meet all those who seek the Absolute and yearn for Peace."[32] The rules of this type of language exclude relativities, marginalia, and the subverted and subverting subject. Fixity of meaning is paramount. Destabilizing self-formations (for example, polymorphous sexuality and its rhetoric) are external to "truth." They stand as sins based on false premises.

The pontificate of Pope John Paul II has been characterized by major shifts in the direction of Vatican policy. Prior to his election, liberalization was well under way through three tenets of reform enunciated during the 1960s and institutionalized over the next decade: collegial ecclesiatical governance by the bishopric at regional, national, and international levels rather than through the centralized hierarchy of the Roman Curia; ongoing, widespread exegetical and doctrinal debate, involving non-Church members, in place of papal authority; and diverse practices of worship, pastoralism, and administration. Under Wojtyła, there has been a careful reversal of these trends. First, he has made more than fifty overseas trips to nearly one hundred countries since 1978 as part of a reinstatement of central authority; this is pope as touring orientalist, able to indicate that the world starts wherever he may be. Second, the Curia has been strengthened. And third, new lay movements have been endorsed that work toward a restoration of traditional values.

Wojtyła's approach is classically logocentric in its "desire for a direct, given *hold* on meanings, being and knowledge. It requires an assured access to, and mastery of, a presence conceptual, significatory, sexual or ontological of identity."[33] This is a need to know that functions from an oppositional, but nondialectical, logic. Good and bad are juxtaposed. There is no acknowledgment that the privileged end of this couplet is dependent on its opposite for meaning. Nor is there any consideration of the silent element, the mediating difference, which stands between them.

Much is made of the fact that Wojtyła argues that priests may not marry because they must given themselves totally to Jesus Christ. It is not unreasonable to draw from this interdiction that Christ receives, as a consequence, something that otherwise would be reserved for wives. Clearly, a physical loving of Christ is part of this line. What, then, are the implications for the papal body?

Bryan Turner's survey text on the sociology of belief starts from the position that: "Questions about religion cannot . . . ever be divorced from questions of the body . . . [because of the] finitude of our corporeality."[34] This can rarely have been truer than in the case of the pope. Knowledge about Wojtyła's body as pontiff and person circulates in contradictory and powerful ways that nevertheless permit him to be established as an exemplary cultural subject. He is a man of civility, but not servility, precisely because of his ability to be both a living, material human and a *Geist* in himself. Public accounts of him are routinely dedicated to the production of Wojtyła as the embodiment and the ideal of both virile Romantic and sage Enlightenment thinking. It is perhaps not surprising that Weber regards the nineteenth-century emergence of the doctrine of papal infallibility as an indication of the drive to set up a careful bureaucratic distinction between pope as officeholder and pope as individual man. Now, as part of an attempt to reconcile the public and private dichotomy in a marketable way, Wojtyła's biography has been dedicated to the ancient priestly role of exemplifying perfection and thus embarking on what Nietzsche referred to as "the task of forming men in whom selfishness was dead."[35] I shall proceed to consider some further productions of Wojtyła that do this work.

The *Australian Women's Weekly* is a mass circulation magazine aimed at women working "at home," performing child- and husband-minding duties. Its major article on Wojtyła's visit provides information about the architecture of his home; his diet; his taste in music; his domestic servants and their gendered division of labor; his soldiers; his feelings toward children; and his propensity for undressing and dressing (in which he is rivaled, it seems, only by Rudolph Valentino). Three paragraphs dedicated to the types of clothes he wears are followed by the single-sentence paragraph: "Pope John Paul II has never had much regard for clothes."[36]

This turn between a fetishization of the everyday decorated body and its higher order eschewal typifies the uncomfortable intersection of Wojtyła's phenomenology and spirituality. Unease surrounding the body and desire parallels the fudging of a conflict between the material and the nonmaterial. An official visit program fetishizes the precautions undertaken to protect Wojtyła—a boys' game about officialdom, importance, professionalism, and gun toys—and concludes the section by stating that the pope "makes no demands for security himself."[37] The simple man, untrammeled by the obsessions of the corporeal, is to be rendered significant by attention to his security, and worthy by his own lack of concern about it. Readers are positioned as worried about his physical safety, whereas Wojtyła is above such tribulations.

His biography is routinely written in terms of the Wojtyłan body. He is the only former industrial worker to be made pope, coming from "unpretentious" surroundings ("Log Cabin to See"). As a young man, his hard work scholastically was balanced by a love of sport ("a natural athlete"): a series of self-disciplinings. "Passion" for studies was matched by "Zest for life" in sport. In what could otherwise be read as an aberrant statement of unreconstructed Maoism, Wojtyła is quoted as finding two years of laboring more valuable than two doctorates.[38]

A constant involvement as a boy in association football, swimming, canoeing, and acting can be constructed as signs of vitality. But it can also be read as a series of acts of sublimation, avenues for the safe expression of desire. During the visit, a former Australian professor of sociology recalled meeting Wojtyła at a summer camp for Polish Catholics in 1938, describing him as "a ruggedly handsome and athletic boy." This was highlighted in an official account of the Australian tour. At the same time, endorsed publications mystify Wojtyła's wartime point of entry into the priesthood: "EXACTLY WHAT TRANSPIRES THAT DAY IN WAUVEL CASTLE MAY NEVER BE KNOWN." His election to the pontificate in 1978 was hailed in part because he was said to be "manly."[39]

What happens if these accounts are put alongside what he said to the inmates of a Melbourne seminary—namely, "that their commitment to celibacy was a positive expression of a special capacity to love. It was a gift from God that was not given to everyone, and it was the priests' gift of their whole self to Christ and the Church"? As he put it, this capacity "is a gift that is made over and over again . . . it must be continually renewed."[40] Here, nothingness is a gift, absence a donation. But if it is denial, how can it be regiven? It is simply a matter of continued abstention unless there is a psychosexual intercession with Jesus Christ (who is held to be both man and god, of course).

By putting the statements together in that way, I have set up a new cultural subject. This cultural subject is contradictory. It is false to itself, and necessarily so. In other words, a form of logic now holds sway that appears to designate the pope as a "repressed homosexual." This is not my belief. I simply seek here to illustrate the contingency of cultural subjectivity, how quickly it can be altered by changing the intersection of certain statements. One could just as easily use the knowledges circulating about his youthful exuberance to parody his current institutional power, for example. Instead of making either move, I want now to address the actual ecclesiastical formation of sexed subjects and the pope's part in that process.

The Sexed Subject

"Patriarch of the West" is one of Wojtyła's titles of office. He is regularly positioned as deserving of that moniker in both its pejorative and positive senses. Michael Costigan's hagiographic treatment uses referents of difference ("Anglican") and expertise ("psychiatrist") to valorize Wojtyła's speaking for others through the following formulation: "An Anglican psychiatrist, Dr Frank Lake, has concluded that 'both the Church and the world stand in ever greater need of Pope John Paul II as a physician of the corporate soul.'" This patriarchal vision is differently—and more specifically—exemplified in Wojtyła's statement of policy to Roman Catholic bishops during the Australian visit. He criticized a "levelling out of Catholic life" in some places, to the point of an acceptance of abortion. And one of his acolytes has explained Wojtyła's line on surrogate motherhood in these terms: "Do not expect a pope to call virtue what is sinful."[41]

These absolute moral imperatives of the body are constantly reproduced to define "unconventional" women as Other. Wojtyła's treatise *Love and Responsibility* is cited as a classic statement in support of permanent marriage as the only proper forum for sex, and the home as the only proper forum for women. The book was "said to have directly influenced" Pope Paul VI's *Humanae vitae,* the archetypal modern Vatican statement on gender. After Wojtyła's election in 1978, he introduced a high-level consultative/policymaking machine on these questions, via the creation of a Council on Family Matters, and initiated a new Inquisition, which has brought proceedings against both a priest from the Catholic University of America, for questioning the ban on certain forms of contraception, and twenty-four nuns who took out an advertisement in the *New York Times* in opposition to the Church's stance on abortion. The director of Planned Parenthood in Rhode Island was excommunicated for her position on terminations.[42]

It is a conventional critical wisdom to derogate "religion" as an opponent of homosexuality, particularly the Catholic Church and its pope. Dennis Altman's description of churchpeople as "Ideologues of Oppression" is a classic statement of this formulation.[43] And certainly Wojtyla in particular can be seen as repressive in the areas of sex and morality. But it is necessary to go behind such easy categorizing to investigate Catholic formations of the homosexual subject, for their genealogy is a picture of epistemological ruptures; in other words, of changes in cultural policy.

A 1975 "Declaration on Certain Questions concerning Sexual Ethics" from the Vatican advised that "according to the objective moral order, homosexual relations are acts which lack an essential and indispensable finality." (This finality referred to the impost that sexual relations always be conducted under the sign of procreation.) It was also held, however, that homosexuality may be innate in some people and therefore irrevocable. Such persons should be treated with understanding and tolerance in the interests of "overcoming their personal difficulties and their inability to fit into society." Similarly, the archbishop of Westminster had argued in the 1950s that while homosexual acts were "grievously sinful," it was up to individual Catholics to decide whether their prosecution would be more harmful than the acts themselves. It may be best to "tolerate without approving."[44]

The wellsprings of this duality are manifold, and their policy outcomes equally varied. In biblical terms, the New Testament provides only minimal textual guidance. Jesus' teachings do not touch on the subject, while Paul's merely reiterate traditional Hebraic and Hellenic objections to the threat to social renewal of all nonprocreative sexual practices. The argument is essentially a functionalist one; and in any case, it has been suggested that such a reading of Paul is based on a decidedly problematic translation. In fact, only Leviticus provides a really clear condemnation of sodomy. But it remains the case that even radical parts of the Anglican Church continue to condemn "homosexual practices of the genital kind" as "a major blemish on a person's conduct."[45] The Australian Uniting Church is often regarded as a very progressive institution, but it continues to exclude gays from positions in the clergy.

It is important to recognize the dependence of much theology on an extra-biblical set of "natural" laws, beyond obsessive scriptural exegesis and content analysis. Aquinas is a key figure in this. Writing in the thirteenth century, he warned that orgasm was a problem because it diverted the mind from more serious matters. The quest for it became a total one that would brook no interruption. Furthermore, since children were original sinners because of their creation through sex, orgasm begat evil. Nevertheless, he acknowledged that gestation was, ipso facto, a good. The act could be redeemed and rendered "without sin." It was theoretically possible to counteract the egregious anti-cogitative force of sex by continuing to reason at all times during the deed. Specifically, the dispersal of semen must be managed "in the way befitting the end for which it is needed. . . . Copulating with the wrong sex, male with male or female with female" was second only to bestiality in wickedness, as it did not act to sustain the species.[46]

It has also, of course, been argued that monotheism is marked by homophobia, whereas polytheism historically supported "the ambiguous and the anomalous."[47] This may be connected to a wider discursive shift during the Hellenistic and later Roman empires toward a privileging of asceticism. Actual punishment of homosexual acts dates only from the Middle Ages and is connected to the Gregorian reforms, which marked a movement toward a centralized monarchy and class conflict within city-states. A growth in world trade saw the spread of monotheism and asceticism, and the emergence of the city disempowered polytheistic appeals to agricultural and fertility gods.

In any case, Aquinas's line has acquired the status of both law and nature in Catholic teachings. But it has been significantly problematized at a practical, extra-discursive level by the need to deal with a "problem" that is not removable. Gay sex has been rendered objectively a sin, but subjectively not a sin. A structural theory of homosexuality, removing the notion of individual choice at the level of desire, informs the position that gays are normally not responsible for their "condition." And it is also important to draw a distinction between the church *qua* institution and the church *qua* community of believers.

These contradictions are present in Wojtyła's positions on the topic. During his 1987 tour of North America, he told a gathering of AIDS patients, including two Catholic priests, that God loved them. But just a year before, he had officially reiterated the turpitudinous nature of homosexuality. Gays are, he can say, "not outcasts . . . like all people who suffer, they are inside the Church"; but he can also claim that the "future of Australia and the Church" is "in the family."[48] Catholicism is thus positioned as an all-encompassing doctor and parent, combining technical competence to decree the health of a subject with ownership of that subject.

It therefore becomes enunciatively possible to align apparently incommensurate statements under the one speaker, if always at different times. The statements are not allowed to meet in a dialogic fashion. Their separateness provides the space for differing logics to operate independently of one another. The first set of statements, the logic of support for gays, permits some play to an accepting liberal humanism where this is necessary to provide a picture of tolerance. But the second set of statements, the set surrounding "nature," can be operationalized to legitimize control and surveillance. These positions also operate differentially at different sites of administrative power. Raymond Hunthausen, a Seattle archbishop, was stripped of many of his powers by the Vatican in 1987 for a variety of liberalisms, notably a relaxation of the disciplining of gays. And the American Catholic Church exerted immense pressure on a publisher to excise material on homosexuality from the biography of a cardinal in the mid 1980s. But a priest has had official pastoral responsibility for South Australian gay people since 1985 and "Acceptance" is a successful Roman Catholic gay support group. This may also be seen as a response to a need expressed by gay religious believers, who have mounted a series of sophisticated arguments to be considered seriously by the Church.

The problematic issue of AIDS has clearly drawn these twin strands closer together, especially as the conventional pathologizing of homosexuality now has a supposedly clinical corollary. In their May 1987 message, the Australian Catholic bishops called on Roman Catholic people to respond to sufferers with "love and practical assistance." But this was coupled with its apparently paradigmatic countersentiment, that the "only answer . . . lies in moral renewal and appropriate education" because the epidemic "is one disastrous result of promiscuous sexual behaviour." Significantly, the line is that "what has always been sinful is now becoming suicidal." A "condom culture" is neither "decent or effective." Yet the disease should not be presented as "divine judgement." Homosexuality is, rather, contrary to the laws of nature.[49] The laws of nature are clearly distinct from those of God; there is some let-out for gays, and a way in for Catholics to be compassionate. But this cannot be at the expense of Aquinas's insistence on the need for appropriate seminal finality. In a more positive, productive vein, this gives an epidemiological warrant to the promulgation of the civic cultural subject of sex.

Propagandists for papal consistency simply deny that there are any inconsistencies here, because: "It is not open to a pope to practise the sort of deception that is postulated as diplomacy or said to be useful in the cause of building bridges." These totalizing, absolutist, consistent narratives extend to what is constructed as an "all-inclusive . . . concern for humanity" and respect for human rights and differences of opinion.

The Melbourne *Age* newspaper lauded Wojtyła's capacity to "promote the universal virtues with which all men and women can identify." (Even so, these global certainties are rapidly and suitably tinged with a necessary mystification: "to listen to and absorb John Paul is a challenge. There is never confidence that the real message has been understood, even if it has been received."[50] Not only does this allow for mystery and difference, but it precludes any certainty of logical contradiction in reading Wojtyła. The listener/reader is condemned to incompleteness because the texts of Wojtyła are assigned a never-ending indeterminacy.)

Italo Calvino's story "Desire in November" brings out this duality. A poor Italian man has been given a new undershirt and pants by a Catholic priest. But he steals into a clothes shop and passes a cold night wrapped in fine furs, emerging in the morning without the furs but with the donated underclothing. He is left feeling "as comfortable as a Pope."[51] At one level, the Church stands for a donor of untied aid that gives without requiring a particular return. But this unconditional giving is in a nexus with a gluttonous appetite for control and luxury. The apparently antonymical sacerdotal subjects—priest as donor, priest as recipient—can be accommodated only within a vertically, horizontally, and historically differentiated institution. Western Catholicism acts as an umbrella of discursive piety over positions that are in fundamental conflict with one another. As Kenneth Leech puts it, there is cover for those who could otherwise be characterized as "Marxist and anarchist groups, movements of non-violent protests . . . and fighters for racial justice" alongside those devoted to "the defence of established structures of oppression."[52] It is not always possible to keep the subjects apart, and their meeting can be disquieting. Steve Bell satirizes Wojtyła's semi-acceptance of the former Pinochet regime in Chile by proposing that people render to Caesar and to God what they are due, and use whatever is left over to start a small business.[53] This encourages a further consideration of the intersection of church and state, and the latter's formations of homosexuality.

Church and State

Religion is central to modernity in two areas. First, the freedom to follow a faith or not is one of the critical definitional markers of modern tolerance. And second, this freedom of conscience is considered to be private. This division positions the Church in a subordinate public role to the state. Questions of sexuality, its definition, its field of significance, its performativity, and its relationship to a public-private split of conscience and performance are examples of the tense boundary points between the institutions. And as moves are made to increase gay rights, bodies such as the Oregon Citizens' Alliance and participants in the "straight pride" rally at the University of Massachusetts emphasize other types of community in their efforts to exclude homosexuals from the provisions of anti-discrimination machinery, to recapture the moral high ground of identity politics. Attempts to enshrine protection for gay men and women through human rights legislation have been partially successful across the European Community, but continue to meet with opposition from various countries.

State policy on gays in Australia represents a set of disaggregated events. Recent decriminalization in some parts of the country has had a variety of effects, not the least of which has been a greater public acceptance of homosexuality. But the story has not always been so harmonious. What follows is a very brief overview.

Prior to white invasion two hundred years ago, homosexuality in Australia had been deeply embedded via ritual. But under the first white governorship, the penalty for sodomy became death, in keeping with a continuing use of British precedent to establish Australian law and the metonymic use of anti-sodomy laws by the British monarchy to take over domains that had previously been ecclesiastical. A subculture of gays around religion is on record from the 1830s, but the state continued to pursue them vigorously for the next hundred and fifty years. The first public agitation for reform of the law stemmed from the 1930s, but received a major setback with the crackdown on "deviance" during the Cold War that characterized Britain and the United States as well. With the development of an identity-based politics in the 1960s, various parts of Sydney had effectively become gay from the late 1970s. This is in keeping with the achievements of lesbian and gay occupation of urban space and the creation of distinct public identities. But these occupations have been contingent and problematic. The first of what are now annual Gay Mardi Gras in Sydney, in 1978, saw over fifty arrests. Serious police violence marred the festivities. Yet the sheer weight of a formative culture, combined with a pervasive discourse of liberalism and the politicization of sufferers, made for change. This subculture was comprised of material objects of particular exchange- and use-value: gay papers, bars, restaurants, plumbers, clerics, pharmacists, undertakers, and so on. It developed along the lines of a mini-civil society. By 1988, the official program of the Mardi Gras was replete with messages of support from the Police Community Relations Bureau, Police-Gay

The Well-Tempered Self

Liaison, and the Department of Community Services and Health. But in order to make sense of the various arms of the state and their operation on November 26, 1986, we need a further theorization and some examination of how the state responded to Wojtyła's visit in general.

For all its internal differentiation, the state takes policing to be its fundamental mode and logic of operation. As Foucault puts it

> an entire series of utopias or projects for governing territory . . . developed on the premise that a state is like a large city; the capital is like its main square. . . . At the outset, the notion of police applied only to the set of regulations, that were to assure the tranquillity of a city but at that moment the police became the very *type* of rationality for the government of the whole territory. The model of the city became the matrix for the regulations that apply to a whole state.[54]

This view of the effect of regulation contrasts with knowledge of the state as responsive to its citizens. Such a sovereign view would make for a more sanguine set of statements about, as it were, the opportunity to make statements. So the Catholic Enquiry Centre takes as a given that in a "democratic society, such as we have in Australia, laws are drawn up by the will of the people. Citizens have the right to express their views and to influence and form public opinion by demonstrations, or protests, provided these do not interfere with the freedom or rights of others, or promote unnecessary violence."[55]

A classic liberal discourse on the rights of speech simply operates on another grid from policing practices. Yet official accounts of Wojtyła's trip place great importance on the repressive state apparatus as a guarantor of the civility of each event. Thus: "The police and the hundreds of volunteer marshalls and supervisors were without complaint after the ceremony."[56] And the very accusation made of the Sisters resonates with the intellectual and social activity of policing, the disciplinary complex of manners, family, and control that operates through the civil policing that is known as good conduct.

Of course, the Catholic Church is the most secular of all religious institutions. It sets its governing body up as an independent nation, complete with diplomatic presences. The papacy uses its sovereign status to play a special part in international relations. And this in part accounts for the unique status afforded Wojtyła by government officials across different sites: his capacity to mobilize a set of different discourses of the secular and the spiritual and give them an apparent unity in his person. He came to Australia technically "as the guest of the Australian national government in his capacity as Head of State of the

Holy See." An official welcome from the then Australian prime minister, Bob Hawke, was in just these terms, although modified by the set of knowledges about Wojtyła as pope. Thus: the "Australian Government is delighted" by the visit, as Wojtyła "has repeatedly affirmed the dignity of the individual and a belief in the principle of freedom." Hawke found it noteworthy that the tourist would be spending "the greater part of his time meeting people from all walks of life." "Freedom" is here present as a fixed absolute, Wojtyła's catholic approach to greeting people its guarantee across sites. In a farewell speech in Perth, the prime minister decreed that the trip had been "an inspiration and a cause for great joy," an event proving that "this is a country prepared to support the cause of peace and justice."[57]

The combination of Irish and Italian migration referred to earlier ensures an attentive audience for any pope visiting Australia. The public aura surrounding such visits becomes akin to a royal tour. So Hawke is a republican, but he welcomes Elizabeth Windsor. And he is an agnostic by way of Protestantism, but he welcomes Karol Wojtyła. While eschewing the core political ideology of monarchy and religion, he pays complete obeisance to their traveling iconography. It is through such moves that it becomes possible for the Australian government to act as the publisher for Wojtyła's speech to Aboriginal people. Two messages are sent out by this: first, Hawke is following the Weberian ideal type of the distinterested public sector worker who fulfills duties of office regardless of personal belief. And second, he is following an electorally pragmatic line, seeking to avoid offending significant parts of the voting population. Once more, the incommensurate becomes acceptable. A syntagm is made of paradigmatic nonrelations: the republican welcomes a reigning monarch, the nonbeliever welcomes the apotheosis of high faith. To bring these types of contradiction to the fore, in a way that does not necessarily seek to impose a synthesis on their junction, is to refuse both the orderliness and the mystification of the civic cultural subject. To do so in public, in a way designed to confront and to play, is to embark on a politics of parody.

Performing the Unruly Subject:
Parodic Politics

EVENT 1: The Sydney journal *Gay Information* utilized a picture of gay male nuns in its subscription drive in 1984.

The Well-Tempered Self

EVENT 2: The Tea Towels d'Art Company marketed an A $10 "Come back to Catholicism" towel in 1986 depicting Wojtyła mounted on a horse in the Australian bush, clutching a boomerang.

EVENT 3: The comedian Pamela Stephenson advertised her tour of Australia in 1987 as "Not a Papal Tour." She was depicted in newspaper graphics clothed in priestly robes and wielding a chainsaw.

These three events are part of parodic politics, the playful satire of symbolic irreverency that sends messages of subversion as much through its mode of address as its substantive content. This is not to suggest that such parody has any status outside prevailing social relations, that it is in some sense sealed off and sanitized from them. A common element among these objects is that each is a commodity. It is worth noting that Stephenson's tour was sponsored by an airline and a commercial radio station. The secular interests of business can find such appropriation acceptable. There is nothing specifically anti-capitalist about unruly discourses of sex and gender that argue against dominant codes. But their very appeal is distinctively organized around making fun of religion, and particularly the Catholic Church, via two sacred icons: the gender of nuns and the peripatetic neocolonialism of Wojtyła.

Similarly, the soubriquet "The Sisters of Perpetual Indulgence / an order of gay male nuns" makes syntagms of signifiers that are normally in paradigmatic relation to one another. Men are sisters, nuns are male, religion is indulgent, gay is ordered. Signs are scrambled, but in a way that borrows from a variety of grammars to bring together binary opposites that generally define each other through difference. To invert is to subvert when you are showing that doctrines of decency desperately need living examples of indecency. This forwards one of the critical confusions of postmodernity. The irony is that a sense of gender confusion sees the medical model of congenital maladjustment producing a subcultural corollary that plays with identity. The appearance of the homosexual as a category of person, as opposed to the description of particular sexual practices that offers no wholesale key to identity, is now said to be a nineteenth-century European invention, not a nineteenth-century European finding. It is an invention to be mocked.

Of course, there are controversies within gay and feminist politics about this mocking mode because of its uneasy adjacency to misogyny. In acknowledgment of this, the Sisters have rules about referring to each other as "he." The discourses of "effeminacy" often applied to and by the gay subject are not accepted; so to refer to one another as "she" or "bitch" is infra dig. And yet such codes are hinted at in their linguistic formations and habiliments. It is just that the misogynistic meanings of "effeminacy" and cross-dressing are said to be eschewed. Cross-dressing clearly references a trope of the 1980s, what Showalter calls "a fin-de-siècle ambiance in which sex-roles are under attack."[58] This also recalls practices from the nineteenth-century city. The ambivalent freedom of anonymity it provided included the space for clandestine gay groups to form themselves. Transvestism was often a central component of this process. The idea behind such activities clearly involves parodying a version of femininity, but not merely imitating it in order to derogate and differentiate. Rather, the aim is to develop what Lynne Segal calls "a positive aesthetic sensibility" that can bring pleasure and pain together in a new order of value that works with categories of perceived oppression of Self and Other rather than denying or negating them outright.[59] Gaylyn Studlar draws a useful distinction between different modes of cross-dressing in film texts. Whereas Divine in *Pink Flamingos* (John Waters, 1972) threatens phallic power via an association with femininity that emphasizes the abject side of the sign of woman (a "multiple-sited morass of dissolute perverse sexuality" that is determinedly incoherent), Frank-N-Furter in Jim Sharman's *The Rocky Horror Picture Show* (1975) reinscribes normalcy—despite his dress—by being active, decisive, and powerful.[60] Not all male cross-dressing mocks women; some emphasizes a shared exclusion from the public performance of a self of choice. As in much gay culture, a deep ambiguity seems to reside here, in a liminal state between an appropriating quotation from women and a strong sense of identification with them.

However unconsciously, these moves heed Guattari's call to problematize the binary oppositions established in the course of categorizing people sexually. He seeks to "destroy notions which are far too inclusive, like woman, homosexual. . . . When they're reduced to black-white, male-female categories, it's because there's an ulterior motive, a binary-reductionist operation to subjugate them."[61] For Sennett, the most devastating legacy of the Victorian era's classifications of sexuality was the myth that "sex is a revelation of the self."[62] Refusing such categorizations also breaches the older European cultural tradition that establishes hierarchies across four critical symbolic domains: psychic forms; the body; space; and the social order. Each is interconnected, such that disturbances within one sector have significant implications elsewhere. This is part of the process of manufacturing *différends de soi*.

"Carnival," a new point of celebration in cultural studies, offers a means of organizing our thinking about the Sisters. Peter Stallybrass and Allon White, after Rabelais and Mikhail Bakhtin, define it as "the repeated, periodic celebration of the grotesque body—fattening food, intoxicating drink, sexual promiscuity, altered ego-identity, the inverse and the heteroglot."[63] The sacred was to be desecrated and the spoken word profane, such that an ill-disciplined vulgate displaced *politesse*. The *charivari* of the sixteenth century saw objects of derision—such as bishops or husbands—"paraded through the streets and ridiculed by the community," often through a cross-dressing mockery.[64] Britain's carnivals of the Industrial Revolution through to late in the nineteenth century involved courtship, dancing, eating, and drinking in public; in short, they involved display in a way that frequently evoked official displeasure and repression.

The grotesqueries of carnival serve to destabilize boundaries that define bodies and their differences. Parading these differences often involves distorting them into hideously deformed exaggerations through abnormal size or the reversal of inside and out, particularly through cross-dressing. Although the grotesque is necessarily something unusual and perverse, its popularity in a wide variety of popular cultural forms is apparent, in part because of its uncanny, magical qualities, its very excess that plays with the distance between pleasure and pain, "the droll and the fearsome." The grotesque refuses sympathy; instead, it works via a complex of distantiation and identification for an uncomfortably empathetic reaction.[65] It would be quite opposed, for example, to Wojtyła's geopolitics, which calls for Europe to "find yourself, be yourself," to become one and undertake a mission to civilize the world.[66] For carnival is dedicated to a world that is inevitably split. Where the diurnal world is serious and prohibitive, this festival world is frivolous and developmental, in a nondisciplinary way. The contemporary Brazilian *carnaval* is routinely valorized as a moment when the drabness of the everyday is colored and invigorated by a sensual, sexual reinvention that celebrates bodily exchange and caress. *Carnaval* turns decency and decorum on their heads in the name of "a single overriding ethic: the conviction that in spite of all the evidence to the contrary, there still exists a time and place where complete freedom is possible." The notion of play is critical here in a double sense: it returns participants to a lost world of childhood even as it imparts a knowing sexualization to the practices it licenses. The dominant symbolic feature is cross-dressing, a metonym for the transformative claims of the event available across gender and age.[67] This is less to do with hysterical acting-out revealing the truth of a hidden complex than it is a displacement of social oppression onto parodic, emetic conduct.

The Australian Sisters follow a carnival-like anti-program. Their activities are not to be part of a plan. That would buy into conventional structures and modes. Similarly, Foucault's advocacy of "a gay culture" of "polymorphous, varied and individually adjusted relationships" is based upon the rejection of "a set of propositions," because "as soon as a program is presented, it becomes law and stops people from being inventive." Ultimately, he says, the task in forming the subject anew is to "make the following question into an incontrovertible challenge: 'What game could we play, and how do we make up the rules?' "[68] Playfulness as a process is here raised to the status of policy, an end in itself because of its destabilizing effect.

The Sisters, in operation in Australia since 1981, describe themselves as "an order of gay male nuns dedicated to the promulgation of universal joy and the expiation of stigmatic guilt through public manifestation and habitual perpetration." The language is a combination of the (conventionally distinct) sacred and profane. The combination works to indicate the logocentric interdependence of such binary oppositions: the "oppressive effect of gender roles" is to be countered by an attempt "to exorcise the gloom." The medicalization of sexuality is rejected. Negative internalizing by gays is seen as a necessary response to "centuries of systematic scapegoating," but it must now be reversed through a process of "public manifestations," a turning back out through the reclamation of public spaces. But again, highly formal language is coined punningly to signify satire. It is a fundamental precept that the Sisters should "show forth their vocation wherever people gather but most of all in the market place. They do not always wait for an invitation."[69] Foucault resuscitates this site as a critical space for redefining the division of private and public. He recounts the "scandalous gesture of Diogenes . . . : when he needed to satisfy his sexual appetite, he would relieve himself in the marketplace. Like many of the Cynics' provocations, this had a double meaning." This doubling expressed itself in the performance of a "private" act in the public domain. Diogenes was problematizing the notion that a public manifestation of sexual pleasure necessarily implied an ignoble temperament, via what Foucault calls "performance" criticism."[70] And much gay sex is the closest to market bargaining of all male sexual conduct because of its casual anonymity.

The Sisters' notion of the marketplace is also akin to the unruliness of the early English fair, where the marketplace represented a disturbance

The Well-Tempered Self

to localism, a recognition of change and difference and a source of fluidity, of coming and going. Identity is here loosened from its official moorings and replaced by a disrespectful public modeled on the pleasure of commonality-with-differences. Space is to be contested, and special efforts made to move outside, to get away from the always-already-institutionalized nature of public buildings. What is set up in that space will be determined by the outcome of processes predicated on difference:

> The Order is collective in its decision making and anarchistic in its practice . . . membership reflects the wide variety of beliefs, philosophies and ideologies that are present in the gay community and movement. There are radical faerie nuns who are Marxist, Haute Couture nuns, nuns who are Christian, atheist nuns who drink alcohol, gourmet nuns and nuns who won't listen![71]

They share a commitment to be "specialist demonbusters." Categories are rendered problematic in their taxonomic components, constituted as they are of supposed oxymorons or non sequiturs (Radical : faerie; nun : Marxist; Haute Couture : nun; nun : won't listen). Contradictions are exposed and then leavened (atheist : nuns who drink alcohol). Various different discourses are permitted intertextual meeting without resolution being a necessary *telos*. The seams of their habits have an overt weave. Contradictions are further exemplified in Sisterly titles: Mother Inferior, Sister Sit on My Face, Sister Mary Armageddon to Be a Habit with You, Sister Monsterio Deliciosa Hysterica, Sister Avon Calling, Sister Airpsly Fair Billis, Sister Ophelia Dick, Sister Amyl Nitrate, Sister Maria von Stoop 'entakit, Sister Mary Third Secret of Fatima, and Sister Fellatio Obliviata, for example. A register of names and skills is kept at the Nun Speakers' Bureau, the titles in themselves counting as further signs of a deliberate fossicking out of "tastelessness" and its eponymic glorification.[72] The sacred and the profane are rendered as a couplet, a couplet that insists on the interdependence of the polite and the grotesque. Functioning in this way manufactures *différends de soi*. It sees the subject making, to redeploy Marx, "his own life . . . an object for him," an object beyond the alienation that is produced by defining the self in terms of the prevailing mode of governance and its categories of existence.[73] A similar task is prescribed by G. H. Mead. He calls on the subject to treat the self "as an object to itself" and thus to mix subject-object formulations in such a way that the self correctly identifies the communities to which it belongs via a process of matching ideal types from the social with its own self-view and developing a fully achieved capacity for intersubjective recognition and conduct.[74]

Inside postmodernity, this can, at its best, be an overtly pluralized cultural self with a lineage that can be dated back to periods prior to the disciplining of theatrical spaces in the seventeenth century, before tight distinctions were drawn between performer and audience and collective grotesqueries excised from the public sphere. With the Enlightenment, order and cleanliness arrived as tropes of culture, with everything accorded a proper, polite place. To move outside this is to conjure a reverse world (cross-dressing is another trope in such counterspheres) in which transgression is quite literally achieved by being in the interstices between categories, in a life founded on undecidability. For Baudrillard, cross-dressing emblematizes artifice. As such, it establishes the possibility of fashioning ourselves anew in a distinctively postmodern way, a form of kitsch that transcends the opposites of beauty and ugliness to inaugurate a "transaesthetic."[75]

One thinks here of a rallying cry for gay rights in the 1970s: "Think we're lowdown and disgusting? Damn right we are." Such logic is exemplified by Eric Michaels's decision to have his AIDS diaries illustrated by a photograph of himself in an advanced state of physical decay and distress.[76] To speak in a collective way that problematizes the categories of taste ("disgusting" as per Michaels) and methodological individualism ("behavior" as per the terms of the charge against the Sisters) is to work toward a communal definition of homosexuality that begins to form a new account of the self. Hence the formation of a lesbian and gay reading group called "the Bad Object Choices" parodies the terms by which its members have been made into the subjects of psy-discourses. Parody offers a new turn in what has been termed the career of the homosexual. It references Oscar Wilde's "transgressive aesthetic" of "the reverse: insincerity, inauthenticity, and unnaturalness." So Paul's biblical requirement that we not utter the crime of sodomy has been routinely troped, most epically by Lord Alfred Douglas in 1894 with "*I am* the Love that dare not speak its name," and latterly by the badge on sale at the Oscar Wilde Memorial Bookstore that reads: "I KNOW YOU KNOW."[77]

This parody is closely and deliberately implicated with the critique it is seeking to unsettle. Hocquenghem argues that the ultimately private part of a man—the anus, that which must be hidden—is a constitutive component, perhaps the crucial bodily emblem, of the division between public and private. Where the phallus is a public, symbolic display of penile power (and vice versa) the anus has no such representative. It is

The Well-Tempered Self

precisely and indefatigably individual, private: "one does not shit in company." The anus must not be public, and making it so is allowing its produce to flow.[78] The popular identification of gay sex with the anus clearly has this effect, perhaps ineradicably so. One response is to deny the fact, another to play up to it and expose its workings and their overlapping with definitions of legitimate public activity. This is to realize Hannah Arendt's maxim, "One can resist only in terms of the identity that is under attack";[79] but to take this resistance a step further by overstressing that identity and magnifying it out of all proportion. Stuart Hall has shown how the concept of blackness was brought into being as a political category by Jamaicans and the Jamaican-English by appropriating its connotations:

> You have spent five, six, seven hundred years elaborating the symbolism through which Black is a negative factor. Now I don't want another term. I want that term, that negative one, that's the one I want. I want a piece of that action. I want to take it out of the way in which it has been articulated in religious discourse, in ethnographic discourse, in literary discourse, in visual discourse. I want to pluck it out of its articulation and re-articulate it in a new way.[80]

For Leo Bersani, gay men define themselves by turning homophobia into a force of desire, a force that jumbles up drives and identifications in a cathectic project of excitement.[81] The desire to offend is not autotelic, in that it desires a reaction of self-questioning from the sweet reasonableness of mannered tolerance. Such a logic informs D. A. Miller's search for "a gay writing position" that eschews the special pleading of identity miserabilism that can "bore or terrorize with a 'positive image.'"[82]

Playing with negativity and linking anti-homosexuality with other political questions sets the Sisters apart from other types of gay public life. The association of gay and radical is a contingent one. It must be in a search for publicness by a group for whom secrecy was for so long the touchstone of identity. Older gays found the politics of declaration of the 1970s not only personally uncomfortable but threatening to their carefully produced and maintained privacy. This manufactured an early division between moralisms of declaration and moralisms of denial. The 1990s have seen the emergence in the United States of those apparent oxymorons the gay Republican and the anti-abortion lesbian separatist. Their politics, rather than their sexual preferences, have been hidden in the past. The National Log Cabin Federation has over four thousand members, and a "homocon" ran Pat Buchanan's San Francisco presidential campaign in 1992. As Bersani puts it, "To want sex with another man is not exactly a credential for political radicalism."[83]

Nevertheless, this form of parodic gay politics rejects authoritarian models. The Sisters' 1989 *White Paper* (complete with brown cover) seeks to promulgate some ideas of the Order that may have been "lost" with an expansion of numbers. But it equally proclaims its partiality and conditionality:

> It is of concern that this paper does not hamper or direct the thinking and evolution of the Order. So this paper is to be seen as a guide to the thinking of some sisters at one point and not a piece of dogma to direct the thinking of the Order . . . it is not necessarily a piece of right thinking . . . it is not to be dragged out as proof or support for an argument or an idea.

The *Paper* calls for a joyful life via an "expiation from self" of guilt. The Order's choice of title is significant here. It plays with two meanings of "indulgence": the playfulness of consensual and enjoyable bodily pleasures; and the tradition of ecclesiastical payment for failure to be sufficiently moral. The "perpetual" element is the timeless expiation of guilt. Again, the marketplace is invoked for its publicness: "It is there that we take on meaning."[84]

The words spoken by the two Sisters at the November event were carefully chosen, selected because of the Vatican's opposition to homosexuals, to homosexual civil rights, and to women, via the rejection of female ordination into the priesthood. The word *fascist* was applied in opposition to Wojtyła's repression of dissent. One of the men, Fabian Lo Schiavo, then Mother Inferior in charge of the Convent, was on the Anglican Synod of Sydney for nine years until 1986. In December of that year, some three weeks after the arrest, he was sacked from his parish positions and formally required to worship elsewhere because of his other selves and practices. These included actions taken under a variety of personae, such as the Reverend Oral Richards, who preaches the "Four Square Gospel of Socialism, Feminism, Gay Liberation and Ethnic Pride"; Dean Lance Sheraton-Hilton, a play on the name of a former senior Anglican official in New South Wales; and Monsignor Porca Madonna.

These titles and associated practices do not signify levity alone; the levity is predicated on an automatic association with capacity to shock. Definite material effects may flow from them: arrest and rejection have already been noted. And when Porca Madonna appeared at the launching of a book by Don Dunstan (who as South Australian premier in the

1970s had orchestrated decriminalization of homosexuality in that state) the uproar was such that Dunstan was forced to resign from his then position as a senior bureaucrat in the tourism sector in the state of Victoria. But these costs may be offset by gains made at the level of signification, and the possibilities for alliance. The San Francisco Chapter of the Sisters pulled a mock Wojtylan popemobile in the 1987 Gay Pride Parade, later joining in anti-papal protest with the Whores of Babylon group of prostitutes, whose leader Scarlet Harlot sang "Pope, Don't Preach, I'm Terminating My Pregnancy." Such actions mirrored the Sydney Sisters' "special tribute to a megastar Pope" on his arrival there in 1986.[85] These loose international links—links at the level of signifier and parodic practice—are fully appropriate to the "charterless character" of the Sisters. It is just this polymorphously perverse organizational anti-structure that destabilizes a conventional secular and religious masculine subject.

So for *Sydney Morning Herald* investigative journalist Evan Whitton, they are the "so-called Sisters of Perpetual Indulgence."[86] Of course, the title "Sisters" is no more a self-investiture than is the title "Sydney Morning Herald." The appellation "so-called" attests to the Sisters' value as irritants to conventional metadiscourses on naming. In his epistemic discussion of differing ways of writing about François Mitterand's election in 1981, Michel Pêcheux suggests that the struggle over discourse is more than one of paraphrase. Referentiality exists in the same event, whether in an article written from the left or the right. But signification in the reporting of the event is a site of struggle as much as signification in the event itself.[87] The Sisters are bringing into question even this structuralist notion of the mutual impact of signifying elements. Theirs is a more radically shifting system of meaning.

This capacity to disturb is not an unbridled license to shock. With some of the ideological mystification surrounding "casual sex" as a way of life rent asunder by the advent of AIDS, the Sisters perform dual functions of health education, via their distribution of male prophylactics, and ideologizing, an acceptance of sexual difference that includes different modes and tempi of sexualizing. But critically, while their activities are heavily marked out through excess, there is no account of "the true homosexual" underpinning them. There is no "whole, true person" to emerge. The Sisters are using categories of outrage from the margins and blending them with categories of decency from the center to break up the logic of a unified cultural subject. They desiccate Lyotard's formula for keeping sexual identity well-ordered: "Virility claims to establish order and feminity [*sic*] is the compulsion to deride order.

There is chattering in the gynaeceum and silence among the troops."[88] To break up this bifurcation is to go back to some of the ancient reasons for criticizing the love of boys by men. The critique was not connected to any essential condemnation of the morality of such relationships, but rather for what they indicated about the men's preparedness to be leaders in other spheres of life and to distinguish themselves from other categories of person, such as slaves, boys, and women. Calling such divisions into question was dangerous.

Of course, the Sisters are not autotelic. When they dress and speak as they do, their form of communication sets up a desire for recognition. The pope is a particular target of those disturbing and disrupting the codes of religious orders precisely because of the closed-shop, gendered labor market that his bureaucracy produces, and its correlation with a rejection of homosexuality. For Christians amongst the Sisters, this is a serious case of neglect by a wanted but tyrannical Other. "Desire finds its meaning in the desire of the other, not so much because the other holds the key to the object desired, as because the first object of desire is to be recognized by the other," Lacan observes.[89] And Wojtyła simply denied their presence at Sydney. But the Other here is not necessarily a psychological category. It may become manifest in a public sphere, which may be the preferred site to form contradictoriness. The act of prohibited persons dressing in a code sanctioned/enforced by the papacy for others is something more than a conscious parody; it is almost a move calling for recognition of misrecognition, an inscription of self-incompleteness for which no resolution is required. One might consider here the account Ed Cohen gives of submitting an article from the field of gay literary studies to *PMLA* and the terpsichories entered into between himself and the editorial board. That dance could be described by reference to the complexities of ambition, autonomy, defense of the realm, and the breaking of *politesse:* Cohen wanted the credibility of a *PMLA* publication in order to assist his job prospects; he wanted to do this self-consciously as a gay scholar; the board wanted him to remove a political coda at the end of his essay and allow it to stand on the basis of its "literary argument"; and he proceeded to rewrite the article.[90] He required recognition and approbation, but on his own terms of self. The relevant liberal institution could not agree and had to act to define gay literary studies as insufficiently literary. (Recalling the earlier critiques of Foucault, perhaps *PMLA* would not qualify as a liberal institution for Rorty.)

To return to the ecclesiastical, it is clear that the regendering of religious codes problematizes churches at a very profound level. "Man can

The Well-Tempered Self

exist because God helps him to define his genre, to situate himself as a finite being in relation to the infinite (the regrowth of the religious can in fact be interpreted as man defending the notion of man)," Luce Irigaray suggests. A male, never-ending God has been a key referent for masculinity, justification for its certainty and guarantor of its eternity. The self-reproduction of God, his status as parthenogene, obviates the requirement for men to be biologically or discursively dependent on women.[91] Nuns are supposedly married to Christ, who is simultaneously the son of God and God himself. The implications of Oedipal conflicts become more profound when a tribe of Jocastas is found to be all-male. (In the New Testament, Jesus remains unmarried. He has no real physical mother, and therefore no woman to contest possession with the father in an Oedipal sense.) Again, one does not have to hold to notions of unconscious interiorities to use this logic. For it is as an institutional force and a warrant for manners that the seemingly non-contradictory logics of the Church have operated. Simply to work to point out the mutual dependency of supposed antonyms is to problematize unifying notions of the subject and extant systems of individual categorization. We do not need a theory of masculinity that assigns meaning inside either the performance of a role or the denial of the unconscious to understand such actions. Rather, we should note that the practices in which men engage are frequently to be associated with other means of description, such as cartoonist, parent, patient, or campanologist. Masculinity becomes an issue not in terms, then, of adherence to either overt or covert norms. Rather, it is an issue on occasion, where problems arise such as the freedom for two men to touch in public, or when discussion sustains a doctrine of inappropriate and appropriate maleness. When the Sisters appear, masculinity appears, because this is just such an occasion. There is no indeterminacy of masculinity here. On the contrary, this is a definite occasion. But its definiteness resides in the circumscription of the event marked by clothing and naming rather than in the sustenance of stable gender identity or a relationship to hegemonic masculinity.

Rituals of Distinction

In October 1978, Wojtyła drafted a letter from Polish Catholic bishops to their congregations. It read in part: "Not allowing people with a different social and political ideology to speak, as is the practice of the State, is unjust."[92] But the freedom to speak in public is always a conditional freedom. At some level, everyone knows about what Foucault calls the "taboo on the object of speech" that makes certain statements unmakable in certain places, most prominently at the points where politics and sex meet. This is achieved through three technologies: the rules of discourse that allow and prohibit discussion; the practices of division that distinguish between good and mad behavior; and the clinical separation of truth from falsehood. Wojtyła knows about them, as my analysis of his speech has demonstrated. For they are also what Foucault identifies as the three axes that provide the available means of knowing oneself via the conventional subjectivity of discourses of "sexuality."[93]

Eight years after the 1978 letter, Wojtyła watched as organs of another state acted in just the way that he had once condemned. So did hundreds of academics and others whose livelihoods might be said to bear testimony to liberalism as a discourse of dominant moment within Australia. When the two men leapt to their feet and shouted, "Anti-woman / Anti-gay / Fascist pope / Go away," they were brutalized, arrested, and charged with offensive behavior. They had stood up, interrupted, and disagreed gratuitously. Conversely, when a much larger group, dressed in "Polish national costume," broke through barriers and interrupted, they were greeted with grins by the officers of the repressive state apparatus.

This could be interpreted as follows: resistance through the breaking of ritual is against the law, but support through the breaking of ritual is legitimate. The act or behavior of interrupting, shouting, or moving into spaces closed off for others is irrelevant. It is the message contained or enunciated within that appropriated space that matters. Liberalism depends on the classification of the utterer and the utterance before it can admit of tolerance. Or more specific to this site, the avowedly liberal state can be illiberal when the particular discourse it is privileging is fundamentally illiberal.

Alternatively, one could concentrate on the incivility of the Sisters' address: its haranguing, ugly, angry tone; its failure to be polite; and its association of public debate with unruliness. The error of those two men was not that of breaking the convention of sitting in silence for the speaker and rising while others sat; or raising a placard and seeking attention. For others were not penalized for so doing. Nor was it a question of their being public supporters of "homosexuality." Elsewhere, government-sanctioned and -salaried workers were writing and implementing critiques of anti-abortion, anti-homosexual, and generally discriminatory policies segregating women and people of color from various occupations. Or put another way, the same government that arrested the two men for expressing these views was also providing more than an awning for the expression of similar opinions (if not always stated at the designated expense of Wojtyła). But one space was Sydney University on a pope's day, and others may have been hospital wards; women's divisions within a range of bureaucracies; other parts of the university; or other segments of the academy. And the mode of expression would mostly have been a measured, considered, *decent* subjectivity of instrumental rationality.

Occupying a space reserved for others is legitimate when it serves to assist the interests of the discourse for which that space was originally marked out and is a "jolly" distraction. Occupying a reserved space against those interests in an unseemly manner is not permissible, although working against them from spaces sanctioned by the state is acceptable. In no sense could the Sisters' actions be seen to threaten papal physical security; the future of the Catholic Church; the Australian state; the university; the nexus between them; or in fact any thing or body. But a message had been given in a distasteful fashion in a space assigned by the state for messages of an opposing character. The interdicted message contradicted various points of view expressed by the sanctioned speakers in a way that forwarded a "new" politics of the self and its public performance. This is the problem that Habermas identifies as a central tenet of Foucault's investigations: "Those limit experiences in which Western logos sees itself, with extreme ambivalence, faced with something heterogeneous."[94] As Godard wryly said in explanation of his decision to remove *Hail Mary* (1985) from exhibition in Rome after an outburst from Wojtyła: "It's the house of the church, and if the Pope didn't want a bad boy running around his house, the least I could do is respect his wishes. This Pope has a special relationship to Mary; he considers her a daughter."[95] Godard knows about how to keep things apart that some people want to bring together.

One could argue that the Sisters' sin was to interrupt ideologically, but they could not be charged in those terms because of freedom of speech. Their actions were therefore personalized and pathologized as "behavior" that was "offensive." Systemic unruliness, an uncivic mode of conduct, was their real crime. The inoffensiveness implicitly contrasted to this is not silence (*vide* the Polish supporters); it is conduct that evidences respect. Hence the inconsistency in the treatment of the pope's interruptors.

The relative legitimacy of the actions taken on November 26 by Sisters, Poles, security guards, and police was set by the *donnés* of circumspect authority. Even Mill acknowledged that "permission to differ" was only granted on an absolute basis by those in marginal positions. Its uptake by the dominant was always contingent.[96] But he saw this in terms of access to an object called power, rather than as an outcome of the need of that dominant group to form itself and its subjects by exclusion. This is the source of the difficulty experienced when, as Mother Inferior Lo Schiavo put it in 1989, "We are happy to poach church ritual and the aspects of religious tradition which we like and put them to good use. . . . Straight society says, 'If you people were discreet to the point of invisibility we'd accept you.' The Sisters reject that completely. We're determined to be as visible as it's possible for a moustachioed male face in a wimple to be."[97]

Three years later, the former Mother Inferior emerged from a personal retreat transmogrified into Mother Abyss to publicize on the national youth radio network the Sisters' decision to exclude military personnel from the Order. (The Australian government had just announced that its defense forces would continue to prohibit gay people from employment, despite trends in more than a dozen countries over the 1980s in the other direction.) The Sisters had already proscribed military membership because of concerns about the influence that such people could wield over the "younger novices," for whom the elders considered themselves to be *in loco parentis*. The ban applied only in the novitiate, a group noted for its "susceptibility" to military ideology. Mother emphasized the Sisters' readiness to negotiate with the defense forces over their exclusion from the Order. This knowing reversal of terminology emphasized that "we are in the frontline of the war against homophobia." In explaining the Order for new listeners, Mother said that it consisted of people sharing a "fondness for dressing-up and same-sex grouping" whose "collective and respectful" precepts were inimical to military logic. He also noted that the tenth anniversary in 1991 had seen a redefinition into a "coalition Order" and the appointment of the first "lesbian monk."

It is of the essence for the Sisters' actions to be critical in an unruly way and unruly in a critical way that breaks rituals of distinction between categories of person and conduct in order to produce what Durkheim calls "illegitimate mixings."[98] This is the nature of the Order's account of the resistive gay as a misbehaving public cultural subject working to form the means toward a technology of the self. The Sisters' rules of conduct may be positioned within what Habermas has called "autonomous public spheres." These spheres, unlike "the" public sphere discussed earlier, arise from the generation of meanings within

The Well-Tempered Self

subcultures. Their meanings then enter "public discourses and higher-level forms of intersubjectivity"; in this instance, with a shocking impact that has often been the modus operandi of marginal groups when they call into question a politics ordered around the conventions of the economic, the spiritual, the sovereign, or the psychological as means of knowing a society.[99] This new form of politics is a politics of hypallage, a reversal of terms. But it is more than an inversion. It can also be understood as the need for freedom, not merely from the state or capital, but from the *doxa* of what it is to be a person, from a particular and limiting "type of individualization." The new freedom serves "to promote new forms of subjectivity" distinct from the notions of individuality that currently obtain.[100] This is the freedom to speak *différends de soi*.

◆

CONCLUSION

I HAVE SOUGHT to argue that culture is a significant area in the daily organization of fealty to the cultural-capitalist state. More specifically, it has been my contention that various technologies of subjectivity are the very stuff of cultural policy inside postmodernity; that the formation and functioning of citizenship is a central concern of the times. These are hardly findings; more a banal recitation of the obvious. The claim of the argument to innovation rests, first, on the primacy it gives the protocols of textual theory, and, second, on the possibilities it outlines for political action under the rubric of citizenship. These two elements are crucially interconnected.

Cultural critique principally operates via the interpretation of texts. This is as true of the anti-capitalist, anti-patriarchal, and anti-racist stances of much tertiary level training in cultural studies as it is of the diurnal drills in how to read characteristic of much secondary school training in literature. The overtly politicized and theorized domain of the first is connected to the overtly conserving and empiricist domain of the second. They share a methodology that seeks to find ethical incompleteness in textual characters and transfer that incompleteness to readers. This methodology works to concentrate the subject on self-improvement. It sets up a never-ending dialectic between an ideal adequacy of self-knowledge and service in the public purpose on the one hand and an already-extant riddle of insufficiency and self-serving consumption in the individual purpose on the other. Between these agonistic poles there are further tensions at work, between knowing oneself and knowing one's place in the social structure. The notion that understanding begins with the subject means that the subject is forever a complex to be undone and remade. This is the ironic Cartesian link between social movements of identity politics, aesthetic autoexpression, and the prosperous economic calculator. This link becomes visible in the life of cultural policy. Such policy thrives on the subject's incompleteness, precisely because the subject is never fully present in the dyadic sign of art and society, a sign that expresses the relevance of that subject, as its imagined interpreter, but excludes it via the distance presumed to separate language from the social.

We can see a preoccupation with the playing out of these issues across a wide variety of sites. I have shown how, at a foundational level, textual analysis sets up a reflectionist protocol based on this process of inscribing incompleteness by forming a readership required to do continuous work on itself. This can easily lead to a mode of subjection, rather than a politics of the self. I have indicated how this mode of subjection operates within cultural policy that seeks to form national sovereignties via television drama. The argument has also been made with reference to the philosophical and pragmatic tension between the notions of the selfless citizen and the selfish consumer, caught between maximizing utility for the general and the particular interest. These chapters have stressed the mutability of cultural subjectivity formed by the operation of ethical incompleteness.

They are chapters that sit alongside the account of social and cultural theory given earlier in chapter 1, "Civic Culture and the Postmodern Subject." That chapter's explanations of the morphology of the citizen, the role of cultural policy, the concept of a social surface, and the operation of postmodern knowledge indicate both the plasticity of citizenship and the limits within which it functions. It is these limits, and possible ways of dealing with them, that I wish to stress in this Conclusion. What are the settings and relationships of resistance and adherence that differentiate the self as an autoinvention from the subject as an imposition? How far can a politics of identity proceed in search of *dif-*

fěrends de soi before it must work with the ethically indeterminate sub-jection of cultural citizenship?

Citizenship is clearly a term whose time is here. Since 1989 in eastern and central Europe, citizenship has been a popularly conceived and applied concept that appears to transcend rhetoric. At least temporar-ily, it describes a powerful civil society. And after the work of various social movements in the older cultural-capitalist democracies, it is a popularly conceived and applied idea that appears to challenge both conventional party politics and critical theory, as broadly defined. Half the world now lives under democracy, an increase of 10 percent on 1988. No longer a reformist trope or the hidey-hole of institutionalist politi-cal science, citizenship is a new move, a revived idea of sovereignty that is itself always on the move. It appears to have made a shift away from *Das wohltemperierte Klavier* of my Introduction and toward the *différends de soi* of chapter 5.

There are, however, very definite limits to what this move can achieve. For it continues to function as a technology of subjection. Citizenship is tied to doctrines of representativeness that define the public in very general terms. These terms may be contradictory (such as the citizen-consumer couplet) but their significatory home ultimately resides in this metaphor: citizens are public. And this unitary public—not a series of public spheres of dialogue and difference—will continue to have ide-alized general needs spread across it by the cultural-capitalist state in-side very particular logics of appropriate individual and collective iden-tity and conduct. These logics define the terms of subjectivity. They may not be harmonious among themselves, but the contradictions they harbor will mostly be kept unseen. When Rousseau published his "Social Contract, or Principles of Political Right" in 1762, he dealt with this issue in what remains a definitive manner. That document described the "essence" of the "social compact" forged between person and pol-ity in the following language: "Each of us puts his person and all his power in common under the supreme direction of the general will, and, in our corporate capacity, we receive each member as an indivisible part of the whole." A "corporate and collective body" henceforth displaces "the individual personality of each contracting party" and problema-tizes particular interests that fail to conform to the "general will" as outside the tacitly agreed preconditions for the exercise of citizenship.[1]

I do not wish to say that this is always and everywhere undesirable. If nothing else, it ensures policies are generated that can be put into oper-ation and discourages purely expressive forms of politics that fail to attend to general collective needs. But even as such a position lends itself very well to the generation of cultural citizens that are civil in their subjection to the public good, it is not usable for producing selves that are otherwise outside convention. These are selves that, inside post-modernity, may become manifest on the terrain of cultural politics and therefore, at least in part, contest cultural policy.

Civil society has come to serve as a "code word" covering a multitude of practices to do with economic restructuring and, frequently, a reduction in state services. This is hardly surprising for a "conceptual portmanteau" that provides semantic shelter for practices all the way from "households and voluntary associations to the economic systems of capitalism," recalling the economic subtext to Woodrow Wilson's announcement in 1917, "We have come to redeem the world by giving it liberty and justice." Consider the irony signified by the existence of a 1990 "Batman" story in which ancient curses left by an occult group—which included Jefferson amongst its members—plague American cities.[2]

There will always necessarily be a master command in the discourse of citizenship, that where we are constitutionally equal, we can suffer other forms of inequality with equilibrium, because in this ultimate court of personage, we are identical. The means of ensuring this equilibrium is a doctrine of equivalence that denies difference. While such a doctrine can work very well at the point of distributing rights, because it refuses to distinguish between categories of person, it does less well at the point of forming those rights, the stage when rights and obligations are defined and divided. The tendency within this doctrine of equivalence is to delineate sectional from general interests very early on in such deliberations, in ways that typically function within the command metaphors of citizenship as we find it; which is to say, a white, male, heterosexual, and polite capitalist norm projected out onto the world via the twin struts of private property as a model of the rights of the individual and fatherly property as a model of the rights of the state. To be branded a "sectional interest" is utterly disabling under these circumstances.

Against this, as Stephen Heath notes, the success of theorizing difference means that it is no longer easy for men to see themselves as "the universal agents of a common sex." Instead, the seeming neutrality and universalism of doctrines of equivalence in fact mask a profound and skewed specificity at their source. The supposed openness—he even uses the word *indeterminate* to describe their work—of human science doctrines of rights and logic in fact conceals a history of contestation.[3]

Nevertheless, there are still problems associated with a complete withdrawal from the domain of ontic or epistemic logic in favor of the postmodern. Seyla Benhabib identifies the retreat from doctrines of the principled, autonomous subject and the march of history toward a thoroughgoing dialectic of critique and legitimacy as inimical to women's agency and their senses of self. For her, a utopia, to be understood as a regulatory principle of hope, is essential. The establishment of norms is basic if ethical conduct is to prevail, and those norms should be concerned with empathy, pacific sentiment, ecology, fluidity, and solidarity.[4] It is not my purpose here to disavow the utility of such technologies for initiating and sustaining social change. Rather, I am seeking to ask whether the project of reconciliation of the subject and society that forms the basis for such reflection is architecturally different from the project set up by cultural policy. And to establish whether the postmodern position enunciated in chapter 5 might be useful in establishing some movement between the politics of self-formation and the politics of subject-formation. This involves a dialectic between the particular and the universal. Doctrines of the universal are always reasoned from a definite place; they necessitate exclusion; they require, therefore, to be forced open at the moment of their operation. To find that point, we might ask what can be salvaged from the ideals of modernity.

For Jeffrey Isaac, the modern is characterized by a nexus of power and freedom rather than their separation, a nexus that looks less than appealing following global conflict in war and ecology. Because the average person now looks far beyond the everyday toward the international, that everyday is lost to politics: "Citizenship has become an experience of powerlessness before the seemingly inexorable imperatives of economic and political systems." Progress seems to be stultifyingly antithetical to its avowed purposes because it is determined at a macro level even as its effects are experienced locally. Nevertheless, there are equally significant, more positive aspects of the Enlightenment's legacy, such as penal reform, universal suffrage, and an end to slavery. The identifiably shared—in fact, universal—features of the citizen are the greatest part of this inheritance, because of the inalienable stature of the rights that form its gift to a world public. Modernity and democracy, on this reading, are the sole spaces of history that allow equal rein to utterly dissimilar ethical presumptions, permitting private choice in the field of dress, diet, partnership, and association. Democracy gives the technology within which differing, opposed conceptions of these questions can exist and even talk with one another in search of commonality or when their positions correspond.[5]

The technology of citizenship, of shared rights, has been the principal arguing point shared by modern movements of emancipation. The idea that political rights are granted to all by the fact of birth has animated the claims of every category of the oppressed since the eighteenth century. Even so, the struggle once won has rarely satisifed. Equal access to citizenship has not led to equal social justice for all, because of the propensity toward economic anarchy and political oligarchy and because the discourse of justice increasingly presumes a space of autonomy between person, economy, and polity rather than a policy of assurance by the last on behalf of the first, or some other variant. It is for this reason that Iris Marion Young proposes "*differentiated* citizenship." This acknowledges the value of universalism in terms of "a general will and common life" but is critical of the exclusion of groups from dialogue under such totalities. Too often, the notion of citizenship functions as a "demand for homogeneity." This can be avoided if access to political decisions is institutionalized for all categories of person, however different.[6]

Action inside the apparatus of the state is essential for subcultural groups if they are to achieve wide-ranging reform in a variety of important areas. But the means of self-definition, the politics of identity, will tend to serve an unsatisfactory set of protocols if they are thought through and practiced within these terms. For the civic cultural subject—the citizen—is produced as a polite and obedient servant of etiquette, within limited definitions of acceptable behavior. The indeterminacy inscribed onto subjects through cultural policy can be particularly disabling in the area of defining the self. For it tends to work via technologies of power inside a general model of ethical incompleteness and pedagogic dependence. The return of the desire to forge well-tempered subjects is inevitable with citizenship. In this sense, it is quite wrong to equate cultural policy with "totality" and describe it as an attempt to "restrict and stabilize meaning."[7] For this even temper depends on the uncertainty that is civility's stock in trade.

Paradoxically, it is against this tendency that we may pose the polysemic, polyvalent notions of postmodernity, a sign frequently denounced for its depoliticizing effect, but one that bears recuperation. The valuable idée fixe of postmodernity is to manufacture identity, not to accept the existing identities on offer. Hence the emphasis of my final chapter. It aims to explain a cultural politics that inscribes its own sense of indeterminacy, that not only refuses a logic of self-truth, but disavows any search for such a singular truth. In their acceptance of contradiction and rejection of *politesse,* the Sisters of Perpetual Indulgence are dedicated to expunging notions of self-definition through sexuality and even the search for any ultimate self. By accounting for homosexuality as a set of practices that should be divorced from an overarching account of the person, the Sisters abjure the reflexive engagement with one's ethical incompleteness that animates cultural subjects. They seek their own *différends de soi*.

If we accept the anti-essentialist accounts of postmodernity, their one point of concert—namely, the implausibility of a throughgoing model of the subject—then where is the space to move? Indeed, who or what could be said to be moving? We do not have to return to the carping metaphysicians arrayed against Foucault in order to face such a question. To identify *différends de soi* is to assert the existence of agency. It assumes that people can organize their own emancipation from definition and enclosure, in search of selves that are not transactions with the deeply secreted truth, but rather rejections or appropriations of surface categories. Such a move takes us away from queries as to the identity of the subject and toward tactics for utilizing it. This involves making do with the acceptable components of existing technology, even as new ones are made to appear through the action of producing hybrids that combine conventional subjectivity and impolite selfhood.

For marginal or resistive groups to function, it is clearly necessary for them to harness both a reformism that knows the subjectifying technologies of the cultural-capitalist state and a means of fashioning their own technologies of the self. The state will routinely use the concepts of the nation and the individual as tropes to engender fealty. But even these homogenizing categories may be usefully deployed by various subordinate groups, because the heterogeneous composition of populations necessitates a certain state regard for difference. For the state is ultimately a grid of governance, an analytic tool that brings together and unites some really quite distinct forces in the management of people. In particular, cultural-capitalist democracies specialize in "action at a distance." They seek to organize the social world, not merely through institutional agencies of the state, but through a very broad band of knowledge across a spectrum that includes public health, social work, auditing, accountancy, and other modes of modulation operating in very dispersed ways. There are always opportunities for the expression of difference in so dispersed a set of actions. That space of opportunity is not emphasized, after the manner of a sanguine political science, by the notion that such states are pluralistic. Rather, such openings arise because the very act of government involves problematizing, bringing into doubt, carving and slicing in order to render social issues smaller and hence create more and more difficulties in need of resolution.[8]

The inescapable contradictions in the model of the originary social contract become evident when its favored method of animation—the

The Well-Tempered Self

creation of abstract subjects in the form of objects of knowledge—is coupled with the move toward intervening in all areas of life. That shift has complex manifestations and meanings. While it enables a monumental training and surveillance, it simultaneously divides subjects up so carefully that they cease to be rallied under the clarion call of the citizen, looking outside representative democracy for public definitions and political technologies of identity. This opportunity derives from the manifold activities of the state that in fact challenge the subject outside the technical role of the citizen: working, living, and birthing subjects are of more poignant, consistent, and pregnant moment on a diurnal basis than is the occasional voter. Governments finally yearn for a social efficiency, "a happy, healthy, virile and integrated social body."[9]

The state appears more and more to be a series of disaggregated agencies of organization, rather than a center of distributional politics. As such, minority politics becomes one focus of activity, even under universalist democratic doctrines. So the efflorescence of citizens' charters in Britain, which saw the three major parties producing such documents in July 1991, was a very mixed affair. We have already noted the reactionary tone of the Conservatives' document, which granted citizens the right to take action against trade unions, for instance, but not against companies. The Labour Party charter guaranteed the following: women were to have the right of access to female public sector doctors; the subjects of rape or domestic violence were to be interviewed by specially trained women police; nursery places were to be available for all young children; and public tenants were to be provided with the opportunity to purchase their residences through the reallocation of rent payments. Discrimination was to be outlawed and minority ethnic groups provided with special services of advocacy. Conversely, equivalent new accounts of citizenship and civil society in Poland have involved moves to outlaw abortion, partly the work of Karol Wojtyła.

To repeat, the sine qua non of citizenship, which appears to guarantee status and service via sovereignty, is tied to doctrines of nation, economy, and person that do not develop the politics of identity prerequisite to participation in defining public spheres and their processes in broad terms that go beyond equivalence at the level of defining rights. It will remain the task of subcultural groups both to form their identities through technologies of the self and then to articulate those sensibilities, or their material policy corollaries, to the state. This is a double movement, a paradox that sees the self still tied in to a relationship with the subject. To do otherwise would be to utilize identity politics as an end in itself. But this is not feasible after modernity, when self-contemplation gives way to the work of mimetic desire. Any "pleasing image of the self" is resumed via "the disquieting presence of a supplementary audience whose gaze fractures the auto-erotic reverie," as Stephen Bann puts it.[10] Subcultural groups are inevitably called back to seeking to influence the dominant and achieve some recognition, much like the Sisters in chapter 5. The hope is that they may be able to influence the dominant in return. This is to reciprocate the process of ordination, or naming rights, which has served to rank signifiers in a way inimical to their concerns.

We might consider here Heath's call for a "non-representative representation." He is interested to encourage an ethics of difference in its stead. Beginning from the understanding that there are three types of representation (the image, the argument, and the deputy), he suggests that the first two of these conventionally combine in the third form, that of the plenipotentiary. This ambassador for the people adopts a generalized mode. Heath insists that there must be a more open model, in which representativeness flows down additional tributaries. But he is aware that this still involves a sense of the plenipotentiary engaging in an exercise of pleading performed in front of the perennially dissatisfied forces of the dominant. In place of this endless gymnastic repetition, these forces should themselves be repositioned to account for sameness and difference.[11] Similar questions are posed when we consider the contribution of the human sciences to division, as opposed to unity. There is a clear consanguinity of race and racism inside the representational and policy protocols of the modern. But, of course, the means of responding to such travesties reside precisely in universalist doctrines of justice. These are not to be ditched, surely; for it is in their breach rather than their observance that difficulties lie and appeal becomes possible.

The processes to prevent these iniquities are integral to Young's revised model of citizenship: first, organization by minorities to identify themselves and forge a critique of the social; second, formal arrangements allowing the initiation and discussion of social policy proposals; and, finally, the power of veto over policies with a direct impact on the designated minority. This appears to address something Marx always had such difficulty with—namely, the activation of a transcendent dialogue between the specific and the particular, articulated both by the state and within each citizen.

These are similar difficulties to those identified in feminist debates over the notion of androgynous ethics. These debates involve the drawing of a distinction between characteristics that connote moral value and those that are more clearly inside the register of personal style.

Virtues that are gendered (reason, principle, and justice for men; benevolence, modesty, charm, and compassion for women) often work to exclude people's choices in life between the public and the private. A new, feminist-inflected definition of ethical completeness should require equal and interactive amounts of each quality instead of a paradigmatic selection founded on their opposition. This form of virtue should be a *donné*, not something amenable to negotiation. But this presumes the prospect of delimiting the ground of the purely interior from the purely exterior, the personal from the social. The preconditions for this investment in classification are not present because of the overweening sexism of contemporary life, which clouds any possibility of distinguishing nonmoral from moral virtues. The desired end point of feminist justice must instead be what Rosemarie Tong refers to as "equal repect for, consideration of, and delight in difference." Conventional definitions of virtue find it to be "a cultivated behavioral disposition that results in habitual acts that make a person socially acceptable." In place of that understanding, Tong prefers to substitute "acts that make a person not merely *acceptable* in his or her own society, but *good* in any recognizably human society." We can then begin the business of differentiating moral virtues from those outside that register. This is particularly significant because "nonmoral virtues" are normally those that women and men have been required to display as part of the psychology of femininity or masculinity. So (feminine) humility and (masculine) hardiness can now be catalogued as virtues that belong with the nonmoral, and benevolence and honesty with the moral. The latter can be valorized as nongendered prerequisites for virtue, with the former understood as maneuvers in search of personal performance, which are unrelated to the legitimate demands of public virtue.[12]

The best option for converting between the subject and self, while being able to move back in order to utilize citizenship where possible, is to uncouple ethics from the doleful tasks set by the human sciences. As Ian Hacking puts it: "At present rhetoric about the good life is almost always based on some claim to know the truth about desire, about vitamins, about humanity or society. But there are no such truths to know." This moves the project onto Kantian terrain, in the sense that ethics and freedom become intertwined, without a status for freedom inside knowledge. Rather, it is simply present. Hence Foucault's difficulties with social movements claiming to have uncovered enduring truths of the person, for this was to implicate them in the very labor of the human sciences that had worked to oppress them.[13]

Said argues that the wave of imperialism that commenced at the conclusion of the eighteenth century stressed questions of identity for both colonized and colonizing, mostly in an antagonistic manner. This depth of epistemological division into races and nations was imperialism's startling debt to its future. The debt insists that everyone is of a category, with its own inner truth. He calls this "exceptionalism." The differences that imperial nations insisted upon in their categorization of others then became available as rallying points and research interests for the catalogued, for the accusative as much as its nominative. Examples include attempts to turn this type of definitive classification of subordinate alterity into an anti-colonial virtue such as *négritude*. These were necessary moves in the staging of resistance. But once the colonizer has departed, a discourse of resistance based on these tactically useful categories must be replaced by a new form of social rhetoric that abjures the inevitable subjection of nationalism. The value of an emphasis on symbolic systems of identity and independence cannot, in Said's view, be allowed to go on for too long, lest it subside into "an ultimately uninteresting alternation of presence and absence."[14] The emancipatory narrative that underpins modern law is founded on sovereign power being assigned upward by the people as citizens. But it fails to tell adequately the story of those people's lives as public agents, concentrating "the political"—as it must—as the exclusive province of the parliamentary-political and the constitutional mythology of foundational contracts. The new social movements have demands that cannot be encompassed, either definitionally or administratively, inside the norms of democratic theory, because they do not aim to control state power. And their very existence emerged from the exercise of bio-power by the state in the first place. They are creatures of its practices of division, practices that underscore collective ethnic, gender, and age tropes of organization in place of an individual citizen-consciousness. An effect of state power has come to speak more loudly than the supposed warrant for that power. No longer can it be understood via a universalist rule of law: for governmentality has overreached the limitations of government. As Mark Crispin Miller puts it, a "disavowal of public movements has itself become a public movement."[15] The intimacy that sees the world from the perspective of someone else has become part of public sympathy.

In this sense, the task of founding technologies of the self that are ethical, but do not subjugate, and allow for movement between the categories, is complex and currently unsatisfying. For this to be otherwise, a new mode of producing knowledge—including economic knowledge and hence the economic system—would need to come into being.

The Well-Tempered Self

For now, it seems best to accept certain regulating principles as tools that are acceptable to prevailing logics and useful for groups that need to work both with and against them. Such precepts would include legality, free speech, free association, and guarantees that the state will not intervene in everyday life. Of course, this can be a recipe for capitalism based on the sovereignty of individual choice, particularly if "democracy" is substituted as the desired end point for, say, "socialism." This could easily be the outcome of the lifestyles logic of certain social movements. But without changes to the discourse of an individualism founded on doubt and laboring in the promise and service of an infinitely deferred certainty, the shared logic of the human sciences and capitalism will remain intact. Otherwise marginality will always involve expulsion from only partially relativized norms, consigned to live in "the abstraction of the secondhand."[16]

The seductiveness of forming a self in opposition to the ordinations of others is undoubted. But only fantasy can permit an absolute heroization of identity politics. As Eve Kosofsky Sedgwick notes, even the most careful of social movements are bound up with practices of exclusion. Identifying as something necessitates a criss-crossing in order to identify both with and against, and hence the promotion of a moral righteousness of inclusion in denial of differences that in other walks of life would clearly divide members of such a community.[17] Paradoxically, the standardization of such a politics might be seen to reference the difference-crushing machines of universalism that it was designed to counter. It inevitably downplays or denies either particular traits of conduct or whole categories of person. Hall has demonstrated both the utility of "Black" as a reversed, renewing trope and its more negative coefficients: the exclusion of Asian people of color and black people who have other coordinates of collective identification. United fronts adopted for the purposes of external conflictual engagement always have "differences . . . raging behind."[18] One recalls here Bersani's explosion of the caring and sharing myths of sex parlors for gay men. For him, far from being anti-hierarchical spaces of equality, they were sites for the playing-out of customized sex characterized by a harsh gradation of persons, "ruthlessly ranked" and marked by intense competition.[19]

In conclusion, we bring to mind Elias's "civilizing process," subsequently redefined by Zygmunt Bauman as "the typically modern discourse of power." The displacement of ignorance by reason, of barbarism by decency, of chaos by order, of passion by civility, of chance by security is to be seen as the advent, over many centuries, of revised forms of management. Now the will of the producing and consuming subject is a desired object of control, where the sense of identification is with an internalized obedience. Modernity enshrined constitutionalism and individualism simultaneously, a double move of unification and division that created a centrally ordered account of individualism even as it insisted on conditions for the subordination of that individual.[20]

Ultimately, cultural-capitalist states cannot enshrine differential accounts of the person in their doctrines of sovereignty, because that would require a revolution in the liberal, humanist, proprietorial subject that underpins their laws of property and methods of collecting and distributing revenue and service. This would, in its turn, imply a new economy and polity. The discourse of citizenship is therefore limited because its indeterminacy—the questioning it encourages—only goes to the spread of services within a given type of social organization, not to the shape of that society or the means of defining and dividing it up. And the work of cultural policy inside this discourse, while relatively autonomous from issues of capital accumulation and state security, does not finally encourage different, dissident cultures of conduct. Its need to form a singular public is too pressing to be that supple. Hence, for example, the ultimately pastoral nature of efforts to liberalize views on sex. Such right-minded attempts presume that there will be a sanitation of the sexual and social spheres when transgression is rendered legitimate. But it has been just such an idealization of sex, its transformation into the properly sanitary and into a representative sign for the identity of a human subject, that has ostracized gay people in the past.

Instead of this process of annihilation of difference, Foucault preferred to approach points of experience that were limit cases, toward the bounds of possibility, in areas of existence that tested to the full one's ability to combine "intensity and impossibility." Experience at the limit necessitates performing "the task of 'tearing' the subject from itself in such a way that it is no longer the subject as such, or that it is completely 'other' than itself so that it may arrive at its annihilation, its dissociation."[21] This aim is to be achieved at the site of the limit experience, that place of the ultimate in ethics, the extreme that insists on the repeated invocation of the past in the present, whether it is easily integrated into common understandings or not. The problematization of the originary subject that this involves is achieved in the name, not of speculation, but of political pragmatism. And that imperative produces the realization that we should not devote our energies to reassembling or reintroducing a subject previously divided or gone missing in anomie.

Distancing ourselves from some reconciliation of the split subject with its real self, "we must produce something that doesn't yet exist and

The Well-Tempered Self

about which we cannot know." This leaves us, according to Foucault, at a moment of change akin to the period of Europe's modernization. Just as the government of people changed across the fifteenth and sixteenth centuries via the emergence of the sovereign state, of Protestantism, of authoritarian monarchies, and of administered territories, so contemporary sources and systems of authority are now in question. This is "the beginning of a huge crisis of a wide-ranging reevaluation of the problem of 'government.' "[22] To be agile in such a crisis necessitates putting an end to attempts to embrace one's incompleteness in the service of obedience. In order to begin again, we must lose ourselves, and do so in sight of danger.

Notes

Introduction

1. Lawrence Grossberg, "Patrolling the Frontiers: The Articulation of the Popular," in Tony Fry et al., *It's a Sin: Essays on Postmodernism, Politics and Culture* (Sydney: Power Publications, 1988), 64.

2. Theodor W. Adorno, "On Jazz," trans. Jamie Owen Daniel, *Discourse* 12, no. 1 (1989–90): 46.

3. Mark Crispin Miller, *Boxed In: The Culture of TV* (Evanston, Ill.: Northwestern University Press, 1988), 180.

4. Malcolm Barr, "The Labour Party's Policy for the Arts: Is It Socialist?" *Red Letters* no. 19 (1986): 36, 40.

5. Adorno, "On Jazz," 53.

6. Roland Barthes, "The Grain of the Voice," trans. Stephen Heath, in *Image Music Text* (London: Flamingo, 1984), 179, 182–83, 188.

7. Jacques Derrida, "Of an Apocalyptic Tone Recently Adopted in Philosophy," trans. John P. Leavey, Jr., *Oxford Literary Review* 6, no. 2 (1984): 12.

8. Quoted in Roy Armes, *The Cinema of Alain Resnais* (London: Zwemmer, 1968), 66.

9. Vincent P. Pecora, "Ethics, Politics, and the Middle Voice," *Yale French Studies* no. 79 (1991): 204.

10. Michel Foucault, "How We Behave," *Vanity Fair,* November 1983, 66–67.

11. Michel Foucault, "Technologies of the Self," in *Technologies of the Self: A Seminar with Michel Foucault,* ed. Luther H. Martin et al. (London: Tavistock Publications, 1988), 18.

12. Michel Foucault, "The Order of Discourse," trans. Ian McLeod, in *Untying the Text: A Post-Structuralist Reader,* ed. Robert Young (Boston: Routledge & Kegan Paul, 1981), 73.

13. Michel Foucault, *The Archaeology of Knowledge,* trans. A. M. Sheridan Smith (London: Tavistock Publications, 1985), 32–33.

14. Georg Simmel, *The Problems of the Philosophy of History: An Epistemological Essay,* trans. Guy Oakes (New York: Free Press, 1977), ix.

15. Isaiah Berlin, "Two Concepts of Liberty," in *Readings in Social and Political Philosophy*, ed. Robert M. Stewart (New York: Oxford University Press, 1986), 94.

16. F. R. Leavis, *The Common Pursuit* (London: Chatto & Windus, 1965), 203.

17. Michel Foucault, *Remarks on Marx: Conversations with Duccio Trombadori*, trans. R. James Goldstein and James Cascaito (New York: Semiotext(e), 1991), 56–58, 63–65, 85–86.

18. David Saunders and Ian Hunter, "Lessons from the 'Literatory': How to Historicise Authorship," *Critical Inquiry* 17, no. 3 (1991): 482.

19. Michel Foucault, "The Subject and Power," trans. Leslie Sawyer, *Critical Inquiry* 8, no. 4 (1982): 777–78.

20. John Stuart Mill, *On Liberty* (Harmondsworth: Penguin Books, 1974), 59.

21. Jacques Lacan, "The Function and Field of Speech and Language in Psychoanalysis," trans. Alan Sheridan, in *Ecrits: A Selection* (London: Tavistock Publications, 1985), 47.

22. Louis Althusser, "Montesquieu: Politics and History," trans. Ben Brewster, in *Politics and History: Montesquieu, Rousseau, Hegel, Marx* (London: New Left Books, 1977), 25; id., "Rousseau: The Social Contract," in ibid., 125; Robert Michels, *Political Parties: A Sociological Study of the Oligarchical Tendencies of Modern Democracy*, trans. Eden and Cedar Paul (London: Jarrold & Sons, 1915), 236.

23. Jacques Derrida, "Women in the Beehive: A Seminar with Jacques Derrida," in *Men in Feminism*, ed. Alice Jardine and Paul Smith (New York: Methuen, 1987), 200.

24. Althusser, "Rousseau: The Social Contract," 148.

25. Jean-Jacques Rousseau, "A Discourse on Political Economy," trans. G. D. H. Cole, in *The Social Contract and Discourses* (London: J. M. Dent & Sons, 1975), 124, 123.

26. Herbert Spencer, "The Study of Sociology," in *Sociological Perspectives: Selected Readings,* ed. Kenneth Thompson and Jeremy Tunstall (New York: Penguin Books, 1976), 37.

27. Jürgen Habermas, "The New Obscurity: The Crisis of the Welfare State and the Exhaustion of Utopian Energies," in *The New Conservatism: Cultural Criticism and the Historians' Debate,* ed. and trans. Shierry Weber Nicholsen (Cambridge, Mass.: MIT Press, 1989), 65.

28. Quoted in John Bloomfield, "Citizen Power in Prague," in *Citizenship,* ed. Geoff Andrews (London: Lawrence & Wishart, 1991), 113–14.

29. Michels, *Political Parties,* 232.

30. Karl Marx, "Alienated Labour," in *Sociological Perspectives,* ed. Thompson and Tunstall, 52.

31. Immanuel Kant, "An Answer to the Question: 'What Is Enlightenment,'" trans. H. B. Nisbet, in *Kant: Political Writings,* ed. Hans Reiss, 2d ed. (New York: Cambridge University Press, 1991), 54.

32. Foucault, *Remarks on Marx,* 117–18.

33. Michel Foucault, *The Birth of the Clinic: An Archaeology of Medical Perception,* trans. A. M. Sheridan Smith (New York: Vintage Books, 1975), xiv.

34. Stewart Ranson and John Stewart, "Citizenship and Government: The Challenge for Management in the Public Domain," *Political Studies* 37, no. 1 (1989): 6.

35. Michael Ignatieff, "Citizenship and Moral Narcissism," in *Citizenship,* ed. Andrews, 28.

36. Foucault, "Subject and Power," 790.

37. Fredric Jameson, *Postmodernism, or, the Cultural Logic of Late Capitalism* (London: Verso, 1991), 188.

38. Foucault, *Remarks on Marx,* 70-71, 97.

39. Patricia O'Brien, "Michel Foucault's History of Culture," in *The New Cultural History,* ed. Lynn Hunt (Berkeley and Los Angeles: University of California Press, 1989), 29.

40. Michel Foucault, "La Psychologie de 1850 à 1950," *Revue internationale de philosophie* 44, no. 2 (1990): 159.

41. Foucault, *Archaeology of Knowledge,* 52.

42. Jürgen Habermas, "Neoconservative Cultural Criticism in the United States and Germany," in *New Conservatism,* ed. Nicholsen, 36. Also see his "Obscurity," in ibid., 52-55.

43. Michel Foucault in Pierre Boulez and Michel Foucault, "Contemporary Music and Its Public," trans. Maria Koundoura and Nikos Papastergiadis, *Melbourne Journal of Politics* no. 17 (1985-86): 46.

44. Michel Foucault, *The Order of Things: An Archaeology of the Human Sciences* (New York: Vintage Books, 1973), xi.

45. Foucault, *Remarks on Marx,* 123; id., *Birth of the Clinic,* xiv.

Chapter One.
Civic Culture and the Postmodern Subject

1. Alain Touraine, "What Does Democracy Mean Today?" *International Social Science Journal,* no. 128 (May 1991): 259-60.

2. Claus Offe, "Capitalism by Democratic Design? Democratic Theory Facing the Triple Transition in East Central Europe," trans. Pierre Adler, *Social Research* 58, no. 4 (1991): 866.

3. James Madison, "Federalist 39," in *Readings on the Body Politic,* ed. Fred R. Harris (Glenview, Ill.: Scott, Foresman, 1987), 42.

4. Rousseau, "Discourse on Political Economy," in *Social Contract,* 120-21.

5. Shelley Burtt, "The Good Citizen's Psyche: On the Psychology of Civic Virtue," *Polity* 23, no. 1 (1990): 23-27; Rousseau, "Discourse on Political Economy," in *Social Contract,* 135, 130, 136.

6. Harold D. Lasswell and Abraham Kaplan, *Power and Society: A Framework for Political Inquiry* (London: Routledge & Kegan Paul, 1952), 217.

7. Charles E. Lindblom, *The Policy-Making Process,* 2d ed. (Englewood Cliffs, N.J.: Prentice-Hall, 1980), 105.

8. Lynda Stone, "What Matters for Citizenship Education?" *Theory and Research in Social Education* 20, no. 2 (1992): 207, 215.

9. Henry Wickham Steed, *The Press* (Harmondsworth: Penguin Books, 1938), 8.

10. Juliet Flower MacCannell, *The Regime of the Brother: After the Patriarchy* (New York: Routledge, 1991), 13–17, 20, 32, 36.

11. Anne Phillips, "Citizenship and Feminist Politics," in *Citizenship,* ed. Andrews, 85.

12. Aristotle, *Nichomachean Ethics,* trans. Martin Ostwald (Indianapolis: Bobbs-Merrill, 1962), 1.1.4, 5.6.130.

13. Karl Marx, "The Materialist Conception of History," in *Sociological Perspectives,* ed. Thompson and Tunstall, 44–45.

14. Karl Marx and Friedrich Engels, "Bourgeois and Proletarians," in *Sociological Perspectives,* ed. Thompson and Tunstall, 239.

15. Frederick Engels, *Anti-Dühring: Herr Eugen Dühring's Revolution in Science* (Beijing: Foreign Languages Press, 1976), 362–63.

16. Antonio Gramsci, "The Conquest of the State," trans. John Mathews, in *Antonio Gramsci: Selections from Political Writings, 1910–1920,* ed. Quintin Hoare (New York: International Publishers, 1977), 74; id., "Class Intransigence and Italian History," in ibid., 42.

17. Norbert Elias, *The Civilizing Process: The History of Manners,* trans. Edmund Jephcott (Oxford: Basil Blackwell, 1978), 256.

18. D. E. Apter, "The Passing of Development Studies," *Government and Opposition* 15, no. 3–4 (1980): 271–72.

19. Edward Shils, "The Virtue of Civil Society," *Government and Opposition* 26, no. 1 (1991): 3.

20. Edward Shils, "Observations on Some Tribulations of Civility," *Government and Opposition* 15, no. 3–4 (1980): 528.

21. Christopher Lasch, "Liberalism and Civic Virtue," *Telos,* no. 88 (Summer 1991): 58.

22. Christopher Lasch in Jeffrey Isaac and Christopher Lasch, "Modernity and Progress: An Exchange," *Salmagundi,* no. 93 (Winter 1992): 104–5, 107.

23. Norbert Elias, *The History of Manners* (New York: Pantheon Books, 1978), 53–56; id., *Civilizing Process,* xiv–xv, 3–4, 78, 82.

24. Michel Foucault, "Body/Power," in *Power-Knowledge: Selected Interviews and Other Writings, 1972–77, Michel Foucault,* ed. Colin Gordon (New York: Pantheon Books, 1980), 55.

25. Jean-Jacques Rousseau, "A Discourse on a Subject Proposed by the Academy of Dijon: What Is the Origin of Inequality among Men, and Is It Authorised by Natural Law?" in *Social Contract,* 64, 66 n. 2, 73.

26. Lucian S. Pye, "Foreword," in Leonard Binder et al., *Crises and Sequences in Political Development* (Princeton: Princeton University Press, 1971), vii.

27. Andreas Huyssen, "From Counter-Culture to Neo-Conservatism and Beyond: Stages of the Postmodern," *Social Science Information* 23, no. 3 (1984): 615–16.

28. F. R. Ankersmit, "Historiography and Postmodernism," *History and Theory* 28, no. 2 (1989): 150.

29. Chantal Mouffe, "The Civics Lesson," *New Statesman and Society* 1, no. 18 (1988): 29–30. Also see Nancy Fraser, "Rethinking the Public Sphere: A Contribution to the Critique of Actually Existing Democracy," *Social Text* 8, no. 3–9, no. 1 (1990): 66–67.

30. Léopold Sédar Senghor, "The African Road to Socialism," trans. Mercer Cook, in *On African Socialism* (New York: Praeger, 1964), 93–94, 73–74.

31. Michel Foucault, "Georges Canguilhem: Philosopher of Error," trans. Graham Burchell, *Ideology and Consciousness*, no. 7 (Autumn 1980): 54.

32. Lord Acton, "Nationality," in *The History of Freedom and Other Essays*, ed. John Neville Figgis and Reginald Vere Laurence (Freeport, N.Y.: Books for Libraries Press, 1967), 298.

33. Michael Walzer, "The Idea of Civil Society: A Path to Social Reconstruction," *Dissent* 38, no. 2 (1991): 293.

34. Gabriel Almond, "The Nature of Contemporary Political Science: A Roundtable Discussion," *PS* 23, no. 1 (1990): 34–35.

35. Ernesto Laclau, "Coming Up for Air," *Marxism Today*, March 1990, 27.

36. Barry Hindess, "Political Equality and Social Policy," *Thesis Eleven*, no. 25 (1990): 114, 116.

37. Mouffe, "Civics Lesson," 28.

38. Althusser, "Montesquieu," 62, 45, 80.

39. Touraine, "What Does Democracy Mean Today?" 260–61.

40. Foucault, "Subject and Power," 782–83.

41. Tom Harrisson, "What Is Public Opinion?" *Political Quarterly* 11, no. 4 (1940): 368.

42. Michel Foucault, "Truth and Power," in *Michel Foucault: Power, Truth, Strategy*, ed. and trans. Meaghan Morris and Paul Patton (Sydney: Feral Publications, 1979), 41, 37.

43. Rousseau, "Discourse on Political Economy," in *Social Contact*, 135.

44. Randall McGowen, "Punishing Violence, Sentencing Crime," in *The Violence of Representation: Literature and the History of Violence*, ed. Nancy Armstrong and Leonard Tennenhouse (New York: Routledge, 1989), 140–41, 152–53.

45. Margaret S. Archer, *Culture and Agency: The Place of Culture in Social Theory* (New York: Cambridge University Press, 1989), xvi, 1, 274.

46. Tony Bennett, "Putting Policy into Cultural Studies," in *Cultural Studies*, ed. Lawrence Grossberg et al. (New York: Routledge, 1992), 26.

47. Jacques Donzelot, *The Policing of Families*, trans. Robert Hurley (New York: Pantheon Books, 1979), 6–7.

48. Saunders and Hunter, "Lessons from the 'Literatory,'" 503.

49. Rousseau, "Discourse on Political Economy," in *Social Contract*, 130.

50. David Gross, "Critical Synthesis on Urban Knowledge: Remembering and Forgetting in the Modern City," *Social Epistemology* 4, no. 1 (1990): 3–9.

51. Max Weber, *General Economic History*, trans. Frank H. Knight, (New York: Collier Books, 1961), 234.

52. Jürgen Habermas, "Modern and Postmodern Architecture," in *New Conservatism,* ed. Nicholsen, 8.

53. T. H. Marshall, "The Nature and Determinants of Social Order," in *Sociological Perspectives,* ed. Thompson and Tunstall, 290.

54. Elizabeth Wilson, *The Sphinx in the City: Urban Life, the Control of Disorder, and Women* (London: Virago Press, 1991), 6; and see too Abram de Swaan, *The Management of Normality: Critical Essays in Health and Welfare* (London: Routledge, 1990), 142.

55. Georg Simmel, "The Metropolis and Mental Life," trans. Kurt H. Wolff, in *Sociological Perspectives,* ed. Thompson and Tunstall, 88–89.

56. Jameson, *Postmodernism,* 51.

57. T. A. Wallace, *The Etiquette of Australia* (Sydney: Radcliffe Press, 1922), 8.

58. Woodrow Wilson, "Life Comes from the Soil," in *Virginia Reader: A Treasury of Writings from the First Voyages to the Present,* ed. Francis Coleman Rosenberger (New York: Octagon Books, 1972), 486.

59. Jean-François Lyotard, *La Condition postmoderne: Rapport sur le savoir* (Paris: Editions de minuit, 1988), 54, 56.

60. Quoted in J. D. B. Miller, *Norman Angell and the Futility of War: Peace and the Public Mind* (London: Macmillan, 1986), 56, 59.

61. Anthony King, "Introduction: Spaces of Culture, Spaces of Knowledge," in *Culture, Globalization and the World-System: Contemporary Conditions for the Representation of Identity,* ed. Anthony King (London: Macmillan, 1991), 9.

62. Julia Kristeva, "Postmodernism?" *Bucknell Review* 25, no. 2 (1980): 138.

63. C. Wright Mills, "Culture and Politics," in *Power, Politics and People: The Collected Essays of C. Wright Mills,* ed. Irving Louis Horowitz (New York: Oxford University Press, 1970), 236–37, 244.

64. Daniel Bell, "Post-Industrial Society: The Evolution of an Idea," *Survey* 17, no. 2 (1971): 105. Bell advised that he was working with ideas borrowed from Amitai Etzioni.

65. Janet Staiger, "Future Noir: Contemporary Representations of Visionary Cities," *East-West Film Journal* 3, no. 1 (1988): 21–22, 33.

66. Kristeva, "Postmodernism?" 138.

67. Ernest Gellner in Ernest Gellner and Charles Taylor, "The Tough and the Tender," in *Voices: Modernity and Its Discontents,* ed. Bill Bourne et al. (Nottingham: Spokesman, 1987), 34–35.

68. Friedrich Nietzsche, *The Genealogy of Morals,* trans. Francis Golffing (New York: Doubleday Anchor, 1956), 178–79.

69. Mill, *On Liberty,* 68.

70. Ankersmit, "Historiography and Postmodernism," 139.

71. Matthew Arnold, *Culture and Anarchy,* ed. J. Dover Wilson (Cambridge: Cambridge University Press, 1971), 44–45, 47.

72. Vassilis Lambropoulos, "Violence and the Liberal Imagination: The Representation of Hellenism in Matthew Arnold," in *Violence of Representation,* ed. Armstrong and Tennenhouse, 173, 175–76, 179, 191.

73. "The Corporate Collector," *Australian Director,* March–April 1988, 28.

74. Tim Rowse, *Arguing the Arts: The Funding of the Arts in Australia* (Ringwood: Penguin Books, 1985), 11, 35, 37, 41.

75. Quoted in *Shooting the Pianist: The Role of Government in the Arts,* ed. Philip Parsons (Sydney: Currency Press, 1987), 50.

76. Ronald Dworkin, *A Matter of Principle* (Cambridge, Mass.: Harvard University Press, 1985), 221–22, 225, 229–30, 232–33.

77. *Australian Labor Party Platform, Resolutions and Rules* (Canberra: Australian Labor Party, 1986).

78. Quoted in John Brademas, "The Arts and Politics: A Commentary," *Mediterranean Quarterly* 1, no. 2 (1990): 95, 104–5.

79. Saul Bellow in Saul Bellow and Martin Amis, "The Moronic Inferno," in *Voices,* ed. Bourne et al., 12, 23; Octavio Paz in Octavio Paz and Leszek Kolakowski, "Lost Illusions," in ibid., 92, 97.

80. Quoted in Catharine R. Stimpson, "Federal Papers," *October,* no. 53 (Summer 1990): 34.

81. Karl Marx, *The Eighteenth Brumaire of Louis Bonaparte* (Beijing: Foreign Languages Press, 1978), 27, 35.

82. Loren Kruger, "Attending (to) the National Spectacle: Instituting National (Popular) Theater in England and France," in *Macropolitics of Nineteenth-Century Literature: Nationalism, Exoticism, Imperialism,* ed. Jonathan Arac and Harriet Ritvo (Philadelphia: University of Pennsylvania Press, 1991), 244, 246–47, 249–50, 262, 245.

83. Tony Bennett, *Outside Literature* (New York: Routledge, 1990), 50, 290 n. 17, 163–64.

84. Foucault, "Truth and Power," 35.

85. Louis Althusser, "Ideology and Ideological State Apparatuses (Notes Towards an Investigation)," trans. Ben Brewster, in *Lenin and Philosophy and Other Essays* (London: New Left Books, 1977), 129 n. 5.

86. Louis Althusser, *For Marx,* trans. Ben Brewster (Harmondsworth: Penguin Books, 1969), 256.

87. Michel Foucault, "The Discourse of History," trans. John Johnston, in *Foucault Live: Interviews, 1966–84,* ed. Sylvère Lotringer (New York: Semiotext(e) Foreign Agents Series, 1989), 14.

88. Althusser, "Ideology and Ideological State Apparatuses," 129–30.

89. Ibid., 136–38. Also see Emile Durkheim, "The Division of Labour in Society," trans. G. Simpson, in *Sociological Perspectives,* ed. Thompson and Tunstall, 104.

90. Anthony Giddens, *The Consequences of Modernity* (Cambridge: Polity Press, 1991), 14.

91. Foucault, "Subject and Power," 782; id., "Body/Power," in *Power-Knowledge,* ed. Gordon, 58.

92. Foucault, "Subject and Power," 786–87; id., "Questions of Method: An Interview with Michel Foucault," trans. Colin Gordon, *Ideology and Consciousness,* no. 8 (Spring 1981): 5.

93. Quoted in "P. L.," "T. H. Marshall, 1893–1981," *International Social Science Journal,* no. 91 (February 1982): 157.

94. Craig A. Rimmerman, "The 'Post-Modern' Presidency—A New Presidential Epoch?" *Western Political Quarterly* 44, no. 1 (1991): 221–38.

95. Gary S. Marshall and Orion F. White, Jr., "The Blacksburg Manifesto and the Postmodern Debate: Public Administration in a Time without a Name," *American Review of Public Administration* 20, no. 2 (1990): 71–72.

96. Althusser, "Ideology and Ideological State Apparatuses," 152–54, 158, 160, 162–64.

97. Michel Foucault, *Discipline and Punish: The Birth of the Prison,* trans. Alan Sheridan (New York: Vintage Books, 1979), 222.

98. Michel Foucault, *The History of Sexuality: An Introduction,* trans. Robert Hurley (New York: Penguin Books, 1984), 60, 170, 73, 192, 194.

99. Jacques Donzelot, "The Poverty of Political Culture," trans. Couze Venn, *Ideology and Consciousness,* no. 5 (Spring 1979): 76–77.

100. Steven Lukes, *Power: A Radical View* (London: Macmillan, 1974), 34.

101. Foucault, "Truth and Power," 39.

102. Foucault, *History of Sexuality,* 95.

103. Michel Foucault, "The Archeology of Knowledge," in *Foucault Live,* ed. Lotringer, 51.

104. Umberto Eco and Stefano Rosso, "A Correspondence with Umberto Eco: Genoa-Bologna-Binghamton-Bloomington, August-September 1982–March-April 1983," trans. Carolyn Springer, *Boundary 2* 12, no. 1 (1983): 7.

105. Aristotle, *Nichomachean Ethics,* 6.4.150.

106. Auguste Comte, "The Positive Philosophy," trans. Harriet Martineau, in *Sociological Perspectives,* ed. Thompson and Tunstall, 18–20.

107. Herbert Spencer, "The Study of Sociology," in *Sociological Perspectives,* ed. Thompson and Tunstall, 38.

108. Emile Durkheim, "Thought and Reality," in *Emile Durkheim: Selected Writings,* ed. and trans. Anthony Giddens (New York: Cambridge University Press, 1972), 251.

109. Jean Baudrillard, "For a Critique of the Political Economy of the Sign," trans. Charles Levin, in *Jean Baudrillard: Selected Writings,* ed. Mark Poster (Stanford: Stanford University Press, 1988), 71, 81.

110. Foucault, *Archaeology of Knowledge,* 91.

111. Max Weber, "The Ideal Type," in *Sociological Perspectives,* ed. Thompson and Tunstall, 65, 63; id., "The Definitions of Sociology, Social Action and Social Relationship," trans. A. M. Henderson and Talcott Parsons, in ibid., 128.

112. Simmel, *Problems of the Philosophy of History,* xi, 76–77, 201.

113. Max Weber, *Basic Concepts in Sociology,* trans. H. P. Secher (New York: Citadel Press, 1964), 48–49; id., "Power and Bureaucracy," trans. Hans Gerth and C. Wright Mills, in *Sociological Perspectives,* ed. Thompson and Tunstall, 68–69.

114. Gilles Deleuze and Félix Guattari, "Rhizome," trans. Paul Foss and Paul Patton *Ideology and Consciousness,* no. 8 (Spring 1981): 52–53, 54, 57.

115. Jacques Derrida, "Signature Event Context," trans. Samuel Weber and Jeffrey Mehlman, *Glyph* no. 1 (1977): 179, 182, 185–86.

116. Jean Baudrillard, "Symbolic Exchange and Death," trans. Jacques Mourrain, in *Jean Baudrillard*, ed. Poster, 145–46; Ankersmit, "Historiography and Postmodernism," 143.

117. Scott Lash, *Sociology of Postmodernism* (New York: Routledge, 1990), 11, 8.

118. Simmel, "Metropolis and Mental Life," 87, 83.

119. Foucault, *Order of Things*, 248, 318.

120. Kristeva, "Postmodernism?" 136.

121. Jürgen Habermas, "The New Intimacy between Culture and Politics: Theses on Enlightenment in Germany," in *New Conservatism*, ed. Nicholsen, 203.

122. Jean-François Lyotard, "The *Différend*, the Referent, and the Proper Name," trans. Georges Van Den Abbeele, *Diacritics* 14, no. 3 (1984): 7.

123. Jean-François Lyotard, interview by Georges Van Den Abbeele, *Diacritics* 14, no. 3 (1984): 18.

124. Michel Foucault, "The Political Technology of Individuals," in *Technologies of the Self*, ed. Martin et al., 145.

125. Saul Bellow in Bellow and Amis, "Moronic Inferno," 20.

126. Mills, "Culture and Politics," 240–41.

127. Søren Kierkegaard, "The Individual and 'The Public,'" in *A Kierkegaard Anthology*, ed. Robert Bretall (New York: Modern Library, 1974), 265.

128. Jameson, *Postmodernism*, ix.

Chapter Two.
Textual Theory

1. Jean-Jacques Rousseau, "A Discourse on the Arts and Sciences," in *Social Contract*, 15, 4–19.

2. "The Mexico City Declaration on Cultural Policies," *Cultures* no. 33 (1983): 190.

3. Canadian Commission for UNESCO, "A Working Definition of 'Culture,'" *Cultures* 4, no. 4 (1977): 81.

4. Umberto Eco, interview by Adelaida Lopez and Manthelma Costa, trans. Donald Tucker and Adelaida Lopez, *Diacritics* 17, no. 1 (1987): 50–51.

5. Geoffrey Thurley, *The Romantic Predicament* (Melbourne: Macmillan, 1983), 5, 7–9, 29–32.

6. John Hinde, *Other People's Pictures* (Sydney: Australian Broadcasting Commission, 1981), 5, 8, 26.

7. Terry Lovell, *Pictures of Reality: Aesthetics, Politics, Pleasure* (London: British Film Institute, 1983), 6.

8. Raymond Williams, *The Politics of Modernism: Against the New Conformists* (London: Verso, 1989), 93, 178.

9. Geoff Hurd, "Notes on Hegemony, the War and Cinema," in *National Fictions: World War Two in British Films and Television*, ed. Geoff Hurd (London: British Film Institute, 1984), 18.

10. Andy Medhurst, "1950s War Films," in *National Fictions*, ed. Hurd, 35.

11. Colin McArthur, "National Identities," in *National Fictions*, ed. Hurd, 55.

12. Laura Mulvey, "Visual Pleasure and Narrative Cinema," *Screen* 16, no. 3 (1975): 6–10.

13. Tessa Perkins, "Struggles over the Meaning of 'The Imitation Game,'" in *National Fictions*, ed. Hurd, 50.

14. Homi K. Bhabha, "Interrogating Identity," in *Identity Documents 6* (London: Institute of Contemporary Arts, 1988), 5.

15. Yi-Fu Tuan, "Cultural Pluralism and Technology," *Geographical Review* 79, no. 3 (1989): 270.

16. Williams, *Politics of Modernism*, 112.

17. Jean-Luc Godard quoted in Brian Henderson, *A Critique of Film Theory* (New York: Dutton, 1980), 65.

18. Michel Foucault, "Powers and Strategies," trans. Paul Patton, in *Michel Foucault*, ed. Morris and Patton, 54.

19. Horace Newcomb, *TV: The Most Popular Art* (Garden City, N.Y.: Anchor Books, 1974), 256.

20. Douglas Kellner, "Television, Mythology and Ritual," *Praxis* no. 6 (1982): 133, 152.

21. Rupert Murdoch, *Freedom in Broadcasting*, MacTaggart Lecture at the Edinburgh Television Festival (N.p.: News Corporation Ltd., 1989), 5; John Tulloch, *Television Drama: Agency, Audience and Myth* (New York: Routledge, 1990), 3.

22. Tulloch, *Television Drama*, 9–10, 215–16, 70–71, 91–92.

23. Stuart Cunningham, "Textual Innovation in the Australian Historical Mini-Series," in *Australian Television: Programs, Pleasures and Politics*, ed. John Tulloch and Graeme Turner (Boston: Allen & Unwin, 1989), 46–47.

24. Albert Moran, "Crime, Romance, History: Television Drama," in *The Australian Screen*, ed. Albert Moran and Tom O'Regan (Harmondsworth: Penguin Books, 1989), 252, 255.

25. Aristotle, *Poetics*, trans. S. H. Butcher (New York: Hill & Wang, 1961), 68, 111.

26. Louis Althusser, "Cremonini, Painter of the Abstract," in *Lenin and Philosophy*, 210, 213, 218.

27. Aristotle, *Poetics*, 62–63; Jean-Luc Godard, *Pierrot le Fou*, trans. Peter Whitehead (London: Lorrimer Publishing, 1969), 63.

28. Stuart Cunningham, "Style, Form and History in Australian Mini-Series," *Southern Review* 22, no. 3 (1989): 318.

29. Tulloch, *Television Drama*, 124.

30. Michel Foucault, "I, Pierre Rivière," in *Foucault Live*, ed. Lotringer, 133–36.

31. James Donald, review of *Channels of Discourse*, ed. Robert C. Allen, and *Television Culture*, by John Fiske, *Screen* 31, no. 1 (1990): 117.

32. Terry Eagleton, *Literary Theory: An Introduction* (Oxford: Basil Blackwell, 1983), 60.

33. Edward Said, "Figures, Configurations, Transfigurations," *Race and Class* 32, no. 1 (1990): 16; Dominick LaCapra, "Culture and Ideology: From Geertz to Marx," *Poetics Today* 9, no. 2 (1988): 386–87; Wayne C. Booth, "The Company We Keep: Self-Making in Imaginative Art, Old and New," in *Television: The Critical View*, ed. Horace Newcomb, 4th ed. (New York: Oxford University Press, 1987), 395; Errol Simper, "Academic [Leonie Kramer] Urges 'TV Rationing' for Young," *Australian*, September 4, 1990, 4.

34. John Frow, "Golgotha . . ." *Southern Review* 17, no. 2 (1984): 143.

35. Catherine Belsey, "The Plurality of History," *Southern Review* 17, no. 2 (1984): 140–41.

36. Roger Chartier, "Texts, Printing, Readings," in *New Cultural History*, ed. Hunt, 154–57.

37. Rita Felski, *Beyond Feminist Aesthetics: Feminist Literature and Social Change* (London: Hutchinson Radius, 1989), 159, 162, 180.

38. Parveen Adams et al., "*m/f* Editorial," *m/f* no. 2 (1978): 3; Elizabeth Cowie, " 'Woman as Sign,' " *m/f* no. 1 (1978): 49, 62–63.

39. Elizabeth Cowie, "The Popular Film as a Progressive Text—A Discussion of *Coma* Part 1," *m/f* no. 3 (1979): 63.

40. Ian Hunter, "On Reflection Theory: Including Remarks on John Docker's *In a Critical Condition*," *Australian Journal of Cultural Studies* 3, no. 1 (1985): 9.

41. Elizabeth Riddell, "Entertainment," in *Ten Years of Television*, ed. Mungo MacCallum (Melbourne: Sun Books, 1968), 27.

42. David Hume, *An Inquiry concerning Human Understanding*, ed. Charles W. Hendel (Indianapolis: Library of Liberal Arts, Bobbs-Merrill, 1955), 26.

43. Foucault, *Order of Things*, 221.

44. Julia Kristeva, *Desire in Language: A Semiotic Approach to Literature and Art*, ed. Leon S. Roudiez, trans. Thomas Gorda et al. (New York: Columbia University Press, 1980), 98.

45. Raymond Williams, "A Lecture on Realism," *Screen* 18, no. 1 (1977): 63–64; György Lukács, "Notes on the Theory of Literary History," trans. Ian Fairley, *Comparative Criticism: An Annual Journal*, no. 13 (1991): 240.

46. Ihab Hassan, "Quest for the Subject: The Self in Literature," *Contemporary Literature* 29, no. 3 (1988): 420.

47. Caren J. Deming, "For Television-Centred Television Criticism: Lessons from Feminism," in *Television and Women's Culture: The Politics of the Popular*, ed. Mary Ellen Brown (Sydney: Currency Press, 1990), 51.

48. Jonathan Dollimore and Alan Sinfield, "Culture and Textuality: Debating Cultural Materialism," *Textual Practice* 4, no. 1 (1990): 92.

49. Hassan, "Quest for the Subject," 420.

50. Ian Hunter, "The Concept of Context and the Problem of Reading," *Southern Review* 15, no. 1 (1982): 91 n. 18.

51. Michel Foucault, "Friendship as a Way of Life," in *Foucault Live*, ed. Lotringer, 207.

52. E. M. Forster, *Aspects of the Novel*, ed. Oliver Stallybrass (New York:

Penguin Books, 1984), 25; Graham Hough, "Crisis in Literary Education," in *Crisis in the Humanities,* ed. J. H. Plumb (Baltimore: Penguin Books, 1964), 97.

53. Frederic [*sic*] Jameson, "Marxists and the University," *New Political Science* 1, no. 2–3 (1979–80): 35.

54. Ian Hunter, "The Occasion of Criticism: Its Ethic and Pedagogy," *Poetics* 17, no. 1–2 (1988): 159–60.

55. Hans-Georg Gadamer, "The Expressive Power of Language: On the Function of Rhetoric for Knowledge," trans. Richard Heinemann and Bruce Krajewski, *PMLA* 107, no. 2 (1992): 348–49.

56. Hunter, "Occasion of Criticism," 163–65; Jean-François Lyotard, *The Postmodern Explained to Children: Correspondence, 1982–1985,* trans. Don Barry et al., ed. Julian Pefanis and Morgan Thomas (Sydney: Power Publications, 1992), 118.

57. George Steiner, "To Civilize Our Gentlemen," in *George Steiner: A Reader* (New York: Oxford University Press, 1984), 27.

58. Daniel R. Schwarz, "Review-Essay: Canonicity, Culture, and Pluralism—A Humanistic Perspective on Professing English," *Texas Studies in Literature and Language* 34, no. 1 (1992): 151, 169, 173. See also Gary Shaw, "Using Literature to Teach Ethics in the Business Curriculum," *Journal of Business and Technical Communication* 6, no. 2 (1992): 187–99.

59. Walter Benjamin, "The Storyteller," trans. Harry Zohn, in *Illuminations: Essays and Reflections,* ed. Hannah Arendt (London: Jonathan Cape, 1970), 89–90; id., "The Task of the Translator: An Introduction to the Translation of Baudelaire's *Tableaux parisiens,"* in ibid., 69–70; Hans-Georg Gadamer, "Aesthetics and Hermeneutics," trans. Karl Ameriks, in *Postwar German Culture: An Anthology,* ed. Charles E. McClelland and Steven P. Scher (New York: Dutton, 1974), 146.

60. Geoffrey Hartman, *The Fate of Reading and Other Essays* (Chicago: University of Chicago Press, 1985), 8, 19.

61. Patricia Spacks, "The Novel as Ethical Paradigm," *Novel* 21, no. 2–3 (1988): 181–82, 184.

62. Foucault, *Order of Things,* 327–28.

63. Catherine Greenfield, "Psychoanalysis and Literary Criticism," *Southern Review* 14, no. 3 (1981): 198.

64. Joseph Brodsky, "Poetry as a Form of Resistance to Reality," trans. Alexander Sumerkin and Jamey Gambrell, *PMLA* 107, no. 2 (1992): 221.

65. Charles Altieri, "Life after Difference: The Positions of the Interpreter and the Positioning of the Interpreted," *Monist* 73, no. 2 (1990): 269–72.

66. Walter Benjamin, "The Work of Art in the Age of Mechanical Reproduction," in *Illuminations,* 237–38; Lyotard, *Postmodern Explained to Children,* 14–15.

67. Maria Lauret, "Seizing the Time and Making New: Feminist Criticism, Politics and Contemporary Feminist Fiction," *Feminist Review,* no. 31 (Spring 1989): 95.

68. Irving Howe, "The Self in Literature," *Salmagundi,* no. 90–91 (Spring-Summer 1991): 59–60.

69. Foucault, *Order of Things,* 262.

70. Elaine Showalter, "Critical Cross-Dressing; Male Feminists and the Woman of the Year," in *Men in Feminism,* ed. Jardine and Smith, 130.

71. Cheryl Walker, "Feminist Literary Criticism and the Author," *Critical Inquiry* 16, no. 3 (1990): 568, 571.

72. Michael Bywater, "Tastes Like Soap," *Listener* 119, no. 3059 (1988): 6.

73. Stuart Hall and John O'Hara, "The Narrative Construction of Reality: An Interview with Stuart Hall," *Southern Review* 17, no. 1 (1984): 9.

74. Mary J. Piccinillo, "An Isocratean Rhetoric of Television," *Communication* 12, no. 1 (1990): 4–5, 8–9, 11, 14–15.

75. Philip Abrams, "Television and Radio," in *Discrimination and Popular Culture,* ed. Denys Thompson, 2d ed. (Baltimore: Penguin Books, 1973), 129; Denys Thompson, "Introduction," in ibid., 17.

76. Nicholas Garnham, "TV Documentary and Ideology," in *Screen Reader I: Cinema/Ideology/Politics* (London: Society for Education in Film and Television, 1977), 59–60.

77. Lauren Rabinovitz, "Sitcoms and Single Moms: Representations on American TV," *Cinema Journal* 29, no. 1 (1989): 16; Forster, *Aspects of the Novel,* 58.

78. Jerry Palmer, *The Logic of the Absurd: On Film and Television Comedy* (London: British Film Institute, 1987), 11, 25–26, 115–16, 148, 167–68, 171.

79. Frank Kermode, *A Commentary on "Hamlet" by Professor Frank Kermode* (N.p.: Shakespeare's Globe and Greater Union Distributors, 1991), unpaginated.

80. Michèle Mattelart, "Can Industrial Culture Be a Culture of Difference: A Reflection on France's Confrontation with the U.S. Model of Serialized Cultural Production," trans. Stanley Gray and Nelly Mitchell, in *Marxism and the Interpretation of Culture,* ed. Cary Nelson and Lawrence Grossberg (Urbana: University of Illinois Press, 1988), 430. Also see Steve Best and Douglas Kellner, "Watching Television: Limitations of Post-Modernism," *Science as Culture,* no. 4 (1988): 45; Hartman, *Fate of Reading,* 34.

81. Ariel Dorfman, *The Empire's Old Clothes: What the Lone Ranger, Babar, and Other Innocent Heroes Do to Our Minds* (London: Pluto Press, 1983), ix–x.

82. Ian Hunter, "Personality as a Vocation: The Political Rationality of the Humanities," *Economy and Society* 19, no. 4 (1990): 396.

83. Michel Foucault, "Order of Discourse," 57–58; id., "Monstrosities in Criticism," *Diacritics* 1, no. 1 (1971): 58.

84. Leavis, *Common Pursuit,* 200.

85. James Sloan Allen, "The Existential Reader: Or Reading, Rumination, and the Classics," *Sewanee Review* 99, no. 1 (1991): 87, 90.

86. Stephen Heath and Gillian Skirrow, "Television: A World in Action," *Screen* 18, no. 2 (1977): 7, 56, 9.

87. Gregory Ulmer, *Teletheory: Grammatology in the Age of Video* (New York: Routledge, 1989); David Bordwell, *Making Meaning: Inference and Rhetoric in the Interpretation of Cinema* (Cambridge, Mass.: Harvard University Press, 1989); Terry Eagleton, *The Ideology of the Aesthetic* (Oxford: Basil Blackwell, 1990).

88. Eagleton, *Ideology of the Aesthetic,* 26.

89. Ibid., 26, 32, 51–53, 63.

90. Michel Foucault, "The End of the Monarchy of Sex," in *Foucault Live,* ed. Lotringer, 148; id., "Body/Power," 55.

91. Eagleton, *Ideology of the Aesthetic,* 64–65.

92. Ibid., 75, 84, 106; Ludwig Wittgenstein, *Notebooks, 1914–1916,* ed. G. H. Wright and G. E. M. Anscombe, 2d ed. (Oxford: Basil Blackwell, 1979), 78.

93. Tuan, "Cultural Pluralism and Technology," 272.

94. Ulmer, *Teletheory,* 33–34, 36, 43, 60.

95. Ibid., 68, 85, 89, 99, 106 and 124.

96. Bordwell, *Making Meaning,* xi–xii.

97. Ibid., 2, 8–9, 16–17, 22–23, 45–46.

98. Ibid., 58–59, 65.

99. Foucault, "Psychologie de 1850 à 1950," 168.

100. Peter Stallybrass and Allon White, *The Politics and Poetics of Transgression* (Ithaca, N.Y.: Cornell University Press, 1986), 106.

101. Jean Baudrillard, "On Seduction," trans. Jacques Mourrain, in *Jean Baudrillard,* ed. Poster, 149; id., "The Masses: The Implosion of the Social in the Media," trans. Marie Maclean, in ibid., 214.

102. Wittgenstein, *Notebooks, 1914–1916,* 80.

103. Bordwell, *Making Meaning,* 72, 75–76, 83, 110.

104. Ibid., 151–52, 166–67, 172.

105. Ibid., 257–58.

106. Foucault, *Birth of the Clinic,* xvi–xvii.

107. Tony Bennett and Graham Martin, "Series Editors' Preface," in Steve Neale and Frank Krutnik, *Popular Film and Television Comedy* (New York: Routledge, 1990), vii.

108. Meaghan Morris, *Ecstasy and Economics: American Essays for John Forbes* (Sydney: EM Press, 1992), 73.

109. Michel Foucault, *The Use of Pleasure,* vol. 2 of *The History of Sexuality,* trans. Robert Hurley (New York: Vintage Books, 1986), 34–35, 38.

110. Jürgen Habermas, "The Idea of the University: Learning Processes," in *New Conservatism,* ed. Nicholsen, 125.

111. Michel Foucault in Noam Chomsky and Michel Foucault, "Human Nature: Justice versus Power," in *Reflexive Water: The Basic Concerns of Mankind,* ed. Fons Elders (London: Souvenir Press, 1974), 146.

112. Michel Foucault, "How Much Does It Cost to Tell the Truth?" in *Foucault Live,* ed. Lotringer, 245–46.

113. Jameson, *Postmodernism,* xi.

Chapter Three.
Nation, Drama, Diplomacy

1. Peter Brimelow, "The Dark Side of 1992," *Forbes* 145, no. 2 (1990): 85.

2. Quoted in Guy Pineau, "L'Europe audiovisuelle de l'après-directive," *Dossiers de l'audiovisuel,* no. 35 (January–February 1991): 10–12.

3. "GATT: Plenty of Talk, Answers Yet to Come," *AFC News* no. 87 (October 1990): 1.

4. Quoted in Ian Jarvie, "Dollars and Ideology: Will Hays' Economic Foreign Policy, 1922–1945," *Film History* 2, no. 3 (1988): 215.

5. Ronald Grover, "The World Is Hollywood's Oyster," *International Business Week* 3186, no. 516 (1991): 57; David Waterman et al., "Television Program Trade in Ten Asian Countries: Does U.S. Fare Dominate?" (paper presented at International Communication Association Conference, Chicago, 1991), 9, 11–12; "Data Box," *Screen Digest,* August 1992, 192.

6. Richard Gold, "Globalization: Gospel for the '90s?" *Variety,* May 2, 1990, S-1.

7. Quoted in Ian Jarvie, "The Postwar Economic Foreign Policy of the American Film Industry: Europe, 1945–1950," *Film History* 4, no. 4 (1990): 280; "U.S. Pics at Home and Abroad," *Variety,* January 4, 1993, 56.

8. Sandra Braman, "Trade and Information Policy," *Media, Culture and Society* 12, no. 3 (1990): 372.

9. A. Frank Reel, *The Networks: How They Stole the Show* (New York: Charles Scribner's Sons, 1979), xiii.

10. Quoted in Jarvie, "Dollars and Ideology," 211.

11. Victor de Grazia, "Mass Culture and Sovereignty: The American Challenge to European Cinemas, 1920–1960," *Journal of Modern History* 61, no. 1 (1989): 53.

12. Quoted in Richard Collins, "Wall-to-Wall *Dallas:* The U.S.–U.K. Trade in Television," in *Global Television,* ed. Cynthia Schneider and Brian Wallis (New York: Wedge Press; Cambridge, Mass.: MIT Press, 1988), 79–80.

13. Jarvie, "Dollars and Ideology," 207.

14. Herbert I. Schiller, "Not Yet the Post-Imperialist Era," *Critical Studies in Mass Communication* 8, no. 1 (1991): 14.

15. John Sinclair, "From 'Modernization' to Cultural Dependence: Mass Communication Studies and the Third World," *Media Information Australia,* no. 23 (February 1982): 8.

16. Industries Assistance Commission, *International Initiatives to Liberalise Trade in Services,* Inquiry into International Trade in Services Discussion Paper 3 (Canberra: Australian Government Publishing Service, 1989), 6.

17. Quoted in Aramand Mattelart et al., "International Image Markets," in *Global Television,* ed. Schneider and Wallis, 19–20.

18. Foucault, *Use of Pleasure,* 220.

19. Richard Collins, "Television and National Identity on Both Sides of the Atlantic," *Round Table,* no. 318 (April 1991): 175.

20. John Corner and Sylvia Harvey, "Heritage in Britain: Designer-History and the Popular Imagination," *Ten-8* no. 36 (1990): 16.

21. David Russell, "A World in Inaction," *Sight and Sound* 59, no. 3 (1990): 177.

22. Brimelow, "Dark Side of 1992," 89.

23. Heinz Ungureit, "Le Groupement européen de production: Rassembler les forces du service public . . . ," *Dossiers de l'audiovisuel,* no. 35 (January–February 1991): 16.

24. Quoted in Lisa C. Cohen, "Conflict and Consensus: Television in Israel," in *Global Television,* ed. Schneider and Wallis, 51.

25. Jan Nederveen Pieterse, "Fictions of Europe," *Race and Class* 32, no. 3 (1991): 3, 5, 6.

26. Quoted in Philip Schlesinger, *Media, State and Nation: Political Violence and Collective Identities* (London: Sage Publications, 1991), 184.

27. Michèle Mattelart, "Can Industrial Culture Be a Culture of Difference," 430.

28. Lyotard, *Postmodern Explained to Children,* 46–47.

29. Hans Kohn, *The Idea of Nationalism: A Study in Its Origins and Background* (New York: Macmillan, 1945), vii.

30. J. D. B. Miller, "The Sovereign State and Its Future," *International Journal* 39, no. 2 (1984): 284 n. 1.

31. Harold Anderson, "Exporting TV Know-How—A Case History," *Television Quarterly* 4, no. 1 (1965): 21.

32. Chin-Chuan Lee, "The International Information Order," *Communication Research* 9, no. 4 (1982): 618.

33. Sinclair, "From 'Modernization' to Cultural Dependence," 5–8.

34. Quoted in Coco Fusco, "Telepictures: An Interview with Josh Elbaum," in *Global Television,* ed. Schneider and Wallis, 40, 43.

35. Asu Aksoy and Kevin Robins, "Hollywood for the 21st Century: Global Competition for Critical Mass in Image Markets," *Cambridge Journal of Economics* 16, no. 1 (1992): 18.

36. Marshall Dimock, "The Restorative Qualities of Citizenship," *Public Administration Review* 50, no. 1 (1990): 22.

37. Collins, "Television and National Identity," 173.

38. David Plowright et al., "The Togetherness Approach to World TV," *Broadcasting Abroad,* March 1989, 9.

39. Immanuel Wallerstein, "Culture as the Ideological Battleground of the Modern World-System," *Hitotsubashi Journal of Social Studies* 21, no. 1 (1989): 6–8, 10–11, 15, 18.

40. Jonathan Friedman, "Being in the World: Globalization and Localization," *Theory, Culture, and Society* 7, no. 2–3 (1990): 312.

41. Ulf Hannerz, "Cosmopolitans and Locals in World Culture," *Theory, Culture, and Society* 7, no. 2–3 (1990): 239–40, 244, 236, 249.

42. Stuart Hall, "The Local and the Global: Globalization and Ethnicity" and "Old and New Identities, Old and New Ethnicities," in *Culture, Globalization and the World-System,* ed. King, 24–25, 67.

43. Schiller, "Not Yet the Post-Imperialist Era," 15.

44. Murdoch, *Freedom in Broadcasting,* 1.

45. Industries Assistance Commission, *International Initiatives,* 1–2.

46. R. Negrine and S. Papathanassopoulos, "The Internationalization of Television," *European Journal of Communication* 6, no. 1 (1991): 12–13.

47. "Oz Production: Meat in Trade Sandwich?" *Communications Update,* no. 59 (September 1990): 8.

48. Industries Assistance Commission, *Assessing Barriers to International*

Trade in Services, Inquiry into International Trade in Services Discussion Paper 2 (Canberra: Australian Government Publishing Service, 1989), 13.

49. "GATT: The Fight That Was Almost Lost before It Started," *Filmnews* 20, no. 8 (1990): 3.

50. Quoted in Richard Collins, *Culture, Communication, and National Identity: The Case of Canadian Television* (Toronto: University of Toronto Press, 1990), 251.

51. David Williamson, "Arts 1: Aussie Content at Risk," *Australian,* November 9, 1989, 16.

52. Phillip Adams, "Response," *Cinema Papers,* nos. 44–45 (April 1984): 71, 70.

53. John McLaren, "Cultural Independence for Australia: The Need for a National Literature," *Australian Studies,* no. 14 (October 1990): 7–8, 10.

54. P. R. Stephenson, "Queensland Culture," *Meanjin* 1, no. 6 (1942): 7–8.

55. "Interim Report of the Film Committee, Australian Council for the Arts," in *An Australian Film Reader,* ed. Albert Moran and Tom O'Regan (Sydney: Currency Press, 1985), 171.

56. Sylvia Lawson, "Not for the Likes of Us," in *Australian Film Reader,* ed. Moran and O'Regan, 154–55.

57. Albert Moran, *Images and Industry: Television Drama Production in Australia* (Sydney: Currency Press, 1985), 11.

58. Communications Law Centre, *The Representation of Non-English Background People in Australian Television Drama* (discussion paper prepared for Actors Equity, Sydney: n.p., 1992).

59. Quoted in Moran, *Images and Industry,* 51–52.

60. Susan Dermody and Elizabeth Jacka, *Anatomy of a National Cinema,* vol. 2 of *The Screening of Australia* (Sydney: Currency Press, 1988), 20; Sylvia Lawson, "General Editor's Preface," in Moran, *Images and Industry,* 6.

61. Gillian Appleton, *Attitudes to Television: A Survey of Advertisers* (Sydney: Australian Film Commission, 1989), 14, 20, 23.

62. Suzanne Pingree and Robert Hawkins, "U.S. Programs on Australian Television: The Cultivation Effect," *Journal of Communication* 31, no. 1 (1981): 104.

63. Sylvia Bashevkin, "Does Public Opinion Matter? The Adoption of Federal Royal Commission and Task Force Recommendations on the National Question, 1951–1987," *Canadian Public Administration* 31, no. 1 (1988): 395, 397, 400.

64. Mark Lawson, "Playing Safe," *Marxism Today,* March 1990, 46.

65. Elizabeth Jacka, "Australian Cinema: An Anachronism in the '80s?" in *The Imaginary Industry: Australian Film in the Late '80s,* ed. Susan Dermody and Elizabeth Jacka (Sydney: Australian Film, Television and Radio School, 1988), 126.

66. Jean Baudrillard, "Simulacra and Simulations," trans. Paul Foss, Paul Patton, and Philip Beitchman, in *Jean Baudrillard,* ed. Poster, 68–71.

67. Ernesto Laclau, "Coming Up for Air," *Marxism Today,* March 1990, 27.

68. Jock Given, "Cultural Policy and the Broadcasting Tribunal," *Culture and Policy* 1, no. 1 (1989): 35.

69. Ibid., 35–36.

70. Australian Film Commission, "G.A.T.T. Services Framework: Comments on the Application to Audio-Visual Industries of the Draft Multilateral Framework for Trade in Services" (Photocopy, 1990), 10, 14.

71. Australian Broadcasting Tribunal, *Australian Content Inquiry Discussion Paper: Amounts of Time Occupied by Different Program Categories* (N.p., 1988), 3.

72. Australian Broadcasting Tribunal, *Draft Television Program Standard 14,* November 6, 1989, 1.

73. Anne Davies, "Hollywood Attacks Aust-Content TV Rule," *Australian Financial Review,* September 15, 1989, 8.

74. Heath and Skirrow, "Television," 8.

75. Foucault, *Order of Things,* 353.

76. Mungo MacCallum, "Drama," in *Ten Years of Television,* ed. MacCallum, 67.

77. Quoted in Moran, *Images and Industry,* 95–96.

78. Tom Weir, "No Daydreams of Our Own: The Film as National Self-Expression," in *Australian Film Reader,* ed. Moran and O'Regan, 144.

79. Quoted in Collins, *Culture, Communication, and National Identity,* 250–51.

80. Aristotle, *Poetics,* 56.

81. Stuart Hall, "Cultural Identity and Cinematic Representation," *Framework* no. 36 (199): 69–70.

Chapter Four.
Making Citizens and Consumers

1. John Carter, "Parliamentary Education: A Challenge for All Parliaments," *Legislative Studies* 4, no. 1 (1989): 37.

2. British Broadcasting Corporation in association with *The House Magazine, The BBC Guide to Parliament* (Rugby: BBC, 1979), 42.

3. Norman St. John-Stevas, "Government by Discussion," in *Parliament and Bureaucracy: Parliamentary Scrutiny of Administration: Prospects and Problems in the 1980s,* ed. J. R. Nethercote (Sydney: Hale & Ironmonger, 1982), 24. See also *BBC Guide to Parliament,* 44.

4. Lesley Johnson, *The Unseen Voice: A Cultural Study of Early Australian Radio* (London: Routledge, 1988), 193.

5. See Benjamin, "Work of Art in the Age of Mechanical Reproduction," in *Illuminations,* 249 n. 12; the quotation in the text is from "Max Brod's Book on Kafka and Some of My Own Reflections," in ibid., 145.

6. Charles Taylor, "Modes of Civil Society," *Public Culture* 3, no. 1 (1990): 95.

7. Jonathan Clark, "Magna Carta for Our Times," *Times,* July 23, 1991, 14; "Mimicking the Market," *Times,* July 23, 1991, 15; John Pienaar, "Consumer Rights 'to be central theme of 1990s,' " *Independent,* July 23, 1991, 3.

8. See Geoff Andrews, "Universal Principles," *Marxism Today,* August 1990, 16–17; Dimock, "The Restorative Qualities," 21–22, 24; Ranson and Stewart,

"Citizenship and Government," 11. The comment by Christopher Lasch quoted in the text is in Lasch and Cornelius Castoriadis, "The Culture of Narcissism," in *Voices,* ed. Bourne et al., 50–51.

9. Jürgen Habermas, "The Horrors of Autonomy: Carl Schmitt in English," in *New Conservatism,* ed. Nicholsen, 138; id., *Moral Consciousness and Communicative Action,* trans. Christian Lenhardt and Shierry Weber Nicholsen (Cambridge, Mass.: MIT Press, 1990), 3–4.

10. Quoted in Patricia Aufderheide, "Public Television and the Public Sphere," *Critical Studies in Mass Communication* 8, no. 2 (1991): 174.

11. Bob Franklin, "Televising the British House of Commons: Issues and Developments," in *Televising Democracies,* ed. Bob Franklin (New York: Routledge, 1992), 3, 19.

12. John Hartley, "Invisible Fictions: Television Audiences, Paedocracy, Pleasure," *Textual Practice* 1, no. 2 (1987): 121–38.

13. J. Cooper, "Television to Stay Out of ICAC Hearings," *Australian,* July 11, 1990, 4; editorial, *Sydney Morning Herald,* March 29, 1990, 16; S. Rodgers, "House of Reps TV Bid Fails," *Courier-Mail,* June 2, 1990, 8.

14. Austin Mitchell, "Beyond Televising Parliament: Taking Politics to the People," *Parliamentary Affairs* 43, no. 1 (1990): 2, 7.

15. Peter O'Keeffe, "Towards Better Parliamentary Education," *Legislative Studies* 5, no. 1 (1990): 19.

16. Plutarch, *The Rise and Fall of Athens: Nine Greek Lives by Plutarch,* trans. Ian Scott-Kilvert (Baltimore: Penguin Books, 1976), 73.

17. C. Yronwode, "Viewing With Alarm," *Reid Fleming: World's Toughest Milkman* 2, no. 1 (1989): frontispiece.

18. Paul McLean, "Towards Better Parliamentary Education," *Legislative Studies* 5, no. 1 (1990): 15; Errol Simper, "Media Seeks Right to Film Judicial Hearings," *Australian,* March 27, 1990, 2.

19. Herman Wigbold, "Holland: The Shaky Pillars of Hilversum," in *Television and Political Life: Studies in Six European Countries,* ed. Anthony Smith (London: Macmillan, 1979), 215–18. The quotation in the text is from Antoine de Tarlé, "The Monopoly That Won't Divide," in ibid., 44, 60.

20. Bryan Boswell, "Perot Hits Hustings via Satellite," *Australian,* June 1, 1992, 10.

21. Sonia M. Livingstone and Peter K. Lunt, "Expert and Lay Participation in Television Debates: An Analysis of Audience Discussion Programmes," *European Journal of Communication* 7, no. 1 (1992): 9–10, 14.

22. Carl Bernstein, "The Idiot Culture," *New Republic* 206, no. 23 (1992): 28.

23. Robert Karl Manoff, "Statist Discourse in the Public Realm: Some Notes on the End of History and the Fate of Journalism" (paper presented at International Communication Association Conference, Dublin, 1990), 29–31.

24. The quotation in the text is from Mildred Amer and Ilona Nickels, "The Congress: From Quill to Screen," *Congressional Research Service Review* 10, no. 2 (1989): 31–32. See, too, Peter M. Lewis and Jerry Booth, *The Invisible Medium: Public, Commercial and Community Radio* (London: Macmillan, 1989), 38.

25. Richard Bolton, "Advertising Democracy," *Ten-8* no. 35 (1989–90): 35.

26. J. R. Odgers, *Australian Senate Practice,* 5th ed. (Canberra: Australian Government Publishing Service, 1976), 525.

27. Quoted in "TV Comes to the Commons," *Australian Financial Review,* June 14, 1989, 52.

28. Quoted in Janine Perrett, "Made-for-TV Convention Turns into a Ratings Flop," *Australian,* July 28, 1988, 15.

29. Joan Child, speech as Madam Speaker in the House of Representatives, *Commonwealth Parliamentary Debates Daily Hansard,* May 29, 1989, 3069.

30. Jenny Hutchison, *The Big Picture on the Small Screen,* Papers on Parliament 5 (Canberra: Department of the Senate, 1989), 9.

31. Quoted in Keith Tribe, "The Representation of the Real," *Cambridge Anthropology,* 1977, 56.

32. Francesco Casetti and Roger Odin, "De la paléo- à la néo-télévision," *Communications* no. 51 (1990): 9–11.

33. R. Ayres et al., *Guide to Video Production* (Sydney: Allen & Unwin, 1990), 87–88; Graeme Turner, *Film as Social Practice* (London: Routledge, 1988), 62.

34. John Hinde quoted in Peter Laud, "Watching Brief," *Sunday Times TV Guide,* April 14, 1991, 3.

35. Casetti and Odin, "De la paléo- à la néo-télévision," 11–12.

36. Lyotard, interview (cited chapter 1, n. 123, above), 7; id., "Plastic Space and Political Space—," trans. Mark S. Roberts, *Boundary 2* 14, nos. 1–2 (1985–86): 211.

37. "MPs Subdued as Commons Goes Live on TV," *Australian,* November 23, 1989, 10.

38. John Biffen, "The Shampoo Approach," *Listener* 122, no. 3119 (1989): 8.

39. Quoted in Brian Lamb, "The American Experience: C-SPAN and the US Congress," in *Televising Democracies,* ed. Franklin, 222.

40. Janet Powell, speech in the Senate, *Commonwealth Parliamentary Debates Daily Hansard,* May 31, 1990, 1630.

41. Robert Ray, speech in the Senate, *Comonwealth Parliamentary Debates Daily Hansard,* May 31, 1990, 1626.

42. Quoted in L. Taylor, "Hawke to Allow Television Cameras into Lower House," *Australian,* August 20, 1990, 1.

43. Quoted in David Culbert, "Presidential Images," in *Readings on the Body Politic,* ed. Harris, 386.

44. Quoted in Franklin, "Televising the British House of Commons," 22.

45. Madonna interviewed by Glenn O'Brien, *Interview* 20, no. 5 (1990): 127.

46. D. Harbrecht and P. Dwyer, "Congress. It Doesn't Work. Let's Fix It," *Business Week* 3148, no. 478 (1990): 55.

47. Australia, Senate Estimates, *Committee A,* May 14, 1990 (*Hansard* proceedings).

48. Quoted in *West Australian,* August 21, 1990, 15.

49. O'Keeffe, "Towards Better Parliamentary Education," 18.

50. Max Harris, "It's Question Time: Who Are These Nonentities?" *Weekend Australian,* September 1–2, 1990, REVIEW 2.

51. J. Shelley, "Television 2," *Blitz* 88 (April 1990): 34.

52. Jean-Luc Godard, "Passion (Love and Work)," *Camera Obscura,* nos. 8–9–10 (Fall 1982): 125.

53. Australia, National Training Council, *Report for 1982–84* (Canberra: Australian Government Publishing Service, 1985), iii, viii–x, 54, 57, 58.

54. Sir Alastair Pilkington, "Business in the Community: Where Do We Go from Here?" *Policy Studies* 4, no. 4 (1984): 12, 12 n. 13, 19.

55. Foucault, *Discipline and Punish,* 122–23.

56. Georg Simmel, "Prostitution," in *On Individuality and Social Forces* (Chicago: University of Chicago Press, 1971), 126.

57. Comte, "The Positive Philosophy," 23.

58. Max Weber, "The Ideal Type," in *Sociological Perspectives,* ed. Thompson and Tunstall, 63.

59. Karl Marx, *A Contribution to the Critique of Political Economy* (Moscow: Progress Publishers, 1977), 192.

60. Trevor Prescott, *Speech to Printing Industry Symposium: Training—Focus on the Future* (Canberra: National Training Council, 1985), 1.

61. Ibid., 2–5.

62. Ibid., 10, 8.

63. Ibid., 11–13.

64. Brian Pickett, *Industry Education: Cost or Benefit? Speech to Hardware Unity South Pacific* (Canberra: National Training Council, 1985), 2, 9, 5–6.

65. Ibid., 9, 12.

66. Trevor Prescott, *The TAFE/Industry Interface: Speech to a Conference on the Changing Context of TAFE* (Canberra: National Training Council, 1985), 3–7, 11.

67. Ibid., 21.

68. Weber, "Power and Bureaucracy," 77.

69. Saunders and Hunter, "Lessons from the 'Literatory,' " 479.

70. David Lodge, "Milan Kundera, and the Idea of the Author in Modern Criticism," *Critical Quarterly* 26, no. 1–2 (1984): 105–21.

71. Jean-Jacques Rousseau, "A Discourse on a Subject Proposed by the Academy of Dijon: What Is the Origin of Inequality among Men, and Is It Authorised by Natural Law?" in *Social Contract,* 106–7.

72. Michel Foucault, "Politics and the Study of Discourse," trans. Colin Gordon, in *The Foucault Effect: Studies in Governmentality,* ed. Graham Burchell et al. (London: Harvester Wheatsheaf, 1991), 58.

73. *Washington Post:* "Speakes with Forked Tongue," reprinted in *Guardian Weekly* 138, no. 17 (1988): 89.

74. "Carter, Ford Appraise Relations between Press, President," *Broadcasting* 116, no. 5 (1989): 44.

75. Peggy Noonan, "My Word, Mr President," *Good Weekend,* January 27, 1990, 49.

76. "Wordsmith Rampant," *Economist* 314, no. 7643 (1990): 90.

77. Robert Pear, "Focusing on Welfare: Bush Plays Private Acts of Decency against the Government as a Helper," *New York Times,* May 11, 1991, 8.

78. Cited by Mark Mellman in "Symposium on Presidential Campaigns and Elections," *Journal of Law and Politics* 8, no. 2 (1992): 247.

79. Richard Sennett, *The Fall of Public Man* (New York: Vintage Books, 1978), 4.

80. Wolfgang Hager, "Political Implications of US–EC Economic Conflicts (II): Atlantic Trade—Problems and Prospects," *Government and Opposition* 22, no. 1 (1987): 57.

81. Mill, *On Liberty,* 142.

82. John Stuart Mill, *Principles of Political Economy with Some of Their Applications to Social Philosophy* (New York: Longman, Green, 1896), 575.

83. Sandford F. Borins, "Public Choice: 'Yes Minister' Made It Popular but Does Winning the Nobel Prize Make It True?" *Canadian Public Administration* 31, no. 1 (1988): 13.

84. A. W. McHoul, "Sociology and Literature: The Voice of Fact and the Writing of Fiction" (paper presented at Sociological Association of Australia and New Zealand Conference, Sydney, 1987), 2.

85. Brian Head, "Economic Rationalism: The New Orthodoxy in Australian Public Policy?" (paper presented at Australasian Political Studies Association Conference, Armidale, 1988), 2.

86. Michael Pusey, "From Canberra the Outlook Is Dry," *Australian Society,* July 1988, 21.

87. Quoted in Eliot Marshall, "Nobel Economist Robert Solow," *Dialogue,* no. 82 (1988): 8–9.

88. Thea M. Lee, "Contradictions in the Teaching of Neoclassical Theory," *Review of Radical Political Economics* 20, nos. 2–3 (1988): 8–9.

89. Roger L. Kerr, *Ideas, Interests and Experience: Some Implications for Policy Advice* (Sydney: Centre for Independent Studies; Auckland: New Zealand Centre for Independent Studies, 1988), 2, 10, 12, 14; Ian Castles, "Facts and Fancies of Bureaucracy," *Canberra Bulletin of Public Administration,* no. 53 (December 1987): 44.

90. Morris, *Ecstasy and Economics,* 141 n. 53, 76.

91. Castles, "Facts and Fancies of Bureaucracy," 39–40; Pusey, "From Canberra the Outlook Is Dry," 22; Brent Davis, "Hitting the Right Lobby Target," *Australian Business* 8, no. 35 (1988): 125.

92. Australia, Committee of Inquiry into Labour Market Programs, *Report* (Canberra: Australian Government Publishing Service, 1985), 49.

93. Neil Marshall, "Bureaucratic Politics and the Demise of the Commonwealth Tertiary Education Commission," *Australian Journal of Public Administration* 47, no. 1 (1988): 26.

94. Senator Nick Bolkus, "Alarmed Australia Bans Political Ads," *New York Times,* May 10, 1991, A30; Darrell M. West, "Reforming Campaign Ads," *PS* 25, no. 1 (1992): 74; Mellman in "Symposium on Presidential Campaigns and Elections," 229.

95. George Armstrong Kelly, "Who Needs a Theory of Citizenship?" *Dædalus* 108, no. 4 (1979): 28.

96. Karl Marx and Friedrich Engels, "Bourgeois and Proletarians," in *Sociological Perspectives,* ed. Thompson and Tunstall, 239.

97. Murray Milgate and John Eatwell, "Economic Theory and European Society: The Influence of J. M. Keynes," *History of European Ideas* 9, no. 2 (1988): 215.

98. Plato, *The Laws,* trans. Trevor J. Saunders (Baltimore: Penguin Books, 1972), 1.1.48.

99. Michels, *Political Parties,* 257; Bryan S. Turner, *Citizenship and Capitalism: The Debate over Reformism* (Boston: Allen & Unwin, 1986), 109–110.

100. Offe, "Capitalism by Democratic Design?" 881–82.

101. Stephen Sestanovich, "The Hour of the Demagogue," *National Interest,* no. 25 (Fall 1991): 3–4, 6.

102. Peter Golding and Graham Murdock, "Pulling the Plugs on Democracy," *New Statesman and Society* 2, no. 56 (1989): 11.

Chapter Five.
New Technologies to Form New Selves

1. Michel Foucault, *The Care of the Self,* vol. 3 of *The History of Sexuality,* trans. Robert Hurley (New York: Vintage Books, 1988), 85.

2. Anthony Giddens, *Power, Property and the State,* vol. 1 of *A Contemporary Critique of Historical Materialism* (London: Macmillan, 1983), 170–73.

3. Monique Plaza, "Our Costs and Their Benefits," trans. Wendy Harrison, *m/f* no. 4 (1980): 28–39.

4. Michael Walzer, "The Politics of Michel Foucault," *Dissent* 30, no. 4 (1983): 481, 483–87.

5. See Foucault, *Use of Pleasure,* 22–23, 83–85, 127–29, 143–51, 158; id., *Care of the Self,* 121–22, 128, 146–85, 222–23.

6. Barry Smart, "Theory and Analysis after Foucault," *Theory, Culture, and Society* 8, no. 2 (1991): 152.

7. See John Frow, "Some Versions of Foucault," *Meanjin* 47, no. 1 (1988): 149.

8. Foucault, "Politics and the Study of Discourse," 55.

9. Larry Ray, "Foucault, Critical Theory and the Decomposition of the Historical Subject," *Philosophy and Social Criticism* 14, no. 1 (1989): 98.

10. Foucault, "Politics and the Study of Discourse," 65.

11. Richard Rorty, "Foucault/Dewey/Nietzsche," *Raritan* 9, no. 4 (1990): 3, 1, 3–5, 7.

12. Charles Taylor, *Sources of the Self: The Making of the Modern Identity* (Cambridge, Mass.: Harvard University Press, 1989), 23, 77, 93, 490, 518–19, 99, 488–90.

13. Thomas McCarthy, "The Critique of Impure Reason: Foucault and the Frankfurt School," *Political Theory* 18, no. 3 (1990): 450; Leslie Paul Thiele,

"The Agony of Politics: The Nietzschean Roots of Foucault's Thought," *American Political Science Review* 84, no. 3 (1990): 919; Jerrold Seigel, "Avoiding the Subject: A Foucaultian Itinerary," *Journal of the History of Ideas* 51, no. 2 (1990): 275, 295–96. Also see James Miller, "Foucault; The Secrets of a Man," *Salmagundi,* no. 88–89 (Fall–Winter 1990–91): 311–32.

14. Foucault, *Remarks on Marx,* 11–12, 159; Teresa de Lauretis, "The Violence of Rhetoric: Considerations on Representation and Gender," in *Violence of Representation,* ed. Armstrong and Tennenhouse, 243–44.

15. Foucault, *Remarks on Marx,* 169–72.

16. Jean-François Lyotard, *Le Différend* (Paris: Editions de minuit, 1983), 29.

17. Guy Hocquenghem, *Homosexual Desire,* trans. Daniella Dangoor (London: Allison & Busby, 1978), 104.

18. Pierre Bourdieu, *Outline of a Theory of Practice,* trans. Richard Nice (Cambridge: Cambridge University Press, 1977).

19. Deborah Gordon, "Writing Cultures, Writing Feminism: The Poetics and Politics of Experimental Ethnography," *Inscriptions,* nos. 3–4 (1988): 7–24; Frances E. Mascia-Lees et al., "The Postmodernist Turn in Anthropology: Cautions from a Feminist Perspective," *Signs: Journal of Women in Culture and Society* 15, no. 1 (1989): 11, 14.

20. Jacques Derrida, "Structure, Sign and Play in the Discourse of the Human Sciences," trans. Alan Bass, in *Modern Criticism and Theory: A Reader,* ed. David Lodge (New York: Longman, 1988), 112, 109.

21. Meaghan Morris, "Banality in Cultural Studies," *Discourse* 10, no. 2 (1988): 17. The activity under scutiny is in evidence in John Fiske, *Understanding Popular Culture;* id., *Reading the Popular* (Boston: Unwin Hyman, 1989).

22. Lyotard, *Condition postmoderne,* 21–22.

23. Steven Grant, *The Life of Pope John Paul II* (New York: Marvel Comics, 1986), 1, 56–57.

24. Quoted in Jim Clarke and Michael Costigan, *John Paul II: The Journey through Australia* (Melbourne: Australia Pacific 1986), 16.

25. Raymond Lémieux, "Charisme, mass-média et religion populaire: Le Voyage du pape au Canada," *Social Compass* 34, no. 1 (1987): 11.

26. Clarke and Costigan, *John Paul II,* 31, 16; Helen Trinca, "Pope's Progress," *Australian,* December 1, 1986, 11.

27. Evan Whitton, "Boisterous Reception at Sydney Uni," *Sydney Morning Herald,* November 27, 1986.

28. Trinca, "Pope's Progress," 11.

29. "The Prince of Peace," *New Idea,* December 13, 1986, 6; George Pell, "The Pope Comes to Australia," in *John Paul II: Welcome to Australia 1986* (Sydney: Playbill, 1986), 48.

30. *John Paul II: Welcome to Australia 1986,* 64, 30. See also Michael Costigan, "Pope John Paul II: The Man and His Travels," in ibid., 10, 14; Clarke and Costigan, *John Paul II,* 103.

31. James Oram, *The People's Pope: The Story of Karol Wojtyla of Poland* (Sydney: Bay Books, 1979), 76, 81.

32. *John Paul II: Welcome to Australia 1986,* 62.

33. Elizabeth Gross, "Derrida and the Limits of Philosophy," *Thesis Eleven* no. 14 (1986): 26–27.

34. Bryan S. Turner, *Religion and Social Theory: A Materialist Perspective* (London: Heinemann Educational Books, 1983), 1.

35. Friedrich Nietzsche, "History of Moralization and Dismoralization," trans. Walter Kaufman and R. J. Hollingdale, in *The Will to Power* (New York: Random House, 1967), 786, 415.

36. Mollie McGee, "The Private World of Pope John Paul II," *Australian Women's Weekly* 54, no. 11 (1986): 66, 68–69.

37. *John Paul II: Welcome to Australia 1986*, 56.

38. Costigan, "Pope John Paul II: The Man and His Travels," 8, 11; Grant, *Life of Pope John Paul II*, 4; Mark Lane, "The Philosophy of a Pope," in *John Paul II: Welcome to Australia 1986*, 28.

39. Evan Whitton, "The Road to Rome," *Sydney Morning Herald*, November 22, 1986; Clarke and Costigan, *John Paul II*, 46–47; Ralph Della Cava, "Vatican Policy, 1978–90: An Updated Overview," *Social Research* 59, no. 1 (1992): 176; Grant, *Life of Pope John Paul II*, 21.

40. Quoted in Clarke and Costigan, *John Paul II*, 78.

41. Oram, *People's Pope*, 150; Costigan, "Pope John Paul II: The Man and His Travels," 16; Clarke and Costigan, *John Paul II*, 30–31; J. René Marcel Sauvé, letter to *Guardian Weekly* 136, no. 16 (1987): 2.

42. Paul Collins, *Mixed Blessings: John Paul II and the Church of the Eighties* (Melbourne: Penguin Books, 1987), 164, 170–72; Oram, *People's Pope*, 85; Grant, *Life of Pope John Paul II*, 59; Joel Kovel, "The Theocracy of John Paul II," in *Socialist Register, 1987*, ed. Ralph Miliband et al. (London: Merlin Press, 1987), 448–49, 458–59.

43. Dennis Altman, *Homosexual: Oppression and Liberation* (Sydney: Angus & Robertson, 1972), 43–44.

44. Ruth Tiffany Barnhouse, "Homosexuality: A Synthetic Confusion," in *Homosexuality and Ethics*, ed. Edward Batchelor (New York: Pilgrim Press, 1980), 85; Vatican, "Congregation for the Doctrine of the Faith," in ibid., 239; Archbishop of Westminster, "Statement," in ibid., 240, 239.

45. Bishop John Reid, quoted in Bruce Stannard and Kevin Murphy, "More than a Million Australians—Still Glad to Be Gay?" *Bulletin*, October 10, 1989, 54.

46. Thomas Aquinas, "Summa Theologica," excerpted in *Homosexuality and Ethics*, ed. Batchelor, 39–41, 44, 47.

47. Richard J. Hoffman, "Vices, Gods, and Virtues: Cosmology as a Mediating Factor in Attitudes toward Male Homosexuality," *Journal of Homosexuality* 9, no. 2–3 (1983–84): 36–37.

48. Quoted in "Political Intrigue Fills Air as Miami Welcomes Pope," *Sydney Morning Herald*, September 12, 1987; Clarke and Costigan, *John Paul II*, 106.

49. Australian Catholic Bishops, "The AIDS Crisis: A Message to the Australian People," *Australasian Catholic Record* 64, no. 3 (1987): 293–94.

50. James Murray, "The Megastar Pope," *Weekend Australian*, November 22–23, 1986, 23; Clarke and Costigan, *John Paul II*, 79, 52, 1, 108.

51. Italo Calvino, "Desire in November," trans. Archibald Colquhoun and Peggy Wright, in *Adam, One Afternoon and Other Stories* (London: Picador, 1983), 132.

52. Kenneth Leech, *The Social God* (London: Sheldon Press, 1981), 15.

53. Steve Bell, cartoon, *Guardian Weekly* 136, no. 16 (1987): 7.

54. Michel Foucault, "Space, Knowledge and Power," in *The Foucault Reader,* ed. Paul Rabinow (Harmondsworth: Penguin Books, 1986), 241.

55. Catholic Enquiry Centre, *The Catholic Religion: A Course of Twenty Lessons* (Maroubra: 1987).

56. Clarke and Costigan, *John Paul II,* 19.

57. Ibid., 1, 112; R. J. L. Hawke, in *John Paul II: Welcome to Australia 1986,* 4.

58. Showalter, "Critical Cross-Dressing," in *Men in Feminism,* ed. Jardine and Smith, 120.

59. Lynne Segal, *Slow Motion: Changing Masculinities, Changing Men* (London: Virago Press, 1990), 139–40, 145.

60. Gaylyn Studlar, "Midnight S/excess: Cult Configurations of 'Femininity' and the Perverse," *Journal of Popular Film and Television* 17, no. 1 (1989): 8–9.

61. Félix Guattari, "Becoming-Woman," *Semiotext(e)* 4, no. 1 (1981): 86–87.

62. Sennett, *Fall of Public Man,* 7.

63. Stallybrass and White, *Politics and Poetics of Transgression,* 189.

64. Peter Stallybrass, "'Drunk with the Cup of Liberty': Robin Hood, the Carnivalesque, and the Rhetoric of Violence in Early Modern England," in *Violence of Representation,* ed. Armstrong and Tennenhouse, 46, 48–49, 54.

65. Bernard McElroy, *Fiction of the Modern Grotesque* (London: Macmillan, 1989), 1–2, 5, 14, 20.

66. Della Cava, "Vatican Policy, 1978–90," 192.

67. Richard G. Parker, *Bodies, Pleasures, and Passions: Sexual Culture in Contemporary Brazil* (Boston: Beacon Press, 1991), 139–42, 145–46, 163.

68. Michel Foucault, "Friendship as a Lifestyle," *Gay Information,* no. 7 (Spring 1981): 6.

69. Sisters of Perpetual Indulgence, *Who Are the Sisters of Perpetual Indulgence?* (n.p.: n.p., 1986), n.p.

70. Foucault, *Use of Pleasure,* 54.

71. Sisters of Perpetual Indulgence, *Who Are the Sisters of Perpetual Indulgence?* n.p.

72. Ibid.; id., *White Paper* (N.p., 1989), 2; "Sisters Six Years Old," *Sydney Star Observer,* no. 63 (October 20, 1987): 3; Larry Galbraith, "While There's Still a Wimple," *Outrage* no. 50 (1987): 11.

73. Karl Marx, "Alienated Labour," trans. T. B. Bottomore, in *Sociological Perspectives,* ed. Thompson and Tunstall, 57.

74. George Herbert Mead, "Self," in *Sociological Perspectives,* ed. Thompson and Tunstall, 145–47, 152, 155.

75. Jean Baudrillard, "Transpolitics, Transsexuality, Transaesthetics," trans. Michel Valentin, in *Jean Baudrillard: The Disappearance of Art and Politics,* ed. William Stearns and William Chaloupka (London: Macmillan, 1992), 20.

76. I owe this reference to personal information provided by the late Eric

Michaels. Also see the photograph in his *Unbecoming: An AIDS Diary* (Sydney: EM Press, 1990), 8.

77. Jonathan Dollimore, *Sexual Dissidence: Augustine to Wilde, Freud to Foucault* (Oxford: Clarendon Press, 1991), 14; Eve Kosofsky Sedgwick, *Epistemology of the Closet* (Berkeley and Los Angeles: University of California Press, 1990), 74, 164.

78. Hocquenghem, *Homosexual Desire*, 83.

79. Quoted in Larry Gross, "The Contested Closet: The Ethics and Politics of Outing," *Critical Studies in Mass Communication* 8, no. 3 (1991): 377.

80. Hall, "Old and New Identities," in *Culture, Globalization and the World-System*, ed. King, 54.

81. Leo Bersani, "Is the Rectum a Grave?" *October*, no. 43 (Winter 1987): 208.

82. D. A. Miller, "Bringing Out Roland Barthes," *Raritan* 11, no. 4 (1992): 41.

83. Bersani, "Is the Rectum a Grave?" 205.

84. Sisters of Perpetual Indulgence, *White Paper*, 2, 5–6, 8.

85. Helen Trinca, "Starstruck Sydney's Shot of Adrenalin," *Australian*, November 26, 1986, 3.

86. Whitton, "Boisterous."

87. Michel Pêcheux, "Discourse: Structure or Event?" trans. Warren Montag et al., in *Marxism and the Interpretation of Culture*, ed. Nelson and Grossberg, 634.

88. Jean-François Lyotard, "One of the Things at Stake in Women's Struggles," trans. Deborah J. Clarke et al., *SubStance* no. 20 (1978): 10.

89. Lacan, "Function and Field," in *Ecrits*, 58.

90. Ed Cohen, "Are We (Not) What We Are Becoming? 'Gay' 'Identity,' 'Gay Studies,' and the Disciplining of Knowledge," in *Engendering Men: The Question of Male Feminist Criticism*, ed. Joseph A. Boone and Michael Cadden (New York: Routledge, 1990), 163–65.

91. Luce Irigaray, *Divine Women*, trans. Stephen Muecke (Sydney: Local Consumption Publications, 1986), 3–4.

92. Quoted in Oram, *People's Pope*, 113.

93. Foucault, "Order of Discourse," in *Untying the Text*, ed. Young, 52; id., *Use of Pleasure*, 4.

94. Jürgen Habermas, *The Philosophical Discourse of Modernity: Twelve Lectures*, trans. Frederick G. Lawrence (Cambridge: Polity Press, 1990), 240.

95. Quoted in Stuart Cunningham and Ross Harley, "Scandal to the Jews, Folly to the Pagans: A Treatment for *Hail Mary*," *Continuum* 1, no. 2 (1988): 34.

96. Mill, *On Liberty*, 66.

97. Quoted in Stannard and Murphy, "More than a Million Australians," 57.

98. Emile Durkheim, "The Functions of Ritual," in *Emile Durkheim*, ed. Giddens, 233.

99. Habermas, "New Obscurity," in *New Conservatism*, ed. Nicholsen, 66–67.

100. Foucault, "Subject and Power," 785.

Conclusion

1. Jean-Jacques Rousseau, "The Social Contract or Principles of Political Right," in *Social Contract,* 175, 177.

2. Ellen Meiksins Wood, "The Uses and Abuses of 'Civil Society,'" in *Socialist Register, 1990,* ed. Ralph Miliband et al. (London: Merlin Press, 1991), 65; Robert N. Bellah et al., *The Good Society* (New York: Knopf, 1992), 35; Alec McHoul and Tom O'Regan, "Towards a Paralogics of Textual Technologies: Batman, Glasnost and Relativism in Cultural Studies," *Southern Review* 25, no. 1 (1992): 16.

3. Stephen Heath, "The Ethics of Sexual Difference," *Discourse* 12, no. 2 (1990): 134, 138.

4. Seyla Benhabib, *Situating the Self: Gender, Community and Postmodernism in Contemporary Ethics* (Cambridge: Polity Press, 1992), 228–30.

5. Jeffrey Isaac and Christopher Lasch, "Modernity and Progress: An Exchange," *Salmagundi,* no. 93 (Winter 1992): 85–87, 92.

6. Iris Marion Young, "Polity and Group Difference: A Critique of the Ideal of Universal Citizenship," in *Feminism and Political Theory,* ed. Cass R. Sunstein (Chicago: University of Chicago Press, 1990), 117–19, 126.

7. Teresa L. Ebert, "The "Difference" of Postmodern Feminism," *College English* 53, no. 8 (1991): 887.

8. Nikolas Rose and Peter Miller, "Political Power beyond the State: Problematics of Government," *British Journal of Sociology* 43, no. 2 (1992): 174–75, 180–81.

9. Anne Barron, "Legal Discourse and the Colonisation of the Self in the Modern State," in *Post-Modern Law: Enlightenment, Revolution and the Death of Man,* ed. Anthony Carty (Edinburgh: Edinburgh University Press, 1990), 109, 116–17.

10. Stephen Bann, "René Girard and the Revisionist View of Narcissism," *Comparative Criticism: An Annual Journal* no. 12 (1990): 92–93.

11. Heath, "Ethics of Sexual Difference," 149–50.

12. Rosemarie Tong, "Feminist Justice: A Study in Difference," *Journal of Social Philosophy* 22, no. 3 (1991): 81–83.

13. Ian Hacking, "Self-Improvement," in *Foucault: A Critical Reader,* ed. David Couzens Hoy (Oxford: Basil Blackwell, 1986), 239.

14. Edward Said, "The Politics of Knowledge," *Raritan* 11, no. 1 (1991): 21–24.

15. Miller, *Boxed In,* 183–84.

16. Susan Stewart, *On Longing: Narratives of the Miniature, the Gigantic, the Souvenir, the Collection* (Baltimore: Johns Hopkins University Press, 1984), 173.

17. Sedgwick, *Epistemology of the Closet,* 61.

18. Stuart Hall, "Old and New Identities," in *Culture, Globalization and the World-System,* ed. King, 56.

19. Bersani, "Is the Rectum a Grave?" 206.

20. Elias, *Civilizing Process;* Zygmunt Bauman, "Ideology and the *Weltan-*

schauung of the Intellectuals," *Canadian Journal of Political and Social Theory* 15, no. 1–3 (1991): 108–10; Jean Baudrillard, "Modernity," trans. David James Miller, *Canadian Journal of Political and Social Theory* 11, no. 3 (1987): 66–67.

21. Foucault, *Remarks on Marx,* 31.

22. Ibid., 31, 46, 139, 121, 176.

Select Bibliography

Where no translation was available, the English version quoted in the text, given in brackets following the original, is my own.

Acton, Lord [John Emerich Edward Dalberg-Acton, 1st baron]. *The History of Freedom and Other Essays*. 1862. John Neville Figgis and Reginald Vere Laurence. Freeport, N.Y.: Books for Libraries Press, 1967.

Adams, Parveen, Beverley Brown, and Elizabeth Cowie. "*m/f* Editorial." *m/f* no. 2 (1978): 2–4.

Adorno, Theodor W. "On Jazz." 1936. Trans. Jamie Owen Daniel. *Discourse* 12, no. 1 (1989–90): 45–69.

✓ Aksoy, Asu, and Kevin Robins. "Hollywood for the 21st Century: Global Competition for Critical Mass in Image Markets." *Cambridge Journal of Economics* 16, no. 1 (1992): 1–22.

Allen, James Sloan. "The Existential Reader: Or Reading, Rumination, and the Classics." *Sewanee Review* 99, no. 1 (1991): 86–100.

Almond, Gabriel. "The Nature of Contemporary Political Science: A Roundtable Discussion." *PS* 23, no. 1 (1990): 34–36.

Althusser, Louis. *For Marx*. 1966. Trans. Ben Brewster. Harmondsworth: Penguin Books, 1969.

———. *Lenin and Philosophy and Other Essays*. Trans. Ben Brewster. London: New Left Books, 1977.

———. *Politics and History: Montesquieu, Rousseau, Hegel, Marx*. Trans. Ben Brewster. London: New Left Books, 1977.

✓ Altieri, Charles. "Life after Difference: The Positions of the Interpreter and the Positioning of the Interpreted." *Monist* 73, no. 2 (1990): 269–95.

Altman, Dennis. *Homosexual: Oppression and Liberation*. Sydney: Angus & Robertson, 1972.

Anderson, Harold. "Exporting TV Know-How—A Case History." *Television Quarterly* 4, no. 1 (1965): 19–21.

✓ Andrews, Geoff. "Universal Principles." *Marxism Today,* August 1990, 16–17, 19.

✓ ———, ed. *Citizenship.* London: Lawrence & Wishart, 1991.

Ankersmit, F. R. "Historiography and Postmodernism." *History and Theory* 28, no. 2 (1989): 137–53.

Appleton, Gillian. *Attitudes to Television: A Survey of Advertisers.* Sydney: Australian Film Commission, 1989.

Apter, D. E. "The Passing of Development Studies." *Government and Opposition* 15, no. 3–4 (1980): 263–75.

✓ Arac, Jonathan, and Harriet Ritvo, eds. *Macropolitics of Nineteenth-Century Literature: Nationalism, Exoticism, Imperialism.* Philadelphia: University of Pennsylvania Press, 1991.

Archer, Margaret S. *Culture and Agency: The Place of Culture in Social Theory.* 1988. New York: Cambridge University Press, 1989.

Aristotle. *Nichomachean Ethics.* Fourth century B.C. Trans. Martin Ostwald. Indianapolis: Bobbs-Merrill, 1962.

———. *Poetics.* Fourth century B.C. Trans. S. H. Butcher. New York: Hill & Wang, 1961.

Armstrong, Nancy, and Leonard Tennenhouse, eds. *The Violence of Representation: Literature and the History of Violence.* New York: Routledge, 1989.

Arnold, Matthew. *Culture and Anarchy.* 1869. Ed. J. Dover Wilson. Cambridge: Cambridge University Press, 1971.

Australia. Australian Broadcasting Tribunal. *Australian Content Inquiry Discussion Paper: Amounts of Time Occupied by Different Program Categories.* N.p., 1988.

———. *Draft Television Program Standard 14.* N.p. November 6, 1989.

Australia. Committee of Inquiry into Labour Market Programs. *Report.* Canberra: Australian Government Publishing Service, 1985.

Australia. Industries Assistance Commission. *Assessing Barriers to International Trade in Services.* Inquiry into International Trade in Services. Discussion Paper 2. Canberra: Australian Government Publishing Service, 1989.

———. *International Initiatives to Liberalise Trade in Services.* Inquiry into International Trade in Services. Discussion Paper 3. Canberra: Australian Government Publishing Service, 1989.

Australia. National Training Council. *Report for 1982–84.* Canberra: Australian Government Publishing Service, 1985.

Ayres, Rowan, Martha Mollison, Ian Stocks, and Jim Tumeth. *Guide to Video Production.* Sydney: Allen & Unwin, 1990.

Bann, Stephen. "René Girard and the Revisionist View of Narcissism." *Comparative Criticism: An Annual Journal* no. 12 (1990): 89–104.

Barthes, Roland. *Image Music Text.* Trans. Stephen Heath. London: Flamingo, 1984.

Bashevkin, Sylvia. "Does Public Opinion Matter? The Adoption of Federal

Royal Commission and Task Force Recommendations on the National Question, 1951–1987." *Canadian Public Administration* 31, no. 1 (1988): 390–407.

Batchelor, Edward, ed. *Homosexuality and Ethics*. New York: Pilgrim Press, 1980.

Baudrillard, Jean. *Jean Baudrillard: Selected Writings*. Ed. Mark Poster. Trans. Jacques Mourrain, Charles Levin, Marie Maclean, Paul Foss, Paul Patton, Philip Reitchman, and Mark Poster. Stanford: Stanford University Press, 1988.

———. "Modernity." 1985. Trans. David James Miller. *Canadian Journal of Political and Social Theory* 11, no. 3 (1987): 63–72.

———. "Politics of Seduction." Interview by Suzanne Moore and Stephen Johnstone. *Marxism Today,* January 1989, 54–55.

Bauman, Zygmunt. "Ideology and the *Weltanschauung* of the Intellectuals." *Canadian Journal of Political and Social Theory* 15, no. 1–3 (1991): 107–20.

Bell, Daniel. "Post-Industrial Society: The Evolution of an Idea." *Survey* 17, no. 2 (1971): 102–68.

Bellah, Robert N., Richard Madsen, William M. Sullivan, Ann Swidler, and Steven M. Tipton. *The Good Society*. New York: Knopf, 1992.

Belsey, Catherine. "The Plurality of History." *Southern Review* 17, no. 2 (1984): 138–41.

Benhabib, Seyla. *Situating the Self: Gender, Community and Postmodernism.* Cambridge: Polity Press, 1992.

Benjamin, Walter. *Illuminations*. 1955. Ed. Hannah Arendt. Trans. Harry Zohn. London: Jonathan Cape, 1970. English translation first published by Harcourt, Brace & World. New York, 1968.

Bennett, Tony. *Outside Literature*. New York: Routledge, 1990.

Bersani, Leo. "Is the Rectum a Grave?" *October,* no. 43 (Winter 1987): 197–222.

Best, Steve, and Douglas Kellner. "Watching Television: Limitations of Post-Modernism." *Science as Culture* no. 4 (1988): 44–70.

Binder, Leonard, James S. Coleman, Joseph LaPalombara, Lucian W. Pye, Sidney Verba, and Myron Weiner. *Crises and Sequences in Political Development*. Princeton: Princeton University Press, 1971.

Boone, Joseph A., and Michael Cadden, eds. *Engendering Men: The Question of Male Feminist Criticism*. New York: Routledge, 1990.

Bordwell, David. *Making Meaning: Inference and Rhetoric in the Interpretation of Cinema*. Cambridge, Mass.: Harvard University Press, 1989.

Borins, Sandford F. "Public Choice: 'Yes Minister' Made It Popular but Does Winning the Nobel Prize Make It True?" *Canadian Public Administration* 31, no. 1 (1988): 12–26.

Boulez, Pierre, and Michel Foucault. "Contemporary Music and Its Public." 1983. Trans. Maria Koundoura and Nikos Papastergiadis. *Melbourne Journal of Politics* no. 17 (1985–86): 42–50.

Bourdieu, Pierre. *Outline of a Theory of Practice*. 1972. Trans. Richard Nice. Cambridge: Cambridge University Press, 1977.

Bourne, Bill, Voi Eichler, and David Herman, eds. *Voices: Modernity and Its Discontents*. Nottingham: Spokesman, 1987.

Brademas, John. "The Arts and Politics: A Commentary." *Mediterranean Quarterly* 1, no. 2 (1990): 93–105.

Braman, Sandra. "Trade and Information Policy." *Media, Culture and Society* 12, no. 3 (1990): 361–85.

Brodsky, Joseph. "Poetry as a Form of Resistance to Reality." Trans. Alexander Sumerkin and Jamey Gambrell. *PMLA* 102, no. 2 (1992): 220–25.

✓ Brown, Mary Ellen, ed. *Television and Women's Culture: The Politics of the Popular*. Sydney: Currency Press, 1990.

✓ Burchell, Graham, Colin Gordon, and Peter Miller, eds. *The Foucault Effect: Studies in Governmentality*. London: Harvester Wheatsheaf, 1991.

✓ Burtt, Shelley. "The Good Citizen's Psyche: On the Psychology of Civic Virtue." *Polity* 23, no. 1 (1990): 23–38.

Canadian Commission for UNESCO. "A Working Definition of 'Culture.'" *Cultures* 4, no. 4 (1977): 78–85.

✓ Carter, John. "Parliamentary Education: A Challenge for All Parliaments." *Legislative Studies* 4, no. 1 (1989): 37–38.

✓ Carty, Anthony, ed. *Post-Modern Law: Enlightenment, Revolution and the Death of Man*. Edinburgh: Edinburgh University Press, 1990.

Casetti, Francesco, and Roger Odin. "De la paléo- à la néo-télévision." *Communications* no. 51 (1990): 9–26.

Clarke, Jim, and Michael Costigan. *John Paul II: The Journey through Australia*. Melbourne: Australia Pacific 1986, 1986.

Collins, Richard. *Culture, Communication, and National Identity: The Case of Canadian Television*. Toronto: University of Toronto Press, 1990.

✓ ———. "Television and National Identity on Both Sides of the Atlantic." *Round Table*, no. 318 (April 1991): 173–78.

Communications Law Centre. *The Representation of Non-English Background People in Australian Television Drama*. Discussion Paper prepared for Actors Equity. Sydney, 1992.

Corner, John, and Sylvia Harvey. "Heritage in Britain: Designer-History and the Popular Imagination." *Ten-8* no. 36 (1990): 14–21.

Cowie, Elizabeth. "The Popular Film as a Progressive Text—A Discussion of *Coma* Part 1." *m/f* no. 3 (1979): 59–81.

Crimp, Douglas. "To Our Readers." *October,* no. 53 (Summer 1990): 108–10.

Cunningham, Stuart. "Style, Form and History in Australian Mini-Series." *Southern Review* 22, no. 3 (1989): 315–30.

Deleuze, Gilles, and Félix Guattari. "Rhizome." 1976. Trans. Paul Foss and Paul Patton. *Ideology and Consciousness,* no. 8 (Spring 1981): 49–71.

Della Cava, Ralph. "Vatican Policy, 1978–90: An Updated Overview." *Social Research* 59, no. 1 (1992): 169–99.

Dermody, Susan, and Elizabeth Jacka. *The Screening of Australia*. Vol. 2 of *Anatomy of a National Cinema*. Sydney: Currency Press, 1988.

————, eds. *The Imaginary Industry: Australian Film in the Late '80s*. Sydney: Australian Film, Television and Radio School, 1988.

Derrida, Jacques. "Of an Apocalyptic Tone Recently Adopted in Philosophy." 1983 Trans. John P. Leavey, Jr. *Oxford Literary Review* 6, no. 2 (1984): 3–37.

————. "Signature Event Context." Trans. Samuel Weber and Jeffrey Mehlman. *Glyph* no. 1 (1977): 172–97.

Dimock, Marshall. "The Restorative Qualities of Citizenship." *Public Administration Review* 50, no. 1 (1990): 21–25.

Dollimore, Jonathan. *Sexual Dissidence: Augustine to Wilde, Freud to Foucault*. Oxford: Clarendon Press, 1991.

Dollimore, Jonathan, and Alan Sinfield. "Culture and Textuality: Debating Cultural Materialism." *Textual Practice* 4, no. 1 (1990): 91–100.

Donald, James. Review of *Channels of Discourse*, ed. Robert C. Allen, and *Television Culture*, by John Fiske. *Screen* 31, no. 1 (1990): 113–18.

Donzelot, Jacques. *The Policing of Families*. Trans. Robert Hurley. New York: Pantheon Books, 1979.

————. "The Poverty of Political Culture." 1978. Trans. Couze Venn. *Ideology and Consciousness*, no. 5 (Spring 1979): 73–86.

Dorfman, Ariel. *The Empire's Old Clothes: What the Lone Ranger, Babar, and Other Innocent Heroes Do to Our Minds*. London: Pluto Press, 1983.

Durkheim, Emile. *Emile Durkheim: Selected Writings*. Ed. and trans. Anthony Giddens. New York: Cambridge University Press, 1972.

Dworkin, Ronald. *A Matter of Principle*. Cambridge, Mass.: Harvard University Press, 1985.

Eagleton, Terry. *The Ideology of the Aesthetic*. Oxford: Basil Blackwell, 1990.

————. *Literary Theory: An Introduction*. Oxford: Basil Blackwell, 1983.

Ebert, Teresa L. "The 'Difference' of Postmodern Feminism." *College English* 53, no. 8 (1991): 886–904.

Eco, Umberto. Interview by Adelaida Lopez and Manthelma Costa. Trans. Donald Tucker and Adelaida Lopez. *Diacritics* 17, no. 1 (1987): 46–51.

Eco, Umberto, and Stefano Rosso. "A Correspondence with Umberto Eco: Genoa-Bologna-Binghamton-Bloomington, August-September 1982–March-April 1983." Trans. Carolyn Springer. *Boundary 2* 12, no. 1 (1983): 1–13.

Elders, Fons, ed. *Reflexive Water: The Basic Concerns of Mankind*. London: Souvenir Press, 1974.

Elias, Norbert. *The Civilizing Process: The History of Manners*. 1939. Trans. Edmund Jephcott. Oxford: Basil Blackwell, 1978.

————. *The History of Manners*. 1939. New York: Pantheon, 1978.

Elkin, Stephen L. "Citizenship and Constitutionalism in Post-Communist Regimes." *PS* 23, no. 2 (1990): 163–66.

Engels, Frederick. *Anti-Dühring: Herr Eugen Dühring's Revolution in Science.* 1877–78. Beijing: Foreign Languages Press, 1976.

Felski, Rita. *Beyond Feminist Aesthetics: Feminist Literature and Social Change.* London: Hutchinson Radius, 1989.

Forster, E. M. *Aspects of the Novel.* 1927. Ed. Oliver Stallybrass. New York: Penguin Books, 1984.

Foucault, Michel. *The Archaeology of Knowledge.* 1969. Trans. A. M. Sheridan Smith. London: Tavistock Publications, 1985.

———. *The Birth of the Clinic: An Archaeology of Medical Perception.* 1963. Trans. A. M. Sheridan Smith. New York: Vintage Books, 1975.

———. *The Care of the Self.* Vol. 3 of *The History of Sexuality.* 1984. Trans. Robert Hurley. New York: Vintage Books, 1988.

———. *Discipline and Punish: The Birth of the Prison.* 1975. Trans. Alan Sheridan. New York: Vintage Books, 1979.

———. *Foucault Live: Interviews, 1966–84.* Ed. Sylvère Lotringer. New York: Semiotext(e), 1989.

———. *The Foucault Reader.* 1984. Ed. Paul Rabinow. Harmondsworth: Penguin Books, 1986.

———. "Friendship as a Lifestyle." *Gay Information,* no. 7 (Spring 1981): 4–6.

———. "Georges Canguilhem: Philosopher of Error." Trans. Graham Burchell. *Ideology and Consciousness,* no. 7 (Autumn 1980): 51–62.

———. *The History of Sexuality: An Introduction.* 1976. Trans. Robert Hurley. New York: Penguin Books, 1984.

———. "How We Behave." *Vanity Fair,* November 1983, 61–70.

———. *Michel Foucault: Power, Truth, Strategy.* Ed. Meaghan Morris and Paul Patton. Sydney: Feral Publications, 1979.

———. "Monstrosities in Criticism." *Diacritics* 1, no. 1 (1971): 57–58.

———. *The Order of Things: An Archaeology of the Human Sciences.* 1966. New York: Vintage Books, 1973.

———. *Power-Knowledge: Selected Interviews and Other Writings, 1972–77, Michel Foucault.* Ed. Colin Gordon. New York: Pantheon Books, 1980.

———. "La Psychologie de 1850 à 1950." 1957. *Revue internationale de philosophie* 44, no. 2 (1990): 159–76.

———. "Questions of Method: An Interview with Michel Foucault." 1977. Trans. Colin Gordon. *Ideology and Consciousness,* no. 8 (Spring 1981): 3–14.

———. *Remarks on Marx: Conversations with Duccio Trombadori.* 1981. Trans. R. James Goldstein and James Cascaito. New York: Semiotext(e), 1991.

———. "The Subject and Power." Trans. Leslie Sawyer. *Critical Inquiry* 8, no. 4 (1982): 777–95.

————. *Technologies of the Self: A Seminar with Michel Foucault.* Ed. Luther H. Martin, Huck Gutman, and Patrick H. Hutton. London: Tavistock Publications, 1988.

————. *The Use of Pleasure.* Vol. 2 of *The History of Sexuality.* 1984. Trans. Robert Hurley. New York: Vintage Books, 1986.

Franklin, Bob, ed. *Televising Democracies.* New York: Routledge, 1992.

Fraser, Nancy. "Rethinking the Public Sphere: A Contribution to the Critique of Actually Existing Democracy." *Social Text* 8, no. 3–9, no. 1 (1990): 56–80.

Friedman, Jonathan. "Being in the World: Globalization and Localization." *Theory, Culture, and Society* 7, no. 2–3 (1990): 311–28.

Frow, John. "Golgotha . . ." *Southern Review* 17, no. 2 (1984): 142–46.

————. "Some Versions of Foucault." *Meanjin* 47, no. 1 (1988): 144–56.

Fry, Tony, Ann Curthoys, Lawrence Grossberg, and Paul Patton, *It's a Sin: Essays on Postmodernism, Politics and Culture.* Sydney: Power Publications, 1988.

Gadamer, Hans Georg. "The Expressive Power of Language: On the Function of Rhetoric for Knowledge." 1983. Trans. Richard Heinemann and Bruce Krajewski. *PMLA* 107, no. 2 (1992): 348–52.

Giddens, Anthony. *The Consequences of Modernity.* 1990. Cambridge: Polity Press, 1991.

————. *Power, Property and the State.* Vol. 1 of *A Contemporary Critique of Historical Materialism.* 1981. London: Macmillan, 1983.

Given, Jock. "Cultural Policy and the Broadcasting Tribunal." *Culture and Policy* 1, no. 1 (1989): 35–36.

Godard, Jean-Luc. "Passion (Love and Work)." *Camera Obscura* nos. 8–9–10 (Fall 1982): 125–29.

————. *Pierrot le Fou.* 1965. Trans. Peter Whitehead. London: Lorrimer Publishing, 1969.

Gordon, Deborah. "Writing Cultures, Writing Feminism: The Poetics and Politics of Experimental Ethnography." *Inscriptions* nos. 3–4 (1988): 7–24.

Gramsci, Antonio. *Antonio Gramsci: Selections from Political Writings, 1910–1920.* Ed. Quintin Hoare. Trans. John Mathews. New York: International Publishers, 1977.

Grant, Steven. *The Life of Pope John Paul II.* 1982. New York: Marvel Comics, 1986.

Greenfield, Catherine. "Psychoanalysis and Literary Criticism." *Southern Review* 14, no. 3 (1981): 195–211.

Gross, David. "Critical Synthesis on Urban Knowledge: Remembering and Forgetting in the Modern City." *Social Epistemology* 4, no. 1 (1990): 3–22.

Gross, Elizabeth. "Derrida and the Limits of Philosophy." *Thesis Eleven,* no. 14 (1986): 26–43.

Gross, Larry. "The Contested Closet: The Ethics and Politics of Outing." *Critical Studies in Mass Communication* 8, no. 3 (1991): 352–88.

Grossberg, Lawrence, Cary Nelson, and Paula Treichler, eds. *Cultural Studies*. New York: Routledge, 1992.

Guattari, Félix. "Becoming-Woman." *Semiotext(e)* 4, no. 1 (1981): 86–88.

Habermas, Jürgen. *Moral Consciousness and Communicative Action*. 1983. Trans. Christian Lenhardt and Shierry Weber Nicholsen. Cambridge, Mass.: MIT Press, 1990.

———. *The New Conservatism: Cultural Criticism and the Historians' Debate*. Ed. Shierry Weber Nicholsen. Cambridge, Mass.: MIT Press, 1989.

———. *The Philosophical Discourse of Modernity: Twelve Lectures*. 1985. Trans. Frederick Lawrence. Cambridge: Polity Press, 1990.

Hager, Wolfgang. "Political Implications of US–EC Economic Conflicts (II): Atlantic Trade—Problems and Prospects." *Government and Opposition* 22, no. 1 (1987): 49–63.

Hall, Stuart. "Cultural Identity and Cinematic Representation." *Framework* no. 36 (1989): 68–81.

Hall, Stuart, and John O'Hara. "The Narrative Construction of Reality: An Interview with Stuart Hall." *Southern Review* 17, no. 1 (1984): 3–17.

Hannerz, Ulf. "Cosmopolitans and Locals in World Culture." *Theory, Culture, and Society* 7, no. 2–3 (1990): 237–51.

Harris, Fred, ed. *Readings on the Body Politic*. Glenview, Ill.: Scott, Foresman, 1987.

Harrisson, Tom. "What Is Public Opinion?" *Political Quarterly* 11, no. 4 (1940): 368–83.

Hartley, John. "Invisible Fictions: Television Audiences, Paedocracy, Pleasure." *Textual Practice* 1, no. 2 (1987): 121–38.

Hartman, Geoffrey. *The Fate of Reading and Other Essays*. 1975. Chicago: University of Chicago Press, 1985.

Hassan, Ihab. "Quest for the Subject: The Self in Literature." *Contemporary Literature* 29, no. 3 (1988): 420–37.

Hawkesworth, M. E. *Beyond Oppression: Feminist Theory and Political Strategy*. New York: Continuum, 1990.

Head, Brian. "Economic Rationalism: The New Orthodoxy in Australian Public Policy?" Paper presented at Australasian Political Studies Association Conference, Armidale, 1988.

Heath, Stephen. "The Ethics of Sexual Difference." *Discourse* 12, no. 2 (1990): 128–53.

Heath, Stephen, and Gillian Skirrow. "Television: A World in Action." *Screen* 18, no. 2 (1977): 7–59.

Henderson, Brian. *A Critique of Film Theory*. New York: Dutton, 1980.

Hinde, John. *Other People's Pictures*. Sydney: Australian Broadcasting Commission, 1981.

✓Hindess, Barry. "Political Equality and Social Policy." *Thesis Eleven* no. 25 (1990): 114–21.

Hocquenghem, Guy. *Homosexual Desire*. 1972. Trans. Daniella Dangoor. London: Allison & Busby, 1978.

Hoffman, Richard J. "Vices, Gods, and Virtues: Cosmology as a Mediating Factor in Attitudes toward Male Homosexuality." *Journal of Homosexuality* 9, no. 2–3 (1983–84): 27–44.

Howe, Irving. "The Self in Literature." *Salmagundi,* no. 90–91 (Spring–Summer 1991): 56–77.

Hoy, David Couzens, ed. *Foucault: A Critical Reader*. Oxford: Basil Blackwell, 1986.

Hume, David. *An Inquiry concerning Human Understanding*. 1748. Ed. Charles W. Hendel. Indianapolis: Library of Liberal Arts, Bobbs-Merrill, 1955.

Hunt, Lynn, ed. *The New Cultural History*. Berkeley and Los Angeles: University of California Press, 1989.

Hunter, Ian. "The Concept of Context and the Problem of Reading." *Southern Review* 15, no. 1 (1982): 80–91.

———. "The Occasion of Criticism: Its Ethic and Pedagogy." *Poetics* 17, nos. 1–2 (1988): 159–84.

———. "On Reflection Theory: Including Remarks on John Docker's *In a Critical Condition*." *Australian Journal of Cultural Studies* 3, no. 1 (1985): 3–28.

———. "Personality as a Vocation: The Political Rationality of the Humanities." *Economy and Society* 19, no. 4 (1990): 391–430.

Hurd, Geoff, ed. *National Fictions: World War Two in British Films and Television*. London: British Film Institute, 1984.

Hutchison, Jenny. *The Big Picture on the Small Screen*. Papers on Parliament 5. Canberra: Department of the Senate, 1989.

✓Huyssen, Andreas. "From Counter-Culture to Neo-Conservatism and Beyond: Stages of the Postmodern." *Social Science Information* 23, no. 3 (1984): 611–24.

Institute of Contemporary Arts. *Identity Documents 6*. London: Institute of Contemporary Arts, 1988.

Irigaray, Luce. *Divine Women*. Trans. Stephen Muecke. Sydney: Local Consumption Publications, 1986.

✓Isaac, Jeffrey, and Christopher Lasch. "Modernity and Progress: An Exchange." *Salmagundi,* no. 93 (Winter 1992): 82–109.

Jameson, Frederic [*sic*]. "Marxists and the University." *New Political Science* 1, nos. 2–3 (1979–80): 31–36.

Jameson, Fredric. *Postmodernism, or, the Cultural Logic of Late Capitalism*. London: Verso, 1991.

Jardine, Alice, and Paul Smith, eds. *Men in Feminism.* New York: Methuen, 1987.

Jarvie, Ian. "Dollars and Ideology: Will Hays' Economic Foreign Policy 1922–1945." *Film History* 2, no. 3 (1988): 207–21.

———. "The Postwar Economic Foreign Policy of the American Film Industry: Europe, 1945–1950." *Film History* 4, no. 4 (1990): 277–88.

Johnson, Lesley. *The Unseen Voice: A Cultural Study of Early Australian Radio.* London: Routledge, 1988.

Kant, Immanuel. *Kant: Political Writings.* Ed. Hans Reiss. 2d ed. New York: Cambridge University Press, 1991.

Kellner, Douglas. "Television, Mythology and Ritual." *Praxis* no. 6 (1982): 133–55.

Kelly, George Armstrong. "Who Needs a Theory of Citizenship?" *Dædalus* 108, no. 4 (1979): 21–36.

Kierkegaard, Søren. *A Kierkegaard Anthology.* Ed. Robert Bretall. New York: Modern Library, 1974.

King, Anthony D., ed. *Culture, Globalization and the World-System: Contemporary Conditions for the Representation of Identity.* London: Macmillan, 1991.

Kohn, Hans. *The Idea of Nationalism: A Study in Its Origins and Background.* New York: Macmillan, 1945.

Kristeva, Julia. *Desire in Language: A Semiotic Approach to Literature and Art.* Ed. Leon S. Roudiez. Trans. Thomas Gora, Alice Jardine, and Leon S. Roudiez. New York: Columbia University Press, 1980.

———. "Postmodernism?" *Bucknell Review* 25, no. 2 (1980): 136–41.

Lacan, Jacques. *Ecrits: A Selection.* 1977. Trans. Alan Sheridan. London: Tavistock Publications, 1985.

LaCapra, Dominick. "Culture and Ideology: From Geertz to Marx." *Poetics Today* 9, no. 2 (1988): 377–94.

Lasch, Christopher. "Liberalism and Civic Virtue." *Telos,* no. 88 (Summer 1991): 57–68.

Lash, Scott. *Sociology of Postmodernism.* New York: Routledge, 1990.

Lasswell, Harold D., and Abraham Kaplan. *Power and Society: A Framework for Political Inquiry.* London: Routledge & Kegan Paul, 1952.

Lauret, Maria. "Seizing the Time and Making New: Feminist Criticism, Politics and Contemporary Feminist Fiction." *Feminist Review,* no. 31 (Spring 1989): 94–106.

Lawson, Mark. "Playing Safe." *Marxism Today,* March 1990, 46–47.

Leavis, F. R. *The Common Pursuit.* 1952. London: Chatto & Windus, 1965.

Lee, Chin-Chuan. "The International Information Order." *Communication Research* 9, no. 4 (1982): 617–36.

Lee, Thea M. "Contradictions in the Teaching of Neoclassical Theory." *Review of Radical Political Economics* 20, no. 2–3 (1988): 7–11.

Levin, Thomas Y. "Walter Benjamin and the Theory of Art History." *October* no. 47 (1988): 77–83.

Lindblom, Charles E. *The Policy-Making Process.* 2d ed. Englewood Cliffs, N.J.: Prentice-Hall, 1980.

Livingstone, Sonia, and Peter K. Lunt. "Expert and Lay Participation in Television Debates: An Analysis of Audience Discussion Programmes." *European Journal of Communication* 7, no. 1 (1992): 9–35.

Lodge, David. "Milan Kundera, and the Idea of the Author in Modern Criticism." *Critical Quarterly* 26, no. 1–2 (1984): 105–21.

———, ed. *Modern Criticism and Theory: A Reader.* New York: Longman, 1988.

Lovell, Terry. *Pictures of Reality: Aesthetics, Politics, Pleasure.* 1980. London: British Film Institute Publishing, 1983.

Lukács, György. "Notes on the Theory of Literary History." 1910. Trans. Ian Fairley. *Comparative Criticism: An Annual Journal,* no. 13 (1991): 211–43.

Lukes, Steven. *Power: A Radical View.* London: Macmillan, 1974.

Lyotard, Jean-François. Interview by Georges Van Den Abbeele. *Diacritics* 14, no. 3 (1984): 16–21.

———. *La Condition postmoderne: Rapport sur le savoir.* 1979. Paris: Editions de minuit, 1988.

———. *Le Différend.* Paris: Editions de minuit, 1983.

———. "The *Différend,* the Referent, and the Proper Name." Trans. Georges Van Den Abbeele. *Diacritics* 14, no. 3 (1984): 4–14.

———. "One of the Things at Stake in Women's Struggles." Trans. Deborah J. Clarke, Winifred Woodhull, and John Mowitt. *SubStance* no. 20 (1978): 9–18.

———. "Plastic Space and Political Space—." 1970. Trans. Mark S. Roberts. *Boundary 2* 14, nos. 1–2 (1985–86): 211–23.

———. *The Postmodern Explained to Children: Correspondence, 1982–1985.* 1986. Ed. Julian Pefanis and Morgan Thomas. Trans. Don Barry, Bernadette Maher, Julian Pefanis, Virginia Spate, and Morgan Thomas. Sydney: Power Publications, 1992.

MacCallum, Mungo, ed. *Ten Years of Television.* Melbourne: Sun Books, 1968.

MacCannell, Juliet Flower. *The Regime of the Brother: After the Patriarchy.* New York: Routledge, 1991.

McCarthy, Thomas. "The Critique of Impure Reason: Foucault and the Frankfurt School." *Political Theory* 18, no. 3 (1990): 437–69.

McClelland, Charles E., and Steven P. Scher, eds. *Postwar German Culture: An Anthology.* New York: Dutton, 1974.

McElroy, Bernard. *Fiction of the Modern Grotesque.* London: Macmillan, 1989.

McHoul, A. W. "Sociology and Literature: The Voice of Fact and the Writing of Fiction." Paper presented at Sociological Association of Australia and New Zealand Conference, Sydney, 1987.

McHoul, A. W., and Tom O'Regan. "Towards a Paralogics of Textual Technologies: Batman, Glasnost and Relativism in Cultural Studies." *Southern Review* 25, no. 1 (1992): 5–26.

Manoff, Robert Karl. "Statist Discourse in the Public Realm: Some Notes on the End of History and the Fate of Journalism." Paper presented at International Communication Association Conference, Dublin, 1990.

Marshall, Gary S., and Orion F. White, Jr. "The Blacksburg Manifesto and the Postmodern Debate: Public Administration in a Time without a Name." *American Review of Public Administration* 20, no. 2 (1990): 61–76.

Marshall, Neil. "Bureaucratic Politics and the Demise of the Commonwealth Tertiary Education Commission." *Australian Journal of Public Administration* 47, no. 1 (1988): 19–34.

Marx, Karl. *A Contribution to the Critique of Political Economy.* 1859. Moscow: Progress Publishers, 1977.

———. *The Eighteenth Brumaire of Louis Bonaparte.* 1852. Beijing: Foreign Languages Press, 1978.

Mascia-Lees, Frances E., Patricia Sharpe, and Colleen Ballerino Cohen. "The Postmodernist Turn in Anthropology: Cautions from a Feminist Perspective." *Signs: Journal of Women in Culture and Society* 15, no. 1 (1989): 7–33.

"The Mexico City Declaration on Cultural Policies." *Cultures* no. 33 (1983): 189–96.

Michaels, Eric. *Unbecoming: An AIDS Diary.* Sydney: EM Press, 1990.

Michels, Robert. *Political Parties: A Sociological Study of the Oligarchical Tendencies of Modern Democracy.* Trans. Eden and Cedar Paul. London: Jarrold & Sons, 1915.

Milgate, Murray, and John Eatwell. "Economic Theory and European Society: The Influence of J. M. Keynes." *History of European Ideas* 9, no. 2 (1988): 215–25.

Miliband, Ralph, Leo Panitch, and John Saville, eds. *Socialist Register, 1987.* London: Merlin Press, 1987.

———. *Socialist Register, 1990.* London: Merlin Press, 1991.

Mill, John Stuart. *On Liberty.* 1859. Harmondsworth: Penguin Books, 1974.

———. *Principles of Political Economy with Some of Their Applications to Social Philosophy.* New York: Longman, Green, 1896.

Miller, D. A. "Bringing out Roland Barthes." *Raritan* 11, no. 4 (1992): 38–49.

Miller, J. D. B. *Norman Angell and the Futility of War: Peace and the Public Mind.* London: Macmillan, 1986.

———. "The Sovereign State and Its Future." *International Journal* 39, no. 2 (1984): 284–301.

Miller, James. "Foucault: The Secrets of a Man." *Salmagundi* 88–89 (Fall-Winter 1990–91): 311–32.

Miller, Mark Crispin. *Boxed In: The Culture of TV.* Evanston, Ill.: Northwestern University Press, 1988.

Mills, C. Wright. *Power, Politics and People: The Collected Essays of C. Wright Mills.* Ed. Irving Louis Horowitz. New York: Oxford University Press, 1970.

✓ Mitchell, Austin. "Beyond Televising Parliament: Taking Politics to the People." *Parliamentary Affairs* 43, no. 1 (1990): 1–14.

Moran, Albert. *Images and Industry: Television Drama Production in Australia.* Sydney: Currency Press, 1985.

Moran, Albert, and Tom O'Regan, eds. *An Australian Film Reader.* Sydney: Currency Press, 1985.

———. *The Australian Screen.* Harmondsworth: Penguin Books, 1989.

✓ Morris, Meaghan. "Banality in Cultural Studies." *Discourse* 10, no. 2 (1988): 3–29.

✓ ———. *Ecstasy and Economics: American Essays for John Forbes.* Sydney: EM Press, 1992.

Mulvey, Laura. "Visual Pleasure and Narrative Cinema." *Screen* 16, no. 3 (1975): 6–18.

Neale, Steve, and Frank Krutnik. *Popular Film and Television Comedy.* New York: Routledge, 1990.

Negrine, R., and S. Papathanassopoulos. "The Internationalization of Television." *European Journal of Communication* 6, no. 1 (1991): 9–32.

Nelson, Cary, and Lawrence Grossberg, eds. *Marxism and the Interpretation of Culture.* Urbana: University of Illinois Press, 1988.

Newcomb, Horace. *TV: The Most Popular Art.* Garden City, N.Y.: Anchor Books, 1974.

———, ed. *Television: The Critical View.* 4th ed. New York: Oxford University Press, 1987.

Nietzsche, Friedrich. *The Genealogy of Morals.* 1887. Trans. Francis Golffing. New York: Doubleday Anchor, 1956.

———. *The Will to Power.* 1887. Trans. Walter Kaufman and R. J. Hollingdale. New York: Random House, 1967.

O'Connor, James. *Accumulation Crisis.* 1984. New York: Basil Blackwell, 1986.

Offe, Claus. "Capitalism by Democratic Design? Democratic Theory Facing the Triple Transition in East Central Europe." Trans. Pierre Adler. *Social Research* 58, no. 4 (1991): 864–92.

Palmer, Jerry. *The Logic of the Absurd: On Film and Television Comedy.* London: British Film Institute, 1987.

✓ Parker, Richard G. *Bodies, Pleasures, and Passions: Sexual Culture in Contemporary Brazil.* Boston: Beacon Press, 1991.

Parsons, Philip, ed. *Shooting the Pianist: The Role of Government in the Arts.* Sydney: Currency Press, 1987.

✓ Pecora, Vincent P. "Ethics, Politics, and the Middle Voice." *Yale French Studies* no. 79 (1991): 203–30.

Piccinillo, Mary J. "An Isocratean Rhetoric of Television." *Communication* 12, no. 1 (1990): 1–18.

Pickett, Brian. *Industry Education: Cost or Benefit? Speech to Hardware Unity South Pacific*. Canberra: National Training Council, 1985.

✓ Pieterse, Jan Nederveen. "Fictions of Europe." *Race and Class* 32, no. 3 (1991): 3–10.

Pineau, Guy. "L'Europe audiovisuelle de l'après-directive." *Dossiers de l'audiovisuel,* no. 35 (January–February 1991): 10–12.

Pingree, Suzanne, and Robert Hawkins. "U.S. Programs on Australian Television: The Cultivation Effect." *Journal of Communication* 31, no. 1 (1981): 97–105.

Plato. *The Laws*. Fourth century B.C. Trans. Trevor J. Saunders. Baltimore: Penguin Books, 1972.

Plaza, Monique. "Our Costs and Their Benefits." 1978. Trans. Wendy Harrison. *m/f* no. 4 (1980): 28–39.

Plutarch. First century A.D. *The Rise and Fall of Athens: Nine Greek Lives by Plutarch*. Trans. Ian Scott-Kilvert. Baltimore: Penguin Books, 1976.

Prescott, Trevor. *Speech to Printing Industry Symposium: Training—Focus on the Future*. Canberra: National Training Council, 1985.

———. *The TAFE/Industry Interface: Speech to a Conference on the Changing Context of TAFE*. Canberra: National Training Council, 1985.

Rabinovitz, Lauren. "Sitcoms and Single Moms: Representations on American TV." *Cinema Journal* 29, no. 1 (1989): 3–19.

✓ Ranson, Stewart, and John Stewart. "Citizenship and Government: The Challenge for Management in the Public Domain." *Political Studies* 37, no. 1 (1989): 5–24.

Ray, Larry. "Foucault, Critical Theory and the Decomposition of the Historical Subject." *Philosophy and Social Criticism* 14, no. 1 (1989): 69–110.

Rimmerman, Craig A. "The 'Post-Modern' Presidency—A New Presidential Epoch?" *Western Political Quarterly* 44, no. 1 (1991): 221–38.

Rorty, Richard. "Foucault/Dewey/Nietzsche." *Raritan* 9, no. 4 (1990): 1–8.

✓ Rose, Nikolas, and Peter Miller. "Political Power beyond the State: Problematics of Government." *British Journal of Sociology* 43, no. 2 (1992): 173–205.

Rousseau, Jean-Jacques. *The Social Contract and Discourses*. 1755. Trans. G. D. H. Cole. London: J. M. Dent & Sons, 1975.

Rowse, Tim. *Arguing the Arts: The Funding of the Arts in Australia*. Ringwood: Penguin Books, 1985.

✓ Said, Edward. "Figures, Configurations, Transfigurations." *Race and Class* 32, no. 1 (1990): 1–16.

✓ ———. "The Politics of Knowledge." *Raritan* 11, no. 1 (1991): 17–31.

Saunders, David, and Ian Hunter. "Lessons from the 'Literary': How to Historicise Authorship." *Critical Inquiry* 17, no. 3 (1991): 478–509.

Schiller, Herbert I. "Not Yet the Post-Imperialist Era." *Critical Studies in Mass Communication* 8, no. 1 (1991): 13–28.

✓ Schlesinger, Philip. *Media, State and Nation: Political Violence and Collective Identities.* London: Sage Publications, 1991.

Schneider, Cynthia, and Brian Wallis, eds. *Global Television.* New York: Wedge Press; Cambridge, Mass.: MIT Press, 1988.

Schwarz, Daniel R. "Review Essay: Canonicity, Culture, and Pluralism—A Humanistic Perspective on Professing English." *Texas Studies in Literature and Language* 34, no. 1 (1992): 149–75.

Sedgwick, Eve Kosofsky. *Epistemology of the Closet.* Berkeley and Los Angeles: University of California Press, 1990.

Segal, Lynne. *Slow Motion: Changing Masculinities, Changing Men.* London: Virago Press, 1990.

Seigel, Jerrold. "Avoiding the Subject: A Foucaultian Itinerary." *Journal of the History of Ideas* 51, no. 2 (1990): 273–99.

Senghor, Léopold Sédar. *On African Socialism.* Trans. Mercer Cook. New York: Praeger, 1964.

Sennett, Richard. *The Fall of Public Man.* 1974. New York: Vintage Books, 1978.

Shaw, Gary. "Using Literature to Teach Ethics in the Business Curriculum." *Journal of Business and Technical Communication* 6, no. 2 (1992): 187–99.

✓ Shils, Edward. "Observations on Some Tribulations of Civility." *Government and Opposition* 15, nos. 3–4 (1980): 528–45.

———. "The Virtue of Civil Society." *Government and Opposition* 26, no. 1 (1991): 3–20.

Simmel, Georg. *On Individuality and Social Forces.* Chicago: University of Chicago Press, 1971.

———. *The Problems of the Philosophy of History: An Epistemological Essay.* 1892. Trans. Guy Oakes. New York: Free Press, 1977.

Sinclair, John. "From 'Modernization' to Cultural Dependence: Mass Communication Studies and the Third World." *Media Information Australia*, no. 23 (February 1982): 5–11.

Sisters of Perpetual Indulgence. *White Paper.* N.p., 1989.

———. *Who Are the Sisters of Perpetual Indulgence?* N.p., 1986.

Smart, Barry. "Theory and Analysis after Foucault." *Theory, Culture, and Society* 8, no. 2 (1991): 145–55.

Smith, Anthony, ed. *Television and Political Life: Studies in Six European Countries.* London: Macmillan, 1979.

Society for Education in Film and Television. *Screen Reader I: Cinema/Ideology/Politics.* London: Society for Education in Film and Television, 1977.

Spacks, Patricia. "The Novel as Ethical Paradigm." *Novel* 21, no. 2–3 (1988): 181–88.

Staiger, Janet. "Future Noir: Contemporary Representations of Visionary Cities." *East-West Film Journal* 3, no. 1 (1988): 20–44.

Stallybrass, Peter, and Allon White. *The Politics and Poetics of Transgression*. Ithaca, N.Y.: Cornell University Press, 1986.

Stearns, William, and William Chaloupka, eds. *Jean Baudrillard: The Disappearance of Art and Politics*. London: Macmillan, 1992.

Steiner, George. *George Steiner: A Reader*. New York: Oxford University Press, 1984.

Stewart, Robert M., ed. *Readings in Social and Political Philosophy*. New York: Oxford University Press, 1986.

Stewart, Susan. *On Longing: Narratives of the Miniature, the Gigantic, the Souvenir, the Collection*. Baltimore: Johns Hopkins University Press, 1984.

Stimpson, Catharine R. "Federal Papers." *October*, no. 53 (Summer 1990): 24–39.

Studlar, Gaylyn. "Midnight S/excess: Cult Configurations of 'Femininity' and the Perverse." *Journal of Popular Film and Television* 17, no. 1 (1989): 2–14.

Sunstein, Cass R., ed. *Feminism and Political Theory*. Chicago: University of Chicago Press, 1990.

Swaan, Abram de. *The Management of Normality: Critical Essays in Health and Welfare*. London: Routledge, 1990.

Taylor, Charles. "Modes of Civil Society." *Public Culture* 3, no. 1 (1990): 95–118.

———. *Sources of the Self: The Making of the Modern Identity*. Cambridge, Mass.: Harvard University Press, 1989.

Thiele, Leslie Paul. "The Agony of Politics: The Nietzschean Roots of Foucault's Thought." *American Political Science Review* 84, no. 3 (1990): 907–25.

Thompson, Denys, ed. *Discrimination and Popular Culture*. 2d ed. Baltimore: Penguin Books, 1973.

Thompson, Kenneth, and Jeremy Tunstall, eds. *Sociological Perspectives: Selected Readings*. New York: Penguin Books, 1976.

Thurley, Geoffrey. *The Romantic Predicament*. Melbourne: Macmillan, 1983.

Tong, Rosemarie. "Feminist Justice: A Study in Difference." *Journal of Social Philosophy* 22, no. 3 (1991): 81–91.

Touraine, Alain. "What Does Democracy Mean Today?" *International Social Science Journal*, no. 128 (May 1991): 259–68.

Tribe, Keith. "The Representation of the Real." *Cambridge Anthropology* 1977, 56–66.

Tuan, Yi-Fu. "Cultural Pluralism and Technology." *Geographical Review* 79, no. 3 (1989): 269–79.

Tulloch, John. *Television Drama: Agency, Audience and Myth*. New York: Routledge, 1990.

Tulloch, John, and Graeme Turner, eds. *Australian Television: Programs, Pleasures and Politics*. Boston: Allen & Unwin, 1989.

Turner, Bryan S. *Citizenship and Capitalism: The Debate over Reformism.* Boston: Allen & Unwin, 1986.

———. *Religion and Social Theory: A Materialist Perspective.* London: Heinemann Educational Books, 1983.

Ulmer, Gregory. *Teletheory: Grammatology in the Age of Video.* New York: Routledge, 1989.

Ungureit, Heinz. "Le Groupement européen de production: Rassembler les forces du service public . . ." 1988. *Dossiers de l'audiovisuel,* no. 35 (January–February 1991): 16–17.

Walker, Cheryl. "Feminist Literary Criticism and the Author." *Critical Inquiry* 16, no. 3 (1990): 551–71.

Wallace, T. A. *The Etiquette of Australia.* Sydney: Radcliffe Press, 1922.

Wallerstein, Immanuel. "Culture as the Ideological Battleground of the Modern World-System." *Hitotsubashi Journal of Social Studies* 21, no. 1 (1989): 5–22.

Walzer, Michael. "The Idea of Civil Society: A Path to Social Reconstruction." *Dissent* 38, no. 2 (1991): 293–304.

———. "The Politics of Michel Foucault." *Dissent* 30, no. 4 (1983): 481–90.

Weber, Max. *Basic Concepts in Sociology.* Trans. H. P. Secher. New York: Citadel Press, 1964.

———. *General Economic History.* 1923. Trans. Frank H. Knight. New York: Collier Books, 1961.

Williams, Raymond. "A Lecture on Realism." *Screen* 18, no. 1 (1977): 61–74.

———. *The Politics of Modernism: Against the New Conformists.* New York: Verso, 1989.

Wilson, Elizabeth. *The Sphinx in the City: Urban Life, the Control of Disorder, and Women.* London: Virago Press, 1991.

Wittgenstein, Ludwig. *Notebooks, 1914–1916.* Ed. G. H. Wright and G. E. M. Anscombe. 2d ed. Oxford: Basil Blackwell, 1979.

Young, Robert, ed. *Untying the Text: A Post-Structuralist Reader.* Boston: Routledge & Kegan Paul, 1981.

Index

Bazin, André, 89
Bell, Daniel, 23, 24
Bell, Steve, 199
Bellow, Saul, 31, 47
Belsey, Catherine, 63–64, 65
Benhabib, Seyla, 221–22
Benjamin, Walter, 61, 68–69, 74, 76, 86, 133–34
Bennett, Tony, 15, 32
Berlin, Isaiah, xv
Bernstein, Carl, 142, 188
Bersani, Leo, 209, 229
Bhabha, Homi, 57
Biden, Joseph, 144
Black, Herman, 185–87
Blitz, 153
Bolton, Richard, 144
Bonaparte, Napoleon, 167
Booth, Wayne C., 63
Bordwell, David: *Making Meaning,* 83, 88–91
Borins, Sandford, 165
Bourdieu, Pierre, 182
Brademas, John, 31
Bradley, A. C., 64
Braman, Sandra, 102
British Arts Council, 28
BBC, 56, 83, 145
British Film Institute, 53, 88
Broadcasting Abroad, 112
Brodsky, Joseph, 75–76
Brook, Peter: "Moderato Cantabile," xi
Buchanan, Pat, 209–10
Bundestag, 136
Bureau of Agricultural Economics, 116
Burke, Edmund, 84
Burtt, Shelley, 2
Bush, George, 163–64
Business in the Community, 155
Business Week, 152
Bywater, Michael, 79
Byzannes, Thérèse, 186–87, 190

C-SPAN, 143–44
Cabinet Office (U.K.), 103
Caesar, Julius, 199
Cahiers du Cinéma, 88
Cain, 123
Calvino, Italo: "Desire in November," 199
Campaign for Nuclear Disarmament, 54
Canadian Commission for UNESCO, 50
Cannes Film Festival, 100
Capitalism: and art, 27, 28, 29, 53; and history, 18, 21–22, 47, 64, 109, 142, 155, 158, 230; and the novel, 64; and television, 59, 79, 82, 106, 109, 112,

115, 122–23, 170. *See also* Global economy
Capra, Frank: *Mr. Smith Goes to Washington,* 144
"Case For Television," 144
Casetti, Francesco, 148
Castles, Ian, 168
Catholic University of America, 195
Catholic University of Lublin, 191
CBS, 144
Central Intelligence Agency, 182
Cervantes, Miguel de: *Don Quixote,* 64
Channel Four (U.K.), 145, 146
Channel Nine (Australia), 138
Character: literary, xxiv, 50–51, 58, 69, 74, 76, 82, 219; social, 7–8, 67, 76, 80, 144, 165, 185; and television drama, 58, 79–80, 124–25
Charter 88, 135
Chartier, Roger, 64
Church, 12–13, 188, 212–13, 215; and state, 12–13, 199–202. *See also* Religion
Churchill, Winston, 136
"Citizens' Charter," 134, 225
Citizenship, ix, xi–xii, xv, xvii–xxi, xxvi–xxviii, 3–7, 10, 12, 14–20, 22, 24–26, 36, 48, 50, 61, 72, 79, 82, 89, 92–93, 103–4, 109, 112, 115, 119, 129–39, 141, 144–48, 156, 159–61, 165, 169–72, 177–78, 180, 186, 201, 219–20, 222–23, 225, 226, 228; active, 3, 129–30, 131, 135, 146; cultural, xii, xxi, 38, 219–21; and education, x, xi, xxv, 3, 17, 21–22, 70, 82, 85–86, 91, 131, 143, 146; feminist critiques of, 3–5, 221–23, 226–27; Marxist critiques of, 5–6; morphology of, xxiv, 2–14, 219–20. *See also* Education, Pedagogy, Training
Civic culture, xi, xxiv, 219; and education, 7, 143, 162; subjects, 49–50, 96, 156, 168, 169, 170–71, 173, 202
Civic Forum, xix, 141; and "Rules of Dialogue," xix
Civics, xxiv, 6, 17, 132, 160, 164, 167, 171, 215
Civil Society, 4, 5, 8–9, 10–11, 85, 134, 156, 178, 200 221, 225
Civilization, 8, 10, 19, 31, 42, 82, 115, 165, 205, 229–30
Civility, xi, 6–10, 11–12, 21, 22, 85, 110, 156–57, 159, 177, 180, 186, 193, 201, 223, 229. *See also* Incivility
Class, 35–36, 109, 110, 175
Cleinias, 171
Coca-Cola, 107, 112
Cohen, Ed, 212

Collins, Richard, 112
Columbia Prix Entertainment, 102
"Come Back to Catholicism," 203
Committee on Comparative Politics of the United States' Social Science Research Council, 9
Commonwealth Tertiary Education Commission (CTEC), 169
Comte, Auguste, 41, 43, 157
Congress (U.S.), 30–31, 37, 101, 102, 107, 141, 142–44, 152, 163
Congress of People's Deputies (U.S.S.R.), 141
Consciousness, 35, 53, 59, 73, 75–76, 89, 93, 161, 176
Conservative Party (U.K.), 134–35, 145, 151, 225
Coombs, H. C., 28
Coronation Street, 79
Costigan, Michael, 195
Council on Family Matters, 195
Courier-Mail, 137
Cowie, Elizabeth, 66–67
Crawford, Hector, 127
Cremonini, Leonardo, 61
Crichton, Michael: *Coma,* 66
Criticism, xiii, 45, 49, 52–53, 56, 62–65, 66, 68, 70–71, 76–93, 123–26, 160–61, 183, 218–19; ethical, x–xxiv, 69–76, 81, 91; performance, 206–7
Cultural capitalism: and citizenship, 38, 219–21; and democracy, ix, xxiii, 16, 20, 29, 130, 132, 164, 179, 220, 224; and the state, xii, xiii, xxii, xxv, 12, 20, 49, 177, 180, 224, 230. *See also* State
Cultural imperialism, 50, 95–96, 103–6, 110, 122–23; critiques of, 106–10, 115
Cultural nationalism, 28, 84, 96, 100, 105–6, 118–20, 122, 124, 127–28; critiques of, 100–101, 124, 127–28
Cultural policy, xxi, 14–32, 40, 48, 93, 95, 97, 116–28, 154, 173, 196, 218, 219, 221, 222, 223; and Australia, 28–29, 30, 117–28; and Canada, 50, 118, 122, 128; defined, 14–17; history of, 15, 17–23, 28, 31–32, 100, 103–4, 106, 107, 119–20, 122, 127–28; and international organizations, 104–9, 118; and Israel, 108; setting, xi–xii, xxiii–xxiv, 14, 26, 28–32, 50, 103, 123–24, 230; and the U.K., x, 28, 107; and the U.S., 30–31, 102, 105, 127. *See also* Policy
Cultural studies, 53, 62, 74, 77, 182–83, 205, 218. *See also* Screen studies, Television, studies

Culture: anthropological, 14–16, 57, 58; artistic, 14–17, 30–31, 51–52, 57, 58; defined, 14–15, 26–27, 50, 57, 70, 84, 96, 107, 113, 218
Culture, popular: and education, 17, 65, 82, 92, 148; and reason, xiii, 160, 169, 171, 209, 220; and sovereignty, 25, 172, 175
Cunningham, Stuart, 60–61, 65, 68
Curia, 185, 192

Daily Express, 103–4
Daily Mirror, 67
Daimler-Benz, 115
Dallas, 79, 106, 107
Days of Hope, 61–62
de Lauretis, Theresa, 179
de Rojas, Fernando: *Celestina,* 64
de Saussure, Ferdinand, xv, 62
de Sica, Vittorio, 120
Declaration of the Rights of Man, 17
"Declaration on Certain Questions Concerning Sexual Ethics," 196
Deleuze, Gilles, 43–44
Democracy: and gender, 4; individual, xxiii, 101, 129–30; new, 1, 8, 11, 110, 157, 172, 220; and parliament, xxv, 1, 5–6, 130–31; and television, 130–54; theorized, 175–79, 222–23, 228
Democrats (Australia), 138
Democrats (U.S.), 143, 151
Demosthenes, 106
Department: of Commerce (U.S.), 101; of Community Services and Health (New South Wales), 201; of Education (Australia), 162; of Employment and Industrial Relations (Australia) (DEIR), 154, 160, 162, 163, 164, 169–70; of Finance (Australia), 168; of Foreign Affairs and Trade (Australia) (DFAT), 117; State (U.S.), 101; of the Treasury (Australia), 168
Derrida, Jacques, xi, xvii–xviii, 44, 86, 133, 141, 182
Descartes, René, 10, 219
Dick Clark Company, 152
Différends de soi, 176, 178, 179–80, 204, 207, 217, 219–20, 224
Diogenes, 106, 206
Diplomacy, 16, 95–106, 109, 116–17, 198, 201–2
Dirty Harry, 144
Disciplines, xxvii–xxviii, 38, 81–82, 86, 88–89, 102–3, 156
Discourse: academic, x, xv, xx, xxiii, 65, 69, 85, 88, 89–92, 181, 187; and

Gadamer, Hans-Georg, 72, 74
Gaudeamus Igitur, 184
Gay Information, 202
Gellner, Ernest, 24–25
General Agreement on Tariffs and Trade
(GATT), xxv, 95–101, 105, 116–18, 128
General Hospital, 144
General Motors, 107
Giddens, Anthony, 34, 174, 175
Gilliam, Terry: *Brazil,* 23
Global economy: and Australia, 155–56;
and history, 21–22; and labor, 164–
65; theorized, 16, 106–7, 111–12,
114, 186, 222
Godard, Jean-Luc, 153; *Hail Mary,* 215;
La Chinoise, 58; *Pierrot le Fou,* 61
Gorbachev, Mikhail, 172
Gramsci, Antonio, 6, 34
"The Great Society,"163–64
Greenfield, Catherine, 75
Gross, David, 18
Grossberg, Lawrence, x
Guattari, Félix, 43, 204

Habermas, Jürgen, xviii–xix, xxvi, 18–19,
46, 48, 65, 93, 135, 150, 176, 215,
216–17. *See also* Public sphere
Hacking, Ian, 227
Hall, Stuart, 79, 115, 128, 209, 229
Hancock's Half Hour, 80
Harlot, Scarlet: "Pope, Don't Preach,
I'm Terminating My Pregnancy,"
211
Harris, Max, 153
Hartman, Geoffrey, 74
Hassan, Ihab, 70, 71
Hawke, Bob, 202
Hays, Will, 101, 102
Heath, Stephen, 126, 221, 226
Hegel, Georg Wilhelm Friedrich, xii, 5,
8, 67, 75, 85, 174
Heidegger, Martin, xvii
Herder, Johann Gottfried, 73
High Court of Australia, 170
Hill, Anita, 143
Hills, Carla, 108
Hinde, John, 52
Hindess, Barry, 12
Hobbes, Thomas, xv, 156
Hocquenghem, Guy, 180, 208–9
Holocauste, 62
Horne, Donald, 28–29
Hough, Graham, 71
House: of Commons (Canada), 152; of
Commons (U.K.), 145–46, 151; of
Lords, 153; of Representatives (Aus-
tralia), 131–32, 137, 147–49, 153; of

Representatives (U.S.), 101; Un-
American Activities Committee, 143
Human sciences, xxviii, 45, 69–71, 75, 85,
127, 227–29
Hume, David, 67, 84
Hunter, Ian, xvi, 16, 67, 71, 72, 81, 161
Hunthausen, Raymond, 198
Hurd, Douglas, 135
Hurd, Geoffrey, 53–54; *National Fictions,*
53–55, 56
Husserl, Edmund, 75
Huyssen, Andreas, 9

Identity politics, 15, 200–201, 206–9, 219,
225–26, 229
Ideology, 33–39
Ignatieff, Michael, xx
The Imitation Game, 56
Imperial Economic Conference, 103
Incivility, xxvi, 173, 181, 214–15
Independent, 134–35
Independent Commission Against Cor-
ruption (ICAC), 136–37, 138
Indeterminacy: alternatives to, 213,
220–31; defined, xii, 44–46; and
subjectivity, xiv; and texts, xxiv–
xxv, 62, 70, 77–78, 81
Industries Assistance Commission (IAC),
116, 118
"Industry," 155–63
Inquisition, 195
International Cultural Order, 103–13
Irigaray, Luce, 212–13
Isaac, xii
Isaac, Jeffrey, 222
Isocrates, 79

Jacka, Elizabeth, 123, 124
Jameson, Fredric, xxi, 20, 47, 48, 71, 93
Jarvie, Ian, 104
Jefferson, Thomas, xvii, 21, 133, 141, 221
Jennings, Keith, 184, 185
Jesus Christ, 188, 193, 194, 196, 213
Jocasta, 213
John of the Cross, Saint, 191
John Paul II, xxvi, 180–81,184, 190, 193,
199. *See also* Wojtyła
Johnson, Lesley, 132–33
Johnson, Lyndon, 136, 163
Joint Committee on the Broadcasting of
Parliamentary Proceedings (Aus-
tralia), 147

Kant, Immanuel, xii, xix–xx, 10, 85,
92–93, 227; "What is Enlightenment?", xx
Kaplan, Abraham, 3

Kellner, Douglas, 59
Kelly, George Armstrong, 170
Kennedy-Miller, 60
Kermode, Frank, 80–81
Keynes, John Maynard, 166, 167
Kierkegaard, Søren, xii, 48
King, Martin Luther, Jr., 161
Kirby Committee of Inquiry into Labour
    Market Programs, 154–55, 157, 169
Kohn, Hans, 109
Kramer, Leonie, 63
Kristeva, Julia, xi, 22, 24, 69; "Post-
    modernism?", 46
Kundera, Milan, 161

L'Art pour l'art, 77
LA Law, 121
Labour Party (U.K.), 225
Lacan, Jacques, xv, xvii, 75, 90, 212
LaCapra, Dominick, 63
Laclau, Ernest, 11, 124
Lake, Frank, 195
Lang, Jack, 105–6, 108, 110, 111
Lanson, Gustave, 88
Lasch, Christopher, 7, 135
Lash, Scott, 44
Lasswell, Harold, 3
Lawson, Sylvia, 120, 121
League of Nations International Film
    Congress, 103
Leavis, F. R., xv, 64, 78, 79–80, 82, 160
Lee, Thea, 167
Leech, Kenneth, 199
Legislative Teleconferencing Network,
    141
Lémieux, Raymond, 189
Levi's, 107
Lévi-Strauss, Claude, xv, 90, 182
Leviticus, 196
Lindblom, Charles: The Policy-Making
    Process, 3
Listener, 23
Literary history, 17, 51–52, 63–64, 69,
    72–73
Literary studies: and citizenship, xv,
    xxiv, 50, 81, 88–91, 218–19; and iden-
    tity, 57, 69–78, 81–83, 93; and mean-
    ing, 62–63
Loach, Ken: Cathy Come Home, 80
Lo Schiavo, Fabian (also known as Mon-
    signor Porca Madonna, Mother
    Abyss, Mother Inferior, Dean
    Lance Sheraton-Hilton, Reverend
    Oral Richards), 207, 210, 215–16
Locke, John, 156
Lodge, David, 161
Lovell, Terry, 52–53

Lukács, György, 67, 69
Lukes, Steven, 39
Lyotard, Jean-François, 21, 46–47, 73,
    76–77, 109, 150, 180, 185, 211–12

m/f, 65–66
MacCallum, Mungo: Ten Years of Televi-
    sion, 127
MacCannell, Juliet Flower, 4
Madonna, 152
Maguire, Frank, 123
Maguire, Len, 123
Mandel, Ernest, 47, 165
Manoff, Robert Karl, 142
Market: and art, 27–28, 29–30, 75–76; and
    citizenship, 134–35, 156–57, 171–72;
    and culture, 15, 16, 28–29; develop-
    ment, 6–7, 22, 113–15; government,
    129–30, 155–56; screen, 95–113, 116–21;
    training, 154–60, 162–63, 169–70
Marlowe, Philip, 188
Marshall, T. H., 19, 36
Mary, 210
Marvel Comics, 362–63
Marx, Karl, xiv, xix, 19, 31, 39, 46, 65, 75,
    78, 88, 183, 199, 207; and citizenship,
    3–6, 11, 226; criticisms of, 33–36, 39,
    175; and economics, 157, 165, 170–71
Mattelart, Michèle, 81, 109
Max Headroom, 23
McArthur, Colin, 55–56
McLaren, John, 119
McLean, Paul, 138
McLuhan, Marshall, 114
Mead, G. H., 207–8
Medicaid, 163
Medicare, 163
Melville, Herman, 127
Miami Vice, 60
Michaels, Eric, 208
Michelet, Jules, 32
Michels, Robert, xix, 171
Midler, Bette, 111
Milgate, Murray, 171
Mill, John Stuart, 26, 39, 156, 165, 216; On
    Liberty, xvii
Miller, D. A., 209
Miller, J.D.B., 109
Miller, Mark Crispin, x, 228
Mills, C. Wright, 23, 48
Mitchell, Austin, 137
Mitterand, François, 211
Modernity: and citizenship, 4, 133–34,
    222–23; defined, 6–7, 22, 27, 34, 44,
    45, 75, 77, 93, 113–14, 136, 156, 199,
    222, 229–30; and self, xxvi, 68–69;
    and subjectivity, xiv–xv, xix, xxii,

158, 162, 194, 211, 212, 214; and citizenship, 12–13, 19–22, 24–25, 27,
60–62, 119–20, 129–30, 135, 155–57,
165, 170–71; and politics, 65, 147,
176–77; theorized, xxvii–xxviii, 46,
55–57, 69–77, 81, 84–88, 92–94,
113–14, 128, 175–80, 182–83. *See also*
Technologies of the self
Self-formation, xxv, xxvi, 12, 49–50, 58,
63, 70, 71, 72–73, 83, 113–15, 119,
124–25, 138, 153, 192, 222, 229
Senate: Australian, 131, 137, 138, 147, 148,
151; Judiciary Committee's Judge
Thomas Confirmation Hearing
(U.S.), 143; Select Committee on
Presidential Campaign Activities
(U.S.), 143; Select Committee on
Television (Australia), 120; U.S., 143
Senghor, Léopold Sédar, 10
Sennett, Richard, 164, 204
Sesame Street, 138
Sexuality: and citizenship, 106, 152,
221–22; and crime, 174–75; defined,
180; and religion, 188, 192–99, 200
Shakespeare, William, 64, 81; *Hamlet,*
80–81; *Othello,* 63
Sharman, Jim: *The Rocky Horror Picture
Show,* 204
Shils, Edward, 7, 9, 12
Showalter, Elaine, 77–78, 204
Simmel, Georg, xiv, 19, 42, 45, 156
Sinfield, Alan, 70, 71
Sisters of Perpetual Indulgence, 180–81,
182, 190, 201, 205, 226; and Nun
Speakers' Bureau, 207; signification
of, 203–4, 206–9, 210–13, 214–17,
223–24; *White Paper,* 210
Skirrow, Gillian, 126
Smart, Barry, 175
Smith, Adam, 115–16, 171
Social contract, xix, 39, 133, 179–80,
220–21, 224–25
Social surface, xxiv, 33–40, 219
Solidarity, 181
Solon, 137–38
Solow, Robert, 167
Sony, 112, 115
Sophocles: *Antigone,* 85
Sound and Vision Office: *Code of Ethics,*
153
Spacks, Patricia, 74
Spanish International Network, 112
Speakes, Larry, 163
Spencer, Herbert, xviii, 22, 41–42
Spycatcher, 145
St. John-Stevas, Norman, 132
Staiger, Janet, 23

Stallybrass, Peter, 205
State: defined, 12–13, 15, 24–25, 38–40,
109, 110, 134, 175–76, 221; and Marxism, 5–6, 33–34, 84–85; and subjectivity, xvii–xix, xx–xxi, xxii–xxiii,
xxv, 7–9, 26–29, 92–93, 133, 170, 217,
224–25, 228–29
Steiner, George, 73
Stephenson, Pamela: and "Not a Papal
Tour," 203
Stephenson, P. R., 119
Stewart, John, xx
Stimpson, Catharine, 31
Studlar, Gaylyn, 204
Subjectivity: alternatives to, 221–31; formation of, ix–x, xi–xiv, xvi–xvii,
xxi–xxvii, 6, 10, 13–14, 15, 16, 33–35,
178–80, 193; national, 96, 109–10,
114–15, 118–20, 127–28; postmodern,
xiii–xiv, 23–25, 26, 35–48, 76, 92–94,
114–15, 203, 207–8, 223–24; rational
consuming, 35, 113–14, 130–31, 156–57,
164–66, 168, 170, 171, 189, 215, 219;
religious sexual, 195–99; social theory of, xiv–xvi, xvii–xx, 11–12, 21, 32,
75, 173–77, 181–82; textual theory of,
49–51, 52, 55–56, 65–69, 72–74, 80–81,
84–88, 182–83; unruly, x, xii, 153,
176–77, 202–13, 216–17
The Sweeney, 60
Sydney Gay Mardi Gras, 200–201
Sydney Morning Herald, 137, 190, 211
Sydney University, 180, 183, 185, 186, 189,
212, 215; Society for Welcoming the
Pope, 186
Symposium internationale sur l'Identité
culturelle européene, 107

Taft, William Howard, 152
Taine, Hippolyte, 73
Taylor, Charles, 24, 179; *Sources of the Self,*
177
Tea Towels d'Art, 203
Technical and Further Education
(TAFE), 154, 158–60, 169; Research
and Development Centre, 155
Technologies of the self: defined, xiv;
theorized, xxvi–xxvii, 70, 150, 172,
173–74, 204, 207–10, 213, 215, 216–17,
224–26, 228–29
Telepictures, 111
Television: drama, 56, 58–62, 67, 79–81,
112, 115, 117–28; parliamentary,
131–53; studies, 57–59, 63, 65, 70,
78–79, 86–88, 136–39
Thatcher, Margaret, 145
Their Lordships' House, 145